Stravinsky's Piano

Genesis of a Musical Language

Stravinsky's re-invention in the early 1920s, as both neoclassical composer and concert pianist, is here placed at the centre of a fundamental re-consideration of his whole output – viewed from the unprecedented perspective of his relationship with the piano. Graham Griffiths assesses Stravinsky's musical upbringing in St Petersburg with emphasis on his education at the hands of two extraordinary teachers whom he later either ignored or denounced: Leokadiya Kashperova for piano, and Rimsky-Korsakov for instrumentation. Their message, Griffiths argues, enabled Stravinsky to formulate from that intensely Russian experience an internationalist brand of neoclassicism founded upon the premises of objectivity and craft. Drawing directly on the composer's manuscripts, Griffiths addresses Stravinsky's life-long fascination with counterpoint and with pianism's constructive processes. *Stravinsky's Piano* presents both of these as recurring features of the compositional attitudes that Stravinsky consistently applied to his works, whether Russian, neoclassical or serial, and regardless of idiom and genre.

GRAHAM GRIFFITHS studied musicology at Edinburgh University, and music education at Gonville and Caius College, Cambridge, obtaining his D.Phil. (musicology) in 2008 at Christ Church, Oxford. Between 1989 and 1999 he directed *Grupo Novo Horizonte de São Paulo*, and guest-lectured at Brazilian and Danish universities. In 2005 his article 'Fingering as Compositional Process: Stravinsky's Sonata Sketchbook Revisited' was published by *British Postgraduate Musicology Online*. Recently Griffiths has delivered courses at the universities of Bath ('Stravinsky's Spain'), Bristol ('Performance'), Canterbury Christ Church ('Music since 1900') and Oxford ('Stravinsky and the Twentieth Century'). He has been a Visiting Lecturer at City University, London since 2010.

D1295066

Music Since 1900

GENERAL EDITOR   Arnold Whittall

This series – formerly Music in the Twentieth Century – offers a wide perspective on music and musical life since the end of the nineteenth century. Books included range from historical and biographical studies concentrating particularly on the context and circumstances in which composers were writing, to analytical and critical studies concerned with the nature of musical language and questions of compositional process. The importance given to context will also be reflected in studies dealing with, for example, the patronage, publishing and promotion of new music, and in accounts of the musical life of particular countries.

Titles in the series

Jonathan Cross
The Stravinsky Legacy

Michael Nyman
Experimental Music: Cage and Beyond

Jennifer Doctor
The BBC and Ultra-Modern Music, 1922–1936

Robert Adlington
The Music of Harrison Birtwistle

Keith Potter
Four Musical Minimalists: La Monte Young, Terry Riley, Steve Reich, Philip Glass

Carlo Caballero
Fauré and French Musical Aesthetics

Peter Burt
The Music of Tōru Takemitsu

David Clarke
The Music and Thought of Michael Tippett: Modern Times and Metaphysics

M. J. Grant
Serial Music, Serial Aesthetics: Compositional Theory in Post-War Europe

Philip Rupprecht
Britten's Musical Language

Mark Carroll
Music and Ideology in Cold War Europe

Adrian Thomas
Polish Music since Szymanowski

J. P. E. Harper-Scott
Edward Elgar, Modernist

Yayoi Uno Everett
The Music of Louis Andriessen

Ethan Haimo
Schoenberg's Transformation of Musical Language

Rachel Beckles Willson
Ligeti, Kurtág, and Hungarian Music during the Cold War

Michael Cherlin
Schoenberg's Musical Imagination

Joseph N. Straus
Twelve-Tone Music in America

David Metzer
Musical Modernism at the Turn of the Twenty-First Century

Edward Campbell
Boulez, Music and Philosophy

Jonathan Goldman
The Musical Language of Pierre Boulez: Writings and Compositions

Pieter C. van den Toorn and John McGinness
Stravinsky and the Russian Period: Sound and Legacy of a Musical Idiom

Heather Wiebe
Britten's Unquiet Pasts: Sound and Memory in Postwar Reconstruction

David Beard
Harrison Birtwistle's Operas and Music Theatre

Beate Kutschke and Barley Norton
Music and Protest in 1968

Graham Griffiths
Stravinsky's Piano: Genesis of a Musical Language

Stravinsky's Piano

Genesis of a Musical Language

Graham Griffiths

CAMBRIDGE
UNIVERSITY PRESS

CAMBRIDGE
UNIVERSITY PRESS

University Printing House, Cambridge CB2 8BS, United Kingdom

Cambridge University Press is part of the University of Cambridge.

It furthers the University's mission by disseminating knowledge in the pursuit of education, learning and research at the highest international levels of excellence.

www.cambridge.org
Information on this title: www.cambridge.org/9781316632178

© Graham Griffiths 2013

First published 2013
First paperback edition 2016

A catalogue record for this publication is available from the British Library

Library of Congress Cataloguing in Publication data
Griffiths, Graham, 1954–
    Stravinsky's piano : genesis of a musical language / Graham Griffiths.
        p.   cm. – (Music since 1900)
    Includes bibliographical references and index.
    ISBN 978-0-521-19178-4 (hardback)
    1. Stravinsky, Igor, 1882–1971–Criticism and interpretation.
    2. Stravinsky, Igor, 1882–1971. Piano music.   I. Title.
    ML410.S932G73 2013
    780.92–dc23
    2012031734

ISBN 978-0-521-19178-4 Hardback
ISBN 978-1-316-63217-8 Paperback

For Ana, John and all my family
In Memoriam
Miriam Margaret Griffiths (née Heughan) MBChB (Edinburgh)
(1920–2008)
Lena Amy Baker LRAM, Teacher of Pianoforte and Rudiments
(1905–2004)

Contents

List of figures   x
List of music examples   xi
Acknowledgements   xv

Introduction   1

1   Becoming a Russian musician   9

2   Becoming a neoclassicist   78

3   Stravinsky's piano workshop   131

4   Departures and homecomings   205

Conclusions   249

Notes   260
Bibliography   311
Index   324

Figures

1.1 The first page of Stravinsky's sketches for *The Rite of Spring*, 1911/13 (F-Pmeyer). © Mr John Stravinsky. Reproduced by permission of the Bibliothèque nationale de France and Boosey & Hawkes Music Publishers Ltd.   72–3

3.1 Stravinsky, sketch for *Sonate pour piano* (Biarritz, 13 April 1924), PSS 123–0516/17 (Paul Sacher Stiftung, microfilm 123, pp. 516–17). © The Paul Sacher Stiftung, Basel.   132–3

3.2 Stravinsky, sketches for *Concert pour piano et instruments à vent* (1923/1924): the first page of sketches, PSS 220–0634 (Paul Sacher Stiftung: microfilm 220, p. 634). © The Paul Sacher Stiftung, Basel.   144

3.3 Stravinsky, sketch for *Sonate pour piano* (dated 4 August [1924]). © The Paul Sacher Stiftung, Basel.   148

3.4 Stravinsky, sketch for *Symphony of Psalms* (1930): the first page of sketches, PSS 114–0262 (Paul Sacher Stiftung: microfilm 114, p. 262). © The Paul Sacher Stiftung, Basel.   150

3.5 Malwine Brée, *The Groundwork of the Leschetizky Method* (1902): excerpt from Chapter 16, 'Chords'. © 1902 G. Schirmer, Inc.   162

3.6 Stravinsky's annotation of the peals of St Paul's Cathedral, London (June 1914). © The Paul Sacher Stiftung, Basel.   169

4.1 Stravinsky, *Lied ohne Name für Zwei Fagotten* (1918), complete, PSS 123–0336/7 (Paul Sacher Stiftung: microfilm 123, pp. 336–7). © The Paul Sacher Stiftung, Basel.   227

4.2 Stravinsky, sketch for *Movements for Piano and Orchestra* (1958/9), PSS 222–0603 (Paul Sacher Stiftung: microfilm 222, p. 603). © The Paul Sacher Stiftung, Basel.   243

Music examples

0.1   J. S. Bach, *Das wohltemperierte Klavier*, Book I (edited and fingered by Carl Czerny), Fugue in A minor, bb. 52–4.   3

1.1   Stravinsky, *Tarantella* (fragment, 1898): (a) first sketch; (b) second sketch. © 1970 Izdatelstvo Muzyka, Leningrad.   27

1.2   Stravinsky, *Scherzo* (1902), bb. 72–86. © 1974 Faber Music Ltd.   32

1.3   Stravinsky, Piano Sonata in F♯ minor (1903/4), 1st movement: (a) bb. 33–6; (b) bb. 61–4. © 1974 Faber Music Ltd.   36

1.4   Stravinsky, 'How the Mushrooms Mobilized for War' (1904): (a) bb. 44–52; (b) bb. 136–48. © 1979 Boosey & Hawkes Music Publishers Ltd.   43–4

1.5   Stravinsky, *The Faun and the Shepherdess* (1906), III. 'The Torrent': (a) bb. 50–5; (b) bb. 82–7. © 1964 M. P. Belaieff.   46

1.6   Stravinsky, *Two Melodies of Gorodetsky* op. 6 (1907/8), I. 'La Novice', bb. 1–14. © 1908 Boosey & Hawkes Music Publishers Ltd.   48

1.7a Stravinsky, 'Pastorale' (1908). © 1934, 1962 Schott Music, Mainz, Germany.   52–3

1.7b Stravinsky, *Sonate pour piano* (1924), 'Adagietto', bb. 1–3. © 1925 Hawkes & Son (London) Ltd.   54

1.8   Rimsky-Korsakov, *Principles of Orchestration*, 'Table B. Wind group', pp. 95–6. © 1964 Dover Publications Inc.   59

1.9   Stravinsky, *Fireworks* (1908), Fig. 5. Based on the Critical Edition of *Feu d'artifice*. © 2010 Ulrich Mosch: Schott Music, Mainz, Germany.   65

1.10 Stravinsky, *Petrushka* (revised 1947 version), 'Valse', Fig. 150. © 1912, 1948 Hawkes & Son (London) Ltd.   68

1.11 Stravinsky, *The Rite of Spring* (1911/13), Fig. 17. © 1912, 1921 Hawkes & Son (London) Ltd.   76

2.1a Czerny, *Die Kunst der Fingerfertigkeit* op. 740, 'Fingerwechsel auf einer Taste' ('Changing the Fingers on One Key'), bb. 1–3. © Edition Peters.   80

2.1b Stravinsky, *Four Studies for Piano* (1908), III. Andantino, bb. 1–3. © 1925 Anton J. Benjamin (Leipzig).   80

2.1c Stravinsky, *Petrushka*, 'Danse russe', Fig. 86, bb. 1–3. © 1912, 1948 Hawkes & Son (London) Ltd.   81

2.1d Stravinsky, *Trois histoires pour enfants* (1915/17), 'Tilim-bom', bb. 44–7. © 1917 Chester Music.   81

2.1e Stravinsky, *Trois histoires pour enfants*, 'Les Canards, les cygnes, les oies …', bb.10–12. © 1917 Chester Music.   81

2.1f Stravinsky, *Capriccio* (1928/9), 1st movement, Fig. 10. © 1930, 1952 Hawkes & Son (London) Ltd.   81

2.1g Stravinsky, *Movements for Piano and Orchestra* (1958/9), 1st movement, bb. 27–30. © 1960 Hawkes & Son (London) Ltd.   82

2.2 Stravinsky, *Five Easy Pieces for Piano Duet* (*Right Hand Easy*) (1916/17), II. 'Española', bb.1–19. © 1917 Chester Music.   87

2.3 Stravinsky, 'Valse' *from Histoire du soldat* for pianoforte solo (1922): (a) bb. 16–25; (b) bb. 39–44. © 1917 Chester Music.   89

3.1 Stravinsky, *Les Cinq Doigts* (1920/1), VIII. Pesante, bb. 19–25. © 1917 Chester Music.   136

3.2 Stravinsky, *Concert pour piano et instruments à vent* (1923/4), 1st movement, Figs. 36–7. © 1924, 1960 Hawkes & Son (London) Ltd.   137

3.3 Stravinsky, *Sonate pour piano* (1924), 3rd movement: (a) bb. 1–8; (b) bb. 77–85. © 1925 Hawkes & Son (London) Ltd.   139

3.4 Stravinsky, *Concert pour piano et instruments à vent*: (a) sketch, bb. 1–4; (b) 1st movement, bb. 55–7. © 1925 Hawkes & Son (London) Ltd.   145–6

3.5 Stravinsky, *Sonate pour piano* (Edition Russe de Musique, 1925), 1st movement, bb. 143–5. © 1925 Hawkes & Son (London) Ltd.   149

3.6a Malwine Brée, *The Groundwork of the Leschetizky Method* (1902): excerpt from Chapter 16, 'Chords'. © 1902 G. Schirmer, Inc.   164

3.6b Marie Prentner, *The Leschetizky Method* (1903): excerpt from Chapter 6, 'The Chord'. © 1903 J. Curwen & Sons Ltd.   164

3.7 Stravinsky, *Capriccio*, 1st movement, Figs. 14–16. © 1930, 1952 Hawkes & Son (London) Ltd.   177–8

3.8 Isidor Philipp, *Exercices pratiques (Introduction aux exercices journaliers)* op. 9 (1897), p. 290. © 1897/1948 Editions Durand (Paris). Reproduced by permission of Hal Leonard Corporation.   181

3.9 Isidor Philipp, *Complete School of Technic for the Piano* (1908), from 'Exercises in Velocity', p. 8. © 1908 Theodore Presser Company. Reproduced under licence from United Music Publishers Ltd, England.   182

3.10   Isidor Philipp, *Complete School of Technic for the Piano*, from 'Chords', p. 98. © 1908 Theodore Presser Company. Reproduced under licence from United Music Publishers Ltd, England.   183

3.11   Stravinsky, *Symphony of Psalms* (1930), 1st movement, bb. 1–3. © 1931, 1948 Hawkes & Son (London) Ltd.   194

3.12   Stravinsky, *Symphony of Psalms*, 1st movement, bb. 65–7 (Fig. 12). © 1931, 1948 Hawkes & Son (London) Ltd.   197

3.13   Stravinsky, *Sonate pour piano*, 3rd movement, bb. 89–93. © 1925 Hawkes & Son (London) Ltd.   200

3.14   Stravinsky, *Symphony of Psalms*, 1st movement, bb. 1–3. © 1931, 1948 Hawkes & Son (London) Ltd.   201

4.1a   Adriano Banchieri, 'Canzone italiana per organo', opening, as quoted by Charles-Albert Cingria (1932). © 2003 Editions L'Age d'Homme.   209

4.1b   Stravinsky, *Duo concertant* (1931/2), 'Dithyrambe', line 2. © 1933 Hawkes & Son (London) Ltd.   209

4.2   Stravinsky, *Duo concertant*, 'Eglogue I', opening. © 1933 Hawkes & Son (London) Ltd.   211

4.3a   Isidor Philipp, *Complete School of Technic for the Piano*, 'Linked Trills' exercise, p. 107. © 1908 Theodore Presser Company. Reproduced under licence from United Music Publishers Ltd, England.   215

4.3b   Stravinsky, *Concerto for Two Solo Pianos* (1931/5), 4th movement, 'Preludio e Fuga', bb. 1–8. © 1936, 1964 Schott Music, Mainz, Germany.   216

4.3c   Stravinsky, *Sonata for Two Pianos* (1943/4), 1st movement, 'Moderato', bb. 14–16. © 1945 Schott Music, Mainz, Germany.   216

4.4   Stravinsky, *Concerto for Two Solo Pianos*, Variation III, bb. 18–20. © 1936, 1964 Schott Music, Mainz, Germany.   218

4.5a.   Stravinsky, *Symphony in Three Movements* (1942/5); 1st movement, Figs. 9–10. © 1946 Schott Music GmbH & Co. KG, Mainz, Germany.   222

4.5b   Stravinsky, Violin Concerto in D (1931); reduction by the composer for violin and piano, 4th movement, 'Capriccio', bb. 16–21. © 1931 Schott Music, Mainz, Germany.   223

4.6   Stravinsky, *The Rake's Progress* (1948/51), Act III, scene 2, bb. 1–9. © 1951 Hawkes & Son (London) Ltd.   234

4.7   Stravinsky, Septet (1952/3), 1st movement, bb. 1–5. © 1953 Hawkes & Son (London) Ltd.   238

4.8   Stravinsky, *Movements for Piano and Orchestra*, 5th movement, bb. 175–9. © 1960 Hawkes & Son (London) Ltd.   243

4.9   Stravinsky, 'The Owl and the Pussy-Cat' (1965/6), opening. © 1967 Boosey & Hawkes Music Publishers Ltd.   245

Acknowledgements

'Having my high task performed' – to quote from *Trud* (*The Work*), which Pushkin wrote to mark the completion of *Eugene Onegin*[1] – I wish to thank several people without whom my own 'work' would never have reached the light of day. Its very existence is due to the invitation of Arnold Whittall to whom I am grateful, also, for his wise counsel at key moments during the book's preparation. My sincere gratitude is extended to Vicki Cooper at Cambridge University Press; to my editor, Fleur Jones; my copy-editor, Robert Whitelock; and project editor, Emma Wildsmith; and to all those – including Rebecca Taylor, Emma Walker and Danny Bean – who have so calmly and expertly guided *Stravinsky's Piano* along the road towards publication. I am indebted, also, to Paul Webster for his invaluable assistance with proofreading, and to Guillermo Brachetta for setting the music examples so swiftly, and so skilfully.

I owe a great deal to librarians and archivists. In particular I wish to thank Johanna Blask and the infinitely efficient and courteous staff at the Paul Sacher Stiftung (Basel) who ensured that I made full use of my study-visits to the Stravinsky archive. I am deeply appreciative of the authorization granted me to consult original materials when microfilm alone could not provide the information I required. I especially wish to thank Dr Ulrich Mosch for his advice, at the time and in subsequent correspondence. I am extremely grateful, also, to the librarians of the Music Faculty at the University of Oxford, the School of Slavonic and East European Studies at University College London, and the Music Reading Room of the New Bodleian Library, with whom I have spent so many hours. No researcher could wish for more helpful or more knowledgeable support.

Stravinsky's publishers have been most accommodating. I would like to thank Sarah Hopkins (Music Sales/Chester Music), Sarah Osborn (Schott Music) and Bruce MacRae (Faber Music), whilst acknowledging the extraordinary helpfulness of Andy Chan (Boosey & Hawkes). Parts of Chapters 2 and 3 owe their origins to my D.Phil. thesis, completed at Oxford University in 2008. In this regard I am especially indebted to my doctoral supervisor Professor Jonathan Cross (Christ Church) for his expert and generous orientation.

For innumerable acts of kindness, my profound thanks are extended to Mr John Stravinsky; Marie Iellatchitch-Strawinsky (Fondation Théodore Strawinsky, Geneva); Lidia Ader (N. A. Rimsky-Korsakov Museum, St Petersburg); Nadège Danet, Vincent Reniel and Maud Souffir (Bibliothèque nationale de France); Rosie Perkins and the late Janet Mills (Music Education Research Team, Royal College of Music, London); Rachel Jeremiah-Foulds (*British Postgraduate Musicology Online*); and, for their discreet support during, respectively, the initial and final phases of the book's gestation, Professor Grenville Hancox (Canterbury Christ Church University) and Christian Heinrich (Cumnor House School Trust). Unless otherwise stated, translations are entirely my responsibility. My desire to consult documents relating to Stravinsky's youth in their original language brought me into contact with excellent, and extremely patient, Russian teachers; my sincere thanks go to Dorinda Offord (Russian Department, Bristol University) and Larisa Kosyukhina. In particular, I wish to pay homage to Tetyana Ursulova (New Bodleian Library, Oxford) for her invaluable assistance over many years. *Dulcis in fundo*, words alone cannot express my feelings of gratitude to my parents, who patiently guided me towards this personal landmark; and to my brother and his family for their uniquely uplifting spirit in challenging times. Paternal thanks are due to Nicholas for his abundant skills with the computer when I most needed them and to Anthony for his encouragement from afar. I owe an immense debt to *everyone* who has helped me to 'perform' my own 'high task'.

Yet Pushkin's celebratory stanza is also tinged with regret, particularly at the close when the poet bids farewell to 'night's silent companion, / Golden Aurora's friend, friend of the / household gods'. It would be unrealistic to expect my wife Ana and youngest son John to entertain such nostalgia, for they have watched this 'intruder' engage my silent attention during interminable daylight and nocturnal hours. In grateful recognition of their extraordinary forbearance (and cheerfulness) in the face of my unreasonable sacrifice, I affectionately dedicate *Stravinsky's Piano* to them – indeed, to all my family, young and old, near and dear. For, to borrow one of Stravinsky's most celebrated *mots justes*: 'In order to create there must be a dynamic force, and what force is more potent than love?'

Sources of copyright material

The author and publishers acknowledge the following sources of copyright material and are grateful for the permissions granted. While every effort has been made, it has not always been possible to identify the sources of all material used, or to trace all copyright holders. If any omissions are brought to our notice, we will be happy to include the appropriate acknowledgements on reprinting.

The author would like to thank the following publishers and institutions for kindly granting permission to quote musical excerpts: Bibliothèque nationale de France (Paris), Boosey & Hawkes Music Publishers Ltd, Faber Music Ltd, Music Sales Ltd, Paul Sacher Stiftung (Basel), Schott Music Ltd. Also Dover Publications Inc., Editions L'Age d'Homme, Edition Peters, G. Schirmer Inc., Hal Leonard Corporation, Izdatelstvo Muzyka and United Music Publishers.

The following musical examples are under joint copyright:

Examples 2.1d, 2.1e, 2.2, 2.3 and 3.1. © 1917 Chester Music: worldwide except for the United Kingdom, Ireland, Australia, Canada, South Africa and all so-called reversionary rights territories where the copyright is held jointly by Schott Music GmbH & Co. KG, Mainz, Germany and Chester Music Ltd, London. All Rights Reserved. International Copyright Secured.

Examples 1.7a, 4.3b, 4.4. © 1996 in the United Kingdom and all so-called reversionary rights territories is held jointly by Schott Music GmbH & Co. KG, Mainz, Germany and Chester Music Ltd, London.

Example 1.9. © 2010 in the United Kingdom and all so-called reversionary rights territories is held jointly by Schott Music GmbH & Co. KG, Mainz, Germany and Chester Music Ltd, London.

Example 4.3c. © 1945 Schott Music, worldwide rights except the USA where the copyright is held by Boosey & Hawkes Inc.; and except North America (excl. USA) and South America and Israel where the copyright is held by Associated Music Publishers Inc. (BMI); and except the United Kingdom, Ireland, Australia, Canada, South Africa and all so-called reversionary rights territories where the copyright © 1996 is held jointly by Schott Music GmbH & Co. KG, Mainz, Germany and Chester Music Ltd, London.

Example 4.5a. © 1946 Schott Music, worldwide rights except the United Kingdom, Ireland, Australia, Canada, South Africa and all so-called reversionary rights territories where the copyright © 1996 is held jointly by Schott Music GmbH & Co. KG, Mainz, Germany and Chester Music Ltd, London.

Example 4.5b. © 1931 Schott Music, worldwide rights except the United Kingdom and all so-called reversionary rights territories where the copyright © 1996 is held jointly by Schott Music GmbH & Co. KG, Mainz, Germany and Chester Music Ltd, London.

Il ne faut pas mépriser les doigts; ils sont de grands inspirateurs …

('Fingers are not to be despised; they are great inspirers …')
Igor Stravinsky, *Chroniques de ma vie* (1935)

Смотрите на пользу, а не на красоту. Красота сама придёт.

('Look to utility and not to beauty. Beauty will come by itself.')
(N. V. Gogol, *Dead Souls*, Part II (1842); trans.
Robert A. Maguire (London: Penguin, 2004)

Introduction

On 1 May 1969 Stravinsky was photographed in the Hotel Pierre, New York, sitting at his desk in Room 1716, 'orchestrating Bach'.[1] The next day he was admitted to hospital. He was eighty-six, almost eighty-seven, and 'in a parlous physical condition'. Over the next two days, according to Stephen Walsh's re-telling,

> he underwent two major operations for the removal of enormous blood clots from the leg. Against all prognostications he survived and promptly went down with pneumonia … It seemed impossible that he would reach his birthday in a month's time. Then just as suddenly, on the 26th of May, like the Emperor in *The Nightingale*, he sat up in bed, bid everyone a bright good morning and demanded to be lifted out to continue work on the B minor Fugue.[2]

Only the previous month Stravinsky had begun arranging four minor-key preludes and fugues selected from *Das wohltemperierte Klavier*.[3] They were to be his final creative act. Bach's scores (in the Czerny edition)[4] and Stravinsky's manuscript sheets had accompanied the composer on his recent journey from Los Angeles to New York (where he would be within reach of superior medical treatment). Such was his recently restored appetite for work that, according to the testimony of Robert Craft and Vera Stravinsky, he would 'get out of his hospital bed five or six times each day in order to add a few measures'.[5] The scene brings to mind lines from Gogol: 'A new feeling began to stir in him. In his soul old impressions that had long remained buried began to awaken [and he] now looked upon the beautiful views with curiosity, as if seeing them for the first time.'[6] Or perhaps Stravinsky was stirred to overcome his infirmity by memories of the closing pages from *The Rake's Progress*: 'Rouse yourself, Tom, your travail soon will end. Come, try!'[7]

While these Bach arrangements – for various permutations of wind and string instruments – were more 'in the nature of occupational therapy than practical work' (at least, in Walsh's estimation), and although, following the presentation of these works at the Berlin Festival six months later, Craft and Nicholas Nabokov agreed that they were 'not performable as they stood' and withdrew them,[8] their very existence is still cause for celebration and wonderment. Irrespective of the concert-worthiness of these remarkable labours, the whole episode confirms one vital and inextinguishable aspect of Stravinsky's creative spirit: his profound admiration for 'the radiant idea of pure counterpoint' (as he had been moved to comment, regarding Bach, in an interview with the Warsaw journal *Muzyka* in 1924).[9] In fact Stravinsky retained an intimacy with counterpoint throughout his life, his first acquaintance of fugues dating from 'about the age of eighteen [when he] began to study … alone, with no other help than an ordinary manual', as he later explained.[10] This 'manual' may well have been, or been complemented by, Lyadov's *Twenty-Four Canons* (1898) for Piano or the Fuga (1893), also for piano – to be discussed in Chapter 1.[11] Stravinsky's initial experience of counterpoint, then, was not merely as an intellectual exercise (in silence); it was also sensed physically (as sound) via the 'digital' and, by all accounts, pleasurable unravelling of textures through his fingertips at the piano. How unusual, indeed, was the response of this keen and self-motivated student compared to that of his peers at the Conservatoire, struggling through their weekly counterpoint assignments!

> The work amused me, even thrilled me, and I never grew tired of it. This first contact with the science of counterpoint opened up at once a far vaster and more fertile field in the domain of musical composition than anything that harmony could offer me. And so I set myself with heart and soul to the task of solving the many problems it contains … It was only later that I realized to what extent those exercises had helped to develop my judgement and my taste in music. They stimulated my imagination and my desire to compose.[12]

The Bach arrangements written seventy-five years later might betray some tremulous handwriting but Stravinsky's final engagement with pure counterpoint shows his mental perspicuity to be virtually undiminished.[13] (According to his close family, 'even during this difficult time [February 1969] Stravinsky worked at the piano for forty minutes each day'.)[14] His personal copy of 'The 48' reveals that his curiosity extended beyond those movements specifically earmarked for his (re)creation. On a distant page (to be precise: at b. 54 of the A minor Fugue from Book I) Stravinsky could not resist circling *in red* a most rare example of the dreaded parallel fifths. It is a deliberate act – worthy of any eagle-eyed music student these past two and a half centuries – that barely conceals a delight, tinged by incredulity, that he had found 'one that got away' even from Johann Sebastian himself. It had somehow slipped, as it were, through 'God's fingers', but not through Stravinsky's (Example 0.1).

Of course, the inner (alto) voice reads, from the beginning of the bar: D, D♯, E, E, D♯ (*not* D natural), E – which would suggest that Bach successfully avoided parallel fifths 'on a technicality', but it is a close call. Stravinsky

Ex. 0.1 J. S. Bach, *Das wohltemperierte Klavier*, Book I (edited and fingered by Carl Czerny), Fugue in A minor, bb. 52–4, with Stravinsky's 'correction' (original in red pencil).

was clearly still intrigued with and even entertained by the challenges of counterpoint. This preoccupation has become especially associated with his neoclassical works and with those combative pronouncements of the early 1920s, made with the dual intention of proclaiming and explaining his stylistic re-invention. However, his regard for eighteenth-century counterpoint (and even earlier forms of polyphony) was not an interest suddenly acquired when he reached his forties.[15] Nor was it then abandoned when, in his seventies, he sought an individual response to the challenges of serialism. Rather, Stravinsky's embrace of counterpoint – on occasion, his apparent dependence upon it, especially in his keyboard works – was an integral part of his life-long *affaire* with music. In his autobiography he even discloses, somewhat astonishingly, that the counterpoint exercises he wrestled with as a young man 'laid the foundation of all my future technique [and] prepared me thoroughly for the study of form, of orchestration, and of instrument [*sic*] which I later took up with Rimsky-Korsakov'.[16] The Bach arrangements provided Stravinsky with one last opportunity to indulge his private relish for such contrapuntal stimuli; to walk along the tramlines of the greatest technician of them all; to sense the constructive, inspirational and healing properties of Bach's radiant perfection – and to savour his occasional edgy 'imperfections'. If Stravinsky was no longer well enough to sit at the piano 'rehearsing the right sounds' (to cite Luciano Berio's poetic 'Adieu', written in 1971)[17] then he could at least simulate that 'desire to compose' by moulding 'The 48' to make them his own. The pedagogical properties of Bach's work as compositional *and* clavier exercises would not have been lost on Stravinsky, for this pair of characteristics effectively defines his own two-pronged approach towards composition and pianism. He may not have conceived his act of Bach-arrangement in this way, but Stravinsky's determination to complete the exercises he had set himself was surely 'guided' by advice given him in 1902 by Rimsky-Korsakov: that he should dispense with the formalities of St Petersburg's musical establishment and, instead, by his *own* initiative 'acquire complete mastery in the schooling of craftsmanship'.[18] Judging from Stravinsky's self-imposed work routine in May 1969 he still believed in this practice.

Besides the unusually positive attraction of a teenager to the 'science of counterpoint', Stravinsky also developed an early and equally idiosyncratic relationship with the piano. Composing with the aid of this instrument established itself from the outset as his preferred mode of working, as Rimsky-Korsakov immediately recognized and encouraged. His advice to Stravinsky that 'as for you, you will compose at the piano'[19] can now be adjudged not only to be wise counsel, but also a hugely significant act of prophecy.[20] Stravinsky never forsook the habit, and with good reason. This working method represented a process by which he experienced music's parameters – pitch, texture, articulation, chord-spacing, rhythm and intervals (especially intervals) – vividly and elementally. 'I think it is a thousand times better to compose in direct contact with the physical medium of sound', Stravinsky famously declared, 'than to work in the abstract medium produced by one's imagination'.[21]

Stravinsky published these comments at a time when he was also writing chamber works that featured his own participation as a concert pianist: *Duo Concertant*, which Stravinsky toured extensively with the violinist Samuel Dushkin from 1932, and the *Concerto for Two Solo Pianos*, which Stravinsky premiered with his son Soulima in 1935. Performances of these demanding piano parts inevitably required preparation to a professional level and, to ensure this, Stravinsky's technical practice was supported by constant reference to Isidor Philipp's *Complete School of Technic for the Piano*. His personal copy of this volume bears the dates of the lessons when Stravinsky sought the guidance of Isidor Philipp in Paris in the autumn of 1924 – in the midst of touring his newly completed Piano Concerto and composing the *Sonate pour piano* – both works destined to contribute greatly to establishing the composer's identity in his re-invented neoclassical guise.[22] It is instructive to re-consider just how much critical perception of this 'new Stravinsky' was determined by his neoclassical stance. Following the *Octuor* (1923) and his article 'Some Ideas about My *Octuor*' (1924),[23] this new 'image' was projected almost exclusively by piano works – *Concert pour piano et instruments à vent* (1923/4), *Sonate* (1924), *Sérénade en la* (1925) – and by the composer-pianist's own inimitably objective manner of execution. Judging from a 'miniature essay' released by the composer's London-based publishers one can plainly see that Stravinsky's double-barrelled assault, both verbal and musical, provoked an uncomfortable response:

> It is impossible to-day to consider the work of Igor Stravinsky with the detachment that is the first requisite of a judicious appreciation and to avoid taking part in the violent controversy to which it has given rise, a controversy that is in itself a testimony to its vitality, for Stravinsky's music is so characteristic an expression of the artistic tendencies of our time that even those who most dislike it cannot pass it by in silence.[24]

If the piano is to be considered the vessel through which important aspects of Stravinsky's neoclassicism passed, then, in order to explore this hypothesis, one must review fundamental aspects of both neoclassicism *and* pianism (for example, their 'objectivity' and sense of craftsmanship) as complementary aspects of the one creative 'attitude'. If composition derives its craft from counterpoint, fugue and imitative writing generally, then to what does pianism owe *its* debt? In response, it is intriguing to compare the anti-romantic flavour of Stravinsky's 'objective', often contrapuntal piano writing with the 'mechanistic', non-expressive elements of piano methodologies whose didactic focus – exemplified in the literature of studies, exercises and drills – is generally considered to be 'a dry subject useful only for pedagogical purposes'.[25] But it is hardly new science to draw such parallels.

In 2001 Charles M. Joseph proposed that Stravinsky's neoclassical piano works owe much to Philipp's exercises as 'useful models', and that it is 'impossible to miss' such connections.[26] There is no other author in the literature able to combine extensive knowledge of the composer's archive with insights into the composer's pianism gained via direct access to the composer's son. Yet so far Joseph has been averse to tackling the deeper issues that his observations suggest lie beneath the surface of 'Stravinsky's unique compositional approach to the keyboard'.[27] Related topics such as Stravinsky's self-confessed admiration for Czerny, his habit of composing at the piano, his inordinately large hands and (especially) the awkwardness of his piano writing have also remained objects of similarly tangential, superficial reference. Why have these unexpected, unusual and plain uncomfortable unorthodoxies regarding 'Stravinsky's piano' not provoked more coordinated, more musicological, attention? Perhaps the composer's own reluctance to discuss them is at least partially to blame. Compared with his willingness to expound generously on virtually everything else concerning his life and (non-piano) works, Stravinsky's 'silence' has effectively left his pianistic canon vulnerable to neglect. More damaging than neglect, however, has been the hostility directed at the piano repertoire by some within the Anglo-American Stravinsky community. Eric Walter White's early appreciation of Stravinsky's neoclassicism as his 'sacrifice to Apollo' (1930) dismisses the *Sonate* for its 'ungrateful' writing, declaring that 'the sooner

Stravinsky writes a second Piano Sonata the better' and accusing him of 'chromatic sentimentality [in the third movement] that can only be compared to some of the worst Victorian hymn-tunes'.[28] White later shied away from such direct aggression but negativity is never far below the surface, the *Sérénade*'s attributes serving obliquely to condemn both works:

> [It] is perhaps the most satisfactory of all Stravinsky's works for solo piano. In it he showed he was no longer interested solely in the instrument's percussive qualities. It reveals a deeper sensibility than the earlier keyboard works, and a much wider range of texture and timbre. It is also a more grateful work from the pianist's point of view.[29]

White's comments, regarding Stravinsky's 'sole interest' in the piano's percussive qualities, refer principally to certain passages in the outer movements of the Piano Concerto, for he overlooks the Concerto's Adagio and completely misrepresents the predominantly linear character of the *Sonate*. How can White's critique have been left unchallenged, and for so long? Stravinsky had the opportunity to respond via his *Conversations* with Craft but declined. Perhaps his co-author (who set the agenda for these dialogues) was also less than committed – a suspicion confirmed by Craft's observation, published in 1978 with the silent endorsement of the composer's widow, that the solo piano works represent a concession to Stravinsky's limited technique.[30] In 1996 Richard Taruskin's exploration of the Russian Traditions appears too casually to endorse Prokofiev's view of 'the horrifying *Sonate*'.[31] Are these writers reacting – in the *Sonate*, for example – to that pedagogical aura which this volume intends to address? Why would these works provoke such animus? Is it, perhaps, because performance-related or educational issues are regarded, by some, as sub-disciplines of musicology – beyond (or below) its radar? Taruskin's study singularly fails to engage with those traditions of Russian pedagogy or pianism within whose orbit his young subject first became aware of his Russianness – not only from those around him and from those who taught him, but also from those whose reputations formed the cultural heritage that began to engage his attention. Education surely demands that it be considered as a contributory element of civilization and its national characteristics. Within that context pianism and its pedagogy rank amongst those Russian traditions whose influence Stravinsky sensed most keenly. While left unchallenged such bias conveys a censorious message, and unjustly. The issues raised by Stravinsky's piano compositions deserve to be addressed within the same musicological framework as his other works, not least because of the unique contribution they make to the historiographical and hermeneutical enquiry concerning his neoclassicism. Scott Messing, for example, summarizes neoclassicism in music as a 'sign that accommodated both innovation and tradition'.[32] In response, the present study locates 'Stravinsky's piano' within this broader argument by addressing the innovative manner with which he coopted pianistic, pedagogic traditions for stylistic and aesthetic purposes.

The historical relevance of the early neoclassical solo piano music, in particular, cannot be questioned – if only because of the timing of its emergence. The composition of the Piano Concerto, *Sonate* and *Sérénade* coincides with the publication and aftermath of Stravinsky's first ever article on a musical (or other) topic, 'Some Ideas about My *Octuor*'. This declaration of intent now required implementation through his music via more substantial genres than that provided by the 'occasional' format of eight players. The new works were destined for a more prestigious stage via the piano recital and symphonic concert. That the venue marked for Stravinsky's debut as pianist – and for the premiere of the Concerto – was the Paris Opéra would support the implication behind this reading: i.e. the composer was complicit in engineering a coordinated launch for his new 'brand', and of engaging in thinly disguised musical politics. His re-invention as a concert pianist gave him the ideal means to propagandize his message while also establishing a performance tradition for these works more effectively than via newsprint. Faced with these two objectives he forearmed himself – with a piano – and as 'counsel for his own defence' he set about delivering his message from the concert stage. But his armoury extended far deeper: to the pianism inherent in the very notes themselves which, I suggest, he formulated from pianistic sources whose figurations and gesture derive from those same processes that drive the pianist to laborious study and to public performance – and, even, to inconsequential improvisation. All of these aspects of musical production are presented here as elements accessed by Stravinsky via the long memory of his youth in St Petersburg; and this discourse will inevitably have implications throughout this volume.

Certain readings of the early neoclassical piano works will need to be re-considered: for example, Taruskin's identification of Russian aspects in the *Sonate* and *Sérénade* 'missed by Prokofiev'.[33] However, Taruskin's analysis, thorough as it is, fails to account for the unmistakable signs that these works (as well as the Piano Concerto and *Capriccio*) owe a considerable debt to Stravinsky's synthesis of the methods and materials of Russian pedagogy. In grounding his compositional process upon a pedagogic rhetoric, i.e. by reformulating techniques attributable to the workshop of piano study, Stravinsky would build several neoclassical works upon familiar (to him) 'codes of (piano) practice'. Initially he would construct pianistic and instrumental genres. In due course, elements of this pedagogical re-construction would be utilized in choral, operatic and symphonic contexts: for example in *Oedipus rex*, in *Mavra* and *The Rake's Progress*, and in the *Symphony of Psalms* and *Symphony in Three Movements*. In this way, the neoclassical canon reflects those disciplines and materials of piano study which Stravinsky first experienced in St Petersburg. In middle age, at the time of his pianistic career, he was to draw upon this early experience and use it as a point of reference – as a template from which to fashion a new idiom characterized by down-to-earth attitudes of work, craft and construction. Alexis Roland-Manuel (writing in 1923) describes the neoclassical Stravinsky as 'a musician who has no longer any concern other than technique, and who accords to *métier* alone the right to resolve all difficulties of the aesthetic'.[34] While such interests were not exclusive to Stravinsky, the manner in which he formulated his neoclassicism from the methodology, repertoire and aesthetic of pianism was unmatched. His international persona, therefore, will also need to be reviewed as a(nother) Stravinskian mask – this one concealing an identity characterized by an inescapably Russian musical education.

Stravinsky's Piano: Genesis of a Musical Language is structured to allow its main arguments to be placed repeatedly under scrutiny – and from various angles. For example, issues identified amid the minutiae of fingerings in 'Stravinsky's piano workshop' (Chapter 3) are anticipated in 'Becoming a Russian musician' (Chapter 1) and will be raised again in subsequent deliberations on the broader questions surrounding neoclassicism. Commentary regarding Stravinsky's late music in 'Departures and homecomings' (Chapter 4) provides the ideal opportunity to revisit these same practical issues from the 'intellectual' perspective of serialism. Similarly, Stravinsky's creative engagement with the learning process is initially considered as another sign of his interest in 'rules' and, even, the disciplined callisthenics of musical craft. Later, this interpretation is reviewed in the context of Stravinsky's neoclassical constructions – as a means to base his objectivity upon composition *and* pianism, i.e. upon the two musical acts which form his musical identity from the early 1920s onwards. The main concern of this volume is an exploration of Stravinsky's compositional processes. From the earliest sketches outlined in St Petersburg to the late works meticulously crafted in America, Stravinsky's substantial catalogue (particularly his canon of piano works) was guided, I propose, as much by a pianistic 'attitude' – which this study endeavours to (re)define – as by any stylistic orientation.

1 Becoming a Russian musician

Stravinsky's piano teachers

In recent years there has been a significant shift in the terms of engagement with which Stravinsky is viewed – away from the enclosed workrooms of formalist analysis and outdoors, as it were, into the wide expanses of boundless Rus'. The stale laboratory air of close analytical musicology – hermetically sealed from risk of hermeneutical contamination (or so it can appear) – has been refreshed by an invigorating blast of cultural studies. Such new readings of Stravinsky have cast fresh light upon the persona that the composer had laboriously constructed as a self-made figure on the international stage who owed little or nothing to his provincial roots – a free spirit, a phenomenon without a past.[1] We may now justifiably suspect that, despite some exile-induced remarks to the contrary, Stravinsky was 'really' a committed and knowledgeable Russianist, an expert and sensitive manipulator of Russian sources, a composer extraordinarily indebted to his own past – and beyond his past. For was not this polemicist of neoclassicism, this reluctant (neo)serialist, firmly rooted in Russian traditions all the while? Less clear, however, is which of those Russian 'attitudes' it was that most guided Stravinsky's international trajectory. Interpretations continue to be formulated regarding Stravinsky's place in late-nineteenth-century St Petersburg from which he emerged, and to which he 'therefore' related. As more information emerges about Stravinsky's childhood and youth one may contemplate his maturity from the perspective of his early musical interests and activities. It is now possible, for example, to regard Stravinsky's neoclassicism less as a gesture of re-invention – precipitated by *affaires de mode* in France, or by his Italian epiphany at the hands of 'Pergolesi' – but rather, to use Alexander Herzen's phrase, as a 'mere continuance of the past'.[2] Herzen gives voice to the precious importance of one's youth and reveals why it is such an attractive, if problematic, phase for historians: 'Childhood and the two or three years that follow are … the most truly our own; and indeed they are possibly the most important part, because they fix all that follows, though we are not aware of it.'[3] To address such specific concerns it is necessary to cast the web of enquiry far and wide. Which (other) aspects of Russia's manifold histories did Stravinsky engage with, and to what extent did he consider his present and future as, merely, a continuance of his past? Such issues, therefore, become fundamental to this opening chapter. Initially, some form of answer must be sought to the 'simple' yet paradoxically complex question: 'What kind of Russian was Stravinsky?'

In response to such unsettling interrogation one needs to consider not one but two Russias, as Stravinsky himself made clear during the dinner organized in his honour at Moscow's Metropole Hotel in October 1962. Before a gathering of leading composers and Soviet dignitaries Stravinsky rose to his feet to deliver one of the most poignant testaments that any composer has formulated. Such was the emotion at finding himself surrounded once again by fellow Russians after half a century of exile and at hearing his mother tongue being spoken – in his praise, too; this, at least, is Robert Craft's opinion – Stravinsky (like Chichikov before him) 'felt himself to be a true Russian'[4] and was moved to declare: 'A man has one birthplace, one fatherland, one country – one *can* have only one country – and the place of his birth is the most important factor in his life … I did not leave Russia of my own free will, even though I disliked much in *my Russia* and in *Russia generally*.'[5] There is a delicious ambiguity here that invites further examination, for it may illuminate Stravinsky's duality with regard to his past and to his very identity. The terms that Stravinsky employs to describe the locus of his 'home' are perhaps intended to be synonymous; Stravinsky may indeed have a single birthplace/fatherland/country. One *can* only lay claim to one country, as he emphasizes – but still he refers to *two* Russias: 'my Russia' and 'Russia generally'. From this latter term one assumes that Stravinsky is referring to the Russian nation, its cultural and geographical space – where Europe's sun rises, according to the popular saying[6] – incorporating Tsarist Russia and, latterly, the Soviet Union. As for 'my Russia', he surely means St Petersburg and all that Stravinsky's personal experience in that metropolis embraces – for this was 'the place of his birth'. Not literally of course, for he was born fifty *versts* to the west in Oranienbaum (now renamed Lomonosov); but St Petersburg – his home for the first twenty-eight years of his life[7] – was at the very centre (to borrow Philip Bohlman's term) of his metaphysical map.[8] It is this Russia, 'my Russia', which will be observed and re-interpreted throughout this book.

Stravinsky cannot merely be considered a representative of 'Russia generally'. Since when has a citizen born and bred in St Petersburg been anything other than a case apart? The city's very name defines its singularity. It has even been suggested that the original Dutch spelling and pronunciation of *Sankt Pieter Burkh*, its first official title (dating from 1703), exudes 'a certain foreignness which … somehow sounds correct for such a non-Russian town'.[9] Within those palatial, neoclassical surroundings – devised by Peter the Great to symbolize Russia's integration within eighteenth-century

Europe – it was inevitable that those educated in St Petersburg would develop a differentiated sense of identity. 'Nevsky Prospect is rectilineal because it is a European prospect … Other Russian cities are a wooden heap of hovels. And strikingly different from them all is Petersburg,' declares Andrei Bely in his celebrated portrait of 'this un-Russian, but nonetheless capital city'.[10] Moscow and St Petersburg (and Kiev), Russia's rival capitals, have long indulged in 'irreconcilable' differences. (Parallels can often be found, after all, wherever two cities – one ancient, the other modern – are separated by a comparable abyss, when each lays claim to a superior heritage, legacy and all-round 'authenticity'.) Commenting on this division of loyalties, Orlando Figes recalls Tolstoy's observation in *War and Peace* that 'every Russian felt Moscow to be a mother. There was a sense that it was the nation's "home", even for members of the most Europeanized élite of Petersburg … Moscow was a symbol of the old Russia, the place where ancient Russian customs were preserved … [and whose] history went back to the twelfth century'.[11] To paraphrase verses from *Ruslan and Lyudmila*: there, under the green oak tree, is a Russian spirit and 'it smells of Old Russia!'.[12] By comparison, St Petersburg's exceptional status has always been measured in terms of her westward-looking aspirations, to a degree quite alien to her rival's inward- or eastward-looking orientation. Discussion surrounding her privileged location – balanced, as it were, on the needle of the compass – inevitably registers the wider dimensions to this problem. 'For Russians also conceive of "west" and "east" in ways that mark the human experience generally', write Robert Maguire and John Malmstad in the Introduction to their translation of Bely's *Petersburg* (1916). '"West" stands for reason, order, symmetry; "east" for the irrational, the impalpable, the intuitive.'[13] St Petersburg's contemplation of Europe's ordered horizon was intrinsic to the city's very foundation. Her Internationalism – immortalized in Pushkin's 1833 poem *The Bronze Horseman* – was viewed, no less, as predestined. (The poem's title refers to the statue of Peter the Great, who 'stood, with lofty thoughts / And gazed into the distance'):[14] *Where are you galloping, proud steed, / And where will you drop your hooves? / O powerful commander of destiny?*[15] Moscow, on the other hand, was capable of fostering important initiatives in Russian artistic expression. In the field of the visual arts, turn-of-the-century Moscow was regarded as the centre of the Russian avant-garde. By comparison, as Diaghilev frankly admitted, Petersburg was but 'a city of artistic gossiping, academic professors and Friday watercolour classes'.[16] Coming from such 'an arch-patriot of Petrine culture', as Figes observes, 'this was a remarkable acknowledgement'.[17]

It is unsurprising, therefore, that over the years there fermented a certain rivalry also between the musical communities of these cities. Taneyev,

Director of the Moscow Conservatoire from 1885 to 1889 and well noted for his cosmopolitanism,[18] viewed St Petersburg composers as provincial amateurs who had never received, in Oskar von Riemann's elegant phrase, 'the consecration of the true musical grace which is counterpoint'.[19] It was with an eye to their deficiencies in particular, as much as for the enlightenment of the wider community of Russian musicians, that Taneyev – whom Boris Asaf'yev refers to as 'an incorrigible academic'[20] – dedicated his retirement to writing textbooks on invertible counterpoint and canon.[21] Rakhmaninov, who had studied composition under Taneyev, was to recall many years later how fellow students Arensky and Safanov had almost come to blows in the street upon completing their final counterpoint exam, such was the intensity of their dispute as to whether the subject 'should have been treated as *fuga reale* or *fuga in tono*'.[22] While the Petersburgian 'handful' attempted, it seems, to upstage each other in their claim for 'true Russian' culture, the Muscovite community assumed their sense of cultural superiority by historical right. If late-nineteenth-century Moscow was the incontestable centre of Russian national culture and the seat of a lofty engagement with musical academicism based upon 'iconic' western traditions, what could be left for the St Petersburg circle except an identity as 'lesser' Russians – of appearing fiercely (if inappropriately) nationalist, of representing a 'new town' without sufficient 'truly Russian' history, of being culturally incomplete, of promoting a certain dilettantism with regard to counterpoint and the higher musical arts? Stravinsky, however, was an aspirant symphonist and found Taneyev's example most worthy of his attention. In November 1905 he performed Taneyev's Fourth Symphony (a year after it had been awarded the Glinka Prize) in Rimsky-Korsakov's apartment, in four-hand arrangement. This experience, Taruskin asserts, 'provided Stravinsky with a model for the contrapuntally saturated texture that pervades [the] first movement'[23] of his own Symphony in E♭ op. 1 (1905/7).

That distinctiveness to Stravinsky's Petersburgian sense of identity was to be crucial also to his creative individuality. Writing in 1921 in praise of Tchaikovsky (a fellow St Petersburg composer), Stravinsky would express his admiration by means of a barbed reference to Moscow's reputation: 'Tchaikovsky's music, which does not appear specifically Russian to everybody, is often more profoundly Russian than music which has long since been awarded the facile label of Muscovite picturesque-ness.'[24] Stravinsky signs off his open letter with a hearty endorsement of *The Sleeping Beauty*, his sense of patriotism and pride clearly rekindled by his renewed acquaintance with Tchaikovsky's great ballet: 'I warmly desire that … audiences of all countries may feel this work as it is felt by me, a *Russian musician*.'[25] Two decades earlier, however, Stravinsky had yet to merit that title. From his earliest musical awakenings he would have become conscious of the existence of a musical pantheon presided over by Tchaikovsky and Glinka and, later, of the necessity of entering through its portals if he was to be accepted, similarly, as 'a Russian musician' with all that this implied. Rimsky-Korsakov, alone amongst his contemporaries of the St Petersburg fraternity, wished a share of this admirable Internationalism – particularly a dominion over western musical theory. Stravinsky also desired membership of the same élite – the result (as recounted in the *Autobiography*) of his upbringing in the corridors of the Maryinsky Theatre. But this was also due to the specific cultural imprint he gained as a favoured student of Rimsky-Korsakov. Stravinsky has alluded to the intimate bond, almost as father-to-son, that existed between them at one time. However, once he left Russia – indeed, for the greater part of his career – his references to Rimsky-Korsakov were almost invariably disparaging, venting his defiance in the manner of Pushkin's 'poor madman' who 'became gloomy before the proud monster [the statue of Peter the Great portrayed in *The Bronze Horseman*] and, gritting his teeth, making a fist of his fingers, like someone possessed by dark forces, whispered with a vicious shudder: "Fine, miraculous builder, I'll show you!"'.[26] Despite such attempts to write his teacher out of his biography, Stravinsky shared much with Rimsky-Korsakov including an intense and life-long admiration for Glinka and Tchaikovsky, whom they both regarded as the fathers of 'truly Russian' composition, and for the most Petersburgian of reasons: they had succeeded in marrying their indigenous tastes and talents – the 'Slavic soul' – to the incomparable technical sophistication of western music – the 'European intellect'. (Herzen's description of St Petersburg as being 'the seasoned mind of the [Russian] Empire', 'Russia's brain … encased in a skull of ice and granite', somehow reflects the coolly intellectual aspirations of her artistic community.)[27] How fortuitous that Stravinsky should become the private pupil of the one composer within reach whose views were so similar to his and whose teachings, as a result, would colour his attitudes far into the future: not merely in terms of the orchestration of his Russian works, but also in terms of his view of the eighteenth century, of 'Bach', of craft and objectivity – issues which would become particularly vital to Stravinsky's view of neoclassicism. Under Rimsky-Korsakov's guidance Stravinsky's application of the piano's functions expanded to encompass a tri-faceted role: (1) as a practical aid to composition; (2) as a solo concert instrument; and (3) as an effective vehicle, when used to accompany the voice, for projecting orchestral evocations. Regarding the latter, Stravinsky was later to confirm that it was completely natural for him, at this time, to become acquainted with orchestral sonorities via the piano:

Apart from my improvisation and piano-practice, I found immense pleasure in reading the opera scores of which my father's library consisted … Imagine my joy, therefore, when for the first time I was taken to the theatre where they were giving an opera with which as a pianist I was already familiar. It was *A Life for the Tsar*, and it was then I heard an orchestra for the first time. And what an orchestra – Glinka's! The impression was indelible, but it must not be supposed that this was due solely to the fact that it was the first orchestra I ever heard. To this day, not only Glinka's music in itself, but his orchestration as well, remains a perfect monument of musical art – so intelligent is his balance of tone, so distinguished and delicate his instrumentation; and by the latter I mean his choice of instruments and his way of combining them. I was indeed fortunate in happening on a *chef d'oeuvre* for my first contact with great music. That is why my attitude towards Glinka has always been one of unbounded gratitude.[28]

It was surely a source of great satisfaction for both Stravinsky and his teacher that, apart from their shared vision of the piano and its privileged, multi-functional role within the firmament of instruments, they should also retain a profound affection for their earliest musical memories of Glinka; for Rimsky-Korsakov too had sensed 'his deepest musical impressions … from some numbers of Glinka's *A Life for the Tsar*' which he found at his home.[29] Both of them, therefore, had first accessed Glinka's 'perfect monument' via piano reduction. Of course, it was as an orchestral/operatic work that Glinka's intelligent tonal balance and his 'distinguished and delicate instrumentation' could be savoured to the full. However, they had both acquired an early appreciation of how such a pianistic text could operate as testimony to, and yet remain quite separate from, the eventual aural experience of the composer's fully realized conception. Just as Stravinsky's precocious enthusiasm for Glinka (and Pushkin and Tchaikovsky) nourished the neoclassical opera buffa *Mavra*, so one is drawn to examine other facets of Stravinsky's childhood years and youth 'because [as Herzen reminds us] they fix all that follows'. It is therefore appropriate to proceed with a (re-) consideration of Stravinsky's pianistic formation, such is the potential significance of his early pianistic experiences, 'though we are not [yet] aware of it'.

Speaking through the filter of literary collaborators Stravinsky was less than consistent in his revelations of his Russian childhood, for whatever motive. Therefore the résumé that he himself wrote in March 1908, at the request of the composer and critic G. H. Timofeyev, assumes considerable importance for being the only published writing about his early years that is actually 'by him'.[30] Compared to subsequent, often bitter indictments of the personalities who figured in the composer's youth, the tone of this miniature autobiography is frank and conciliatory. The text possesses a confident, yet unpretentious manner; Stravinsky does not shy away from the honest admission of his former ignorance and indiscipline. Between the lines one perceives the enjoyment Stravinsky derives from his musical activities as well as an understandable pride in his achievements to date. Although modest in scope this first 'autobiography' is useful to our purpose for determining, with accuracy, the sequence of his music teachers for piano and musical rudiments. Given its uniqueness and historical moment, it is worth citing here at length:

> I was born in Oranienbaum on June 18, 1882. At the age of nine I began to take piano lessons with A. P. [Aleksandra Petrovna] Snyetkova, the daughter of the violinist at the Maryinsky Theater orchestra. At eleven I entered St Petersburg School No. 27, where I was a poor student as well as an ill-behaved one. I remained there until the end of the fifth grade, then entered the Gurevich School. Here I completed my intermediate education. I then went to St Petersburg University for a total of eight semesters.
>
> Hoping to make a pianist of me, my parents did not stint on the cost of teachers but gave me the opportunity to study with the very best ones, such as L. A. [Leokadiya Aleksandrovna] Kashperova, from whom I took lessons for two years. But I was attracted to composition before that and have always had a lively interest in the musical classics. I did a large amount of sight-reading, which helped my development. The lack of education in theory became an ever greater obstacle, however, and though I improvised endlessly and enjoyed it immensely, I was unable to write down what I played. I ascribed this to my lack of theoretical knowledge. Until I began to take lessons in harmony with Akimenko, you might say that I ripened in ignorance.[31] But I soon switched from him to Kalafati, with whom I studied harmony and counterpoint.[32] In my university years I became friendly with the Rimsky-Korsakov family and then advanced very rapidly.[33]

The need still to resolve even basic factual divergences becomes apparent when one considers the difficulty in establishing the exact age at which Stravinsky initiated formal piano lessons. From the perspective of his twenty-six years, the composer recalls that '[a]t the age of nine I began to take piano lessons with A. P. Snyetkova', i.e. in 1891, possibly early 1892 – prior, at least, to his tenth birthday in June 1892. Taruskin asserts that 'the boy took lessons from her for most of his teens, *from the fall of 1893*',[34] and Walsh is in agreement.[35] Fyodor Stravinsky's account books make no mention of any music lessons as early as 1891, the first annotation being for May 1892 – some casual piano lessons by a temporary governess, O. A. Petrova.[36] Viktor Varunts also suggests that in the autumn of 1892 the

Stravinsky children received some lessons from Petrova's successor, Y. M. Yanovich – but Fyodor's usually meticulous account books do not state this clearly.[37] Whether or not, in omitting so much information, Stravinsky was demonstrating an early penchant for rewriting his past, or whether he was simply responding to editorial policy, it is clear that many details of his early musical training are still in doubt. More significant data regarding his repertoire, his progress and the manner in which he was taught – information essential for a re-construction of Stravinsky's mature pianistic identity – are, therefore, even more difficult to confirm.[38]

One imagines that Stravinsky developed a natural affection for his piano teachers although this is not a view supported by the composer's bitter comments in his 1935 autobiography and the late *Conversations*. Nevertheless, one need not accept the composer's slant on this period. From what little evidence there is, Stravinsky appears to have made good progress under Snyetkova. By the time he had graduated to tuition under Kashperova in 1899 he was of a sufficient standard for the latter to suggest, sometime within the following two years, that he tackle the considerable challenges of Mendelssohn's opus 25: 'I learned to play the … G minor concerto[39] with Mlle Kashperova, and many sonatas by Clementi and Mozart as well as sonatas and other pieces by Haydn, Beethoven, Schubert and Schumann.'[40] Stravinsky does not ever mention Snyetkova by name though one questions whether by 1960, when the seventy-eight-year-old composer was recalling his early progress on the piano, his memory did not juxtapose the whole learning experience of his adolescence, and credit this in its entirety to Kashperova. The music that Stravinsky cites, especially the 'sonatas by Clementi', suggests repertoire of an earlier phase of his learning when he would have been taught by Snyetkova; indeed, the reference to 'pieces' by Schubert and Schumann may refer to the *Impromptus*, *Novelettes* and other *pièces charactéristiques* that form an intrinsic part of a younger pianist's repertoire. Aside from such speculation very little is known about Snyetkova. Not even L. S. Dyachkova, in a footnote to the Timofeyev letter, can give her dates more completely than '1872–?'.[41] Stravinsky's assertion that his parents 'hoped to make a pianist' of him is surely challenged by the fact that no piano teacher was found for him until he was nine (or ten) – an age when Russian children recognized as possessing musical talent would already have been receiving lessons for some years, even, as is still the custom today, from the age of five. That Stravinsky later attended law school for eight semesters rather than enter the Conservatoire casts further doubt on this claim, though his parents may be forgiven for failing to recognize their son's potential given his disengaged attitude to music studies.

Yet, however tempting it may be 'not to tarry'[42] when information about Stravinsky's early musical education is so sparse, one may still glean an indication of the benefits that he acquired from Snyetkova's tuition. Fyodor Stravinsky's account books indicate, for example, that in November 1897 his son purchased music by Chopin,[43] although no details are given as to which works or volume. This may have been an interest encouraged by Snyetkova and reflected her line of teaching. It would suggest that her fifteen-year-old pupil had reached the level needed to acquire knowledge of the Chopin style with the concomitant demands of this romantic idiom: specifically, a cantabile melodic projection in the right hand and a more advanced pedalling technique than would have been required in classical repertoire. Under Snyetkova's tutelage Stravinsky developed into more than a talented improviser; and by the time he passed into the hands of Kashperova he was evidently an expert sight-reader and experienced in duet-playing.

Stravinsky's studies under Snyetkova may be better understood in a pedagogical sense as a time when he concluded his transition between the two principal phases of cognitive development as defined by John A. Sloboda (1985); that is, enculturation and training.[44] This corresponds to A. N. Whitehead's more contemporaneous terminology (1917): 'the stage of romance' and 'the stage of precision'.[45] From these two processes, writes Sloboda, derive 'the spontaneous acquisition of musical skill'.[46] Enculturation may be described as both a shared set of primitive capacities (potentialities) and a shared set of experiences which a culture provides as children grow up. According to Sloboda, enculturation is typified by a lack of self-conscious effort and a lack of explicit instruction. It is a phase of infancy when young children 'do not *aspire* to improve their ability to pick up songs, although they do improve. Adults do not *instruct* young children in the art of song memorization, yet children come to be able to memorize songs.'[47] Sloboda's second or 'training phase' of cognitive behaviour coincides with the development of specialized musical skills. In this later phase pupils *do aspire* to improve and adults *do instruct* and a person is encouraged to build upon 'the general foundation of enculturation to achieve expertise'. Yet these (musical) experiences are not necessarily shared by all members of a culture. 'Rather, they are specific to the sub-culture where aspiration to excellence in a particular skill is encouraged.'[48] The training phase typically takes place in a self-consciously educational milieu; so, therefore, it may particularly be associated with the years Stravinsky spent as a private pupil of both Snyetkova and Kashperova. In this context it will be useful to assess the theory and practice of the latter's teaching and Stravinsky's response to both.

In his autobiography Stravinsky refers to Kashperova's prohibition of the sustaining pedal and her regimented work-plan, while acknowledging her beneficial influence in terms of piano technique. She clearly instilled in him a responsible attitude towards practice. He strongly disapproved of her interpretative references, which were modelled on Rubinstein. Rather, Stravinsky responded to Kashperova as a training model. She was heir to the long pedagogic tradition in St Petersburg; and her contribution in this regard is based upon the revered methods of Theodor Leschetizky. Kashperova may have been the 'spokesperson', but it was Leschetizky's message that echoed – albeit unacknowledged – through Stravinsky's mature neoclassical idiom and ideological stance. And the impact that this message made upon Stravinsky was surely due, and in no small measure, to the forcefulness and multi-faceted professionalism of 'Mlle Kashperova'.[49] Not only was she a virtuoso pianist and composer herself, but at the time of Stravinsky's lessons she successfully maintained both professions in Russia while rapidly developing her reputation abroad. Kashperova's double-profession was, after all, the same one which Stravinsky would eventually aspire to, becoming – as 'dual-craft' – an integral element of his neoclassical persona. One should not underestimate, therefore, the importance of Kashperova's conscious or involuntary effect upon Stravinsky, given the inevitably intense nature of their master–apprentice relationship – and regardless of his subsequent and cynical revision of that undoubtedly beneficial experience. Research into the imitative, aspirational character of teaching/learning environments would require that Stravinsky's pianistic and emotional development at the hands of Kashperova also be measured in the context of one-to-one, instrumental tuition.

Kashperova was an excellent role model in many respects and Stravinsky would have done well to learn from her example. Indeed, Stravinsky's principal mentor in the pianistic field deserves to be better known and her influence judged alongside that of the personalities already familiar to Stravinsky literature. The entry for L. A. Kashperova in Dyachkova's roster of the musical profession in Russia is brief: 'Kashperova (married name Andronova), Leokadiya Aleksandrovna (1872–1940): pianist and composer, pupil of A. G. Rubinstein'.[50] She graduated from the St Petersburg Conservatoire in 1895, which indicates that she would have been a pupil of Rubinstein in his second and final period there. Her participation in his elite, soloists' class is a measure of her exceptional pianistic qualities. She was thereafter held in sufficiently high opinion in contemporary music circles to be called upon to premiere Glazunov's E minor Sonata in 1902 and Balakirev's B♭ minor Sonata three years later.[51] There is mention of a symphony (published by Bessel) and a piano concerto which she even performed in Berlin;[52] her foreign recital tours included several west European capitals including London. However, Stravinsky's portrayals of Kashperova – from a passing reference in his *Autobiography* to a thorough condemnation in *Memories and Commentaries* – were parsimonious at best. According to Walsh, she has the dubious honour of being 'only the first of several victims of [Stravinsky's] revisionist bent'.[53] In the context of his autobiography – with an eye, surely, to impress his western readers in defiance of his ex-colleagues in Leningrad – the composer chose to recall his experiences as follows:

> I often undertook to defend my principles of the group, and in a most peremptory manner, when I came up against the antiquated opinions of those who did not realize that they themselves had long since been left behind. Thus I had to battle with my second piano mistress, a pupil and admirer of Anton Rubinstein. She was an excellent pianist and good musician, but completely obsessed by her adoration for her illustrious master, whose views she blindly accepted.[54]

Taruskin is right to accuse Stravinsky of giving Kashperova 'short shrift … not even mentioning her by name'.[55] From this reference to her as his 'piano mistress' one imagines Kashperova to be an elderly Victorian dame, not a vigorous twenty-seven-year-old successfully developing her international career as a composer and concert artist. In the decade following her graduation she earned the admiration and affection of several leading musical figures including Rimsky-Korsakov and Nikolay Solovyov (with whom she had studied composition at the Conservatoire).[56] The portrait that Stravinsky paints of her as a musical reactionary is questionable: 'I had great difficulty in making her accept the scores of Rimsky-Korsakov or of Wagner – which at that period I was fervently studying.'[57] This view was later to be contradicted: 'We played Rimsky's operas together four-hands, and I remember deriving much pleasure from *Christmas Eve* this way.'[58] Such a revelation invalidates the composer's complaint against Kashperova's 'narrowness and formulae' made in the same breath.[59] Rimsky-Korsakov's opera after Gogol, *Noch pered Rozhdestvom* (*Christmas Eve*), had been premiered in St Petersburg as recently as December 1895. By reading through its four-hand reduction, Kashperova evidenced neither disinterest in Rimsky-Korsakov's music nor narrowness in her tastes. One wonders how many piano teachers, before or since, would introduce their pupils to the latest in contemporary opera? Stravinsky did have the decency, however grudgingly, to give Kashperova credit for giving him an early sense of *métier*: 'I must say that, notwithstanding our differences of opinion, this excellent musician managed to give a new impetus to my piano-playing and to the development of my technique.'[60] Yet, by 1960 the composer's selective memory had provoked him to a virulent slur upon her name:

> She was an excellent pianist and a blockhead – a not unusual combination. By which I mean that her aesthetics and her bad taste were impregnable but her pianism was of a high order … I am most in Kashperova's debt, however, for something she would not have appreciated. Her narrowness and her formulae greatly encouraged the supply of bitterness that accumulated in my soul until, in my mid-twenties, I broke loose and revolted from her and from every stultification in my studies, my schools, and my family. The real answer to [enquiries] about my childhood is that it was a period of waiting for the moment when I could send everyone and everything connected with it to hell.[61]

The notion that Kashperova 'blindly accepted' Rubinstein's views is also questionable. If her antipathy to Wagner – a posture she is accused of inheriting from Rubinstein – was as heated as her supposed disinterest in Rimsky-Korsakov, this criticism may also be unfounded. Neither should one be concerned with Kashperova's reported ban on the use of the pedals: 'Mlle Kasperova's only idiosyncrasy as a teacher was in forbidding me all use of pedals; I had to sustain with my fingers, like an organist – an omen, perhaps, as I have never been a pedal composer.'[62] Whether or not this was a means primarily to wean the young improviser off the over-use of the pedal,[63] Kashperova employed a perfectly legitimate teaching method – one that can be identified with many virtuoso pianists in the mainstream of the romantic tradition. Chopin was noted for his many fingering innovations, eye-witness accounts confirming that he 'changed fingers upon a key as often as an organ-player'.[64] Nearer still to the piano traditions fostered in Russia during the nineteenth century was the example of Adolph von Henselt, 'a characteristic feature of [whose] technique was to sustain widely arpeggiated figures and chords as much as possible with the fingers, avoiding the use of the pedal'.[65] Thus, the characteristic dry sonority of Stravinsky's neoclassical piano works and those uncomfortably wide stretches, particularly in the left hand, may be read as another nineteenth-century Petersburgian tradition coopted to the cause of the modernist, objective aesthetic. The performance styles of such influential pianists as Henselt and Rubinstein may have differed, yet they were united in the value they attributed to proper use of the pedal. Its expert deployment was regarded in both camps as central to the question of good, contemporary taste. Rubinstein in particular was considered a master of this resource, as Rakhmaninov observed, having heard him play in 1885 when he was twelve years old: 'One of Rubinstein's great secrets was his use of the pedal. He himself has very happily expressed his ideas on the subject when he said, "The pedal is the soul of the piano." No pianist should ever forget this.'[66] Was not a pupil of Rubinstein such as Kashperova, therefore, all the more likely to take the judicious application of this precious and often-abused resource very seriously? To understand better the young Stravinsky's intense and contradictory response to Kashperova's message – and the nature of his own attitudes to the piano, to piano study and to performance – it will be useful to consider the historical context; for, as with the specific issue of the (non-) use of the pedal, much of relevance may be elicited from reviewing the legacy of pianism in St Petersburg – considering firstly the impact of Henselt upon subsequent piano virtuosi, particularly Rubinstein and his disciples. Such was the dominance of this latter's personality in forming cultural traditions concerning the role of the piano virtuoso and the manner of pianistic teaching, Rubinstein's influence may be said to have guided Russian musical and cultural perceptions right up to the present day.

From the considerable volume of literature written about the performance style of the great nineteenth-century virtuosi, it is possible to elucidate which elements of this tradition (indoctrinated into the fabric of the St Petersburg Conservatoire community) may singularly have failed to impress the young Stravinsky – especially when viewed from the perspective of his later aesthetic taste and musical development. Principal amongst these antipathies must surely have been the cult of the 'great virtuoso', for an intrinsic element of this – particularly in the nineteenth century – was the artistic licence that these idolized performers could wield over the composer's material. In the context of St Petersburg this notion undoubtedly derives from Henselt's arrival at court in 1836: 'Henselt does not play Chopin as that master ought to be played, and we can but agree with the great virtuoso, that, when one is a Henselt one has the right to play as one likes, as we once heard him remark.'[67] Wilhelm von Lenz's book from which this quotation is taken was published in 1899 but his observations were originally penned around 1868,[68] by which time the term 'great virtuoso' is evidently in common usage. Furthermore, the virtuoso's privileges are accepted without censure. However, Henselt should not be judged on this one critique. Hearing him play at Broadwood's in London in 1867, Alfred Hipkins (1826–1903) wrote to a Russian acquaintance that Henselt's playing was 'glorious, faultless … Chopin never had a finer interpreter'.[69] It is a fair assumption, though, that this fine interpretation was characterized by much artistic licence.

A half-generation later Anton Rubinstein's interpretative freedom was seen to be his principal strength – one of the foremost characteristics, in fact, that defined him as a 'great virtuoso'. Yet, such attitudes and manner were by no means universally held. Oscar Bie, writing in 1898, compares Rubinstein's performance style with the more clinical approach of Hans von Bülow:

> Rubinstein was the great subjective artist, who gave way entirely to the mood of the moment, and could rush on in an instant in such a way as to leave no room for the cool criticism of a later hour. [However] Bülow was the great objective artist, the teacher and unfolder of all mysteries ... Both artists were of their kind finished and complete, and both were of incalculable influence on whole generations. The impressionist Rubinstein and the draughtsman Bülow had each the technique which suited him.

Bie confirms, in short, that Rubinstein 'rushed and raved, and a slight want of polish was the natural result of his impressionist temperament'.[70] While this impulsive autonomy was clearly recognized as one of the hallmarks of Rubinstein's prowess – and, by implication, endorsed as a sine qua non for all performing artists of subjective persuasion – Rubinstein the pedagogue would not tolerate such playing in his pupils, as Gerig relates: 'Although Rubinstein had often played with considerable liberty himself, he admonished his students: "When you are as old as I am now you may do as I do – if you can."'[71] His pupils were evidently not granted this prerogative, but had to earn it the hard way. Despite this, the message was abundantly clear: interpretative liberty was intensely desirable, was an elevated state of artistry to which one should aspire, and was understood to define the stature and maturity of the performer. One may remark in passing how much more appropriate 'the draughtsman Bülow' would have been as a model for our future neoclassicist, given the description here offered by Oscar Bie: '[he] drew carefully the threads from the keys ... while every tone and every tempo stood in ironbound firmness, and every line was there before it was drawn'.[72] In his programme-planning Bülow anticipated other twentieth-century practices. 'When he gave public recitals he did not, like Rubinstein, crowd a history of the piano into a few evenings.' According to Bie: 'He took by preference a single author, like Beethoven, and played only the five last Sonatas, or he unfolded the whole of Beethoven historically in four evenings ... Great draughtsman as he was, he hated all half-lights and colourations; he pointed his pencil very finely, and his paper was very white.'[73]

The two prime techniques associated with late-romantic mannerism are the frequent arpeggiation of chords and the asynchronization of bass and treble.[74] Stravinsky's overriding contempt in later years for this period of his musical awakening may also relate to his aversion to this sub-set of affectations. Kenneth Hamilton has warned of the dangers of reading too much of the teacher in the pupil's playing; nevertheless (as he illustrates) it is revealing to compare those early recordings from which 'a broad stylistic range' can be perceived.[75] Of particular interest to this study are the recordings of Theodor Leschetizky, who influenced the careers of many distinguished pianists emerging from St Petersburg, and whose performance style was widely emulated across the international musical scene. According to Hamilton, Leschetizky 'played in a left-hand-before-right style easily as extensive as that of his most successful student Paderewski',[76] adding: 'Paderewski arpeggiated chords so frequently, that a chord played together was almost a special effect. Moreover, in [his recording of Chopin's *Nocturne in* E♭ *op. 9, no. 2*] virtually every left hand bass note is played before the melody note with which, according to the notation, it ought to synchronise.'[77] Such a mannerism as this was not explained nor directed through published methods or treatises of the time; this style of playing had become an integral part of late-nineteenth-century performance practice. It was plainly unnecessary for this to be explained via the printed word, just as it would have been well-nigh impossible for this array of chord-arpeggiations and melody-note-delays to be adequately notated. Much less would this have been a requirement of the composer.[78] Nor would this degree of imposition from the composer have been desirable, nor even, one may speculate (given the elevated status afforded the virtuoso performer at that time), would it have been tolerated. It is upon this precious evidence, in conjunction with the ample literature available on Anton Rubinstein, that the teaching methods during those early decades of the St Petersburg Conservatoire can be re-constructed. It is possible, in other words, to compare the opinions of the founding fathers of the Russian pianistic school on a variety of musical and didactic issues, and to speculate from a more informed perspective upon the impact of these values on the adolescent (and adult) Stravinsky.

If Anton Rubinstein, famed for his performances of surging emotion and improvisatory *rubato*, was the model for the younger generation of his pupils (and, one may surmise, *their* pupils in turn), what, then, was Leschetizky's view with regard to the central question of tempo? According to Leschetizky's method, as described by his pupil and teaching assistant Malwine Brée: 'Where an *a tempo* follows [a ritardando] it should quite often not be taken literally at the very outset, but the former tempo should be led up to gradually – beginning the reprise of the theme like an improvisation, for instance. Thus, in the course of one or two measures, one would regain the original tempo.'[79] Such romantic rhetoric would have become anathema to Stravinsky and one senses how this legacy – prevalent in early-twentieth-century performances – may have haunted him. His tempo indications are precise and afford no place for gradual deviation, in the

form of accelerando or ritardando. Such markings in the Violin Concerto –
for example 'poco rit.', 'subito a tempo (ma non accelerare)' – indicate that
he was (even in 1931) alert to such dangers from 'interpreters'.[80] It is to be
expected that Kashperova wore her hard-earned credentials on her sleeve
and delivered piano tuition that, in both spirit and letter, closely modelled
that which she herself received. Neither would her reputation have been
enhanced by offering anything less than proper Conservatoire-standard
training to the son of Fyodor Stravinsky, the Maryinsky's leading bass, and
in his very drawing-room. These were surely the 'antiquated opinions' that
(Igor) Stravinsky 'had to battle with', though by the time of his autobiography
it was a view formed from considerable hindsight and moulded to support
his reputation as a neoclassicist. At the time, however, Stravinsky not only
applied himself under Kashperova's guidance to successful mastery of the
Mendelssohn G minor Concerto, but he embraced a late-nineteenth-century
idiom so completely as to reproduce an opulent and thoroughly convincing
romanticism in his own F♯ minor Sonata (1903–4). As Taruskin has identified, with this work Stravinsky had emulated his idol Tchaikovsky most
skilfully.[81] The early Sonata may be viewed, then, not only as the *Probestück*
(Taruskin's term) by which Rimsky-Korsakov agreed to accept Stravinsky
as his private pupil; it was also the *Probestück* by which Stravinsky achieved
self-acceptance, identifying *himself* as one who is properly qualified to confront the future as a composer, to enter the profession. The F♯ minor Sonata
tends to be dismissed – more, perhaps, to save the composer's blushes –
though it is open to debate whether Stravinsky did not view this *at the time*
as a formidable personal achievement, proof to himself both of his musical
maturity and of his having successfully assumed the expressive idiom of the
Russian masters. Only later, particularly in the neoclassical context, would
such pianism have been anathema to him – this, despite his open letter to
Diaghilev (1921) eulogizing 'our great and beloved Tchaikovsky'.[82]

It may be that Kashperova handled her pupils in a dogmatic fashion,
modelling her approach on Rubinstein, and that Stravinsky's memory
served him well. Such a tense atmosphere would have been difficult for
Stravinsky – already aware of his own musical strengths and potential, yet
insecure about his lack of theoretical knowledge. Furthermore, although
it is a speculative suggestion, the fact that Stravinsky was not a student at
the Conservatoire may also have preyed on his mind; despite appearances
to the contrary, he might have craved the thoroughness of that institution's
education, above all the confidence that this would bring. It was surely to
this that he referred when he wrote of 'the antiquated opinions of those who
did not realize that they themselves had long since been left behind'.[83] He
returns to this theme in the *Conversations*: despite Kashperova's technique

being 'of a high order', 'her aesthetics and bad taste were impregnable'.[84] Perhaps the same models of impregnability and infallibility that he recognized in his youth fuelled Stravinsky's own brand of dogmatic insistence later, in his relationships with his interpreters – famously in his dealings with Arthur Rubinstein. The distinguished Chopin pianist was forced to lament, as Cortot reported sympathetically: 'In the music of Stravinsky one must assume the role of a sad and unquestioning servant, blindly carrying out [*exécuter*] the composer's orders.'[85] Cortot's phraseology of complaint is surely an echo of the St Petersburgian legacy. Stravinsky had levelled his rant against Kashperova's dominance over him, complaining of Anton Rubinstein's dominance over her. Now, twentieth-century pianists must follow Stravinsky's law. He may have replaced some of the old ideologies, but Stravinsky was to perpetuate the nineteenth-century Russian tradition of master–apprentice absolutism, particularly with regards to the performance of his own music.[86]

Early piano solos

Tarantella *(1898): fragment*

It was while learning with Snyetkova that Stravinsky began to compose – in the sense of writing down his musical ideas: the *Tarantella* sketch for piano is dated 14 October 1898.[87] It is possible that the decision to compose a tarantella may have been stimulated by familiarity with romantic models – through Chopin, Liszt, Heller, Auber, Weber or Thalberg, all of whom wrote tarantellas for piano solo. Valeriy Smirnov, who discovered this *chernovoy nabrosok* ('rough sketch'), attributes the 'character and sound' of the sketch to 'images of the Russian musical East' which Stravinsky would have absorbed through the filter of Glinka's *Ruslan and Lyudmila* and *A Life for the Tsar*.[88] More relevant, perhaps, was a late flourishing of 'tarantism' in Russia via Dargomïzhsky (*Slavyanskaya tarantella* for piano duet, 1864–5) and Cui (*Tarantelle* for violin and piano, 1893) – even via Tchaikovsky (*Capriccio italien*, 1880). Dargomïzhsky's amusing work may have featured in Stravinsky's piano lessons, for familiarity with duet repertoire was regarded as an important element of early piano training. If this were the case, credit for directing Stravinsky towards such byways of the piano repertoire (that would appeal to this impish improviser) is undoubtedly due to Snyetkova. It is most unlikely that he would have gleaned knowledge of this music from his stern father, immersed as he was in the operatic milieu; in fact, none of the correspondence between Fyodor and Igor Stravinsky collated by Varunts (1970) or Kutateladze and Gozenpude (1972)[89] makes any reference to piano literature. Evidently his father's encouragement did not extend to the recommendation of specific repertoire; one must assume that Fyodor considered this level of orientation to lie within Snyetkova's remit.

Even so, the *Tarantella* is less likely to have emerged from the formality of the piano course than from Stravinsky's familial terms of reference. Its lack of sophistication is not so much cause for surprise or disappointment but, rather, prompts one to conjecture at the true nature of the boy's improvisations as he struggled to notate, without adequate theoretical knowledge, even the simplest fruits of his fertile imagination.[90] Nor is the work's childish character inconsistent with the probable inspiration for the work: Stravinsky's spider-hunting adventures with his cousin Zhenya on the Yelachich family estate at Pechisky, dating from as far back as the summer of 1893, when Stravinsky was eleven – if not earlier. By 1898, and with any number of improvisations to choose from for an initial attempt at notation, the sixteen-year-old Stravinsky may well have chosen a favourite one based on a holiday escapade that had since become part of family folklore. By the tone of the young boy's letter to his parents it was certainly the stuff that entertaining domestic improvisations are made of:

> Three days ago we went to catch tarantulas; we lowered a string with wax on it, and the tarantula at once grabbed it. I ran and fetched an axe to dig it out, and Zhenya dug a hole six inches deep and poked it with a knife; and suddenly the tarantula appeared, and so abruptly that we all yelled 'Tarantula!' It seemed to take fright and started running off, but Zhenya put a glass over it so that it couldn't get out. We showed it to everyone. Then Zhenya put it back down its hole.[91]

Stravinsky was probably able to improvise any number of tarantellas, scherzos and other dances, many based on actual incidents or on people in his intimate circle, for as he later wrote: 'I could improvise without end, and was passionately fond of doing so.'[92] The models for these improvisations may even have included the characteristic dance movements of much of the duet repertoire – a tradition that Stravinsky was to enhance further, in due course, with his own four-hand compositions. One can only speculate as to whether the bundle of piano scores piled up on top of the old upright at Ustilug included Dargomïzhsky's *Slavonic Tarantella*.[93]

Stravinsky's *Tarantella* may appear unremarkable to observers who seek a work displaying youthful genius. Taruskin may bewail 'the opening period [with its] childish open fifths in the bass and a hackneyed "Russian" cadence that leaps a fourth to the tonic note' (Example 1.1a) and conclude that 'the only thing remarkable about the *Tarantella* is how little talent it displays'.[94] Smirnov's reading of the melody attributes its pentatonic contour

Ex. 1.1 Stravinsky, *Tarantella* (fragment, 1898):

(a) first sketch

(b) second sketch

to the Georgian dance *lezginka* and the left-hand fifths to Glazunov's ballet *Raymonda* (1896/7). However, within the present context it is more pertinent to observe how this passage operates entirely within the interval of the fifth, both hands exploiting the melodic and harmonic possibilities of the five-finger span – in anticipation of similar procedures, twenty-three years later, in *Les Cinq Doigts*. Setting aside his shortcomings in notation, Stravinsky is credited by Smirnov with demonstrating 'melodic logic' and 'harmonic fantasy'.[95] But the sixteen-year-old *pianist* was at a significantly more advanced level than this. As a novice composer, Stravinsky was evidently developing an early fascination for the permutations available within this *ur*-pianistic envelope, which would have constituted (as for all young learners before and since) the basis of his daily practice. Rather than viewing *Tarantella* as an example of immature writing, the sketch may be understood better as an early (possibly initial) attempt at notating improvisation. As such, it suggests that the path by which Stravinsky began to formulate his personal creativity was one within which he transformed the improvised musical idea into a notated musical composition via the terrain of familiar pianistic formulae. The greater significance of this 'work' is not, therefore, as composition, but as process. *Tarantella*'s true worth lies not in its artistic value as finished composition, but as a creative process adopted intuitively by Stravinsky at a time when he was still musically uneducated.

One is reminded that, regarding musical theory, Stravinsky was entirely self-taught at this stage; he was not to commence lessons in rudiments with Akimenko for another three years.[96] Stravinsky's solution was to construct a composition with those technical exercises most familiar to him, to employ the finger exercises of his daily practice and turn them into a musical result.[97] Whether improvised or written down, this mode of transformation became a consistent aspect of Stravinsky's compositional 'method' far into the future. Despite being a juvenile sketch the *Tarantella* might, even so, be considered the moment prior to Stravinsky acquiring any formal degree of compositional literacy when he developed a modus operandi through which he could make the all-important transition from music-by-impulse to music-by-notation. It is no coincidence, surely, that the tool essential to this personally evolved creativity was the piano; thus, together with the piano stool and its jumbled contents, the piano established itself early as Stravinsky's *fons et origo*.

His unfamiliarity with the notation of accidentals hampers the continuation to the initial theme (Example 1.1b). Stravinsky clearly struggles to notate a chordal passage characterized by a surprising enharmonic (un-harmonic) twist. This may possibly have been an intentional, descriptive effect linked to the narrative of the piece; there is no reason to suppose that Stravinsky's improvisations were intended to be rounded imitations of the 'classics'. 'Wrong' notes and 'wrong' harmonies may not be the unintentional result of his lack of theoretical knowledge; they could have been deliberately calculated as an integral aspect of his entertainment. The organ-grinder's squeaky music in *Petrushka* suggests the composer was naturally adept at putting 'wrong' sounds to useful effect. Aided, in this case, by some subtle orchestration, they could be recruited to produce a result admired as much for its artistry as for its artfulness. Furthermore, from Yastrebtsev's account of a party at Rimsky-Korsakov's apartment[98] it is clear that Stravinsky was adept at using his improvisatory skills to entertain; and, like many musical jokers before him and since – from Mozart (in *Ein musikalischer Spass*) to Victor Borge – he would appreciate that smudged chords and sudden shifts of harmony are useful tools, especially when lampooning the musical rudiments. The delicacy of Yastrebtsev's reference (that Stravinsky 'presented some very charming and witty musical jests') may reflect the subtlety with which Stravinsky handled these aural effects. Unfortunately, as Walsh admits, this evidence can offer no more than 'a tantalizing glimpse of the young Stravinsky's lively improvisatory talent'.[99]

Like many young pianists Stravinsky must have fiddled about in frustration at having to plod through the repetitive aspects of his daily routine and he probably enjoyed livening up these otherwise characterless and mechanical repetitions. Finger exercises may thus have become fair game for his improvisatory instinct. However, unlike other children, Stravinsky was already constructing his own bridge across the experiential (and ontological) divide between finger-training and 'pieces', understanding them both as part of the same musical resource. By exploring the permutations of a limited range of notes within a limited interval *Tarantella* provides an indication of how Stravinsky displayed early interest in musical design based upon this aural fascination. Under the professional tutelage of Kashperova he would recognize his 'discovery' as a foundation stone to building a classical piano technique. In due course, these piano drill-patterns – here used merely for entertaining improvisations – would become an intrinsic part of his neoclassical idiom. While Stravinsky's 'theatre' in the form of improvisation – *en amateur* – does not define him as a folk musician, his autobiographical tribute to the inspirational contribution of his fingers reinforces my point: 'Fingers are not to be despised: they are great inspirers, and, in contact with a musical instrument, often give birth to subconscious ideas which might otherwise never come to life'.[100] Stravinsky never disengaged with the creativity of pianistic improvisation. He continued to value this and, to an extent, depended upon it for sourcing material which, with increasing compositional maturity, he ever more skilfully synthesized into 'real' music in the form of competently notated scores.

Whatever hilarity his antics at the keyboard may have provoked, Stravinsky would learn that talent for extemporization was generally disrespected in a cultural milieu. Thus he may be seen as inheriting a late-nineteenth-century sense of shame with regard to improvisation, but only when mature enough to discern the gulf in 'taste'. He would need to turn his back on public displays of this nature – and be seen to reject any association with improvisation – in order to fit into the mould, initially, of the paradigmatic Russian composer and, later, of the objective western European modernist.

Scherzo (1902)

Stravinsky was to comment in his late *Conversations* that he had written several 'short piano pieces, *andantes*, *melodies*, and so forth' during his years as a pupil of F. S. Akimenko and V. P. Kalafati.[101] However, rather than considering the Scherzo (with Charles Joseph) as 'a new starting point',[102] the work might better be described as a chance survivor from this very early period. As a rare, if not unique, fossil it offers precious evidence of Stravinsky's capabilities at this time whilst also providing a glimpse of what Kalafati (as a former pupil of Rimsky-Korsakov) regarded as compositional priorities. Taruskin suggests that the work conforms to a 'general kinship with Tchaikovsky's salon-style piano music', most particularly with the Scherzo of this composer's early C♯ minor Piano Sonata, written in 1865 though only published in 1900. Therefore, he writes, '[as] a "new" work … its impression was fresh'.[103] Ergo Tchaikovsky's Sonata, and specifically its Scherzo, might well have served as the model for Stravinsky's own piano miniature. On this basis Stravinsky came to Rimsky-Korsakov already a 'piano composer', albeit one with very limited experience. There can be little doubt that their earliest conversations would have centred on his Scherzo, written in 1902 and dedicated in January the following year to the pianist N. I. Richter.[104]

It may be tempting to construct unfavourable comparisons between the 'fearful' symmetry of the twenty-year-old Stravinsky's efforts and the relative 'sophistication' of the eleven-year-old Prokofiev 'down in the Ukraine'.[105] However if Taruskin's hunch is correct, one must also credit Stravinsky (and his teacher) for choosing to learn from this specimen of 'contemporary music'. As the critic A. V. Ossovsky wrote in 1904, the more usual path, such as that taken by Moscow-based Rakhmaninov, was to draw upon much earlier romantic models:[106] 'Rakhmaninov has undoubtedly assimilated, perhaps entirely involuntarily, all the peculiarities of present-day piano writing in the second half of the nineteenth century, shaped by intersecting influences, principally those of Chopin, Liszt and Schumann.'[107] 'Present-day piano writing', evidently, was expected to conform to solidly conservative (romantic) influences from the early to middle nineteenth century – at least in regular didactic contexts. On that score Stravinsky's Scherzo, with its blend of historical and recent operatic allusions – to the overture to *Die Meistersinger* (1868) in the Trio, and to Glinka's *Ruslan and Lyudmila* (1842) and Rimsky-Korsakov's *The Maid of Pskov* (1873) in the opening Scherzo theme[108] – would place the work at the very centre of compositional expectations in St Petersburg in 1902. The dominant pedal that characterizes the work's coda may be confirmation, as Taruskin implies, that the student had successfully absorbed the text on the 'organ point' in Chapter 3 of Rimsky-Korsakov's *Practical Manual of Harmony*.[109] However, it also reflects Stravinsky's interest in contemporary, somewhat experimental composition. Coincidentally (perhaps) the dedicatee of Rimsky's *Manual*, A. K. Lyadov, had recently published sets of piano solos in eighteenth-century styles,[110] some of which Stravinsky purchased in 1900 and began to study on his own.[111] Lyadov's Fuga from *Six Pieces* op. 3 (1893) is notable for its chromatically enhanced coda, its final six bars underpinned by a resonant tonic pedal. Stravinsky may also have been familiar with Glinka's keyboard fugues (although no mention of these is made in the *Autobiography*); the latter's *Fuga a 4 voci* had been published by Jurgenson, in a first edition, as recently as 1885. In the *Fuga a 3 voci con 2 soggetti* (also from 1834) Glinka stylishly dresses up his contrapuntal exercise in the most charming Mazurka style (3/4, con moto). The *Fuga a 3 voci* (of the same year) presents more typically 'Bachian' rigour and features increasingly close stretti, artfully combined with the ubiquitous pedal point.[112] Stravinsky's decision to round off his Scherzo with a pedal point may thus have been motivated as much by a desire to emulate these models

of 'Russian composition' as to satisfy any structural, rhetorical or specifically didactic outcome. Moreover, Stravinsky's use of repeated notes in the
coda, injecting a sense of energy to this traditionally static device, is an
imaginative touch and foreshadows its frequent use in works of the neoclassical period (including *Duo Concertant* and the *Concerto for Two Solo
Pianos*) and far beyond (the second movement of *Movements*). Already, in
the Scherzo, one senses Stravinsky's considerable appetite for acquiring the
necessary qualifications of a turn-of-the-century Russian piano composer.
His awareness of stylistic paradigms is acute and, as for mastering the technical demands of composing for the piano, he displays considerable individuality (to borrow Ossovsky's pertinent phrase) in his 'feeling for piano
instrumentation'.[113] Since Ossovsky was an intimate of Rimsky-Korsakov's
musical household for many years – participant, even, in Stravinsky's (lost)
Cantata performed in Rimsky's apartment on the occasion of his sixtieth
birthday – one is tempted to read into his terminology a reflection of his
master's voice. If that were the case, one might also conclude that Rimsky
also offered guidance on writing for the piano.

Stravinsky's modest Scherzo displays other individual traits that, whilst
embryonic, are signs of a widening musical perspective. The coda has been
described somewhat harshly as 'an inept "symphonic" appendage'.[114] Yet,
the sudden transformation of the texture into a series of canonic, imitative
entries may also be viewed as a laudable expansion into contrapuntal territory. (It may even have been part of the compositional 'brief'.) Stravinsky's
construction, piling up in ever closer stretti, reveals knowledge of the subtler
aspects of counterpoint and how these can be harnessed to dramatic effect –
especially over an emphatically climactic tonic pedal (Example 1.2).

As a coda of considerable pianistic energy it is certainly effective. More
importantly, it reveals a characteristic imprint: even at this early date
Stravinsky could address the art of 'piano instrumentation' with a fear-
less disregard for the comforts of the performer. Pianists, especially, might
criticize the 'awkwardness' of the coda and suggest that Stravinsky already
had in mind an orchestral adaptation of the work. However ingenuous the
Scherzo may be in certain formal aspects, it nevertheless confirms – as does
'Tucha' (1902) – Stravinsky's dual approach towards piano composition:
while providing the performer with recognizably pianistic material for most
of the work, the composer will *also*, on occasion, view his two-stave score
as a stage in the instrumentation process – one which carries the potential
for future arrangement should the opportunity arise. In other early piano
parts – particularly in vocal works such as *The Faun and the Shepherdess*
(1906) and *Two Poems of Verlaine* (1910) – a third stave is occasionally
added (as we shall see). This would suggest, more overtly, the degree to
which Stravinsky's concept might expand beyond the confines of keyboard

Ex. 1.2 Stravinsky, Scherzo (1902), bb. 72–86.

sonority to embrace a more sophisticated, instrumental palette – in a clear demonstration that the composer was imagining his work, simultaneously, in orchestral guise. Stravinsky's portfolio would soon include some genuine orchestral scherzi: the *Scherzo fantastique* (1907/8) and *Fireworks: A Fantasy for Large Orchestra* (1908). For now (1902) it is enough for him to complete his scherzo assignment for Kalafati on time.

Piano Sonata in F♯ minor (1903/4)

Besides 'referring' to the literature of Russian *Grandes sonates*, Stravinsky's F♯ minor Sonata is also a brilliantly executed reproduction of late-nineteenth-century piano writing in its own right. Taruskin's vivid account of these 'sources' (including works by Akimenko and Kalafati) sets great store by Tchaikovsky's *Grande sonate* op. 37 and the Fifth Symphony; also Skryabin's Sonata no. 3, Glazunov's Sonata no. 1 (dedicated to Mme Rimsky-Korsakov) and Glazunov's Sonata no. 2, which had been premiered by Kashperova on 31 March 1902 at a concert in the series 'Evenings of Contemporary Music' – 'the very series that, by Stravinsky's own testimony, was such an important factor in his early musical growth'.[115] Stravinsky is now able to express himself via that broader range of rhetorical gestures appropriate to a four-movement work demonstrating an impressive advance in his compositional technique since the Scherzo. His experience with this latter work served him well, for the Vivo (the 'Scherzo' movement) of the Sonata is especially noteworthy.

A fundamental aspect of the romantic rhetoric to which Stravinsky was apprenticed was a need to exploit and to balance the emotional shadings of the sonata-form narrative. His achievement in this regard can be observed particularly well in the opening Allegro – via the lofty 'militarism' of the opening subject and, by comparison, the ardent sensibility (verging on sensuality) of the second theme. The sustained lyricism of the Andante and the exuberantly triumphalist display of the finale confirm that Stravinsky can now respond skilfully to a far wider variety of stylistic and emotional demands than before. Each of the four movements demonstrates that Stravinsky's piano writing has attained a high degree of competence, emulating many of the acknowledged tropes of romantic pianistic virtuosity: (1) The 'heroic' tone of the first movement is ably supported by rapid octave doublings. These can take a variety of forms: in contrary motion, as widely spaced arpeggios (particularly in left-hand accompaniments), and in extreme registers (both high and low). Octaves are employed to great effect in the coda, where they support the increased pace with bombast and brilliance. (2) The transparent passage-work of the Vivo is conveyed via light and flickering textures that include several brief episodes of two-part counterpoint, by extreme registers (especially in the treble), rapid sequential treatment of the material and, at the end, by a showy accelerando al fine. Much of the impression of virtuosity in the Vivo is derived from the control of *piano* and *pianissimo* dynamics despite the movement's extreme velocity. (This is another imprint of nineteenth-century pianism; one recalls the Finale-Presto to Chopin's Piano Sonata no. 2 in B♭, op. 35.) (3) Characteristic of the Andante – besides the invitation, at every corner, for tonal warmth and a singing, melodic projection – is the eminently romantic deception of an inner voice. 'Thalberg's three-handed writing' (as this has become known)[116] is a *trompe d'oreille* intended – by means of virtuosic guile – to conceal the true nature of pianistic production. As the movement progresses Stravinsky explores ever more sophisticated combinations of texture, dynamic and articulation, so as to highlight the independence of these separate lines – further augmenting, via this paradigmatic romantic rhetoric, the illusion of extraordinary dexterity (for which very real dexterity, of course, is required). (4) The final movement's pianistic 'effect', besides its impetuous mood, is almost exclusively due to the employment of octaves whose rhythmic and gestural exploration culminates, agitato, in a coda which is itself crowned by a double-octave, bravura cascade. Most impressive of all, perhaps, is the way that Stravinsky's writing suggests a free sense of 'inspirational' extempore, which is so thoroughly appropriate to this idiom. Given his famed improvisatory skills, Stravinsky was surely able to conceive of, and execute, broad stretches of this work at the keyboard before setting it down on paper.

Faithful to those traditions of piano performance that had long been established in the concert halls of St Petersburg (through the example and teachings of Anton Rubinstein and his colleagues at the Conservatoire), Stravinsky's own 'Grande sonate' provides ample opportunity for the interpreter to indulge in the fullest possible range of *rubato*. The slow movement especially sets the stage for that systematic dislocation of the hands (by delaying the melody note) that Sandra Rosenblum terms 'contrametric *rubato*'.[117] By contrast, the outer movements, with their great surges of energy, encourage an elasticity of tempo that affects the whole texture (in both hands) – Rosenblum's 'agogic *rubato*', i.e. when 'the left hand always follows suit'. Both forms of *rubato* would soon become anathema to Stravinsky: his last solo piano work in romantic vein – the *Four Etudes* op. 7 (1908) – would be subject to the composer's rigid control over tempo. As in the Vivo movement of the Sonata, the extreme velocity of three of these *Studies* obliges the performer to execute the music, principally, as a set of challenges to his or her powers of prestidigitation – i.e. not as a wave of 'subjective outpourings' in the mould of the symphonic-romantic piano sonata where *rubato* is most used to express (to borrow Rosenblum's evocative phrase) 'the individualistic, the different, the seeking, the unending'.[118] In the F♯ minor Sonata, however, this was precisely the expressive goal that Stravinsky sought to attain. He skilfully mixed the correct set of pianistic ingredients and, with these, achieved the desired intensely romantic and highly energized rhetoric. For this reason too, and not just for its accurate modelling of familiar repertoire, the Sonata could be described as 'quintessentially and very consciously Belyayevets' and adjudged a 'pledge of allegiance to the Rimsky-Korsakov circle'.[119] The prize, as Taruskin phrases it, was an admission ticket to acceptability amongst the Belyayevets entourage. If Stravinsky too viewed it in these terms, then one must admire the expertise with which he accomplished his goal. His accurate portrayal of Russian romantic *style* was skilfully and crucially enhanced by his equally impressive absorption of the technicalities of Russian romantic *pianism*. Armed not only with the material but with the means to deploy it, i.e. with a true Belyayevets sense of piano instrumentation, Stravinsky was perfectly able to satisfy the requirements set by his teacher. Early in his career, then, Stravinsky demonstrated a surprising resourcefulness and versatility to his emerging, thoroughly cultured brand of kleptomania.

By the time his grandiose F♯ minor Sonata was premiered in February 1905 Stravinsky was already well aware, from opinions expressed by some within his family circle, of certain hierarchies within the profession of musical composition or, more accurately, the perception of such hierarchies. The previous summer he had recorded a conversation with his supportive and musically knowledgeable uncle, the much beloved Aleksandr Frantsevich Yelachich: 'Yesterday, for example, we were talking about Rakhmaninov. [Yelachich] doesn't want to get to know Rakhmaninov, since he isn't worth it (he's a "piano composer"). So I told him he'd do better to hear and get to know Rakhmaninov's piano concerto than my sonata.'[120] This account of some good-humoured though sincere musical banter would suggest that not only Rakhmaninov's piano writing was the object of Stravinsky's admiration: so was his orchestration – most probably, in fact, the expertly handled combination of lush piano textures and equally luxuriant instrumentation. Stylistically, Rakhmaninov's spell can be heard most clearly in the 'second theme' of the Sonata's opening movement (Example 1.3a). (One can only surmise that the young composer dreamed of hearing this passage, one day, within such a beguiling orchestral surround as he had heard in Rakhmaninov's Second Piano Concerto.) This would 'account for' the resonant, pedalled character of its initial statement. Yet, surprisingly, Stravinsky's elaboration of this romantic material – in the exposition (at b. 61) and in the recapitulation (at b. 243) – displays a marked and prescient shift towards a clarity of texture more redolent of the eighteenth century (Example 1.3b). This (formerly) Rakhmaninovian theme is now presented as a three-part texture, which lends this passage, when performed strictly *à la lettre*, glimpses of a pronounced 'neoclassical' sonority. Such quasi-contrapuntal lines, shared between the hands (two voices in the right, one in the left) will become the characteristic 'piano instrumentation' of the Piano Concerto, especially of its first movement Allegro. In fact, this carefully partitioned articulation (*legato* in the right hand, *staccato* in the left) is also the defining imprint of the *Sonate pour piano* (1924) – its first and second movements – and will feature in several other compositions well into the future.[121]

The F♯ minor Sonata has been described as both, 'pre-eminently an exercise in modelling',[122] and 'a veritable potpourri of near quotations from the work of [Stravinsky's] forebears'.[123] Indeed, it is the prevailing tone in musicological commentary to portray this work as little more than a successfully completed item of homework constructed under the watchful gaze of Rimsky-Korsakov, i.e. written to order, and from formulae. Exhaustive

Ex. 1.3 Stravinsky, Piano Sonata in F♯ minor (1903/4), 1st movement:

(a) bb. 33–6

(b) bb. 61–4

exploration of the many stylistic sources to which Stravinsky 'refers' would suggest that the work presents a precocious illustration of *drobnost'*, that characteristically Eurasian, pre-neoclassical imprint which Taruskin defines as 'the quality of being a sum of parts'.[124] Nevertheless, despite its 'rich post-Tchaikovsky palette … and big, quasi-orchestral keyboard manner',[125] the Sonata also provides a glimpse of directions in piano writing that Stravinsky would explore in more objective contexts, for some of the tools of his later neoclassical pianism have clearly been identified above. Andriessen and Schönberger, referring to this Sonata and to the Symphony in E♭, write of Stravinsky's 'completely impersonal style-copies of Tchaikovsky and Glazunov ... [as] an adept and studied disability that gradually developed irreversibly into an accomplished disability'.[126] The modelling employed by Stravinsky to (re-)create an *echt*-Russian pianistic artwork may also be understood, therefore, as an approach which foreshadows, and is entirely consistent with, the composer's later neoclassical processes. In keeping with his newly acquired objective aesthetic, Stravinsky would continue to construct 'impersonal style-copies' – based, in the first instance, upon keyboard counterpoint and upon 'Bach'. Thus, one may begin to recognize in Stravinsky's early scores the signs of a consistency of engagement that will eventually contribute in no small measure to his neoclassical re-invention. 'Re-invention', so called, despite the composer readily admitting that his contact with (for example) Pergolesi's music encouraged him to 'discern ever more clearly the closeness of my mental and, so to speak, sensory kinship',[127] i.e. with gestures and textures of the eighteenth century that were *already* a part of his vocabulary. Such brief examples from the F♯ minor Sonata (above) would suggest that Stravinsky's creative development had long been accompanied, from its earliest steps, by a sensory kinship with distant forebears. Such evocations may have been included merely for the sake of variety, or to demonstrate virtuosity (the composer's as well as the pianist's); or they may represent Stravinsky's genuine interest in baroque music by 'referring' to this, even in short flashes, within an otherwise overwhelmingly romantic narrative. The ensuing survey of Stravinsky's early music seeks to provide answers to this conundrum. Regardless of the multitude of uncertainties that surround this proposal there emerges, nonetheless, the dawn of a realization that the key to understanding such a consistency of engagement with the eighteenth century is to be found in Stravinsky's consistent engagement with the piano.

Four Studies *op. 7 (1908)*

The set of *Four Studies* represents the last piano composition where Stravinsky had access to Rimsky-Korsakov and could seek his opinion and guidance. In the final months before Rimsky's death (in July 1908) both teacher and pupil must have recalled with considerable pride the extraordinary sophistication that Stravinsky's compositions had acquired as a result of their collaboration. His technique, particularly in writing for orchestra and for piano, had developed immeasurably. Furthermore, in the three years since completing the F♯ minor Sonata Stravinsky had completed several vocal settings: 'How the Mushrooms Mobilized for War' (1904), *The Faun and the Shepherdess* (1906), *Pastorale* (1907) and the *Two Melodies of Gorodetzky* (1907/8). These, together with the two orchestral scherzi – *Scherzo fantastique* (1907/8) and *Fireworks* (1908) – illustrate the astonishingly steep learning curve that defines Stravinsky's early career. The pianistic assurance of the *Four Studies* reflects the experience of writing for the piano in a variety of idioms and accompanying roles. While Stravinsky considered the Scherzo and the Sonata to be apprentice works, he assumed full artistic responsibility for the *Four Studies* and could release them with confidence for publication by Jurgenson (Moscow) in 1910. Thus, Stravinsky's name became known outside St Petersburg, eventually across Europe, in quite another guise than via his orchestral and ballet scores.[128] In their modest way, the *Studies* contributed to Stravinsky's emerging reputation, particularly abroad, as a 'Russian musician' – and, even, as a piano composer. Such was the receptivity of these masterful (and extremely taxing) Skryabin-esque miniatures their copyright was taken up by the publishing house of Anton J. Benjamin (Leipzig and Hamburg) in 1925. By 1931 André Schaeffner could write (in Paris) that 'the [study] in F♯ major [is] the best known of the four and is included in the repertoire of a good many pianists'.[129] Guided perhaps by Stravinsky's renown, ever since *The Rite*, as a composer of complex rhythms Schaeffner prefers to frame his analysis of the *Studies* in terms of their *souffle rhythmique* ('rhythmic breath/spirit') without attempting any stylistic comparison. It is curious, therefore, that he should have found, especially in the first study, the *pathétique* ('pathos') of this work's rhythmic play to be 'peut-être précurseur'.[130] Stravinsky's neoclassicism, after all, is characterized (as is *The Rite*) by its very lack of pathos. One can but speculate that, perhaps, Schaeffner is referring to that aspect of morbid sentimentality to be found within the otherwise dazzling scores of *The Firebird* and *Petrushka*.

Writing in 1918, Boris Asaf'yev (using his pen-name Igor Glebov) would exclaim that 'the phenomenon of Skryabin is a historic wonder: can it really be possible to understand his whole biography in the midst of grey, tedious Russian ordinariness?'.[131] It is quite surprising (as Craft has commented) that so little of Stravinsky's output around this period owes any such debt: 'After all, [Skryabin] was *the* conspicuous vanguard Russian composer at the time of Stravinsky's emergence; he was right there at Stravinsky's front door; and Stravinsky was then [and remained] one of the greatest confiscators-of-surroundings in music history.'[132] Certainly, in this latter capacity, Stravinsky has skilfully forged these studies according to recent, though conservative, Russian models. Taruskin outlines specific points of equivalence, particularly to Skryabin's *Etudes* opp. 8 and 42, while observing that Stravinsky's debt is more to early 'orthodox' Skryabin rather than to his later 'visionary' style.[133]

There is, however, an aspect of the *Four Studies* that clearly anticipates Stravinsky's neoclassical idiom: it is the presence of certain pianistic tropes which will return to define the syntax of the Piano Concerto, the *Sonate* and, even, the *Symphony of Psalms*. Such precursory elements include: (1) the simultaneous presentation of *legato*, in one hand, and *staccato*, in the other (as already noted in the F♯ minor Sonata); this cembalistic effect is inverted in Study no. 2. (2) the obsessive use of the index-finger-over-thumb overlap in Study no. 3; and (3) the tendency for extreme tempi (particularly in Studies nos. 2 and 4) which, besides augmenting the technical difficulty of the music, conveys an apparently excessive test of stamina and (to borrow Bronislava Nijinska's term) 'muscular drive'.[134] This latter effect, producing what might be described in neoclassical terms as a 'virtuoso *ritornello*', is no less the result of modelling Skryabin's breathless 'transcendental' studies than it is a clear allusion to traditional disciplines of Russian pianism – specifically the literature of piano exercises and the whole theatre of piano practice to which the *Four Studies* owe a considerable debt. (This topic will be revisited later, when the opportunity arises to examine the materials and rhetoric of Stravinsky's neoclassical works in more detail.) It would be a mistake, however, to suggest that Stravinsky was intent on 'writing a pot-boiler'.[135] To dismiss the *Studies* on that basis is surely to miss the point. One might more profitably seek its true 'meaning' from the work's title, and ask whether this apprentice composer did not sense as much satisfaction from the skilful construction of these didactic and useful études – intended for the professional pianist – as he would with the *Three Easy Pieces* (1914/15), the *Five Easy Pieces* (1916/17) and *Les Cinq Doigts* (1920/1) – intended for the amateur and (in the first instance, quite literally) domestic market, i.e. his own children.

Despite their late-nineteenth-century provenance Stravinsky's *Etudes* were also perceived as revealing a modernist fascination with rhythmic complexity.[136] Yet, whatever the polyrhythmic multiplicity, the tempo of each Study is held firm and admits no hint of *rubato* – neither agogic nor contrametric. As such, the *Four Studies* are more craft than they are art and provide significant testimony to their composer's inclination towards the practical, objective possibilities of musical composition. Stravinsky's mature neoclassical aesthetic will embrace a return to his early respect for educational piano literature. Indeed, his re-invention as a concert pianist will be characterized by the adoption or (to borrow Craft's term) 'confiscation' of his pianistic surroundings, past and present. This was a skill Stravinsky had acquired under the guidance of both Kashperova (since 1899) and Rimsky-Korsakov (since 1904). By 1908 Stravinsky was experienced enough to make his own decisions regarding the style, technique and topic of his modelling requirements. Furthermore, even at this early stage in his compositional development, there is no reason to suppose that Stravinsky could not *also* be fostering the embryonic seeds of his neoclassical spring. In particular, a certain fascination with technique was already part of Stravinsky's engagement with the musical art and a discernible feature of the 'Stravinsky sound'. Had not Myaskovsky, writing in 1911, complimented the composer of *The Firebird* for his 'irreproachable technique, refined taste and wonderful orchestration'? In fact these were qualities which Myaskovsky felt Stravinsky possessed at the expense of some others, for he continued: 'If we say [that] he is not an extravagant melodist, and his themes are not always arresting … then we are coming nearer to the truth.'[137] The satisfaction of 'making' something useful (the *Four Studies*, for example) whilst also learning from the experience, was already a Stravinskian imprint and would remain with him all his creative life (that is, all his life) – as the Bach arrangements he made in 1969 amply illustrate. One can only concur with Schaeffner and extend his commentary on the fourth study to the entire set: the *Studies* are, for all the above reasons, 'coupé[es] avec le plus de naturel' ('carved out in the most natural way').[138]

Much curiosity has greeted the early piano works (*Tarantella*, Scherzo, Sonata in F♯ minor) since their posthumous rescue from oblivion.[139] While their artistic merit may be open to question, their greater value has been to reveal the paths by which Stravinsky acquired that textural sophistication and technical assurance which characterize the *Four Studies*. The maturity of their idiom and their dependence upon stylistic precedents may remain a matter of conjecture. However, when viewed as an introductory chapter to Stravinsky's mature canon, these early piano solos display laudable competence in the art of composing for this problematic instrument. It was a hard-won achievement – the result of Stravinsky's immersion, over many years, in those Russian pianistic models that he most admired. Without doubt the confident, complex piano writing of the *Four Studies* was the fruit of compositional experience as much *outside* the realm of piano literature as within it. In particular, the vocal works of this same period effectively broadened the foundations upon which Stravinsky could develop his technical skills as a piano composer. While offering a view of this instrument that transcended the overwhelmingly Russian – and romantic – syntax of their narrative, the early songs reveal further tantalizing glimpses of proto-neoclassical tendencies.

Early songs

'Tucha' ('Storm Cloud', 1902)

Stravinsky's apprenticeship under Rimsky-Korsakov witnessed his trans-formation from being a talented improviser-composer, at the piano, to assuming the professional responsibility of preparing keyboard and orchestral works for performance and, even, international reception. If the F♯ minor Sonata represents merely a *Probestück* from the hand of an amateur, then Stravinsky's first publications (*Fireworks*, *The Faun and the Shepherdess*, the *Four Studies*) establish him as a professional Russian composer. This remarkably rapid evolution (between 1904 and 1908) owed much to the vocal works, within whose context Stravinsky augmented and refined his pianistic vocabulary. Thus, his compositional skills could develop on two fronts simultaneously. The task of providing appropriate piano accompaniment to song – of illustrating poetic images by imaginative use of the piano's potentiality for colour and textural variety – was a challenge that Stravinsky accepted with evident relish. His course of studies with Rimsky-Korsakov had primed him to cultivate the use of 'colour' in every possible context. The songs, therefore, present a set of piano accompaniments which often give the impression that they are also part-way to becoming short-scores for future orchestration. Such dual identity is to be found already in 'Tucha' ('Storm Cloud', 1902), Stravinsky's earliest surviving complete work. The accompanist's role within this Pushkin setting is to provide eminently pianistic sonorities whilst simultaneously evoking instrumental, even orchestral textures – or so it seems. The outer sections of the song are characterized by word-painting via an unremittingly 'stormy' tremolo misurato in the right hand. This is underpinned, in the left, by an 'anxious' take on the *gehende Bass*, suggesting that Stravinsky was familiar with *Der Freischütz* and the Wolf's Glen (his father was renowned for his performances as Kaspar).[140] The central section of 'Tucha' delivers a more overtly, if equally rudimentary, pianistic texture: the vocal ascent is supported by triads in the right-hand accompaniment, and by upward semiquaver rushes in the bass. The subsequent vocal descent is shadowed by diminished chords over a dominant pedal (again, *tremolo misurato*) as the storm gradually subsides, leading to a return of the opening music. Concealed beneath the work's artistic and technical *naïveté*, 'Tucha' nevertheless provided Stravinsky with a valuable opportunity. His rudimentary manipulations of simple digital formulae anticipate his later, more sophisticated engagement with the patterns and materials of pianistic methodology.

'How the Mushrooms Mobilized for War' (1904)

Stravinsky's penchant for colouristic evocation is demonstrated with extra-ordinary versatility in 'How the Mushrooms Mobilized for War' (1904) – to the almost total exclusion of the previously dominant *tremolo misurato*. Yet 'The Mushrooms' also confirms Stravinsky's tendency to view the piano as merely a stage on a more ambitious journey – one that was, in this case, never to be completed. (In marked contrast, *The Faun and the Shepherdess* was orchestrated by the composer and premiered, under the direction of Felix Blumenfeld, during Belyayev's 1907–8 season of Russian Symphony Concerts.) Evidence of such an ulterior motive is suggested by the presence of a third stave which offers material unplayable by the one piano accompanist.[141] Rather, this additional line clearly reveals how these passages might be instrumented in a future orchestral version: for example, at the third statement of the song's comical refrain (bb. 44–50). This has been translated as: 'The boletus, / commander of all the mushrooms, / sitting under an oak tree, / surveying the mushrooms, / commanded and directed / that the mushrooms go to war.'[142] As if to emphasize this repeated statement of the punch-line, recalling the song's droll title, Stravinsky seems to have imagined that the trills of a fife – to be represented, perhaps, by flute or piccolo – would enhance his word-setting with a shrill and comic sense of militarism. Taruskin confirms as much from his study of the composing draft, justifying these otherwise curious appendages to the original voice/ piano edition.[143] In fact, there are other pointers that suggest such a dual identity: in the preceding four bars, for example, where the right-hand chords require a trill on the uppermost note (Example 1.4a). This is clearly not piano writing but, rather, a further sign of Stravinsky's instrumental imagination tugging at the short leash of its pianistic restriction.[144]

Another passage similarly amplified in the draft, i.e. with instrumental material clearly outside the pianist's reach, may be found towards the end of the song. This occurs immediately prior to a buffo statement of the refrain (marked 'pochissimo più mosso') where Stravinsky evidently sensed the need to stoke up the piano interlude in anticipation of the ensuing patter-song variant. This 'quick march' parody is quite possibly another allusion to one of his father's bass roles, for it recalls Bartolo's aria 'La vendetta' in Act I, scene 3 of Mozart's *Le nozze di Figaro*. Viewing the song as a whole, Taruskin proposes that 'The Mushrooms' was inspired by Stravinsky's recollections of Varlaam's aria (sung, according to the stage directions, 'with a bottle in his hand') from the first act of *Boris Godunov* – Varlaam, the 'vagabond', being one of Fyodor Stravinsky's most celebrated operatic roles. This might indeed explain why the composer secreted the manuscript amongst

Ex. 1.4 Stravinsky, 'How the Mushrooms Mobilized for War' (1904):

(a) bb. 44–52

Ex. 1.4 (*cont.*)

(b) bb. 136–48

his personal items, taking it with him on his many journeys in exile – even to his eventual home in California. It does indeed appear to be 'a memorial, even a "portrait" [of Fyodor Ignatyevich] by his son'.[145] This is a very plausible reading.

'The Mushrooms' abounds in orchestral effects although, on occasion, their pianistic roots are cruelly exposed. Following the vocal climax (accompanied by grandiose 'orchestral' tremoli) the eight-bar coda (Example 1.4b) scampers to its mock-triumphant conclusion by means of a glaringly pian-istic series of reiterations. While betraying their five-finger origins so bla-tantly, the final bars are crowned by a chain of rising hand-overlaps which bring the curtain down on this entertaining cabaret number in suitably the-atrical fashion. At first, the spotlight is projected, as it were, upon the bass soloist as he makes his hurried exit, leading his mushroom-troops to war. Then (to continue this analogy *ad absurdum*) the spotlight swings round to capture the pianist in its beam, rushing for the (front) line by means of a showy, 'mock-virtuoso' flourish (bb. 140–8). In fact, the final two bars – with their rapid hand-overlapping – recall the Scherzo's similarly frantic coda. By dint of the left-hand 'drum beats' (bars 144–5) – which Ives would surely have appreciated – and the oddly placed final cadence, 'The Mushrooms' brilliantly parodies a concert performance of an operatic aria, including the inevitable discomforts of the piano reduction. Can this remarkable work give us an inkling, perhaps, of Stravinsky's mischievous imagination as an improviser? It certainly reinforces one's suspicions that, had there been a suitable occasion at which the premiere of 'The Mushrooms' might have been given by the Stravinskys *père et fils*, they would have seized the oppor-tunity whatever the instrumentation.

The Faun and the Shepherdess *op. 2 (1906)*

Analysis of the composition dates and performance history of *The Faun and the Shepherdess* (1906) would suggest, most unusually, that the orches-tral suite and its piano version were assembled in a single and parallel act of creation. Prior to the work's first (private) performance by the St Petersburg Court Orchestra in April 1907 it 'had probably already been sung, with piano, at a Rimsky Wednesday in February 1907'.[146] The orches-tration, therefore, may have been completed after the piano 'reduction'. The latter was prepared by Stravinsky himself and includes several refer-ences to instrumentation, suggesting all too clearly that, from the start, the vocal score served merely to reproduce as faithfully as possible the range of instrumental colours that the 'main work' would eventually contain (Example 1.5a). The ubiquitous tremolo is now put to a far wider range of uses than before, creating atmosphere or heightening a variety of natur-alistic and emotional effects such as zephyrs, or a cry for lost love (at the conclusion to no. 2, 'Faun'); or as shadows, dark woods and swirling mist (in the andante introduction to no. 3, 'Torrent'). Furthermore, Stravinsky reveals a seminal interest in ostinato by creating patterns that will form the basis for similar textures in *Petrushka* (1910/11) and the *Trois histoires pour enfants* (1915/17).

Ex. 1.5 Stravinsky, *The Faun and the Shepherdess* (1906), III. 'The Torrent':

(a) bb. 50–5

(b) bb. 82–7

The work's main point of pianistic interest lies in its final bars. Eric Walter White reads into this brief coda (Example 1.5b) a premonition of the finale to *The Firebird* (1909/10).[147] His observation is founded upon the manner in which the harmonies shift about, enveloped by the sonority of a pedal point (on B). Reference has already been made to this aspect of Rimsky's course of harmony; and it is tempting to trace the 'origin' of every Stravinskian pedal point (demonstrating his 'newly-acquired competence in music's rudiments') to this one theoretical source. However, there may also be a more practical, above all, a more *pianistic* influence at work, for such passages also allude to one of the fundamental practising drills of the Leschetizky piano method that had long been revered in St Petersburg. This 'teasing out' of chordal permutations within the octave – for sound didactic reasons – was, for instance, a mode of daily practice recommended by Kashperova and one to which this discussion shall return (see Chapter 3, pp. 161–5).

Two Melodies of Gorodetsky *op. 6 (1907/1908)*

Stravinsky's next vocal work, the *Two Melodies of Gorodetsky* (1907/8), shows the young composer's ever-widening acquisition of musical styles, although Rimsky-Korsakov was famously contemptuous of the first song, 'La Novice (Chanson de printemps)'. In his opinion, its 'lyrical impressionism' was 'contemporary decadence … full of mist and fog, but meagre in content of ideas'.[148] White describes its bell-like figures (Example 1.6) as 'looking forward to the magic carillon passage in *The Firebird*,[149] while Taruskin emphasizes the song's operatic allusions by way of Musorgsky (*Boris Godunov*), Rimsky-Korsakov (*Sadko*) and, even, Grieg (*Peer Gynt*).[150] On past experience, one might expect a piano reduction of orchestral intentions. However, the pianistic thread in these songs demonstrates the composer's familiarity, rather, with didactic literature and with domestic piano and piano-duet repertoire. The opening thirty-nine bars of 'La Novice' present the right hand in 'a kind of jingle bells', to borrow the jibe levelled at Stravinsky's setting by the author of these verses, the symbolist poet S. M. Gorodetsky.[151] Yet this derogatory allusion to chimes may indicate a possible source for this tinkling sonority. The ear-catching triplet oscillations (with the upper note ringing out across the main beats) immediately suggest three works of child's-world repertoire – compositions which would surely have been as familiar to Stravinsky as to every Russian, particularly Petersburgian, piano student of that era: firstly, Dargomïzhky's *Slavyanskaya tarantella* for piano duet, which is characterized by a melody of similar triplet shape. (Its *Seconda* Part of repeated 'A's an octave apart – intended for absolute beginners or, even, non-pianists – is surely the ultimate in pedal-point

Ex. 1.6 Stravinsky, *Two Melodies of Gorodetsky* op. 6 (1907/8), I. 'La Novice', bb. 1–14.

ostinato.)[152] There is also Borodin's *Tarantelle* for piano duet which offers further clangorous triplets, most notably in the *Prima* Part.[153] Likewise, for more advanced players, there is Lyadov's *Muzïkal'naya tabakerka* (*The Musical Snuffbox*) op. 32 (1893) for piano solo, which is characterized by an incessant pattern in 3/8 evoking a delicate bell effect.[154] This too may have provided Stravinsky with the basis for his own carillon in 'La Novice'.

Stravinsky's treatment of bell-figuration, however, is quite distinctive. Whereas Dargomïzhky, Borodin, Lyadov and, even, Chopin in his celebrated *Tarantelle* (op. 43; 1841) all maintain a constant triplet pulse, Stravinsky constantly varies the rhythmic sub-division of his three-note patterns and often expands their intervallic range (compare bb. 1, 2, 7 and 10). One may view this alternation as good compositional practice and no more. Yet, such variation anticipates an intriguing parallel with later neoclassical piano works (for example, *Les Cinq Doigts* and *Piano-Rag-Music)* wherein the musical syntax suggests that Stravinsky is portraying the exploratory processes of musical composition and its constant play of options. The resultant variety strongly evokes the repetitions of piano practice where, for technical reasons, a particularly awkward configuration (or ornament) may be 'ironed out' by means of an exhaustive series of rhythmically contrasted versions whilst maintaining the original note sequence. During the 1920s Stravinsky was to found his piano technique upon such rhythmic variations which were the hallmark of Philipp's methodology (see Chapter 4, pp. 173–85). To recognize allusions to pianistic drilling in 'La Novice' is not, however, to identify 'creative seeds' from the perspective of possibly inappropriate hindsight. Rather, it is to observe a consistently technical aspect to Stravinsky's musical idiom. Thereafter, one may further appreciate that Stravinsky's neoclassical emergence did not represent a drastic shift in method or taste, so much as a realignment of already familiar materials and processes.

Other didactic touches in the Gorodetsky accompaniments include: (1) the separation of *legato* (right hand) and *staccato* (left hand) – it is a sonority only possible with total abstinence from the use of the sustaining pedal (and has already been commented on in relation to the F♯ minor Sonata); (2) changing chordal permutations between an outer pedal-point octave (as observed in the final bars of *The Faun and the Shepherdess*) – both instances may be considered vestiges of Leschetizky's methodology; and (3), towards the end of no. 2, 'La Rosée Sainte (Chant mystique des Vieux-Croyants Flagellants)', a rapid, toccata-like ostinato which betrays Stravinsky's increasing affection for fast, virtuosic ritornelli. Occupying the space vacated by the Scherzo (whether pianistic or orchestral), these rapid textures adopt an increasingly contrapuntal guise and will become a feature of the mature solo piano works. Such 'neoclassical Scherzi' may be found, specifically, in the *Sonate pour piano* (last movement: crotchet = 112), the *Sérénade en la* (second movement: Rondoletto), the Piano Concerto (last movement: Allegro), *Capriccio* (last movement: Allegro capriccioso ma tempo giusto) and *Duo concertant* (fourth movement: Gigue).

'Pastorale' (1907)

With Stravinsky's other vocal setting of 1907, 'Pastorale', the universe of nineteenth-century piano tropes has truly been left behind in favour of a pastiche of *style galant*. The significance of this deceptively inconsequential miniature, with its wordless 'Ah-oo' vocalise, has become more widely recognized.[155] Taruskin claims (with Yastrebtsev) that 'Pastorale' is Stravinsky's 'earliest work to which [the word "original"] may be unequivocally applied'.[156] Not only was this the first 'Stravinsky work' that the composer himself recognized,[157] but from today's distant perspective it is hard not to exaggerate its importance as a herald of his later and very public embrace of the eighteenth century. Taruskin asks tantalizingly whether this charming *musette champêtre* was, in fact, the fruit of Wanda Landowska's visit to St Petersburg in 1907, where her ground-breaking recitals on the harpsichord caused such a stir in artistic circles.[158] Accustomed to hearing baroque music performed on modern-day instruments – Bach's keyboard literature had long been performed on the piano or portrayed via piano transcription – Europe's musical public responded with delight, while professional musicians and composers were effectively challenged to re-think their whole understanding of that vast pre-romantic repertoire.

One must be cautious, with Taruskin, not to 'saddle the little *Pastorale* with too many heavy portents of Stravinsky's creative future'.[159] Nevertheless it is revealing to observe, in the detail of this *pièce de salon*, several of Stravinsky's most entrenched neoclassical imprints – especially those that will re-emerge in his later piano works. Of the 'pianisms' already noted, the extreme separation of articulation between hands is once again very evident in 'Pastorale'. Here, in Stravinsky's self-conscious evocation of the pedal-less harpsichord, the piano is required by dint of stylistic 'authenticity' to observe strict adherence to minutiae of phraseology: the left hand is *sempre staccato* (until the final cadence), as a perfect foil to the vocalist's tender (and *legatissimo*) fioriture. Occupying the middle ground, as if responding to an architect's concept of beauty by pre-judged proportion, the right hand articulates its ornamental counter-theme by judiciously controlled alternations of *legato* and *staccato*. The widely spaced left hand, evoking a strangely modernist take on the Alberti bass, will become the foundation to many of Stravinsky's neoclassical slow movements, the most prominent example being the Adagietto of the *Sonate*, which encapsulates many other stylistic and technical characteristics of the earlier work. These include: a similar disposition of the hands – separating the right's florid *legato* ornamentation from the rhythmically unchanging secco accompaniment; and, also, a variety of 'eighteenth-century' grace-notes and fully notated (as if 'logically constructed') turns and trills (Example 1.7b).

Other fingerprints of pianistic keyboard technique already observed in previous Rimsky-influenced scores may also be appreciated in 'Pastorale' (and will recur in later neoclassical contexts). There is, for example, a preponderance of the organ point in the form of tonic and dominant pedals. Furthermore, in anticipation of similar technical 'extensions' in the *Sonate* (last movement), the left-hand stretches widen as the work proceeds, gradually increasing the difficulty of performance in an apparently deliberate evocation of graded methodologies or progressive studies. The resultant impact of this stylistic/technical *mélange* is a charming yet strangely unnerving *étude* of repressed quasi-baroque emotionalism, tempered by an implacably extreme (icy) classicism (Examples 1.7a). Stravinsky quickly set aside such dissection of Music's humours as he returned to conventional, that is, 'fantastically', orchestrated Russian fare with the *Scherzo fantastique* (1907/8) and with *Fireworks* (1908), subtitled *Fantaisie pour grande orchestre*.

The 'Pastorale' will yet make its mark in a far more significant moment in the Stravinsky narrative. In December 1923 the composer set aside his sketches of the Piano Concerto and returned to 'Pastorale' which had lain, untouched and unperformed, for sixteen years. Out of the soprano and piano original he formulated a chamber work – for voice and wind ensemble of oboe, cor anglais, clarinet and bassoon. The many presentations of this song given by Nadezhda Rimskaya-Korsakova in her father's apartment (with Stravinsky himself at the piano) must have provoked mixed memories. One might indeed ponder Stravinsky's decision to dust off his little cameo. In a programme note he wrote for the work he would state that he 'had always wanted to arrange the piano accompaniment for a small wind instrument ensemble'.[160] But why did he choose to do this at that precise moment? It could just have been a manifestation of that 're-engagement with classicism' which Figes describes as being 'an obvious reaction by the [Russian] émigrés' living in Paris: 'After the chaos and destruction of the revolutionary period, they longed for some sense of order. They looked back to the European values and inheritance of Petersburg to redefine themselves as Europeans and to shift their "Russia" west. They wanted to recover the old certainties from underneath the rubble of St Petersburg.'[161] On the other hand Stravinsky may have been motivated by those 'ideas' which he was

Ex. 1.7(a) Stravinsky, 'Pastorale' (1908).

Ex. 1.7(a) (*cont.*)

Ex. 1.7(b) Stravinsky, *Sonate pour piano* (1924), 'Adagietto', bb. 1–3.

busily formulating at that very moment for his article 'Some Ideas about My *Octuor*', to be published the following month.[162] When considering how best to arrange this little gem of Petersburgian classicism it is quite possible that Stravinsky chose this task as something of a test case, a modest demonstration 'for his ears only' intended to satisfy his new-found affection for wind instruments and their objectively advantageous lack of nuance. In December 1923 Stravinsky's musical and ideological preference for wind instruments, soon to be made public, was completely in accord with his *Concerto pour piano et instruments à vent* – currently under construction.

Without making undue claims for the 'Pastorale' arrangement it evidently played its part during the winter months of 1923–4 – a crucial period in the emergence of Stravinsky's neoclassicism. It is significant that his decision to recruit a woodwind quartet to form his preferred blend of instrumental timbres for this task chimes perfectly with his latest views on the desirability, and neoclassical appropriateness, of wind instruments as opposed to strings, 'which are less cold and more vague'.[163] The felicitous 'coincidence' of these three contrasting, yet complementary, trajectories is striking: the composition and idiosyncratic scoring of the Piano Concerto, the arrangement of the 'Pastorale', and the imminent publication of 'Some Ideas about

My *Octuor*'. In this light, the final 'idea' of Stravinsky's article appears to be particularly significant: 'I must say that I follow in my art an instinctive logic and that I do not formulate its theory in any other way than *ex post facto*.'[164] Coming at the end of lengthy discussions of a technical nature, this one-sentence appendage may appear to be a somewhat unnecessary gesture of self-justification. Yet, it is also a vindication of the composer's long-held attraction to classicism – as he had been reminded via his recent re-acquaintance with 'Pastorale', his earliest essay 'upon' ornamental classical objectivity. Stravinsky was well able to claim for his neoclassical art an 'instinctive logic'. Had he not just demonstrated that, within the genetic code of this 'new' music, there stirred the current of what one might (with some liberty) refer to as his Petersburgian neo-Neva-classicism? Thus, Stravinsky felt emboldened to sign off his article with the assertion that there was ('I must say') proven and durable consistency 'in my art'. The implication behind Stravinsky's final sentence is that his neoclassical credo, as declared in 'Some Ideas', was not formulated upon a whim but was grounded in solid, artistic foundations of long-standing. He knew exactly, to coin a phrase, where he was coming from.

Rimskian principles

Taken literally, the point of origin for Stravinsky's sense of logic was, of course, that 'artificial city' St Petersburg[165] – viewed optimistically by Russia's eighteenth-century authors as a 'magnificent monument to the power of human reason and will', and by Dostoyevsky, more sceptically, as 'the most fantastical and intentional city in the world'.[166] There is a limit to the effect that bricks and mortar can have on the human mind, which responds with far greater alacrity (not unnaturally) to the stimulus of other human minds. The process which enabled Stravinsky to develop so rapidly, eventually setting the seal upon his 'music of intention', was generated by one mortal above all others within that fantastical cultural hub: this was, of course, N. A. Rimsky-Korsakov – dubbed by Taruskin as 'perhaps the most underrated composer of all time'.[167] In so many ways Stravinsky's empowerment can be traced to his increasingly prominent role as a part of Rimsky's milieu. Furthermore, the technical expertise that supported Stravinsky's compositional impetus derived in large part from his regular visits to the Zagorodnïy apartment. We are indebted to Andrey Rimsky-Korsakov for confirmation – via a re-construction of his father's diary – of the hours, the regularity and (above all) the emphasis of Stravinsky's lessons with Nikolay Andreyevich: 'During the year 1907–8 regular work of Rimsky-Korsakov with I. F. Stravinsky (*instrumentation*, in conjunction with *advice on composition*), usually once a week, on Wednesdays, 4–6 p.m.'[168] The curriculum followed by teacher and pupil on those Wednesday evenings would probably have been founded upon material that eventually appeared under the title *Principles of Orchestration*. Specifically, the central 'planks' of Rimsky's thirty-five years' teaching experience are encapsulated in this reference book, for it was begun in 1873 though not published until after his death, in 1913.[169] It is upon this textbook more than any other that Russian music has acquired its reputation for excellence in orchestration. As an attribute of Russia's musical identity, orchestration plays a leading role in defining for Russian composers what 'our music' comprises. In his discussion of music's ontologies, Philip Bohlman makes several observations that help one to understand, firstly, the craft of orchestration within the community of Russian composers and, secondly, the use of the piano as a tool of orchestration within a more refined conception of the 'art' of instrumentation. 'Our music', Bohlman writes,

> comes into existence within the group; the boundedness of the music accords with the boundedness of the group itself, and 'our music' even becomes a means of communication for knowing and familiarity within the group itself. The resulting form of musical knowledge tends toward growing specialisation … [*The*] *group will attempt to intensify its specialisation in order to increase the worth of 'our music'.*[170]

If, as Bohlman proposes, music 'articulates the bulwark that distinguishes one community from another' then orchestration may be seen as the defining feature of Russia's musical fortress. It was a characteristic explored by Russian composers, with Rimsky-Korsakov at their head, precisely to increase the worth of their music – for their own satisfaction and in the eyes and ears of non-Russians. Such embedding of Russia's musical identity via orchestration was fostered not only as a parameter 'owned', i.e. given supreme value, by her composers, but as a specialization enjoyed and shared amongst them. Orchestration was central to their whole conversation about music.

As we embark upon an investigation of some of the major orchestral works of Stravinsky's 'Russian period', it is an opportune moment to consider how his attitude towards instrumentation, particularly his treatment of the orchestral piano, reveals the hand of his teacher. It is worth recalling, at the outset, Rimsky's elevated conception of this creative principle:

> It is a great mistake to say: this composer scores well, or, that composition is well orchestrated, for orchestration is *part of the very soul of the work*. A work is thought out in terms of the orchestra, certain tone-colours being inseparable from it in the mind of its creator from the hour of its birth. Could

the essence of Wagner's music be divorced from its orchestration? One might as well say that a picture is well *drawn* in colours.[171]

Orchestration, then, is not a process of applying colour to sounds that have already been created elsewhere – on the piano, for example. According to Rimsky-Korsakov, musical creation is born as instrumental or vocal sound. He views composition and orchestration as aspects of the *one* creative discipline rather than as two clearly defined subjects – as is the (supposedly erroneous) tradition in western conservatoire and university music departments, and according to western attitudes generally. In due course, it will be instructive to view Stravinsky's orchestral compositions through the same potent and idiosyncratic cultural prism. Firstly, some re-construction is in order.

Rimsky-Korsakov was proud of his privileged and unusual musical background – including an early career in the navy – as is clear from the opening pages of his *Principles of Orchestration*. He acknowledges the valuable opportunity of 'hearing all my works performed by the excellent orchestra of the St Petersburg Opera'; and he clearly appreciated the experience of writing for orchestras of different sizes and varied components, citing his first opera *The May Night* (1878–9) 'which is written for natural horns and trumpets'. More unexpectedly still, Rimsky's trump card is to boast of his experience with wind instruments – where other composers, particularly in the West, might boast of more artistic accomplishments like singing in a cathedral choir as a boy chorister, for example, or giving public concerts at an early age: 'As regards orchestration it has been my good fortune to belong to a first-rate school, and I have acquired the most varied experience. [For example] I conducted the choir of the Military Marine [*sic*] for several years and was therefore able to study wind instruments.'[172]

With this precious, if singular experience, Rimsky evidently felt qualified to outline the four stages by which a composer learns orchestration. However, he warns that 'when the student works alone he must avoid the pitfalls of the first three phases', and proceeds to itemize these as follows: (1) when the composer 'puts his entire faith in percussion instruments'; (2) when he 'acquires a passion for the harp'; (3) when he 'adores the woodwind and horns, using stopped notes in conjunction with strings (muted or *pizzicato*)'. The fourth phase, which Rimsky views as the most advanced, is when the composer 'comes to realise that the string orchestra is the richest and most expressive of all'.[173] Under these terms, Rimsky-Korsakov would surely have regarded Stravinsky's later absorption with wind instruments as merely a passing fascination (which, of course, it was) and an indication of his lack of development or plain immaturity (which, of course, it was not).

It is significant that the treatment of individual orchestral instruments in *Principles of Orchestration* is inseparable from Rimsky's identification of their associated 'expressive capacities': 'As regards expression, the strings come first and the expressive capacity of the other groups diminishes in the above order ['woodwind, brass, plucked strings, percussion producing definite, and those producing indefinite sounds'], colour being the only attribute of the last group of percussion instruments.'[174] The reputation that Russian composers enjoyed as experts in orchestration may be seen to have been founded upon such a text, where this aspect of composition was not left to individual flair alone, but was a taught element of every young composer's education – particularly within the sphere of Rimsky-Korsakov's considerable influence. The language of Rimsky's explanation is factual, assertive even. Conveyed within the terms of his celebrated treatise is the unstated truth that the Russian School is founded upon expert orchestral writing. Furthermore, Rimsky-Korsakov makes it abundantly clear in his opening chapters that issues of instrumental colour also relate to the concept of expressivity and its measurement: i.e. good practice in orchestral writing is founded upon knowledge of the precise levels of expressivity that instruments are capable of producing. With regard to the wind family Rimsky devises a Table (Example 1.8) that effectively throws down the gauntlet: students following his methodology need to learn much more than the bare essentials of an instrument's range and timbre. They need to acquire detailed knowledge of every register of each instrument. They would also be expected to associate instrument selection with *expressive* result, thereby confirming orchestration as a creative element central to the art of composition. As Stravinsky's views on (and use of) wind instruments will assume such an important role in his early neoclassical projection it is relevant to consider the Table that refers specifically to the 'Wind Group'.[175] From this it will be possible to view Rimsky's teachings on this subject as a point of reference: possibly, even, as a template with which to measure how much Stravinsky's later music and aesthetics did or did not conform to Rimsky's paradigm. Within the context of undergraduate courses – at the St Petersburg Conservatoire or amongst Rimsky's private pupils – one can but imagine the sense of authority that these teachings and their scientific format must have transmitted to their student recipients. Few, if any, would have ignored such instruction from (in the words of Rimsky's pupil, and son-in-law, Maximilian Steinberg) 'a master, held so deeply in reverence'.[176]

The minutiae that Rimsky includes in this *Table* do much to clarify and amplify his musical intentions.[177] By means of the information given within square brackets, he indicates what he calls the 'scope of greatest expression'. This he defines as 'the range in which [each] instrument is best qualified

Ex. 1.8 Rimsky-Korsakov, *Principles of Orchestration*, 'Table B. Wind group',
pp. 95–6.

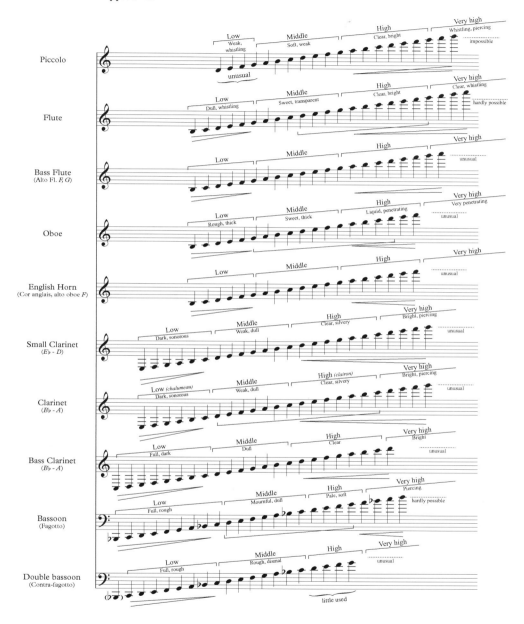

to achieve various grades of tone ('*forte*', '*piano*', '*cresc.*', '*dim.*', '*sforzando*', '*morendo*', etc.) – the register which admits the most *expressive* playing, in the truest sense of the word. Outside this range, a wind instrument is more notable for richness of colour than for expression.' Aware that he was hereby adding to the musical dictionary as well as establishing, he hoped, a novel and excellent principle of orchestration, Rimsky-Korsakov added, not without a little pride: 'I am probably the originator of the term "scope of greatest expression".'[178] Thus, this Table represents, in miniature, Rimsky's task as a whole: to establish a culture where the study of expression is afforded its integral place within the orchestration module, in a sub-category which encourages aspirant composers to treat it knowingly as a desirable and potent tool that should always be identified, measured, explored and applied – but never ignored. Significantly (for this reflects Rimsky's declared specialization in the winds over other orchestral groups) he does not indicate any scope of expression in the equivalent tables for the strings, brass or percussion.[179] The amount of detail given to the wind group in this regard is *unique* to this instrumental family, and must reflect the level of attention that Rimsky-Korsakov afforded wind instruments during his orchestration course, within the context of his teaching generally.

In short, Rimsky-Korsakov views orchestration as an art in the manipulation of expression via the skilled use of those instrumental registers best able to support the composer's fundamental aim. This aim is deemed, tacitly, to be expressivity. Notes that lie outside certain favoured registers are merely capable of offering instrumental colour: i.e. they may even be highly coloured, but their non-expressivity relegates them to secondary status. For example, according to Rimsky's Table (see above), the opening bassoon solo in *The Rite* would certainly be considered outside the 'scope of greatest expression' – the high c″ finds itself within the bracket labelled 'very high, piercing', verging on 'hardly possible'. (This is surely a fairly accurate assessment, even today, a century of mechanical refinements later.) Rimsky is alert to such perils and warns against 'confid[ing] … a sad, plaintive phrase' to the bassoon's high soprano register.[180] In this light, Stravinsky must have savoured his apparent recklessness in allocating the opening phrase of *The Rite* to *Fagotto I*. One recalls the anecdote that, at the first rehearsal, it was suggested to the composer that this solo would 'work better on the saxophone'. However, this may not have been such a mischievous comment as at first appears; the sentiment behind the remark could have reflected the greater danger, as Rimsky himself had foreseen, that 'the mocking character of the bassoon could easily and quite naturally assume a light-hearted aspect'.[181] 'There are also moments', Rimsky-Korsakov continues, 'when a composer's artistic feeling prompts him to employ instruments, the character of which is at variance with the written melody (for eccentric, grotesque effects etc.)'.[182] With regard to the opening tones of *The Rite*, one feels indubitably therefore that, in his 'etc', Rimsky would have embraced (in Cocteau's memorable apophthegm) such 'georgics of prehistory'.[183]

In other contexts Stravinsky follows Rimsky-Korsakov's guidance more literally, for example, in his use of single instruments and 'simple combinations' to obtain colour or, by contrast, in his use of 'compound timbres', which are Rimsky's recommended means for obtaining a 'dull, neutral texture'.[184] Overall, in fact, Stravinsky may be considered an exemplary pupil in the manner he applied his former teacher's colouristic principles throughout his three 'great' Russian ballets (and in *The Nightingale*). Debussy may not have appreciated the provenance of these qualities, but he was an admirer of Stravinsky's command of the orchestra. As he wrote to the Swiss musicologist Robert Godet: '[Stravinsky's] music is full of feeling for the orchestra, conceived directly for the orchestral canvas [*C'est fait en pleine pâte orchestrale*].' Of *Petrushka*, Debussy commented on its 'orchestral infallibility' such as he had 'found only in *Parsifal*'.[185] One might even argue that Stravinsky applied those same skills with still greater ingenuity when writing for small ensembles, as in his Swiss/Turanian chamber and vocal works, culminating in *Histoire du soldat* (1918).[186] Recognizing the special significance of that work, Lukas Foss paid tribute to Stravinsky in 1971: 'With *Histoire* you tore down the notion of orchestration in favour of "writing for instruments".[187] Such a reading of Stravinsky's (apparent) emancipation from the Russian School in the decade following *The Rite* is helpful in constructing the bridge over which Stravinsky strode towards the relative self-abnegation of his early neoclassicism.

Symphonies d'instruments à vent (1920) provides a perfect illustration of the transition from the Russian 'approach' to the neoclassical 'attitude', especially regarding instrumentation. The first part of *Symphonies* offers a striking exposé of instrumental colours and contrasting timbres which contribute greatly to the impact of this music's formal, and very angular geometry. As for its orchestration, the effect is of an almost perverse exploration of those limits (or 'off-limits'), which Rimsky's Bible would never sanction – a sense of daring, of rebelliousness even, at pushing such wisdom to the very edge. The work cries out for the listener's attention, flaunting the audacious modernity of its instrumentation to proclaim its creator's professional emancipation from his Russian heritage. Jonathan Cross makes the point that *Symphonies* is more than an 'assemblage of *objets trouvés*'. Instead, 'in its pragmatism [and in] its experimentation, the structure of [the work] perhaps begins to approach [the] concept of *une musique informelle*'.[188] According to Adorno's definition, this is 'a type of music which has discarded all forms which are external or abstract or which confront it in an inflexible way. At the same time ... [such music] should nevertheless constitute itself in an objectively compelling way, in the musical substance itself, and not in terms of external laws.'[189] *Symphonies* may be seen to conform admirably to this reading, particularly in the way it rejects the 'external laws' of old Petersburgian instrumentation. Yet there is a paradox here. Cross asserts that 'in the *Symphonies* ... its oppositions make little attempt at reconciliation.'[190] In response, one might argue that it is through its singularly unconventional orchestration that *Symphonies* forms a unified and consistent artwork. To borrow from Adorno's definition, *Symphonies* does indeed 'constitute itself'. Furthermore, by straying so far from the established paths of maximum expressivity Stravinsky guarantees that *Symphonies* will do so in an objectively compelling way. The realization that he had achieved this significant feat of artistic and personal independence within the limitations of a work for *wind instruments* must surely have contributed to the conviction with which he penned his novel 'ideas' of objectivity and sent them off to be published for all, particularly his Russian readership, to ponder.

By contrast, the second part of *Symphonies* cultivates an opaque dullness where the neutrality of timbres, created by the dense instrumental combinations, respectfully supports the sonority and funereal mood of the *panikhida*. Here though, in terms of instrumentation, Stravinsky's apparent negation of Russian orchestral tradition is achieved by an equally skilful application of Rimskian know-how. While Taruskin's skilful reading of this work as a rite of Orthodoxy is thoroughly credible, and fascinating, one cannot but also imagine that an ear so receptive as Stravinsky's would have recalled and responded to several stimuli. These might include hearing, for example, the massed bands of the Russian navy (given Rimsky's oft-repeated accounts of his time in the Marines), or, from Stravinsky's own memory of attending a solemn civic occasion with his family, a funeral procession in the open air perhaps, along the Nevsky Prospekt or at St Petersburg's naval dockyard. Alternatively, recalling his trip to Madrid in 1915, Stravinsky may have re-cycled the dignified tones of a *sarabanda* as played by the local *banda militar* whose rehearsals he overheard daily. (Although his autobiography only mentions their paso doble, it is inconceivable that their repertoire would have been limited to that one form of *danza española*.) Then there is that finely calculated passage in *Zvezdoliki* (*Le Roi des étoiles*; 1911–12) marked maestoso tranquillo, where the strings fall silent before the entry of winds and brass en bloc.[191] Most probably, however, Stravinsky's *tombeau* for Debussy is rooted in a score of his own, 'lost' since his exile from Russia and so far never traced: the *Funeral Dirge* op. 5, composed in 1908, was similarly scored for a wind ensemble. It was written in memory of Rimsky-Korsakov and performed at his funeral, 'each instrument laying down its wreath against a deep background of tremolo mournings simulating the vibrations of bass voices', according to the composer. Stravinsky evidently remembered the work in vivid detail, and with affection, as 'the best of my works before *The Firebird*, and the most advanced in chromatic harmony'.[192] It appears that neoclassicism's classicism (via 'Pastorale') and neoclassicism's favoured instrumentation (via the *Funeral Dirge*) were as firmly rooted in the Petersburgian Traditions as their composer's 'carefully crafted and beautifully unreliable' denials.[193]

A certain Rimskian conformity can even be observed in as 'late' a work as *Symphony of Psalms* (1930), wherein Stravinsky may be heard striking out for an extreme neoclassical sonority. The work's syntax is, of course, perfectly Stravinskian in every department except for one. The principle behind the instrumentation of *Symphony of Psalms* is inescapably not Stravinsky's but Rimsky's – twenty-two years after the author's demise (1908) and thirty-nine years after his *Principles of Orchestration* were first published (1891). This proposition can be explored as follows: within the section entitled 'Writing for Orchestral Accompaniment to Chorus' Rimsky-Korsakov writes that doubling choral parts by instruments 'is generally a good plan. In *cantabile* passages such duplication may be melodic in character, and the design more ornamental in the orchestra than in the chorus.'[194] Consultation of the opening choral entry of *Psalms*, for alto voices alone, reveals that this '*cantabile* passage' (Fig. 4 is marked '*mf cant.*') is indeed doubled (by Oboe 1 and 3), and also that this 'duplication' is 'melodic in character'. A glance at the accompaniment figurations in the other wind parts would also confirm that 'the design [is] more ornamental in the orchestra than in the chorus'. This overtly Rimskian solution, once established with 'Exaudi orationem meam, Domine', is maintained for the second phrase, 'Et deprecationem meam' (Fig. 5). Here, the choral melody (sung, principally, by the sopranos and tenors) is doubled by violoncellos *divisi*. As before, the orchestral accompaniment is appropriately, if not also obediently, ornamental.

By way of further illustration, the first oboe (at Fig. 7: 'Auribus percipe lacrimas meas') is employed in its highest and most strident register, two octaves above the vocal line (which, in turn, is doubled at pitch by third oboe). This wide separation between voices lends an unmistakably Stravinskian sonority to this passage due, perhaps, to one's recollection of the lugubrious clarinet/bass clarinet duet in the 'Blackamoor' scene in *Petrushka*.[195] Here, in *Psalms* (and just as Rimsky-Korsakov recommends), both oboes offer melodic doubling of the chorus, while the rest of the orchestra contributes an increasingly ornamental accompaniment ('ornamental' in the sense that it varies previous material). This would again suggest that Stravinsky's approach to orchestration continues resolutely to be based upon Rimskian orchestration theory. Yet, Rimsky-Korsakov's legacy should not be confined within a narrow definition of orchestration, for the piano (not strictly an orchestral instrument) is also subjected to his clinical gaze. Needless to say, Stravinsky's use of keyboards within the body of the orchestra will confirm his reputation as a skilled manipulator of all instrumental laws, whoever wrote them.

The orchestral piano

'The use of a piano in the orchestra (apart from pianoforte concertos) belongs almost entirely to the Russian school.'[196] Such a brazen claim upon this sonority for Russia would explain, at least in part, why Rimsky-Korsakov's treatment of the orchestral piano in his *Principles of Orchestration* is both comprehensive and thought-provoking. It is a mark of his complete knowledge of the subject that he should consider, and contrast, the specific tone qualities of both the grand *and* upright instrument – demonstrating an attention to detail that is lacking in non-Russian treatises, for example Walter Piston's otherwise thorough 1973 guide.[197] Rimsky-Korsakov writes: 'When the piano forms part of an orchestra, not as a solo instrument, an upright piano is preferable to a grand, but today the piano is gradually being superseded by the celesta, first used by Tchaikovsky … When [the celesta] is not available it should be replaced by an upright piano and not by the glockenspiel.'[198] With the notable exception of *Petrushka* Stravinsky's Russian scores do not offer much employment for an orchestral pianist. None of the early works – Symphony in E♭ (1905/7), *Scherzo fantastique* (1907/8), *Fireworks* (1908) or, even, *The Rite of Spring* (1911–13) – requires an orchestral piano at all; and in *The Firebird* (1909–10) and *The Nightingale* (1908–9, 1913–14) the piano plays but a discreet, i.e. not *concertante*, role – its material closely integrated into the harps' traditionally colouristic form of ear-catching punctuation.

Given Stravinsky's status, as a private pupil of Rimsky-Korsakov until 1908, it is unlikely that Stravinsky's decision to exclude the piano from the Symphony in E♭ and the *Scherzo fantastique* would have been taken alone, but, rather, agreed upon in consultation with Rimsky – during his weekly lessons of 'instrumentation' (with 'advice on composition'). Indeed, the *Autobiography* confirms this: 'As soon as I finished one part of a movement [of the Symphony] I used to show it to [Rimsky-Korsakov], so that my whole work, including the instrumentation, was under his control.'[199] Although Rimsky approved of Stravinsky's use of the piano in the process of composition, the true art of orchestration undoubtedly lay in concealing this fact. The piano may be useful to support the composer's inner ear, but

Ex. 1.9 Stravinsky, *Fireworks* (1908): the main theme, as played by six horns (at Fig. 5), transposed to concert pitch – with suggested piano fingerings.

this should not alter the basic premise that 'the orchestral picture should be drawn in colours' and that instrumental tone-colours should be inseparable from the work 'in the mind of its creator from the hour of its birth'.[200] So thoroughly did Stravinsky master this art, it is a rare occasion indeed when one can detect a pianistic origin to any aspect of his Russian scores. One notable exception occurs in *Fireworks*,[201] where the principal theme clearly betrays its five-finger origins. It is offered here, at its first clear statement, in pianistic guise in order to support the conjecture that Stravinsky formulated this material at the keyboard and, unusually, retained its pianistic gestalt through the process of instrumentation (Example 1.9).[202]

Petrushka: Burlesque in Four Scenes *(1910–11)*

> We're not performing some 'Petrushka' out in the streets, we're going to sing an aristocratic romance …
>
> Dostoyevsky, *Crime and Punishment* (1865–6)[203]

Stravinsky's first orchestral work after the watershed of Rimsky's passing was *The Firebird*. Here, the orchestral piano is restricted to adding brilliance to rapid passage-work, especially in the episodes of 'magical' orchestration, where it doubles the harps' wide-ranging glissandi. Overall, the piano is valued for its treble and for its delicacy, rather than for its bass register or chordal mass. More noteworthy than its contribution, however, is the piano's total absence from the second half of the work (from 'The Arrival of Kastchei the Immortal' to the final curtain). The composer does not even call upon the piano to reinforce the orchestral *tutti* at the closing *fortissimo maestoso*, nor the *fff pesante* of the final bars. Stravinsky's later arrangement of the ballet as a concert suite (1919) does not alter the piano's limited participation, so his subsequent interest in writing 'an orchestral piece in which the piano would play the most important part – a sort of *Konzertstück*'[204] – is all the more surprising. The choice of terminology is itself a curiosity for there is no tradition in the Russian catalogue for this form of one-movement *concertino*. Rather, Stravinsky may have encountered Weber's celebrated *Konzertstück* in F minor (1821) in the concert-hall. Alternatively, and as a result of his increasingly professional attitude towards piano study, he may have surveyed the appropriate repertoire (for his level) before opting to study Mendelssohn's G minor Concerto under Kashperova. Several years later, in the context of the 'six lessons' he delivered at Harvard University, Stravinsky was to declare an unexpected admiration for Weber: 'I am thinking of his sonatas, which are of an instrumental bearing so formal that the few *rubati* which they permit themselves on occasion do not manage to conceal the constant and alert control of the subjugator.'[205] (This latter reference is to André Gide's 'salient aphorism' about classical works being beautiful 'only by virtue of their subjugated romanticism'.)[206] However, in 1910 – the year that Stravinsky began to compose *Petrushka* – there is no suggestion that, behind the composer's desire to write a work with such overtly nineteenth-century virtuoso associations, there could possibly lurk an underlying identification with Weber's or Mozart's or anyone else's celebration of this one-movement genre.[207] Rather, the piano is used descriptively and pictorially to support the narrative of this 'burlesque'; and, in the Second Part ('Pétrouchka'), the soloist does his/her best to adopt the identity of this 'droll, ugly, sentimental, shifting personage', to cite Malcolm MacDonald's description – which also neatly summarizes the character of Stravinsky's piano writing.[208] Thereafter, however, the piano retires to a purely orchestral role, following the example of *The Firebird* to the extent, even, of being wiped from the orchestral palette altogether.

Of particular note is one moment in Stravinsky's sketches, which illustrates the aforementioned partnership between piano and harp. This concerns a passage in 'Dance of the Coachmen' when both instruments, situated within the orchestral bloc, are 'merely' occupied with adding to the overall mix of colours. Such is the interchangeability of their contributions that Stravinsky conceives their parts without clear differentiation, indulging in a kind of one-stave-fits-all musical shorthand. The piano material, with its rapid ostinato of repeated chords, resembles a harp part (on one stave) whilst the harp material, with its octave tremolo and wide arpeggios, resembles a piano part (also on one stave).[209] All is clarified by reference to the full score (Fig. 225). Thus, the (solo) piano is no longer personified in the role of Petrushka, but has reverted to fulfilling its customary and impersonal duties as an anonymous element (the orchestral piano) within *Petrushka*. In presentations of the ballet, where the orchestra is in the pit, this is of little consequence. But in concert performances, in full view of the audience, the curious absence of pianistic contributions to the latter half of the work is somewhat problematic. One solution might involve the following piece of theatre at the conclusion of the 'Pétrouchka' scene (which also marks the finale of the *Konzertstück*): the 'soloist' (prominently situated at the grand piano) should stand up and discreetly move across to an upright piano situated in a less conspicuous position. (There is ample time for this during the drumming link.) There, the 'orchestral pianist' will continue, now appropriately re-located physically and metaphorically (above all *timbrally*), i.e. between the harp and the percussion.[210] Nikolay Andreyevich might even have approved.

Petrushka contains one notable 'upright piano moment' – in the 'Valse' – that serves perfectly to illustrate Stravinsky's awareness of his teacher's guidance whilst also demonstrating that any engagement with eighteenth-century style would need, in Stravinsky's view, to be matched by an appropriately adapted 'eighteenth-century instrumentation'. (This will become a consistent feature of his neoclassical re-creations but may already be observed here, in a Russian context.) At the return of the lento cantabile theme (at Figs. 149–51) the tempo di valse material is shared (as at the start of this section) between the trumpet, flute and harp. However, when the music breaks into a 'variation by division' (in a clear reference to classical procedures) the piano enters with semiquaver triplets. This figuration supports and provides ornamentation to the trumpet's melody. At this precise moment (Fig. 150) Stravinsky indicates for the piano part to be played '*left ped*', i.e. *una corda* (Example 1.10). The effect of this imaginative, if unusual, indication is to deny the concert grand its customary resonance and projection. The rationale behind Stravinsky's notation is open to conjecture. The resultant sonority is an altered, slightly muted timbre which might be understood to approximate that of the fortepiano or – more likely, in the aftermath of Landowksa's recitals in St Petersburg – the harpsichord. The *staccato* articulation tends to reinforce the latter reading. This 'tribute to Petersburg's past' is located within the street-fair of hurdy-gurdies and cimbaloms, which makes this reference to Russia's classical age – via a Viennese waltz – a double allusion for the ballet's audience to savour. Those with a western perspective will recognize the *galant* aspect to this charming episode, whilst audiences of a more nationalist sympathy cannot fail to appreciate that Stravinsky's cameo is also evoked through the typically dextrous fingers of a local cimbalom or kantele player. Above all, this scene is a remarkable illustration of how Stravinsky's Russian and neoclassical musics co-existed – here, in an affectionate portrait of Old St Petersburg – long before claims of a 're-invention'.

Petrushka's pianistic sonority is fundamental to a western experience of this work, influenced perhaps by our familiarity with the *Three Movements from Petrushka*. Interestingly, however, the Russian perspective on this

Ex. 1.10 Stravinsky, *Petrushka* (revised 1947 version), 'Valse', Fig. 150.

work is quite different. In the opinion of the critic and composer N. Ya. Myaskovsky, writing in 1912, the piano does not even warrant a mention.[211] He reviews each scene of the ballet, enthusiastically accounting for every last subtlety of its instrumentation – except for the very detail that, for western audiences, gives *Petrushka* its identity *sui generis*. (Indeed, *Petrushka* is so special to its admirers not least for being such a unique conglomerate of genres: ballet, concert suite and concerto.) Nevertheless, Myaskovsky is full of praise in defence of Stravinsky's new work: 'I think that had Rimsky-Korsakov – that exceptional aristocrat of the kingdom of sound – been alive he would have stood up for this work without a moment's hesitation', he writes. Given the laudatory tenor of his critique, Myaskovsky's peroration goes on to pose an oddly rhetorical question. (Yet, given the nationality of its author and his readership, it is a perfectly understandable one.) 'Should one say something about the orchestration? That seems to me unnecessary, for it is altogether obvious now that in Russia at the present Stravinsky is the only person in that line – he feels the orchestra's soul'.[212] Curious it is, indeed, that the readers of Myakovsky's article might only infer the presence of a piano in *Petrushka* from the subtlest of allusions to 'the tinkling *Adagietto* episode – at times joking, at times sad'.[213] One can only speculate whether such a contribution to the orchestra from the piano was, perhaps, just too unremarkable a sonority for Russian ears to warrant more comment. (How different will be the critical reception to Stravinsky's neoclassical piano!) Much more noteworthy for Myaskovsky were Stravinsky's clever tricks: 'the accordion effect obtained by amusing parallel triads in the trombones … a tiny orchestral joke prepared for by an extremely trivial flute cadenza … stupefying fanfares … an almost constant accordion background (scored with inexhaustible inventiveness) [and] the strumming of the balalaikas (a very skilful imitation of their sound)'.[214] A Russian would marvel at Stravinsky's portrayal of St Petersburg's celebrated Shrovetide Fair and its characters, real and fantastical. Petrushka himself was a special focus of Myaskovsky's interest: 'his bowing, the nodding of his long nose and his fussy *falsetto* chatter find in the music a precision of expression which becomes palpable'.[215]

Consistent with our theme, however, the transitional quality of the piano writing in *Petrushka* is more noteworthy still: nineteenth-century gestures of virtuosity, particularly those in scene 2 (with its arabesques, its wide leaps and its harp-like ornamentation) co-habit with modernist effects such as rapidly alternating hands, ostinato figurations of all kinds and a plethora of repeated-note patterns. In fact, Stravinsky's burlesque portrayal of this traditional tale depends for its impact upon both of these stylistic extremes. For all its innovation, the work's greatest surprise (at least, from a pianistic stance) is that the solo piano should recede – as if in evolutionary reversal – until it becomes merely another instrument, its material indistinguishable from that of the harp. Before the moor 'finishes off the ill-starred Petrushka with his cudgel [in Myaskovsky's description]

and the Magician enters [to remove] his lacerated corpse',[216] Stravinsky
(the supreme Master of Ceremonies, after all) has long since exorcized the
puppet of his wicked, pianistic soul and banished him to the orchestral
rank and file.

The Rite of Spring *(1911–13)*

Le Sacre du printemps requires a large orchestra – without piano. However,
we know from one of the most famous narratives in twentieth-century music
that it was composed from beginning to end *at* the piano (in that upper
room in the Hotel Châtelard, Clarens). What relevance, therefore, can this
piano-less work possibly have within the sweep of this book's stated theme?
(Just because the composer tells us, as he 'signs off' on the last page of the
manuscript, that he was suffering from 'an intolerable tooth-ache'[217] should
we seek representation of this in the music – by interpreting *The Rite*'s final,
violent cadence as a gesture of extraction, perhaps?) Yet, despite the absence
of an orchestral piano part in the score, this instrument is still very much an
issue. It is as if the literal pianism of *Petrushka*, which gradually disappears
from sight and sound, now finds its sublimation within *The Rite of Spring*.

According to White (1966) and Goubault (1991) it is considered most
probable that, as with *The Faun and the Shepherdess*, Stravinsky assembled both the orchestral and four-hand scores of *The Rite* in parallel acts of
composition during 1911 and 1912.[218] It is also well documented that the
four-hand score was published in May 1913 (by Edition Russe de Musique,
Berlin)[219] to coincide with the premiere in Paris, so one may assume that
the bulk of the latter score was cared for in the intervening six months.
Whatever the chronology, one recalls that according to Rimsky-Korsakov's
model (see Chapter 1, pp. 56–7) orchestration is a creative process inseparable from composition. It therefore holds that the four-hand *Rite* may
be considered a version or, even, a reduction, but the opposite is not the
case: the orchestral *Rite* cannot, likewise, be considered a version or, even,
an orchestration. In that sense, the chronology is immaterial; if both *Rites*
were conceived in parallel, the order of their notation and any minor dis-
crepancies between the two carry little significance. What *is* significant,
however, is how *The Rite of Spring* displays Stravinsky's extraordinary skill
in producing, from the same material, both an orchestral score that is
wholly orchestral and a piano score that is wholly pianistic. Aside from
a few exceptions (which will be considered in due course) this work is a
masterful demonstration of Rimskian principles, for during the process of
composition Stravinsky bypassed the notion of orchestration altogether
by conceiving the notes already formed with their individual timbres.

That much is abundantly clear from study of *The Rite of Spring: Sketches 1911–1913.*[220] This facsimile edition enables one to gain insight into the Rimskian ideal of musical creation that uses the piano as a sound source only, but which reveals its identity in precise instrumental colours. The first sketches that Stravinsky made of *The Rite* – beginning, quite literally, at the top left-hand corner – demonstrate that the practice of composing with the final instrumentation *already* in his mind was embedded into Stravinsky's mode of working from the very outset (Figure 1.1). The *apparently* pianistic physiognomy of many these initial sketches does *not* mean that Stravinsky's conception first passed through an a-chromic stage for piano from which he would proceed, via a process of orchestration, to colouring in the finished score. He may work his musical ideas in one, two or three staves, and often in the form of a short-score (*particell*), but a modicum of caution is required so as not to read every two-stave sketch as 'piano music awaiting instrumentation' and, on that basis, then to set about tracing its re-appearance in a short-score. Rather, Stravinsky conceives his material as instrumental sound. Whilst his two-stave sketches frequently indicate preparatory thoughts, they are never 'for piano'; such decisions regarding layout and space may only reflect Stravinsky's need to organize his thoughts clearly on pages already cluttered with other sketches. Also, there may be a vertical relationship between two staves for other reasons: here, on the top line (representing the composer's very first sketches for *The Rite*), Stravinsky's initial idea concerns two chords divided between two sections of the woodwind. Following its transposition up a tone, this material is merged into the score of 'The Augurs of Spring' (Fig. 15). No other creative procedure is required to translate this primordial sketch into the final, pagan result. These facsimile reproductions also lead one to conclude that, despite the substantial advance in the musical syntax of *The Rite* over *The Firebird* and *Petrushka*, Stravinsky retained the familiar, fundamentally Rimskian, mode of operation for all three ballets. Orchestration and composition remain indivisible aspects of the one creative process. Stravinsky ensures that his compositional integrity, as a product of the proud Russian tradition of orchestral composition, is never sacrificed.

The art of piano-less composition (which, paradoxically of course, Stravinsky practised at the piano) – this intravenous procedure which accesses directly into the vein of instrumental sonority – is in total contrast to his neoclassical, manifestly pianistic process (see Chapter 3). One reason for this must surely be that, from the beginning of his discussions with N. K. Roerich, Stravinsky conceived 'our child' (as he referred to it in early correspondence with his collaborator)[221] in terms of both music *and* choreography. He even described *The Rite of Spring*, in a commentary sent

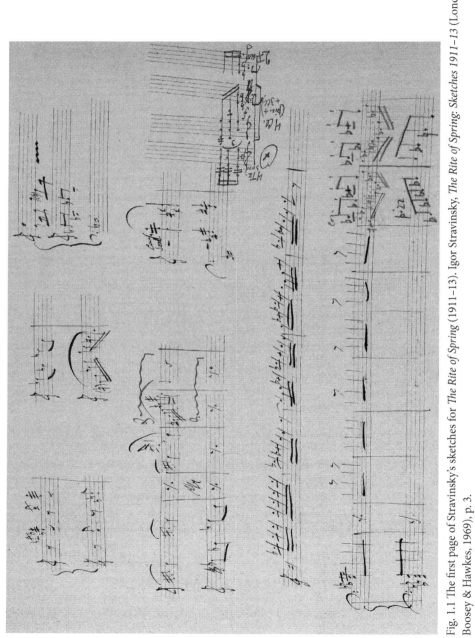

Fig. 1.1 The first page of Stravinsky's sketches for *The Rite of Spring* (1911–13). Igor Stravinsky, *The Rite of Spring: Sketches 1911–13* (London: Boosey & Hawkes, 1969), p. 3.

Fig. 1.1 (cont.)

to the editor of the *Russian Musical Gazette* (in December 1912), as 'my choreodrama'.[222] The extent of his absorption with the visual spectacle and with the details of its rhythmic portrayal was doubtless spurred on by his respect for Roerich's specialist knowledge of his subject ('Who else could help me, who else knows the secret of our ancestors' close feeling for the earth?')[223] and by his own desire, similarly, to 'penetrate the secret of the rhythm of Spring'.[224] 'I want the whole of my work', Stravinsky added, 'to give the feeling of the closeness between me and the earth, between the lives of men and the soil, and I sought to achieve this through the lapidary rhythm of *The Rite*'.[225] Such a powerful rhythmic ingredient would play a crucial role in the portrayal of these rites via dance, just as much as in purely musical terms. This dual focus, the composer wrote in his commentary to the sketchbook, 'greatly surprises me, especially that I could have envisaged synchronisation of music and choreography to such a degree … the dance is almost always in counterpoint to the music'. Clearly his attention – far from the literalness of the piano – was absorbed with the scenic gestures of (what Stravinsky initially called) 'The Great Sacrifice' and with exploiting to the full the vast range of colour permutations that his expanded orchestral palette offered.

This is not to deny that the sketches provide an occasional glimpse of Stravinsky's fluent pianism. For example, at the foot of the first page of sketches one observes material apparently suggestive of pianistic workings, which is rapidly re-formulated in every detail into the final orchestral version. So direct is the process, one can appreciate why Stravinsky was later moved to describe himself as the vessel through which *The Rite* passed. *Le Sacre du printemps* seems to have 'arrived' almost miraculously in its finished state, transforming itself from his imagination as if in one leap, while bypassing the arduous process of revision and refinement that normally characterizes creative work. Perhaps it was due to his experience of this phenomenon that, later, as a neoclassical composer and propagandist for 'objectivity', he became so interested, by complete contrast, in processes of musical construction, exploring questions concerning the laws of music and the craft of composition. Compared to the compositional process of other composers – most notably Beethoven – Stravinsky's input, at least on the page, appears to be minimal. As has been commented by others privileged with the opportunity to examine the Sammlung Igor Strawinsky at first hand, Stravinsky's sketches so closely approximate the finished score as to reveal his extraordinary capacity to organize compositional thoughts in his head with uncommon certainty, prior to committing his decisions to paper.

Two further instances of Stravinsky's seamless creativity are to be found amongst the very earliest sketches: firstly, the celebrated rhythmic pounding that opens 'The Augurs of Spring'. How conveniently these chords fit into the pianist's two hands, and how often are they exhibited as 'proof' that Stravinsky composed, i.e. composed *first*, at the piano! Yet, such was the dual process of their composition and, primarily, such was the composer's complete absorption of Rimskian concepts, the sketches confirm that these chords were, from their earliest inscription on the page, always an orchestral conception *as well*. Let us examine this passage in both the sketch manuscript (Figure 1.1, middle line) and the score (at Fig. 14). The key moment in the sketch is towards the end of this middle line, where the repeated chord in the strings switches to arpeggios (pizzicato quavers in the cellos against semiquavers in the bassoons). Here, Stravinsky writes in shorthand that the upper-stave material is for 'Cor.' and 'Fag.', i.e. cor anglais (not horn) and bassoon. The indication 'pizz.' written over the lower stave confirms that, in accordance with the bass clef and with standard string notation, Stravinsky wished the cellos (and/ or double-basses), who have already been playing the chords since the beginning of the line, to switch from arco to pizzicato. Thus, the 'pianistic' two-stave appearance of this sketch belies a fully instrumental conception, in full (Rimskian) colour. Similarly, it would be tempting to read into another sketch (for 'The Augurs of Spring') evidence that Stravinsky would compose initially for piano if we did not, by now, know better; that is, he might write with pianistic traces but these would be expertly covered under the orchestral mantle, however naturally these might even suggest pianistic fingering. Out of the pianistic 'original' (Figure 1.1, bottom line) Stravinsky has skilfully created three additional flute/piccolo parts. When combined, this wholly orchestral four-part flute-texture masks any trace of pianism most effectively (Example 1.11) As in the earlier consideration of *Fireworks*, fingering has been added to illustrate the natural pianism of this phrase.

Two exceptions that prove the rule ...

The sketches also suggest, however, that the 'Glorification de l'élue' and the 'Danse sacrale' were not only composed *at* the piano, but, exceptionally, they also retained in the composer's imagination a perfectly acceptable *pianistic identity* during their passage from initial spark to final score – and beyond, even, into the 'live' context of the orchestral rehearsal. As Craft informs us, Stravinsky would openly acknowledge the inherent pianism in these sections of the work, primarily as a means to assist orchestras to overcome the complexities of the music with confidence, precision and speed:

> The pianistic aspect of ['The Naming and Honouring of the Chosen One'], with its alternating left-hand right-hand keyboard style, offers an analogy

Ex. 1.11 Stravinsky, *The Rite of Spring* (1911/13), excerpt at Fig. 17 – with suggested piano fingerings.

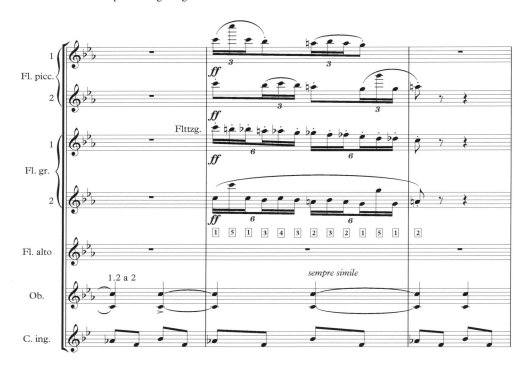

which Stravinsky himself … frequently employed in rehearsals. He would ask timpanists and bassists to think of themselves as a pianist's left hand, and the *tutti* orchestra as the same pianist's right hand; this seemed to improve the rhythmic results, and the same approach did again in the 'Sacrificial Dance'.[226]

That Stravinsky should offer a glimpse of the workmanship that lies behind the finished composition is certainly the exception to the rule, but in this case it was a memory he was content to share publicly whenever the occasion demanded it. Confronted with (what he once called) 'the memory drug of the score'[227] and with a need, in rehearsal, to resolve a problem quickly and practically, Stravinsky seems to have positively enjoyed re-living the pianistic origins that had once formed the prototype for these iconic orchestral passages. His piano duet adaptation of *The Rite* (1913) is testimony to the quasi-vamping pianism that characterizes the music in these two scenes;[228] here, Stravinsky's *Seconda* Part will occasionally make use of the deepest register of the piano. This is especially the case in 'Glorification de l'élue' where these *octavo basso* resonances are not explored in the orchestral work. It represents, therefore, Stravinsky's pianistic extension of this highly proto-pianistic orchestral material. The orchestral composer, as it were, 'embraces' the piano work within. Yet, considering how much of *The Rite* reverts almost effortlessly to a pianistic format, it is remarkable how little of the work in its orchestral splendour suggests a pianistic origin. Neither does *The Rite* ever sound like an orchestration. The very notion is absurd. Yet how extraordinary it is that (with these two exceptions: 'Glorification de l'élue' and 'Danse sacrale') Stravinsky managed so totally to cover over his fingerprints! It is an achievement which is surely as much a tribute to Rimsky-Korsakov's method and his competence as a teacher as it is to his pupil's consummate powers.

Craft has declared *The Rite* to be anti-classical. His case is well made as he observes the gulf which separates this work from 'the iambics of Bach and eighteenth-century classicism and, indeed, [from] European music as a whole during the three centuries preceding our own'. He continues with a particularly acute observation: 'It is surely an achievement of a kind to have created a work of such scope without [dotted rhythms], though I advance the point not for that reason, but as a measure of the rhythmic revolution of the *Rite* and of its anticlassicism.'[229] By comparison, *Petrushka* assumes a privileged role in bridging Stravinsky's Russian past to his Internationalist future – its pianism embedded within the texture of the musical strands, in the very patterning of its notes. With the exception of the above examples, it seems that Stravinsky is attempting to conceal every trace of pianism in *The Rite* behind the mask of his orchestration. *Petrushka*, on the other hand, openly flaunts a range of pianistic styles: from the nostalgia of virtuosity, reflecting the twilight of the long nineteenth century, to the innovation of ostinati – heralding modernism's dawn. There is also a swathe of other references in *Petrushka*, such as the mechanistic barrel-organ or its saccharine variation in *Wiener Walzer* style. Their banal syntax anticipates the composer's future interest in parodying 'low-art' musics as a means of portrayal whilst simultaneously holding the music's expression at an objective distance. Stravinsky's continuing journey towards neoclassicism will be characterized by a series of encounters with popular songs and folk dances. More relevant to our purpose, however, his path will engage with the didactic challenges of children's musical literature; and this will form one of the main topics of Chapter 2, particularly in the section entitled 'Taking the low road', pp. 84–7.

2 Becoming a neoclassicist

Pianistic patterns

The transitional years, between Stravinsky's Russian works and his neo-classicism, provide an opportunity to examine how he became increasingly drawn to the learning processes of music. Perhaps this was a by-product of fatherhood as his children reached an age when they began to have piano lessons and, as a result, Stravinsky felt attracted to the distraction of writing 'easy pieces' for them – with his own participation. It is equally possible that having spent years contemplating his own development, firstly as a pianist then as a composer, he now transferred this curiosity to his young family. By so doing he could observe these gradual generative processes in others, step-by-step and at a distance. For it is from his renewed engagement with the learning path, and by its re-cycling, that Stravinsky found a means to bind his latent classicism to a modernist and more objective aesthetic, thus transforming his long-standing enchantment with *style galant* and with counterpoint into a fruitful relationship. The archetypal neoclassical concept of 'craft' will eventually emerge from Stravinsky's act of deriving procedures of composition from the practicalities of performance – even from the minutiae of music's rehearsal.

To illustrate this, one might examine a fundamentally pianistic pattern and observe how Stravinsky derives a variety of musical textures from this, building a section or even an entire movement from a single pianistic 'brick'. There are countless patterns to choose from, but the index-finger-over-thumb figure – already mentioned regarding the third of the *Four Studies*[1] – is particularly emblematic in this regard. Whilst the left hand delivers a doleful, chromatic melody in quavers, a flowing, semiquaver oscillation in the right hand provides the principal technical element of this study. This *ur-forma* of the index-finger-over-thumb pattern requires a digital deployment of **2**,1,2,5,2,1 – where **2** (in bold) denotes the second finger stepping over the thumb and outside the comfort zone of the octave span. This figure is maintained in the right hand throughout the study. The arrangement of the notes within the octave may vary – for example, to employ the middle or fourth fingers, such as **2**,1,3,5,3,1 or **2**,1,4,5,4,1 – but the index-finger overlap is never abandoned.[2] Whatever the internal arrangement of notes, the 'constant' in terms of piano technique is that the index finger (or, on rare occasions, the middle finger) crosses over the thumb to 'step outside the circle' and immediately step back again.

The extreme technical demands of the *Four Studies* reflect Stravinsky's own attainment of an advanced piano technique by the time of their composition – for he premiered this work himself (in the autumn of 1908). His admiration for Czerny, declared in the autobiography, is likely to be the direct result of studying with Kashperova, who maintained an active career as a concert pianist. From this experience he may even have become familiar with Czerny's *Die Kunst der Fingerfertigkeit* (*The Art of Finger Dexterity* op. 740) and later modelled his own studies upon them; for the pianistic pattern under discussion is a variant, by extension, of a similar figure that features in Study no. 7: 'Fingerwechsel auf einer Taste' ('Changing the Fingers on One Key'; Example 2.1a).[3] The third of Stravinsky's *Four Studies* reflects a similar technical obsession (Example 2.1b), this pattern re-appearing in *Petrushka* (in the 'Danse russe'), where its overlapping aspect is consolidated (Example 2.1c). Czerny's finger-change has evolved, as it were, and assumed a Stravinskian identity. Under the terms of this new choreography the index finger will toy with this extension idea (beyond the octave) onto which Stravinsky stitches a variety of musical costumes. For example: the former, exclusively technical figuration is now used, in *Petrushka*, to portray carnivalesque jollity. Removed, thus, from all didactic responsibilities, the pattern is liberated from the need for such pedantic, unrelenting repetition as witnessed in the study. This lightening of mood is but an initial transformation. The pattern re-appears in the humorous song-cycle *Trois histoires pour enfants* (1917) where Czerny's (same-note) and Stravinsky's (overlap) patterns alternate in 'Tilim-bom' in the right hand (Example 2.1d), and where the overlap variant is used in the left hand in 'Les Canards, les cygnes, les oies …' (Example 2.1e). This characteristic representative of Stravinsky's Swiss output – written at a time when he was immersed in the portrayal of the animal world by way of traditional Russian 'nonsense verse' – marks another stage in the re-cycling process of this versatile and durable pianistic knot. Stravinsky's faith in this motif may be seen to transcend other stylistic boundaries as well. It re-appears, for example, in such neoclassically mature surroundings as the *Capriccio* (1928/9), where it contributes to the *capriccioso* spirit, at Fig. 10, whilst also guaranteeing a respectably technical element to this *concertante* work (Example 2.1f).[4] Preliminary sketch-material for the *Concerto for Two Solo Pianos* (1931/5) indicates this same default fingering (sharing Stravinsky's initial concept) although this will be abandoned in the final draft.[5] The *ur-forma* of this index-finger-over-thumb pattern (dating, one recalls, from the 1907 Study) may even be detected half a century later, in *Movements for Piano* (1958/9).

Ex. 2.1a Czerny, *Die Kunst der Fingerfertigkeit* op. 740, 'Fingerwechsel auf einer Taste' ('Changing the Fingers on One Key'), bb. 1–3.

Ex. 2.1b Stravinsky, *Four Studies for Piano* (1908), III. Andantino, bb. 1–3.

Here, in more introspective mode, it is perfectly suited to conveying this work's widely angular, serial counterpoint, as if in slow motion (Example 2.1g). One of the quirkier moments in Stravinsky's autobiography may once again be savoured: 'Fingers are not to be despised', he wrote. 'They are great inspirers, and, in contact with a musical instrument, often give birth to subconscious ideas which might not otherwise come to life.'[6] Russian romanticism, Eurasianism, neoclassicism, serialism … Stravinsky's main stylistic manifestations all owe something of their thread to this unassuming finger-inspired shape. The variety and ingenuity of its application serve to illustrate Stravinsky's unusual brand of receptivity to musical, especially pianistic, patterning.

While it would be incautious to saddle this little pattern, like 'Pastorale', with 'too many heavy portents', it does suggest that Stravinsky's wide-ranging catalogue may also be viewed in terms of a single (as well as a singular) creative process. Did Stravinsky himself not perceive this? Do not his writings portray a consistency of thought that transcends the stylistic contrasts which characterize his musical journey? Towards the end of the road – in 1962 (the year of his brief return to the Soviet Union) – when confronted

Ex. 2.1c Stravinsky, *Petrushka*, 'Danse russe', Fig. 86, bb. 1–3.

Ex. 2.1d Stravinsky, *Trois histoires pour enfants* (1915/17), 'Tilim-bom', bb. 44–7.

sonn' plus fort. Qui la sonn'? C'n'est plus le __ chat, les gens la sonnent à

Ex. 2.1e Stravinsky, *Trois histoires pour enfants*, 'Les Canards, les cygnes, les oies …', bb. 10–12.

-nais' s'ai-dait aus-si, le pou, trop haut per-ché, la têt' lui a tour-né.__

Ex. 2.1f Stravinsky, *Capriccio* (1928/9), 1st movement, Fig. 10.

leggiero scherzando

Ex. 2.1g Stravinsky, *Movements for Piano and Orchestra* (1958/9), 1st movement, bb. 27–30, with suggested piano fingerings.

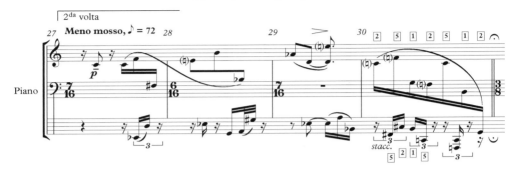

with the overwhelming truth of his eternally Russian identity, he wrote that: 'All my life I have spoken and thought in Russian. I have a Russian style. Perhaps it is not immediately apparent in my compositions; but it is there – latent in my music'.[7] Stravinsky's disarming response confirms that underpinning his entire output there was also an ineluctably Russian attitude. Tracing such a seemingly inconsequential note-pattern across the boundaries of musical idiom – and across the several frontiers of his geographical and cultural exile – enables us to comprehend and to celebrate something of this Stravinskian 'attitude'. More specifically, such a reading supports the view that, of all Stravinsky's styles, neoclassicism provided him with an opportunity to remain in touch with working procedures that date from his Russian past, and to find a way forward via the re-cycling of such fundamentals. This consistency was accomplished by Stravinsky exploiting his abiding interest in the constructive aspects of music, whereby the dual crafts of composition and performance interact as part of the one creative process. The final steps by which Stravinsky arrived at his neoclassical re-launch provide an illustration of this.

The familiar narrative is told of Stravinsky's encounter with the music of Pergolesi (and other Neapolitan composers) at Diaghilev's invitation: of his dissolving the barriers between creation and arrangement through his impulse to write 'his' *Pulcinella* onto the very scores themselves. Such close contact with these 'numerous fragments and shreds of compositions either unfinished or merely outlined' enabled Stravinsky to 'appreciate more and more the true nature of Pergolesi while discerning ever more clearly the closeness of my mental and, so to speak, sensory kinship with him'.[8] Thus Stravinsky declares his mental and sensory kinship with ... *Pergolesi*?! Surely such intellectual and emotional bonding dates from much further back: from

'Pastorale', whose classical demeanour – specifically its persistent Alberti bass and its graceful 'five-hemidemisemiquaver turn-figure'[9] – is echoed in *Pulcinella*'s second movement (Serenata), now in a genuinely (neo)classical context. In 1908 'Pastorale' represented a diversion for Stravinsky, a digression from the true path of a Rimsky pupil – a charming irrelevance, perhaps, though not without a certain *succès de scandale* (on an intimate scale within the Rimsky circle). The year 1919, however, was another context. *Pulcinella*, while similarly engaging with classical models, was to represent no less than 'the epiphany through which the whole of [Stravinsky's] late work became possible'.[10] This oft-cited declaration (made with the benefit of considerable hindsight) is Stravinsky's attempt neatly to situate the starting line for his neoclassicism, the sub-plot being his coy revelation that this was also 'a backward look, of course, the first of many love affairs in that direction'. Reference to Stravinsky's earliest compositions, however, would suggest that *Pulcinella* was not the first but merely the latest such *affaire*. Not only the early piano solos and songs, but also the catalogue of children's pieces that Stravinsky wrote after 1914, enable one to comprehend why he should qualify his admission of looking backwards with 'but it was a look in the mirror, too'. In this mirror's reflection Stravinsky recognized his own long-held fascination with the eighteenth century. It was an interest which, prior to Diaghilev's commission, had remained concealed behind the nursery door of their Swiss home, or, even, 'lost, fortunately lost'[11] in Rimsky's St Petersburg apartment. *Pulcinella*'s image contained traces that Stravinsky surely recognized in his *own* musical physiognomy. For over a decade after all – since 'Pastorale' – he had proved himself to be an observant, skilful and affectionate re-formulator of the classical idiom. *Pulcinella* was not, then, the road-to-Damascus moment that it has often been portrayed as, but represented a continuation of, and liberation from, his past.

Christopher Butler has written of 'stylistic variation' being 'central to the modernist period' and calls on Picasso and Joyce, whose 'development is not linear, but [similarly] cumulative and overlapping'.[12] The experience of working with Picasso (for whom 'there is no past and future in art')[13] provided Stravinsky with the certainty that a part of him had already moved forward through his embrace of the past. *Pulcinella* might represent a 'look backwards' but in doing so it could also provide a revitalizing pointer towards his aesthetic renewal. As he recalled in 1960, 'I created the possibility of the [Pergolesi] commission as much as it created me ... Though it may seem to have been an arbitrary step at the time, [*Pulcinella*] was *an entirely logical step* for me.'[14] The really important difference between 1908 and 1919, i.e. between 'Pastorale' and *Pulcinella*, was that the latter work enabled Stravinsky to declare his engagement with the past openly and in artistic terms. He could claim this new musical territory as his own in a philosophical gesture (to borrow from Y. I. Zamyatin's futuristic novel *We* of 1921) that required Stravinsky 'to line [himself] up on a strong logical axis' in pursuit of 'unimpeachable geometrical beauty'.[15]

Taking the low road

Stravinsky's child's-world literature of songs, arrangements and piano duets occupies a defiantly non-artistic space compared to his main works. The portrayal of childhood, or of objects and emotions that belong to or evoke childhood, inevitably affects one's perception of this composer's subjective aspirations. Our adult response is in direct proportion to the distance that such children's pieces find themselves from the world which we (as mature listeners) inhabit. How should one respond to such works, after all, if they are (for example) mere nonsense (*Pribaoutki*; 1914) or lullabies for cats (*Berceuses du chat*; 1915–16) or *skazki* ('tales') about stumpy tails (*Trois histoires pour enfants*; 1915–17)? Two short examples will suffice:

> Tilim-bom, Tilim-boom,
> Save the goat-shed from its doom!
> Mother goat while grazing,
> Sees her home a-blazing,
> Wags her stumpy little tail,
> Calls for water, pail on pail.
>   ('Tilim-bom',
>   *Trois histoires pour enfants*)[16]

> La punais' s'aidait aussi, le pou, trop haut perché, la têt' lui a tourné.
> Est tombé sur le derrière, s'est fait mal contre un' pierre …
> ['The wood-louse also made his bed, perched too high and turned his head.
> Fell down on his dorsal bone, banged himself against a stone …']
>   ('Les Canards, les cygnes, les oies …',
>   *Trois histoires pour enfants*).[17]

How should one respond? With an appropriate sense of fun is surely the only riposte to that musicologically charged question! However, one might also suspect (with Zamyatin) that children are 'the only bold philosophers' and that – with a sideways glance at Stravinsky – 'bold philosophers will always be children'.[18] Nevertheless, it is not difficult to sense the composer's relaxed attitude to the two sets of piano duets written to educate and entertain 'mon fils Svetik', 'ma fille Mikouchka' and 'mon fils Fedik' – the dedicatees, respectively, of the *Three Little Songs* (1913). Compared to the magnificence of the ballets – with their splendour and their polemic (both emblems of their status as 'high art') – what cultural value can be detected in the childish dance-items that form the *Three Easy Pieces for Piano Duet (Easy Left Hand)* (1914–15),[19] or in such nationalist cameos as 'Española', 'Balalaika' and 'Napolitana' (rounded off by a jolly 'Galop') from the *Five Easy Pieces for Piano Duet (Easy Right Hand)* (1916–17)? Nevertheless, one should not underestimate the degree to which these *divertissements* enabled Stravinsky to develop in several crucial areas, in preparation for his eventual emergence as a neoclassicist. The informality and privacy of this repertoire facilitated Stravinsky's return to music's rudiments and to a fresh engagement with note-on-note relationships at their most transparent. In parallel acts of observation and construction he formulated mechanisms that incorporated dynamics and tempo, and even fingering, in order to provide secure guidelines for his young performers. As a result, Stravinsky's two sets of piano duets and the eight miniatures that comprise *Les Cinq Doigts* resemble construction 'kits' (of a model aeroplane, for example) designed for eager young fingers to assemble step-by-step.

Conceived within, and for, the Stravinskys' domestic environment, these works offered the composer an opportunity to indulge in musical games, far from the madding crowd. There was neither professional feedback nor critical response to anticipate. Thus, more than any other of Stravinsky's works these duets recall Villa-Lobos' description of his own music as letters written for posterity without expecting any reply.[20] In order to write music with a clear didactic purpose, Stravinsky devised a musical syntax of textural clarity and emotional objectivity. This essentially practical music, *hors concours*, is characterized by a tendency towards the gradual *montage* of its materials (rhythms, accompaniments and melodies). Instead of sophisticated instrumentation and the complex textures of adult 'perfected' art Stravinsky's score evokes slip-ups and hesitations, re-starts and repetitions. In short, all the wonky rhetoric of (a child's) piano practice is written into the musical narrative. These duets are 'about music', 'about musical performance' and, even, 'about constructing a musical performance'. They present re-enactments of piano practice as if in 'observational mode' (the term employed in *cinema vérité*) – i.e. the composer, the performers and the listeners all 'regard' the learning process from their own perspective.[21]

Common to these portraits of music's processes is their origin in 'Stravinsky's piano' – for this represents the workshop that they share with the composer's own childhood and with the didactic literature of musical history: from Bach to Clementi to Czerny, and to the exhaustive methods of so many others. Viewed in this context, Stravinsky's duets may be summarized as *pseudo études* which – reflective of *real études* – present a series of pianistic challenges appropriate to the tender age of the performers, e.g. hand position, fingering, counting, dynamic control and the art of just keeping going. Furthermore, they take on the additional responsibility of offering solutions to these technical problems. Within this learning context, the subjectivity of artistic expression is a world away. Instead, the 'object- ivity' of the musical task needs to be addressed. Simple means might lead to simple results but, via such judicious use of a young pianist's five fingers, Stravinsky offers a new perception of familiar musical elements. Thus, the tendency towards *uproshcheniye* – Taruskin's term for the 'radical simplifi- cation of means'[22] – becomes increasingly pervasive in Stravinsky's music in the decade following *The Rite of Spring*. The two sets of piano duets and the *Trois histoires pour enfants* provide him with an unprecedented opportunity to re-evaluate (his) techniques of composition (as creation) and perform- ance (as re-creation) in a non-threatening environment of pure diver- sion (as recreation). In particular, the two-year interlude (1915–17) gave impetus to a process of transition in Stravinsky's musical language which, in due course, would arrive via this unpretentious path to the formation of his neoclassical idiom.

There are several stages to this transition. Firstly: Stravinsky's modelling of his 'easy left hand' two-note ostinati – for example 'Chanson de l'ours' (the third of the *Histoires pour enfants*) and the March (from *Three Easy Pieces for Piano Duet*) – upon historical Russian precedents. Two examples of this device, typical amongst nineteenth-century duet literature intended for amateur (family) use, are Dargomïzhky's *Slavyanskaya tarantella* (men- tioned earlier)[23] and the remarkable quodlibet *Paraphrases on the Theme of 'Chopsticks'* (1878) to which Rimsky-Korsakov contributed several move- ments, as Gerald Abraham puts it, 'to gratify his love of musical tasks'.[24] Secondly, Stravinsky's emerging interest in allocating fingering to his didactic pieces (via the *Five Easy Pieces*). This may be traced to his sketches for the second movement, 'Española', which clearly show how Stravinsky embedded specific finger placements into the 'easy right hand' melody. The fingerings shown in Example 2.2 were written by Stravinsky into his final, neat copy;[25] however, this information is not reproduced in the published edition.

Thirdly, the crucial step up to the adult/professional world (of 'artworks') can be traced, for example, in the concluding bars to 'Canard (Ronde)', the first of the *Quatre chants russes*. Here, Stravinsky engages once more in that particular form of pianistic virtuosity already observed in the Scherzo whereby, in this case, a pair of notes is repeated through the deft exchange of hands.[26] A fourth witness to Stravinsky's transition from child's world to neoclassicism may be observed in his attitude towards piano transcription. By examining one remarkable example in particular we may also recognize

Ex. 2.2 Stravinsky, *Five Easy Pieces for Piano Duet* (*Right Hand Easy*) (1916/17), II. 'Española', bb. 1–19, with the composer's fingerings.

Stravinsky's interest in what might best be termed the choreographic aspects of pianism; for one senses how he became intrigued with the minutiae of fingering and with those related aspects of technique that concern the positioning of the pianist's hands, wrists and arms. Such an extension to the composer's traditional role may also be seen as an example of Stravinsky's increasing desire to control his musical object and to impose laws regarding the manner of its execution.

Transcription and the performer

An additional source of influence upon Stravinsky's mature neoclassical language may be found in the canon of piano transcriptions and arrangements which consistently reward patient study. A sub-species of artistic creation they may be, but the way they thrust into the pianist's hands music and gestures that derive from an entirely different, often theatrical genre makes them objects of pertinent interest. Stravinsky's idiosyncratic fingerings affect the hands and arm movements also, thus widening the debate to include aspects of physicality in Stravinsky's early neoclassical works for the keyboard. To take but one example: the Valse from *Histoire du soldat*, which Stravinsky arranged and edited for publication in 1922.[27] The Valse, one recalls, is the second of three popular dances – the others being Tango and Ragtime – performed during scene 5, the 'Scène de la fille guèrie' ('Scene of the Invalid Girl'). To cite Eric Walter White's synopsis: 'The invalid Princess is lying on a couch. The Soldier enters and plays his fiddle. The

Princess rises and dances a tango, a waltz and a rag-time, at the end of which she falls into the Soldier's arms.'[28] The original instrumentation is characterized by the quantity (and subtlety) of agogic and timbral indications which seem to contradict the music's aura of disarming simplicity. The woodwinds are exhorted to play not just lightly, but *leggierissimo*, the bassist to alternate between arco and pizzicato in close proximity; not only is the violinist's bowing specified in minute detail, the composer resorts to prolix instructions in order to secure the exact manner – both musical and gestural – with which he wishes the violin soloist (as the Soldier) to enact this captivating scene. One fleeting phrase should be played both 'sur la touche' ('on the fingerboard') and 'gliss[ant] avec l'archet de toute sa longueur' ('gliding with the full length of the bow').[29] Whilst these instructions result in modifications to the timbre of violin tone,[30] they also commit the violinist to a physical involvement with the music's projection – by employing expansive, sweeping motions of the bowing arm. Such is the unusual nature of his fingerings in his piano transcription, one is led to believe that Stravinsky was intent on re-creating something of the original's rich timbral detail – and, furthermore, its visual characterization – by means other than purely pianistic. What betrays Stravinsky's physical engagement with his material is the way that his often unexpected fingering obliges the hands to lift and skip about the keyboard in a manner not in the least natural or obvious; that is, pianists left to their own devices would execute these leaps and arabesques differently, and probably more easily. However, by conforming precisely to the fingerings stipulated by the composer, the performer senses that a parallel, gestural work of art is also being spun. While the pianist 'plays the music', a choreography (pianistically, quite unorthodox) is being delineated by the fingers and wrist, guided by Stravinsky's exacting instructions. Facilitate the performance they most certainly do *not*; the competent sight-reader could manage a perfectly satisfactory rendition of this little piece much more comfortably by using whatever comes to hand.

Instead, Stravinsky's fingerings in the following example from the Valse from *Histoire du soldat* (Example 2.3a) reveal the extent of his subtle iconoclasm. For example, the obstinately correct finger alternations on repeated notes – suggestive of methodological models – and the aesthetic arc of hand and arm movement (on approaching and leaving these figures) combine to produce an overall experience which, for the performer, is both demanding in a physical, technical sense and also emphatically gestural – almost, dare one say it, balletic.

Of interest, throughout this passage, are the carefully prescribed indications in the right-hand melody: for example, the repeated thumb from low A to high G (marked x) or the similar leap two bars later (marked y)

Ex. 2.3 Stravinsky, 'Valse' from *Histoire du soldat* for pianoforte solo (1922):

(a) bb. 16–25, with the composer's fingerings.

(b) bb. 39–44

where the grace-note is to be taken by the index finger. One recalls that the original work is scored for violin solo with accompaniment from other instruments. Stravinsky's detailed and calculated fingering for the keyboard version of this melody, with its arching movements up and down, lends the pianist's right hand, wrist and arm an uncanny resemblance to the violinist's bowing gestures. The violinist's more generous movements (as the bow moves from one string to another) find their pianistic equivalent: the choice of fingering obliges the arm to take a wide arc (see Example 2.3a, bb. 17–18, 19–20). Also, the agile and economic (up and down) bowing – near the heel – that is required to play the repeated notes (bb. 17, 19, 22) finds its equivalent on the piano in rapid 3,2,1 repeated-note fingering.

Viewed in this manner, Valse is more than a musical transcription; at times, it verges on pianistic 'choreography'. Particularly unconventional is bar 24. Here, Stravinsky indicates 4,1 for the final right-hand chord where 2,1 would appear to be, at speed, the obvious and comfortable choice. The excerpt illustrated (Example 2.3a) terminates in an emphatic perfect cadence, whose musical simplicity is (again) surprisingly complicated by the composer: the left hand must employ 1,3 where 1,5 would be the natural solution (indeed so obvious that no editor would even indicate it).[31] Example 2.3b illustrates even more startling instances where the composer has marked unexpected fingerings which need to be addressed and from which, again, the diligent performer would undoubtedly gain a sense of Stravinsky's concern with a covert agenda of physicality and corporeal movement.

Both audience and performer are affected. For example, the pianist's 'violin bowing' gestures will be quite evident to those present, while their execution is (naturally) of greater concern to the performer who must experience the work with an acute sense of physical awareness due to the unusual, often uncomfortable fingering. These awkward demands, if respected, will provoke a *technical* mind-set during performance, equivalent to that applied to the study of piano drills and *études* – an environment where the purpose of the fingering is not to find the easiest solution, but rather to avoid it. For thus it is that pianistic, digital dexterity is acquired: i.e. through the exploitation of deliberately taxing figurations for which the student's strict adherence to the given fingering is a key controlling element. In such a context, the method's author is *also* concerned with editorial aspects, for didactic reasons. This blurring of the function of fingering, and of the role of the editor/composer in this regard, is at the heart of this question concerning Stravinsky's fingerings – to be discussed in Chapter 3.

For now, in the Valse, one may observe Stravinsky's carefully annotated indications and ponder the reason why. Note, particularly, the unusual sequence of fingerings for the right hand (in Example 2.3b, bb. 41–3, i.e. the third to fifth bars). It is a novel and disconcerting sensation for one's fingers to be conscripted in this way, though less so if one is familiar with *Les Cinq Doigts*, written the same year as the Valse transcription was published (1922). In *The Five Fingers* Stravinsky pre-determines the finger to be used on every note of these eight short movements by indicating at the head of each piece the exact position of the hand's five fingers on the keyboard.[32] The Valse is thus related to this children's suite, though the former represents a significant advance on the latter. While the fingers are similarly harnessed under the composer's control, the Valse's wide-ranging use of the keyboard reveals a dynamic symbiosis of music and movement. The score is full of conspicuous details where events are allocated unconventional or unexpected fingerings. Whatever their musical or gestural significance, there is the suggestion that Stravinsky identified these events as meriting a differentiated articulation which he achieved through the use of a precisely calculated finger-choreography.

On one level, the Valse from *Histoire du soldat* highlights the extraordinary intimacy with piano technique which Stravinsky had cultivated by 1922, the year before taking into his own hands the premiere of his Piano Concerto. This would suggest that the decision, taken with Sergei Koussevitsky in September 1923, to assume total responsibility for this work – its composition and performance – was not as extraordinary or arbitrary as might at first appear. Stravinsky was already in pianistic mode. Amid the pressures of preparing *Mavra* (1921–2) and the *Octuor* (1922), he had found time to indulge in this innovative little gem: for the Valse is far more than a straightforward transcription; it also reveals an affectionate portrait of pianists' finger-agility and their secret world behind the mask of performance. Stravinsky was clearly in that world himself and must have embraced the opportunity that the Piano Concerto presented to raise the level of his pianistic commitment – for it came at just the right moment.

On another level, this transcription brings to a close a decade of activity wherein Stravinsky, taking a path in parallel to the 'high road' of artistic concert-works, resolved also to unite alternative strands of innovation which contributed, in varying degrees, to his new direction. The Valse is representative of a sub-genre of composition; as such, it may be viewed as a poor relation to 'art' for its endemic incapacity to demonstrate more than craft, however artfully. It is not original work, after all, but an adaptation and, at that, one that suffers from the law of diminishing returns – being a reduction from an instrumental source. How differently one might view this piece of craft had the converse been the case: an original piano solo orchestrated by the composer! That is just the point. Piano transcription, as a genre, occupies a humble position in the musical hierarchy – lowlier even, it could be argued, than arrangement; certainly far below the ingenious and virtuosic concert-paraphrases of Liszt, Rakhmaninov, Horowitz and others. Transcription shares its (lack of) status with the piano duet, with 'nonsense' or 'animal tales', with folk songs and *histoires pour enfants*, with children's piano pieces of the 'Steps to …' variety; in other words with many of the genres associated with Stravinsky's earliest neoclassicism including, in prime location, the wind band. This is represented in varying sizes via *Symphonies d'instruments à vent*, *Concert pour piano et instruments à vent* and the *Octuor*. While string chamber music ensemble may carry with it associations of intellectual refinement, mixed wind–string chamber music and, especially, wind-only chamber music are perceived, for whatever reason, to occupy a lesser artistic status. The Schubert Octet in F major D. 803 (1824; for clarinet, horn, bassoon and string quintet) is a good example of this differentiation. The work is greatly appreciated, adored even, by those who are well acquainted with it (particularly those who perform it); but it does not carry a reputation for revealing profound and fine art as does this same composer's Quintet in C major D. 956 (1828) – or the Mendelssohn Octet in E♭ major op. 20 (1825) – being exclusively for strings. *Pace* Rimsky-Korsakov, one must concede that such artistic expressivity is associated, rightly or wrongly, with the string-instrument repertoire, its performance and its reception. One reason for this may be that the wind-instrument sonority alludes to the world of the divertimento – in tribute, perhaps, to Mozart's memorable legacy in this repertoire – for who could deny the outdoor vigour and charms of the wind Serenades (in E♭ major K. 375; in C minor K. 388) or, indeed, the grandeur of the *Gran partita* (in B♭ major K. 361)? By contrast, however, the listener seeks, expects and defers unhesitatingly to the artistic qualities of the string quartet. A Stravinskian example of this very argument would be the *Symphony of Psalms*, notable (amid so many reasons) for its idiosyncratic scoring. By dispensing with violins – which Rimsky-Korsakov considered expressive, therefore *indispensable* – Stravinsky may be seen to append his adaptation of the symphonic genre also to that roll call of lowly forms with which he made his subtle but decisive re-invention a decade earlier.

One is reminded of Wordsworth, who constructed 'new poetical forms on the basis of models such as the ballad, which had been neglected as a low species of literature'.[33] In the Preface to the second edition of *Lyrical Ballads, with Pastoral and Other Poems* (1802) he inscribed a number of memorable phrases into the English language, including his celebrated definition of 'good poetry' as 'the spontaneous overflow of powerful feelings … [taking] its origin from emotion recollected in tranquillity'. However, Wordsworth's 'principal object' (and one that connects with Stravinsky's portraits of child's-world music-making) is 'to choose situations and incidents from common life … and, at the same time, to throw over them a certain colouring of the imagination, whereby ordinary things should be presented to the mind in an unusual way'. The poet's reason for dwelling on 'low and rustic life' suggests, in its desire for simplicity of delivery, an intriguing commonality with Stravinsky's own move towards, in Taruskin's designation, *uproshcheniye* ('simplification'). 'In that condition', writes Wordsworth, 'our elementary feelings co-exist in a state of greater simplicity, and, consequently, may be more accurately contemplated, and more forcibly communicated'.[34] There can hardly be, in the vast literature of didactic music, a more unusual colouring of those commonplace 'situations and incidents' than in Stravinsky's sets of piano duets, in his song-settings from the animal kingdom, or in his unique contemplation of *Les Cinq Doigts*. In this repertoire Stravinsky breathes new life into tired pedagogic formulae via procedures that are lyrically endorsed by Samuel Taylor Coleridge: 'What is old and worn out, not in itself, but from the dimness of the intellectual eye … [the poet] makes new: he pours upon it the dew that glistens, and blows round the breeze which cooled us in childhood.'[35] In Stravinsky's case his adventures in the nether worlds of music will carry implications for his adult, artistic direction.

As Robert Scholes informs us, this 'raising of "low" forms is noted by the formalists as a typical method of poetic regeneration'.[36] It is one of those remarkable coincidences of history that, contemporaneous with Stravinsky's early forays into the lower genres of music, there should emerge in Russia an artistic movement espousing similar methods, also, in literature. The Moscow Linguistic Circle, founded in 1915, and its St Petersburg counterpart OPOJAZ (an acronym for 'The Society for the Study of Poetic Language'), which was founded the following year, elaborated what has become known as Russian Formalism. Its most celebrated figure in the West is Roman Jakobson (1896–1982), who left Russia, with others, to found the Prague Linguistic Circle in 1926.[37] However, before exploring how Russian Formalist theory might relate specifically to Stravinsky's low forms, it is striking to note their emphasis on the 'literariness' of the text – even to the exclusion of the author. The Formalists regarded the writer 'as a kind of cipher merely reworking available literary devices and conventions'.[38] Indeed, according to J. A. Cuddon, 'OPOJAZ went so far as to suggest that there are no poets or literary figures: there is just poetry and literature.'[39] A leading voice for the movement, Viktor Shklovsky, summarizes this attitude in his definition of literature as 'the sum total of all the stylistic devices employed in it'.[40] One might reflect for a moment upon Stravinsky's comment that he was merely 'the vessel through which *The Rite* passed' in relation to this concept of the writer-as-cipher. By the same token, is not neoclassicism's paradigmatic condition of objectivity also anticipated by the Formalists? For if objectivity is the state of subject-distancing from the artwork, then the negation of the creator, i.e. the non-existence of the subject, must represent the ultimate state of objectivity.

Our focus, however, centres on Stravinsky's regeneration via his use of the piano duet and of other low genres. It is the very familiarity of these genres and the banality of their topics that suggest a further parallel with Formalist theory, specifically with Shklovsky's thesis of Habitualization and its counterpart, Defamiliarization. According to this latter concept, the function of art is to make things unfamiliar, to make forms obscure so as to increase the difficulty and the duration of the perception. (In other words, to cite Stravinsky in correspondence with Charles-Albert Cingria, 'l'art doit être astucieux et dificile'.)[41] In considering a passage from Tolstoy's *Diary*, Shklovsky emphasizes the aspect of this Formalist perspective that most chimes with Stravinsky's re-view of familiar musical genres out of which (and guided by his emergent respect for the craft of music and musical 'construction') he determines his future path towards neoclassicism: 'The act of perception in art', Shklovsky writes, 'is an end in itself and must be prolonged. *In art, it is our experience of the process of construction that counts, not the finished product.*'[42] On the one hand, Stravinsky's subject matter in the decade 1913–23 renders him liable to the accusation of 'Habitualization'. Is not the piano duet, for example, a commonplace of amateur music-making, and was it not especially so at that time, in that pre-media age of domestic music-making? And were not the 'character pieces' – March, Waltz, Polka and the whole gamut of national dance cameos – clichés, all, of mass piano literature? (Just how many collections of little pieces have been written for 'the five fingers' – either by intention, or by carrying this phrase literally in their title?) Yet, in the manner that Stravinsky renders these 'aspects' *unfamiliar* – for example, by increasing their difficulty (did he not require the services of José Iturbi for their premieres?) and by modifying the listener's 'habitual perceptions' – Stravinsky's child's-world music may also be regarded as exemplifying the Formalists' concept of Defamiliarization. In his essay 'Art as Technique' (1917), Shklovsky makes his point crystal clear: 'Art is a way of experiencing the artfulness of an object; the object is not important.'[43] Stravinsky's declaration 'My *Octuor* is a musical object' appears to contradict this. Yet, given his espousal of musical craft, would Stravinsky question the sentiment behind Shklovsky's essay title? Stravinsky may well have been 'as innocent of his contemporaries, the Russian Formalists, as Schönberg was of his, the Viennese Circle', as Milton Babbitt asserts.[44] From a broader perspective, however, by regarding Stravinsky's neoclassicism more as a celebration of musical *process* than as a stylistic return, there are undeniable and intriguing similarities.

From *Svadebka* to *Les Noces*

Throughout the years that Stravinsky spent formulating a Eurasian agenda he was also trying to complete a substantial new composition. *Svadebka* (to give this work its Eurasian, pre-neoclassical title) occupied Stravinsky from 1914 to 1922. It too plays a significant role in Stravinsky's path to neoclassicism via the narrative of its elusive instrumentation. Prior to accepting Diaghilev's teasing invitation ('I want you to look at some delightful eighteenth-century music …')[45] Stravinsky had produced several works which provided him with both the problem and eventual solution to his creative direction. By the time he started work on *Pulcinella* (in 1919), *Svadebka* was all but complete, except for a decision regarding its instrumentation. Finding a solution to this parameter had become the issue upon which the identity of this much-anticipated work now rested.

The eight-year gestation that was required to resolve *Svadebka*'s sonority mirrors Stravinsky's own, gradual re-birth. From several abandoned plans (some with emphatically folkloric resonances) there emerged the final instrumentation in the form of four pianos and percussion. It was a neoclassical solution epitomized in the work's re-christening as *Les Noces*.[46] Orchestral strings, cimbalom and harmonium – all had featured in earlier drafts of *Svadebka*. However, within the context of Stravinsky's evolving re-invention they became the first casualties, and a perfect illustration, of Stravinsky's new concern for homogeneity. By opting instead for four pianos, Stravinsky could hardly have demonstrated better (principally to himself) his emphatic rejection of Russian traditions, both romantic and Eurasian, in favour of an international brand. Stravinsky had found a way forward consistent with his rapidly emerging neoclassical interests. The instrumental sonority that now surrounded these *tableaux* of a traditional Russian wedding transformed the work from being a(nother) pagan *Rite* into an objectivized commentary upon a timeless peasant ritual. *Les Noces* it was and not *The Rite* that provided Stravinsky with the moment to regard his Russian materials as architectonic and to map out his vision of a neoclassical future.[47] The work's spartan soundtrack now perfectly matched the muted colours of Goncharova's revised set, which had formerly been in vivid reds and of bold 'peasant patterns'. As Figes observes, 'the choreography [of *Les Noces*] by Bronislava Nijinska was equally impersonal – the *corps de ballet* moving all as one, like some vast machine made of human beings, and carrying the whole of the storyline … it was the perfect ideal of the Russian peasantry'.[48] More importantly for Stravinsky, he had finally arrived at the consummate blend of idiom and aesthetic that this rite demanded. His eight-year impasse had been resolved by the boldest imaginable decision regarding the work's orchestration: there wasn't to be any! By this simultaneous act of creation and elimination Stravinsky had arrived at a supremely neoclassical result. With the aid of four pianos he had devised a sonority that was (as he famously described it) 'perfectly homogeneous, perfectly impersonal, and perfectly mechanical' – and perfectly neoclassical.[49] Stravinsky's next step in support of his newly formulated ideals, and consistent with views expressed in 'Some Ideas about My *Octuor*', was to write a series of works for wind instruments. Thereafter, out of a determination to distance himself still further from the 'nuances' produced by the strings, his next works explored the inexpressive, objectively extreme potential of the solo piano and piano-as-soloist.

Within a few years, however, the consistency of his neoclassical syntax would not be matched with equivalent rigour in the realm of instrumentation. The strings were soon reinstated, and in the case of *Apollo* (1927/8) Stravinsky even re-lived Tchaikovsky's literature for an exclusively string orchestra. From a Rimskian viewpoint this reverse swerve reflects increased maturity on Stravinsky's part and emphatically endorses his teacher's guidelines: 'We can listen to strings for an almost indefinite period of time without getting tired, so varied are their characteristics (*vide* the number of string quartets, suites, serenades etc. written for strings alone). The addition of a single group of strings will add lustre to a passage for wind instruments.'[50] Nor did Stravinsky wish to re-visit the reduced ensembles of *Pulcinella* or the *Octuor*, which were tailored to evoke, respectively, the early-eighteenth-century suite and the late-eighteenth-century divertimento. Whereas Stravinsky's 'topic' remained neoclassical for several decades into the future, his instrumentation returned almost immediately to the fold of Russian tradition in complete accord with Rimsky's caveat issued via the *Principles of Orchestration*: 'Fairly modern music will teach the student how to score; classical music will prove of negative value to him … such examples are of no further use today.'[51] This dismissal of the eighteenth century betrays Rimsky's bias towards instrumental solutions which intensify the impact of instrumental colour.

The responsibility of liberating music from undesirable nuances would henceforth pass to the piano, the hidden key to Stravinsky's pursuit of objectivity. After *Symphonies d'instruments à vent*, the *Octuor* and the *Concert pour piano et instruments à vent* Stravinsky never more attempted such a literal enactment of his neoclassical claims upon the desirability of winds to the exclusion of strings.[52] With the inclusion of double-basses in the Piano Concerto, cracks were appearing in his argument even before the ink that penned his 'Ideas' had dried. (Stravinsky may have been prepared to make the exception on account of the basses' subtle, almost vibrato-free resonance, and tolerate their presence as string instruments 'of least expression'.)[53] Evidently, the lines of defence presented by 'Some Ideas about My *Octuor*' were subject to erosion by Stravinsky's 'instinctive logic'; he saw no heresy in treating the double-bass as an honorary member of a wind ensemble. Stravinsky's neoclassical campaign was to run for more than three decades, yet within a few years his new politics of instrumentation would revert to Russian conservatism. *Capriccio* (1928/9) flaunts a neo-Baroque (string) concertino recalling the Italian and Handelian concerto grosso,[54] whilst *Oedipus rex* (1926/7) and *The Fairy's Kiss* (1928) both require the services of a string-inclusive nineteenth-century orchestra. The *Symphony of Psalms* (1930), with its neoclassical concession (no violins = less vague) is a rare anomaly in a tendency to ignore his previously trumpeted set of beliefs. Perhaps Stravinsky came to agree with his esteemed teacher that 'the quality of wind instruments soon becomes wearisome'.[55] Stravinsky's musical ear, it seems, remained well attuned to tastes acquired in St Petersburg. Whatever the philosophical ideals, the practical business of finding 'the right sounds' – surely, composition's ultimate craft – was not negotiable.

Thus far, the concerns of this chapter have been manifold. Firstly, Stravinsky's neoclassicism has been re-interpreted as the outcome of a very gradual evolution rather than the result of any sudden response. His declared embrace of this new idiom around the time of *Pulcinella* (1919/20) had been prepared for over a decade by technical procedures that featured, to a greater or lesser degree, in every stylistic engagement since 'Pastorale' (1907). A second avenue of enquiry has been to examine how Stravinsky continued to relate to the teachings of Rimsky-Korsakov after re-locating to western Europe, despite pronouncements to the contrary made throughout his mature career. Specifically, it is of extraordinary pertinence to determine the extent to which Stravinsky viewed his turn towards neoclassicism as, also, a gesture of emancipation and of independence from the influence of his former composition teacher – 'extraordinary' because of the unexpected role of the piano in the process of (as the pupil phrases it) 'obtaining freedom for … his own method of expression'.[56] It seems to have taken time and considerable effort on Stravinsky's part to be free, as he saw it, of influences acquired from his teachers. Yet, was he free and did he ever really wish to be free? His adoption of a new musical aesthetic in the 1920s had become more than a question of idiom; instrumentation was also a central tenet of the neoclassical statement. This was, after all, a very Russian issue.

Stravinsky's re-engagement with the piano seems to have focussed his attention on a key aspect of his problematic relationship with Rimsky-Korsakov's teachings, which appear to have haunted him even at such a geographical and chronological distance. And the crux of this tension was colour or, more precisely, the piano's highly desirable lack of it. Stravinsky and Rimsky-Korsakov relate to this issue from opposite sides, their banners planted at the extremities of the ideological spectrum. Stravinsky's extraordinary comment regarding the *Sonate pour piano* that he wished 'to create drawings at the expense of colour'[57] may be understood as an unambiguous reference to this work's contrapuntal textures, which might also be described as achromatic in its literal sense, i.e. as colour-less. Such is the similarity of Stravinsky's utterance to Rimsky's form of words (quoted earlier) – 'One might as well say that a picture is well drawn in colours'[58] – one can only imagine that, if Stravinsky were not consciously alluding to *Principles of Orchestration*, it was because he was so thoroughly familiar with the sentiment. He was certainly, at least on a subliminal level, 'referring' to Rimsky's teaching, for such matters must have been at the core of their weekly conversations. Furthermore, implicit in Stravinsky's remark is the strong suggestion, if not the frank admission, that throughout his compositional trajectory until that moment, he had indeed been creating colour out of drawings – and joyfully so, as a fully qualified 'graduate' of the Russian School.

Stravinsky's enigmatic remark must also be viewed in the context of his desire (in October 1924) to proclaim his new artistic interests in somewhat provocative fashion: demonstrating his rejection of his entire Russian past. By defining new terms of reference via the *absence* of colour, Stravinsky was allying himself with that more intellectual approach to musical craft he associated with the 'truly Russian' qualities of Tchaikovsky. Furthermore, by using the piano to reduce (or, even, eliminate) music's very 'soul' – defined by Rimsky-Korsakov, one recalls, as comprising 'certain tone-colours … from the hour of [music's] birth' – Stravinsky had taken a significant stride towards denying his own national identity. From this point there was but a short step to the proclamation of his artistic independence in terms of a progressive, supra-national musical aesthetic: neoclassicism. Having also yielded in the past to the temptation of composing according to the gospel of folk-inspired nationalism, it is as if Stravinsky now sought artistic redemption by means of that universally respected musical virtue, counterpoint. (Such a reading is at the centre of Boris de Schloezer's accusation – cf. p. 213 – that Stravinsky's extreme contrapuntal idiom somehow represented the expurgation of previous musical sins.) And the vehicle which guaranteed him the purity of a sonorous blank sheet upon which to design his future career was the piano, whose ideal objectivity steered him far from any association with Rimsky's tables of expression. This instrument, so closely associated in Stravinsky's early career with the *Grandes sonates* of Russian romantic repertoire, would now be employed as a cembalistic tool, indispensable to the construction of spare, contrapuntal textures. The musical result – particularly in the *Sonate* and *Sérénade* – was a comparatively arid musical object. This enabled him more effectively to 'sever the umbilical c(h)ord', i.e. to disassociate himself from his former 'dilettante' compatriots and their predilection for gaudy camouflage. Rather, the piano became a metaphor for Music's pure beginnings employed by Stravinsky to coincide with the return to his own musical origins, as a pianist and – dating from a time even before his lessons with Kashperova commenced – as a lone researcher into the mysteries of counterpoint. Harry Partch's observation that in the eighteenth century 'keyboard instruments became the intellect of the new music'[59] helps one to comprehend Stravinsky's instrumental choice. As he now sought to shun every recollection of former romantic indulgences, Stravinsky's concerns were once again classical, contrapuntal and intellectual, and for all of these reasons frequently polemical.

Stravinsky's neoclassicism re-considered

The argument that portrays neoclassicism as a major force in twentieth-century music is divided along not only stylistic lines, but by a nationalist demarcation. If Dahlhaus chose to end his history of nineteenth-century music in 1907, 'the watershed year of Schönberg's transition to atonality and Richard Strauss's about-face from modernism following *Elektra*',[60] this was because he preferred to consider Schoenberg, and not Stravinsky, as 'the genuine protagonist of twentieth-century modern music'. Those historians who hear remnants of 'romanticism' or 'late romanticism' in Schoenberg's 'modernist works' would find the first manifestation of a genuine twentieth century only later, in the *Neue Klassizität* of the 1920s. Those who share this view, Dahlhaus argues, must then acknowledge as their watershed year not 1907 but 1924, 'the year of the collapse of expressionism. In other words, the limits of the "nineteenth century" as a period in music history depend, among other things, on what phenomena we see as constituting the "genuine" modern music of [the twentieth] century'. The need to define watersheds may be seen as a classic trait of the old positivist historiography. Yet Taruskin, too, is lured into readings of this nature in his 2005 *Oxford History*. His watershed occurred on a specific date, 18 October 1923, and was revealed by one work, Stravinsky's Octet – or, rather, via the impact that this work's premiere cast upon the sensibilities of one young composer who was present, Aaron Copland. That is but one view of when 'the real twentieth century' began.[61] In fact, both readings coincide with the appearance of those foundation stones of Stravinskian neoclassicism in the early twenties: the Octet, Piano Concerto, *Sonate* and Serenade in A.

However it is regarded, the (re-)emergence of (neo-)classicism in the early twentieth century is widely read as a crucial aspect of 'genuine modernism', although, according to the editors of *Canto d'Amore: Classicism in Modern Art and Music*, 'the classicism of the 1920s [might] more correctly be viewed as an "alternative" modernism [for the] changes of direction by such as Picasso and Stravinsky after the First World War were not intended to mark a return to the pre-modernist era but as a continuation of modernism by other means'.[62] Arnold Whittall has observed how the term 'neoclassical', which in the nineteenth century could refer to stylistic or formal considerations, would be tinged in the twentieth with connotations of parody and pastiche[63] – though it is debatable whether Stravinsky could be labelled a *pasticheur*.[64] One may broadly agree with Taruskin that this manifestation was anticipated by a widespread interest throughout the nineteenth century in writing 'fake old music', a trend that was popular in both France and Russia. In the Parisian context he cites the inclusion of imitation eighteenth-century music in the *opéra* (for example, in works by Jules Massenet and Ambroise Thomas), and the re-appearance of these entr'actes and instrumental interludes as concert suites. For a Russian parallel he chooses Anton Rubinstein's encyclopedic (ten-movement) 'baroque' *Suite for Piano* op. 38 (1855), whose inflated dimensions recall the *ordres* of François Couperin. Rubinstein's suite may be seen as typical of the romantic regard to the past, where quasi-modal harmony and ornamental *piquanterie* represent a temporal equivalent of the eighteenth century's position regarding the 'oriental Other'. Whether by timbral 'colour' (percussion-effects, for example) or through rhythmic and melodic inflection, Taruskin argues, the Turkish music of one age can be seen to herald the Spanish music of the next, and so on. Incidentally, it is pertinent that Rubinstein (a St Petersburg-based composer) should favour Gallic forms: for example, Passepied and Bourrée (dances native to France), and Courante, Menuet and Gigue (with their French, rather than Italian, orthography and inflection). Rooted in the same Petrine tradition – more firmly, perhaps, than he was prepared to admit – Stravinsky would also make his pianistic claims on the eighteenth century through the French model.

Nationalist cultural differences were evident not only in original artworks but also in the realm of transcription, a sub-set of arrangement, itself an important sub-genre of neoclassicism.[65] Two concert arrangements of early music by celebrated virtuosi will serve to illustrate the contrasting French and German attitudes to their eighteenth-century models. Isidor Philipp's transcriptions of Rameau in *L'Art pianistique: Collection de pièces célèbres des maîtres anciens et modernes* (1908)[66] are notable, firstly, for their total absence of pedal. Furthermore, the discreet application of expression and articulation markings favours the sonority and rhetoric of the original works (for harpsichord). By contrast, an Arietta by Pergolesi[67] in the same anthology is transformed by Sigismond Thalberg into a veritable *Albumblatt*, the thickly edited result suggesting – not least by its

heavily pedalled resonance – an unfamiliar gem of Schumann. This striking contrast is partly due to the generation gap – Philipp was born in 1863,
Thalberg died in 1871 – but it is also symptomatic of the difference between
nineteenth-century and twentieth-century attitudes.

Yet it is through José Ortega y Gasset that one may still better track the
emergence of neoclassicism in a modernist context. In his consideration
of the term 'expression' – valued, historically, as a quality indivisible from
music and its performance – Ortega lays the foundations for debate by making a useful separation between character and style. Character, he writes, 'is
distinctive of nineteenth-century art', while the eighteenth century, 'which
had so little character, was a past master of style'.[68] Accordingly, he argues, a
condition of realistic art (represented primarily by nineteenth-century evocations of nationalist scenes and old forms) is to demonstrate 'character'. The
opposite is to deform reality, to de-realize, to dehumanize – all these being
the functions, procedures and inherent properties of 'style'. Regarded as the
supreme achievement of the eighteenth century, style is 'the royal road to
art … for this road is called the "will to style"'. Jonathan Cross, while commenting on *Perséphone*, re-phrases this 'will to style' as Stravinsky's 'desire
to achieve a kind of alienation through stylisation',[69] citing Paul Valéry's
enthusiastic response to 'the divine detachment' of this work: 'The point
is, to attain purity through the will.' Stylization or style (the term preferred
by Andriessen and Schönberger) 'implies that the mannerisms are dictated
by an aesthetic attitude'.[70] Such terms contribute to our understanding of
Stravinsky's adoption of pre-romantic forms and a neoclassical ideology. He
appears to follow a 'higher calling', to present his new music within (what he
considered to be) an appropriately inexpressive and pure aesthetic. Writing
in 1925 Ortega was precocious in his grasp of Stravinsky's puzzle, particularly in his comprehension of this desire to re-create something admirable and 'pure'; and it is through the notion of purity that one may further
understand Stravinsky's desire to achieve an objective idiom.[71]

Notes of objectivity

The varied critiques of twentieth-century neoclassicism concede, despite
their differences, that a common denominator of its many readings is the
central role played by objectivity. Such an 'unseen presence' (to use Jim
Samson's term) may occupy a vital role in the revelation of underlying 'aims,
strategies and ideologies'.[72] 'Objectivity' can powerfully affect the terms of
engagement between the score and the performer, both at a practical and
psychological level. In the case of Stravinsky it has been described as 'the
overriding feature of [this composer's] modernism'[73] and may be considered

by implication, therefore, an element central to his legacy. Newspaper interviews and private conversations with Stravinsky in the decade leading up to the publication of *Chroniques de ma vie* (1935) support the argument that his new (neo)classical music was founded upon a conscious desire (cf. Ortega's 'will to style') to 'establish order and discipline in the purely sonorous scheme to which I always give precedence over elements of an emotional character'.[74] Such endorsement of objectivity and constructivism was consistently Stravinsky's tone during the 1920s. Indeed, from the very outset of his new career as a touring concert pianist he had expressed these convictions whenever presented with the opportunity. In the autumn of 1924, for example, he offered – via the medium of the newspaper interview – 'Ideas' consistent with those published 'about my *Octuor*' the previous spring. As Walsh has pointed out, some of this material was syndicated (in translation) in the American press in anticipation of Stravinsky's first visit to the USA in early 1925. In fact, these Ideas were to remain central to his message long into the future – through *Poetics* and the late *Conversations* with Craft. Fresh from completing the *Sonate* (in October 1924) Stravinsky wasted no time in communicating that there was now permanence and consistency to a growing volume of work in this new 'absolute', constructed medium:

> My latest works do not contain any external artistic components …
> 'Symphonies of Wind Instruments', the 'Octet for Wind Instruments'[,] 'The Concerto for the Piano and Winds' and the 'Sonata for the Piano' … all these from beginning to end are absolute music. It is dry, cold and clear like extra dry champagne. It does not give a sense of sweetness, it does not relax like other forms of this drink, instead it burns … The times have passed when I tried to enrich music. Today I would like to construct it.[75]

This interview (conducted in Warsaw in November 1924) goes on to affirm that, while turning his back on 'the methods of musical expression', he aims 'to produce the very essence of music'. In Prague, a week later, he cites these same works as illustrations of his 'musical searches … directed backwards towards Bach's creative works … but in a different sense to that upheld by … pedantic conservationists'.[76] By the time he had reached Berlin in December several commonalities of vocabulary had emerged, linking these initial expressions of Stravinsky's new path to what came to be considered the core issues of modernism. Indeed, Stravinsky took a prime role in defining these issues. There is even a suggestion in these interviews, despite the informality of the medium, that Stravinsky was already convinced of the historic importance of his ideas and of the moment, couching his views in appropriately Wagnerian terms: 'The road I have chosen to follow is the future of music.' Furthermore, in recommending this chosen path as the one 'that contemporary music should follow', he revealed an even loftier ambition to his crusade, adding: 'I recommend, *for the sake of saving the musical soul*, that others be more attentive to the very essence of what I am doing, and try to see what is in my works before they express regret about what is lacking.'[77] From such pronouncements Stravinsky may be said to have provoked three lines of approach and provided fertile material for Stravinsky critiques in the coming years. One will lead to deepening labyrinths of analytical method centred on his music's rhythmic complexity, its pitch organization and his redefinition of diatonicism through 'tonal-centring'. Another will herald the philosophical debate concerning Stravinsky's neoclassicism instigated by Adorno's dialectical reading. And a third path, far into the future, will propose the re-contextualizing of Stravinsky as a Russian (that he, arguably, always felt he was) having long been claimed as a paradigm of musical internationalism.

Yet there remains a hermeneutical impasse which Stravinsky research has circumnavigated – but hardly confronted. How does Stravinsky's classically embedded objectivity measure up in musical as well as ideological terms? Were there certain notes, for example, or combinations of notes or 'pitch-patterns' – in vertical or (more likely) in linear arrangement – that signified for Stravinsky or, better still, *guaranteed* him that burning, cold objectivity he told his Polish readership was like extra-dry champagne? A life-time of defensiveness – whether by dint of interview or manifesto, or hint – may not of itself amount to more than 'some ideas'. But there is sufficient consistency, across the decades and through Stravinsky's recourse to widely varied media, to suggest that this represents a 'body of opinion' deserving of its own critique. At best it is an ideology, at second best a chain of discourses – traceable through utterances, scores and sketches – that, taken together, nuance the established readings of Stravinsky's 'own' objectivity.

Why he should have been so reluctant to address this issue in print *is* a puzzle. One might argue that, after 1924, Stravinsky stated his attitudes towards objectivity via musical 'texts', i.e. through his neoclassical compositions. Another answer may lie in the proposal that Stravinsky based his neoclassical syntax on the language, literature and rhetoric of those pianistic methodologies with which he was familiar, but he just preferred not to discuss something so comparatively lacking in artistic prestige and credibility. Yet, there are similarities between the mechanistic element in his keyboard writing – particularly those fast, 'overlong' *ritornello* movements – and the patterns, the repetitiveness and the sheer endurance of piano drilling. It is hardly material worthy of the term 'quotation' such as when a composer references historical and cultural models. A better way, therefore, to determine Stravinsky's engagement with piano studies might be to consider (with Glenn Watkins) their 'appropriation as a creative stimulus'.[78]

To this end, Stravinsky's youthful musical experiences need to be re-examined, for it is at an early age that one develops affections for familiar modes of working – and they can remain useful for a lifetime. Can one confirm that Kashperova – Stravinsky's foremost piano teacher in St Petersburg – did *not* fuel Stravinsky's interest in the gritty business of technique? His correspondence from the time suggests that she may well have. And would not his first enthusiastic encounter with musical theory and the thrill of his rapid development as a pianist (guided by one of the most brilliant graduates to emerge from the St Petersburg Conservatoire) be as much a part of Stravinsky's 'native culture' as those distant 'abstract' Eurasian sources were at the root of other aspects of his output? Undoubtedly, key elements of his compositional approach (particularly around the time of his emergent neoclassical works in the early 1920s) synthesize seemingly distant past(s) and future(s). There are fundamental consistencies of ideology and compositional process between Stravinsky's earliest engagement with composition in Russia (out of improvisation), and his Swiss/Eurasian–French/neoclassical output, the latter (as suggested above) through engagement with 'modelling' according to a Gallic view of 'les maîtres anciens'. With particular reference to the neoclassical works written for the piano (or, which included the piano in a privileged role), Watkins' phrase – from another context – fittingly describes the manner in which Stravinsky manipulated his methodological models and constructed artworks from the plainest early-learning bricks: 'A personal style was thus coined not so much through the appropriation of ingredients from a particular historical or cultural model as through their fracture and purposeful re-assemblage'.[79]

Viewed from this perspective, the terms 'neoclassicism' and 'objectivity' are neither adequate nor accurate when ascribed to Stravinsky. Both terms, rather, are the by-products of a consistent interest of this composer in process; or, more precisely, in the gradual and essentially constructive processes of composition and performance, those two fundamental foci of musical activity. And it is through the workshop of tuition – both in the form of teaching received from others, and as self-learning – that Stravinsky's life-long absorption with the fracturing and re-assembling processes was grounded. Stravinsky's self-learning (via piano practice) was given an edge owing to his sudden and urgent need to transform himself into a concert pianist in merely eight months over the winter of 1923–4,[80] and owing to his need thereafter to maintain an international performing career over several years. This was, then, a crucial period for the ways in which both of these processes were pushed to the fore with parallel and urgent intensity.

Stravinsky continued composing at the piano, as he had always done, but now his piano practice would share this same workstation – upgraded, as it were, to 'dual-function capability'. On a daily basis, from September 1923 and for the next twenty years or so, the clangorous drills and the many repetitive tools of pianistic methodology would fill the airwaves of Stravinsky's erstwhile near-silent compositional study.

In the light of the above readings, one must re-consider the accepted version of the (apparently) seismic shift in Stravinsky's idiom that came with the arrival of the early neoclassical works. This relates explicitly to the *Symphonies for Wind Instruments*, but also embraces the less aurally shocking, but somehow more perplexing, *Octuor* and the solo piano works. Appearances can deceive. However much the tectonic plates on the surface shifted, the compositional processes underneath remained constant and consistent. Stravinsky's engagement with the purposeful assemblage of music's elements continued apace: the French works share the constructive concerns of the Swiss works. The two sets of piano duets already discussed present a good example of this. On the face of it, these are simple salon-pieces (with a certain didactic feel, it is true) written for the composer's children.[81] The 'didactic feel' is no illusion, however. It is caused by Stravinsky's engagement with those core issues already identified: music's elements, their manipulation, and with musical processes. However, here in the duets (and it is a startlingly clear, and rare, example), the composer reveals his hand. By displaying both the piece and the processes of its creation (including errors or hesitations) *as part of* 'the piece', the effect is of music being composed, rehearsed and played simultaneously before our very ears. Stravinsky is working close to music's point of origin: individual notes played by individual fingers. From these he constructs by a process of combination and assembly. And the learning curve – from the *Three (Very) Easy Pieces* to the *Five* (so-called) *Easy Pieces* – is a steep one. A new process-based music is becoming established.

As for a matching ideology, Stravinsky's manipulative skills would be drawn towards words rather than notes. Before publishing his 'Ideas' in 1924 (these were ostensibly about the *Octet*, although the document has more in keeping with a manifesto of general application to his music as a whole) Stravinsky first set about removing descriptive text from his scores. This cleansing process can be seen clearly in *Les Cinq Doigts* of 1920/1. In keeping with nineteenth-century salon traditions he had named the individual 'pieces' of the earlier piano duets after nationalistic character dances. However, in *Les Cinq Doigts* – a set of (genuinely) easy piano solos which, according to convention, should feature descriptive titles as a stimulus for young pupils – such expressive titles are replaced by purely technical indications.[82] 'Napolitana', 'Balalaika' and similar (in the duets) have now become Andantino and Moderato and the like: i.e. romantic and picturesque titles have been replaced by tempo or stylistic indications, i.e. by instructions. This embryonic though significant manifestation of the neoclassical, objective Idea was soon to be transferred to the public stage: the *Symphonies for Wind Instruments*, the Octet, the Piano Concerto and the *Sonate* all contain sections or entire movements giving *only* metronome indications with no words at all – but merely offering, as it were, numerical (non-verbal) instructions. This is one way that the subject can be distanced and presents a striking similarity to the manner that exercises and drills are marked in piano methods. There, too, 'expression' is not a factor but a *technique* as, for example, when agogic markings are learnt – and applied – as essentials of the process of progress. By the end of 1923, however, Stravinsky clearly felt the necessity to defend his next work and the Ideas behind it through the printed word. The Object he had assembled needed some explanation. The first six sentences of 'Some Ideas about My *Octuor*' present the following keywords: 'object', 'form' (three times), 'marble', 'stone', 'rigidity' (of form), 'cold'. It was with such tools that the composer felt best armed to defend his new essential values in the post-war artistic environment. The way forward was to 'talk up' his new ideology by means of a new and thoroughly pragmatic terminology. There was no dignified option.

But do Stravinsky's compositional concerns parallel this alternative learning universe, one (quite literally) formed from those catchwords (as Andriessen and Schönberger call them): 'order', 'discipline', 'rules', 'elements', 'principles' and 'method'? If so, then Stravinsky's statements trace a thinly veiled confirmation of one underlying preoccupation above all: process. Yet, can one really claim that Stravinsky's compositional materials were mined from piano methodologies? A recurring theme of *The Apollonian Clockwork* is that Stravinsky's oeuvre 'is most similar to a network of roads … each route has characteristics of the other routes, but no two routes could ever be exchanged. The view from the road is always the same but in a different way; always different in the same way.'[83] This commentary illuminates our questions by examining those functions (musical and aesthetical) that guided Stravinsky along his path.

Such debate must also address and contest a related issue. In commenting on the first *Pas d'action* in *Orpheus* (1947) Andriessen and Schönberger propose that Stravinsky's rhythmically monotonous music (four bars after Fig. 99) is 'continually the same … continually slightly different' and represents 'a prophetic premonition of … the music that Steve Reich and his followers would write twenty years later'. One can agree with that, but not with this: 'Random became "process" and pandiatonicism changed into arpeggiating modal chords.'[84] The very opposite is surely the case. Process it was that became random, for process was always there, always at the heart of Stravinsky's method. He could use it in a variety of ways. In the passage quoted from *Orpheus* he makes process become 'random'. I place 'random' within quotation marks because it is a *faux* randomness; there is nothing random about it. The apparently random surface is firmly grounded in discipline, order and method. Similarly, Andriessen and Schönberger's second point must be challenged. Pandiatonicism did not 'change into arpeggiating modal chords', but vice versa. Arpeggiating modal chords were always there in Stravinsky's piano drills (the ultimate minimalist trope). He re-assembled these arpeggiated waves in *Orpheus* – which were first codified at the piano and therefore relate to, if not actually 'emerge from', his pianistic arpeggios – to create his own pandiatonicism. Stravinsky can be seen, therefore, to have formulated and achieved his neoclassicism – a universal, objective result – through the synthesis of his personal, subjective experience. Both the point of departure and the point of arrival are linked by an engagement with process as an ideological current. It is one that consciously unifies the otherwise contrasting – *apparently* contrasting – idioms within Stravinsky's canon.

Poetics, process, *pal'tserazvitiye*

The attitude of the pre-professional/conservatoire student towards study, compared to just playing *anamatyor*,[85] is based upon an appreciative engagement with technical literature having accepted the need for such commitment and, quite possibly, having become stimulated by its challenges. Technical feats per se are admired within the culture of the performing academy. With sights firmly set on a professional career, the aspirant professional may even embrace these (un)musical and psychological rigours as necessary aspects of this career path. Such attitudes and traditions, current even in today's conservatoires, are embedded in the methodologies and values established in the nineteenth century. National schools emerged throughout Europe – the Russian tradition developing a reputation, under the forceful personalities of Anton and Nikolay Rubinstein, for its combination of expressive intensity and technical prowess. Long before his public emergence as a concert pianist Stravinsky had produced a catalogue of works that answered to the same Russian profile. The incomprehension with which his neoclassical 'project' was met is a reflection of this fundamental dichotomy: here was a Russian musician now apparently standing for the negation of all that is personal and forceful and expressive, i.e. of all that was personified as 'Russian' in composition and musical performance.

This thorny issue was clearly at the heart of the first English review of *Chroniques*. If one believes (with the reviewer) that, in music *performance*, 'the personal equation must be a factor',[86] then one is also likely to view the opposite, i.e. the study of piano *technique*, as neither demanding nor requiring such individual expressive input. There is, after all, no audience. While study-material may be regarded as a form of music, it is not musical; and not being in artistic form it is, therefore, not (yet) 'music'. Echoing Kofi Agawu's view that composition is rooted in the pedagogical tradition,[87] Jim Samson has written of musical education forming 'one of the earliest, and most potentially enduring, layers of influence [for any composer]'.[88] Both performer and composer can draw upon their experience in music's workshop, the aim of 'the whole exercise' being, fundamentally, technical. For the performer the benefits acquired may include expressive skills such as tone production and the cultivation of an aesthetically pleasing sonority, via 'beauty of touch'. But within the discipline of technique this represents a minor element, its study withheld until the later, advanced stages. Technical permutations include other apparent tools of expression, such as *crescendo*, *diminuendo* and a widening range of dynamic manipulation. But these of themselves do not signify expression: rather, the development of the technique of dynamic control. Similarly, such expressive devices as *sforzando* or *fortepiano* are treated as muscular/digital skills to be developed within the context of articulation and its refinement. The overriding concern of methods and their teaching, whatever the instrument, is the improvement of technique through emphasis on the physicality of sound production. Technique is acquired via a progressive set of exercises designed to extend the player's reach, develop musculature and improve flexibility. At all stages the mode of presentation is conventionally through 'drills' – short passages designed to be repeated over and over. It is a common feature of Czerny's *Daily Exercises*, for example, to demand thirty or forty repetitions of such two-bar patterns. In much the same way, professional dancers and athletes follow their routines – at the bar or in the gym – mirroring the pianist's engagement with physical endurance as an essential initiation to, and characteristic ritual of, their preparation. Such routines function on both a mental and physical level: to warm up joints and muscles, and as part of a regular, determined programme to develop physical and mental stamina. In a musical context extended drills of this nature may even aspire to an aesthetic position, the most 'musical' of these being the through-composed *étude*. Critical reception of the *étude* has consistently recognized its value over and above that of mere exercises precisely because of its inherent expressive potential – being a step on the road towards the ultimate union of technique and expressivity: the *concerto*.

The late-nineteenth-century view was summarized by Edward Dannreuther, whose entry in *Grove* (first published in 1904 yet considered valid also for the fifth edition, 1954, half a century later) points to the *study* as being 'designed in the first place as a technical exercise, but the better for having artistic value ... over and above [its] executive purpose'.[89] Examples are given, including 'Purcell's and Handel's lessons, D. Scarlatti's esercizi [*sic*], Paganini's capricci [*sic*], [and] Chopin's études'. It is a judgement upheld in *The New Grove*, wherein Howard Ferguson defines the study as 'an instrumental piece ... designed primarily to exploit and perfect a chosen facet of performing technique, but the better for having some musical interest'.[90] The finest examples of these (such as Chopin's two sets, opp. 10 and 25) assumed artistic status – first in the salon, then in the concert-hall. But their genealogy is based in pure mechanics.

Within this re-consideration of Stravinsky's neoclassicism one might profitably trace how he effectively inverted this traditional relationship: his neoclassical works, especially those for or with piano, give every indication of being composed in the mould of artistic genres but aspiring to the (objective) condition of technical exercises. Samson numbers among the myths of Chopin reception the apparent associations between the first two *études* of op. 10 and those of Cramer, Clementi and Moscheles. But there is 'another and deeper influence at work in these pieces'. Chopin, he writes, transcended his more obvious models by 'the inspiration of Bach', particularly his *moto perpetuo*, bravura figurations.[91] Stravinsky, it might be argued, also transcended his apparent debts to Bach by his adoption of the mechanics of pianistic process, thus reducing the fascination of Bach's counterpoint to a purely technical absorption in the sonorous interplay projected (to use Dannreuther's phrase) when 'the changes are rung'. Echoing Samson's regard for Chopin, one may confidently assert that Stravinsky's creative engagement with the procedures of pianistic technique raises 'the whole issue of musical influence, its different levels of operation and the emergence through it of a composer's individual voice'. In the Stravinskian context, Leschetizky's piano method (developed while he taught at the St Petersburg Conservatoire) is a key work and will be discussed at length in Chapter 3, pp. 155–70.

Under Kashperova's direction progress was rapid; and fundamental to this new impetus was a new attitude. Stravinsky put aside the frivolous anarchy of improvisation and embraced serious piano study, his correspondence suggesting that he was stimulated by its self-discipline. On 23 August 1900 he writes of his plans in a letter to his parents who were on vacation in Pechisky.[92] The dominant subject of the letter (occupying thirty-six of its thirty-nine lines) concerns Stravinsky's time-consuming and increasingly desperate efforts to obtain a vaccination against smallpox without which he will not be readmitted to the *Gymnasium*. After spending a whole day searching for a doctor who can offer this service Stravinsky eventually succeeds in making an appointment (by jumping the queue) at the Maximilianovskii Hospital. But the whole business has delayed his return to *pal'tserazvivatel'nïkh* [*zanyatii*] – namely, 'finger-development [exercises]' – and added to his considerable frustration, a flavour of which can be gleaned from his final paragraph: 'You might wonder why we didn't just get the vaccination at the *Gymnasium*. But it's a case of "Don't even mention it!" Instead of a doctor and [medical] assistant they have two complete nincompoops who would very likely have given us the smallpox jab in the cheek. [No] thank you!' Summing up, now that the holidays are over and Stravinsky has arrived back in St Petersburg he is keen to re-engage with what he terms *pal'tserazvitiye* (literally, finger-development). *Pal'tse* derives from *palets*, the Russian for finger. The latter half of this compound, *razvitiye*, may be open to several interpretations all relating to the notion of extension. Whether one translates the end result as finger-evolution, finger-development or finger-stretching it is preferable to use Stravinsky's own term *pal'tserazvitiye*.[93] This mundane expression exerts a powerful and wide-ranging influence upon this volume. I have appropriated it to define several aspects of pianistic study and it will be applied to such material whenever this is identified, in 'synthesized form', within Stravinsky's works. The characteristics of *pal'tserazvitiye* include:

1. The permutation of pitch-combinations (as in chords and arpeggios) used to strengthen fingers and hands and to develop their equanimity and independence.
2. An element of progression through, for example, gradually increased difficulty; it is a feature intrinsic to all didactic journeys.
3. A work-ethic carried, on occasion, to unreasonable lengths. This aspect will re-emerge in Stravinsky's neoclassical compositions for piano as a rhetoric of endurance – as in the *ritornello* movements of the *Sonate*, the *Sérénade en la* and the *Duo concertant*. This seamless, mechanistic flow is also a feature of the *Concert pour piano et instruments à vent* and the *Capriccio*, where the spirit of dialogue between soloist and orchestra, traditional to the genre, is denied.[94]

The term *pal'tserazvitiye* has also been adopted to refer to Stravinsky's attitude towards composition. Whatever the context, it is an attitude based on the methodologies of practical study. A fundamental example of this Petersburgian methodology is Leschetizky's formula, whereby each hand is required to play an extended sequence of arpeggios exploring, en route, numerous permutations within the span of an octave. In one version of this exercise the sequence of arpeggios passes through thirty-three variants; the middle fingers (2–3, or 2–4, or 3–4) stretch and explore the available space between the thumb and fifth finger, within the octave 'envelope'. It is notated in the form of chords and is thus named by Leschetizky's disciples *Accordgruppe*.[95] The exercise emerges from and returns to the unison before shifting up a semitone and setting off again.[96] This drill, more than any other, encapsulates permutation-exploration, process and attitude – the three aspects of *pal'tserazvitiye* that underscore much of Stravinsky's neoclassical idiom. Furthermore, it is the spirit of *pal'tserazvitiye* that is constantly evoked by Stravinsky (suggested, 'but never played') as a sub-text to his central ideologies in *Poetics*.

Such arguments put considerable emphasis on the terminology of *Poetics*, so it is essential, firstly, to address the reliability of that text, particularly in its English translation. It is now established that all of Stravinsky's major writings that bear his name – whether in the form of autobiography, lecture-series or conversations – were essentially prepared in collaboration with others: notably Walter Nouvel (*Chroniques de ma vie*),[97] Roland-Manuel (*Poétique musicale*)[98] – including an important contribution from Pierre Souvtchinsky in the chapter on Russian music – and Robert Craft (the *Conversations*). Having previously exposed the French literary hand behind Stravinsky's autobiography, Taruskin was later to support his study on Stravinsky's Russian traditions by promulgating the influence of Souvtchinsky on *Poétique* and 'the Stravinsky/Craft books – especially the first of them, *Conversations with Igor Stravinsky* (1959)'.[99] Craft has since responded by defending his collaborations as 'the only published writings attributed to Stravinsky, that are actually "by him", in the sense of fidelity to the substance of his thoughts. The language, unavoidably, is very largely mine.'[100] Inevitably, then, one must approach any argument based upon the interpretation of these texts with caution, as Joseph N. Straus has warned: 'Stravinsky certainly approved the sentiments expressed in these documents, but the words should not be taken strictly as his.'[101] Nevertheless, it would be disingenuous to suppose that Stravinsky – famously meticulous with regard to the finer points of verbal meaning and particularly sensitive to the nuances between languages – would have been satisfied with anything less than the closest control over the manner with which his opinions were to be represented. Claude Roland-Manuel's recollection of his father – at the time of his collaboration on *Poétique* – bears this out unequivocally. Returning home exhausted from his working visits to Sancellemoz, 'Roland-Manuel would smile [commenting] "He doesn't let me get away with a thing."'[102]

Regardless of who was holding the pencil, *Poétique* masks a sub-text concerning the underlying presence of *pal'tserazvitiye* in Stravinsky's neo-classicism. In his discussion of 'The Phenomenon of Music' (Chapter 2), for example, he defines 'the general significance of art' as a combination of 'the gifts of nature … and the benefits of artifice'.[103] His train of thought leads him directly to associate the former, intuitive quality 'art' with invent-iveness (and one may further claim this 'creativity' as pianistic or mental improvisation). The second, constructed quality is an acquired knowledge, an 'apprenticeship' wherein Stravinsky encounters the artifice of music: 'Art in the true sense is a way of fashioning works according to certain methods acquired either by apprenticeship or by inventiveness. And methods are the straight and predetermined channels that insure the rightness of our operation.'[104]

It is essential, of course, to be alert to the subtleties of French in the *six leçons* – which one must acknowledge to be the form of words closest to Stravinsky's wishes – and to consider whether the original sense has not been distorted in translation. In the above citation, for example, reference to Stravinsky/Roland-Manuel's terminology suggests another emphasis: 'Et les méthodes sont les voies strictes et déterminées qui assurent la recti-tude de notre opération.'[105] One may prefer to translate 'les voies' as proc-esses rather than channels, 'strictes et déterminées' as strict and worked-out rather than straight and pre-determined – this latter term suggesting to the reader something quite inappropriate, i.e. the pre-planning of the various forms and transpositions of the tone-row characteristic of serial compos-ition. Furthermore the authors' preference for 'rectitude' (over the moralis-tic term *droiture*) is a nuance that emphasizes the practical, down-to-earth sense of correctness with which Stravinsky viewed his working methods.[106] The well-spring of improvisation and the challenging discipline of technical study – both, in Stravinsky's case, 'déterminées' at the piano – were evidently central to his sense of 'la rectitude de notre opération' and were amply rep-resented in the musical experiences that defined his youth. Indeed, these processes continued to be the basis of his attitude towards musical com-position throughout his life. Stravinsky's terminology is redolent of several other references which applaud the role of the *homo faber* and value the craftsman over the artist.

Elsewhere in *Poetics* he makes unfavourable comparison between those artists who are ruled by 'individual caprice and intellectual anarchy – mon-sters of originality', he calls them – and those (like himself presumably) for whom 'the use of already employed materials and of established forms is usually forbidden'.[107] The originality of this latter category is all the more praiseworthy, apparently, for emanating from a restricted freedom. He even raises the status of the artisan to the spiritual, revealing the influence of Jacques Maritain, from whom he had acquired nostalgia for the 'mighty structure of medieval civilization'.[108] Those were 'happy ages', according to Stravinsky, when the practical artisan was valued above the aesthetic artist, when the work of art was prized for its usefulness and the quality of artifice defined its beauty:[109] 'It is not through promulgating an aesthetic, but by improving the status of man and by exalting the competent workman in the artist that a civilization communicates something of its order to works of art and speculation. The good artisan himself in those happy ages dreams of achieving the *beautiful* only through the categories of the *useful*.'[110]

There is solid value, in other words, to be gained from practical work-attitudes. There is quality to be admired in whatever results from freedoms evinced from such restrictions. Baudelaire is summoned to help justify such apparent impositions: '[P]rosodies and rhetorics ... are not arbitrarily invented tyrannies, but a collection of rules demanded by the very organization of the spiritual being ... [to aid] the flowering of originality.'[111] Here, in Stravinsky's intensely felt declaration, is clear exposition of his belief in the sanctity of inventiveness *and* apprenticeship. There is no division, in that deeper sense, between the inspirational flash and the drudge of labour. The divine spark – he seems to be telling us – glistens brighter in the bead of sweat. If practising piano technique is the key to Stravinsky's binaries of inventiveness–apprenticeship and creation–construction, then the spirit of *pal'tserazvitiye* is its triumphant metaphor.

Several of Stravinsky's pronouncements in *Poetics* suggest Leschetizky's most characteristic finger-development exercises and the way in which these drills explore finger-combinations within the narrow frame of the octave: 'The more art is controlled, limited, *worked over*, the more it is free.'[112] Stravinsky later expands on the nature of his idiosyncratic sense of freedom, defined as it is by an unusual response to repetition and constraint: 'It is into this field that I shall sink my roots, fully convinced that combinations which have at their disposal twelve sounds in each octave ... promise me riches that all the activity of human genius will never exhaust ... My freedom thus consists in my *moving about within the narrow frame* that I have assigned myself for each one of my undertakings.'[113] Every element of this message alludes to *pal'tserazvitiye*. Stravinsky exploits the twelve notes of the chromatic scale like any composer, of course. But it is the terminology of his declaration that reveals a confluence of specific features, associating his musical roots with endless 'combinations' obtained within self-imposed limitations. A serial composer might refer to such constraints – as did Schoenberg himself, when referring to composition 'with Twelve Notes' in almost identical terms. Diatonic or non-serial composers, on the other

hand, would be expected to rejoice in their relative freedom. But Stravinsky
is revelling here in the even greater freedom (the combinations that 'promise me riches') that he enjoys 'within the narrow frame'. This is, indeed, a
curious form of expression given that, as a non-serialist, he is supposedly
operating within the maximum sphere of options available. So, where are
the narrow frames? And what are the freedoms that Stravinsky claims for
himself?

As an intuitive and curious improviser Stravinsky would have embraced
pal'tserazvitiye firstly for its harmonic freedom. There is no diatonic direction to such patterns as the finger-development sequences of Leschetizky
based on the exploration of pitch combinations. Such morsels do not have
musical sense as their aim, but are vehicles merely to technical thoroughness. Except for those contrived 'modulations' up a semitone at the end of
each sequence (as the benefits of each exercise are transposed to all keys),
pal'tserazvitiye does not function diatonically at all; its concern is to conduct a survey of pitch-combinations because of the practical need to treat all
finger-positions uniformly. Allusions to the *dis-functional* or *non-functional*
properties of *pal'tserazvitiye* may also be observed in Stravinsky's acceptance of dissonance as the inevitable result: 'parallel dissonant chords …
lose their functional value, and our ear quite naturally accepts their juxtaposition'.[114] Within this context it is perfectly natural to view Stravinsky's
approach to tonality as tonal centring, or polarity. In 'The Phenomenon of
Music' he writes of 'the axis of our music … [which] recogniz[es] the existence of certain poles of attraction'. Furthermore, his description of music as
being 'nothing more than a succession of impulses that converge toward a
definite point of repose' functions too, in a general way, as a description of
pal'tserazvitiye: whether short or extended and however illusive their harmonic implications (in an effort to explore digital combinations), piano
exercises tend to arrive at a final, tonally simple cadence. (This is a consistent feature of the drills devised by Leschetizky and Philipp, for example.)
Thus Stravinsky denies diatonicism in favour of an ontological system of
harmony portrayed as the 'polar attraction of sound, of an interval, or even
of a complex of tones. The sounding tone constitutes, in a way, the essential
axis of music'.[115]

Later, Stravinsky suggests how he views the application of these fundamental concerns to the wider, constructive issues of composition: 'A system
of tonal or polar centres is given to us solely for the purpose of achieving a
certain order, that is to say more definitively, form, the form in which the
creative effort culminates'.[116] This remark illuminates Stravinsky's repeated
exaltation of form, of music's elements and its morphology. Through his
immersion in the characteristic sound-world of *pal'tserazvitiye* Stravinsky's

ear was attuned to harmonic shapes defined by subtle and shifting 'circular' relationships. The opening bars of *Symphony of Psalms*, to take an example, could then be viewed as a synthesis of *pal'tserazvitiye* resulting in a typically neoclassical, Stravinskian outcome. Similarly, on a macro-harmonic plane, the concluding movement to this same work presents a duality of tonal centres, C and E. This, too, may be read as a manifestation of the *pal'tserazvitiye*'s pandiatonicism at its most elemental and elementary, as the music shifts back and forth between two 'sounding tones'. 'In this regard', write Andriessen and Schönberger, 'one could speak of circular melodies: the[y] … whirl around two or three intervals, are not built on harmonic tension and, therefore, have no real beginning or end, but seem to be more or less haphazardly cut from a continuum'.[117] Such features characterize much of Stravinsky's neoclassical music, which (paradoxically) projects a sense of change through a constant effort to impose order upon the seeming limitlessness of an unrestrained (post-tonal) syntax.

It was not just as a young man that Stravinsky indulged in hours of daily practice. These regimented and repetitive actions were to acquire a professional dimension when he launched into that process of metamorphosis from which he would emerge as a concert pianist. This particular re-invention was to coincide with the emergence of the first public neoclassical compositions for piano – i.e. concert-works, as opposed to the duets and other domestic/didactic miniatures of previous years. Now, with renewed intensity, he would become familiar again with the aural stimuli – as well as the physical and psychological demands – of regular, disciplined piano study. In other words, he would immerse himself once more in his universe of finger-development, of *pal'tserazvitiye*. According to Craft it was a habit he kept up for the next twenty years.

Whether (as a pianist) Stravinsky worked within the restrictions of Leschetizky's drills, or whether (as a composer) he constructed a new work within self-imposed limitations, the very act of creating musical interest out of such rigid unity inevitably prioritizes the subtlest manifestation of variety. As a teaching aid – and for sound didactic reasons – a method directs the pupil to 'cover' permutations of pitch, initially in the form of scales, broken chords, arpeggios and their conventional spin-offs (major, minor, melodic, harmonic, diminished, augmented, parallel-motion, contrary-motion etc.). Within a more probing, more comprehensive, more professionally oriented context, a course of study will incorporate more specific and challenging demands. These may commonly involve aspects of dynamic control, variations in articulation and rhythm (this particularly well developed by Philipp)[118] and permutations of fingering (as recommended by Leschetizky and his epigoni of the Russian school). These more advanced exercises are

considered to be essential to the short-term development of finger independence, strength and equality, and to the long-term extension of a wider
span in each hand.

In purely musical terms, the environment generated by *pal'tserazvitiye*
may also be understood as 'a hierarchy of relationships', albeit one that
includes a far wider (more distant) range of relationships than those recognized by strictly diatonic harmony. Stravinsky appears to allude to this
unique digital/aural universe when he writes of the 'true hierarchy of phenomena, as well as the true hierarchy of relationships, [taking] on substance
and form on a plane entirely apart from that of conventional classification'.[119]
One is tempted to accept this invitation to seek out his alternative 'plane' in
unconventional classifications, for example through 'other hierarchies' of
permutations *not* governed by narrow tonal divisions, but by a broader spectrum of possibilities such as *pal'tserazvitiye* offers. Such processes abound
in Stravinsky's neoclassical scores and form an unmistakable feature of
the Stravinskian sound. Their non-expressive, pedagogical (non-musical)
origins, as are here proposed, clearly reflect and support Stravinsky's
intentions towards objectivity and may be considered as another referent
of commodity along with Russian wedding music, opera buffa, jazz and
'Bach'. More important is the consistency with which Stravinsky handles
another 'other'. Basically, he adopts the ways of his adopted homeland and
embraces 'France's venerable tradition of aesthetizing colonial expansion'.[120]
Stravinsky's kleptomania is not conditional upon his own geographical position. It is usually the opposite: he wrote his Eurasian music in Switzerland,
his American (rag) music in France, his Second Viennese (serial) music in
America. Rather, his expansion is chronological – backwards in time, then
forwards again – and by a process which enabled him constantly to evolve.
This, he claimed, was fortuitous, as 'I have the luck to have very little memory, which is what enables me to begin each new step of my life forgetting
the past.'[121] Appropriation was Stravinsky's response to the past – to those
aspects of the past that most interested him. It became his principal means
of renewal and guided the processes by which so much of his new music
was formulated. It remained a constant, whatever the idiom; and for that
reason Stravinsky italicized the labour of construction. Process was where
his art lay. In that sense, he wrote his *pal'tserazvitiye* music everywhere,
irrespective of geographical referents; for it is embedded in the (re-)cre-
ation of all his music.

It is clear, too, that Stravinsky and Roland-Manuel construct their discourse in *Poetics* from the process of searching rather than from the result.
'Searching' may also be judged a sub-text, though this impression is due,
rather, to the dislocated, almost off-hand manner with which Stravinsky

introduces it: 'Composing ... leads to a search for the centre upon which the series of sounds involved in my undertaking should converge. Thus, if a centre is given, I shall have to find a combination that converges upon it.'[122] Searching, either for the 'centre' or for the 'combination', is evidently at the core of Stravinsky's approach to the compositional process. This he defines imprecisely as a quest for 'musical topography',[123] although he does acknowledge the importance of these concerns. Composition is not creation, but the act of creation; music is not static, but fluid.

Stravinsky's response to dramatic works confirms that he was less concerned with human interest, with the development of his characters, than he was with the directions his music would take. He would remark concerning *Oedipus rex* that he 'focussed the tragedy not on Oedipus' (i.e. on the development of his personal fate), 'but on the "fatal development" – that, for me, is the meaning of the play'.[124] Neither was Stravinsky concerned with character development in *Les Noces*, *Mavra* or *Perséphone* but, here too, in their musical unfolding. Stravinsky merely views the dramatis personae as providing the means with which to develop the music. The process is centre stage, 'is the meaning of the play'. Examples of this abound. Designated by the composer himself as a 'musical fairy tale', *The Nightingale* is thus already part-ritual, which may explain the abrupt, unrealistic, dramatically weak but musically satisfactory conclusion. Gripped as the audience is by Tom Rakewell's fate, Stravinsky is making it clear that he was less interested in his rake's progress than in *The Rake's Progress*' process. That is the meaning of his music, as he chose to put it. Performance and composition, as disciplined processes of creation, are both nourished in the workshop of musical pedagogy. They contribute equally to music's meaning. Furthermore, from Stravinsky's unique perspective they are united through the medium of music's processes, of which *pal'tserazvitiye* may be regarded as the catalyst – and the piano, to cite this inveterate piano composer, is the 'fulcrum'.[125]

Later in *Poetics* he refers to the art of composition as a process of 'discovering the work', employing terminology that evokes the gradual, step-wise path of didactic methodologies: 'Step by step, link by link, it will be granted [the composer] to discover the work [culminating in a] chain of discoveries.'[126] It is this chain that provokes the thrill of composition: 'The very act of putting my work on paper, of, as we say, kneading the dough, is for me inseparable from the pleasure of creation.'[127] In this self-portrait 'from the cookhouse' one may better comprehend the naturalness with which Stravinsky assumed the identity of a craftsman and how, from his work-bench in music's atelier, he could critique the term 'artist' as 'pretentious ... and entirely incompatible with the role of the *homo faber*'.[128] He wishes to convince us that the artisan is one whose trade is 'closely bound up with the idea of the arranging of materials'.[129] Stravinsky thus gives supreme value to the simple processes of making. Neither are the materials of creation, for an artisan such as he, the stuff of 'a beautiful landscape … [nor] rare and precious objects'. Rather they are to be found 'in the commonest and humblest thing … always within his reach … familiar things, things that are everywhere attract his attention … if a finger slips he will notice it'.[130]

The qualities of *pal'tserazvitiye* are convincingly evoked in Stravinsky's remarks. The attributes of the craftsman share many similarities with those required of piano students, too, as they learn their craft: endurance, discipline, practice, work ethic, patience and endless repetition. These are all essential elements of the process of progress. The true creator, Stravinsky writes, 'seeks a satisfaction that he fully knows he will not find without first *striving* for it … In order to understand one must *exert* oneself … We are not going around in a vicious circle; we are rising spirally, providing that we have made an initial effort, have even just gone through *a routine exercise*.'[131] Stravinsky's insistence here on the positive effects of a vicious circle is surprising. His assertion that this usually pointless manoeuvre could possibly lead one to 'rise spirally' (heavenwards, perhaps, like Elijah in his chariot) would suggest that he is alluding here to those contexts of musical endurance where, for others, such excessive repetition is dispiriting and unmusical. However, Stravinsky was unusual for the creative impetus he derived from self-reflective practices such as these. His reference to 'routine exercise' surely supports this reading. *Ardua ad astra* indeed.

Stravinsky valued the intimate workshop of the piano, particularly its impersonal, technical discipline, for the same reasons that he was attracted to 'rite, ritual, myth and formal theatres of all kinds'.[132] Stravinsky's dispassionate theatres – 'where the collective was emphasised over the individual, where objective representation was preferred over subjective expression'[133] – are to be found in all genres of his neoclassical canon. Similarly, there is no room for individuality when studying the mechanics of piano playing. The massed ranks of beginner-pianists tend to be treated as one-and-the-same until their artistic aspirations can be served by an adequate technique. They need to complete their tariff, their rite of passage, and often require a drill sergeant to keep them at it. Leschetizky, Essipova and Long, for example, employed assistants for this very purpose: to drive their pupils through these arduous, but essential, preliminary stages.

When *Chroniques de ma vie* first appeared in English translation in 1936 the reviewer for *Music & Letters* identified Stravinsky's ambivalent relationship with his past, noting that this 'extremely vital, pertinacious man [is]

aware not only of the past as a dead weight on the forward-looking creator, but of its importance as the depository of doctrine'.[134] For the artisan
in Stravinsky these 'depositories' offered him a wealth of constructive and
liberating processes; though, contrary to critical reception, these doctrines
from the past would *also* fuel the composer's forward-looking aspirations.[135]
Ramifications in the post-modern era – while not uniquely attributable to
Stravinsky – suggest nevertheless that it was this melt-down of personaliza-
tion that Frederic Jameson would refer to in his reading of John Adams as
'the end … of style'.[136] Indeed, Stravinsky's synthesis of *pal'tserazvitiye* surely
resonates throughout the minimalist works of recent years, rejoicing in the
aural relationships that are struck up 'from within' in seemingly endless
permutations.

The 'pure' character of counterpoint

The *Sonate pour piano* was performed by Jean Wiener on 12 November
1924, in a recital that also featured Bach's *Goldberg Variations*.[137] It is indicative of the contemporary reception of Stravinsky's new-classical pieces
that this programming decision should have been taken. After all, for the
past century composers had indulged in evocations of 'Bach', particularly
as a manifestation of compositional good practice. This had commonly
taken the form of contrapuntal writing in the tradition of Bach's instrumental canon, especial reverence being directed towards 'The 48' (the fugues,
not the preludes). There are, of course, many examples of imposing choral
fugues in classical and romantic repertoire, a common feature of such *hom-
mages* being their inclusion in the final section of a musical work, such as
in Beethoven's Ninth Symphony. In this context, the fugue could provide an
appropriately climactic gesture, effective at injecting and augmenting that
sense of intellectual achievement from which both composer and performer
could gain. Such had been the acceptance of contrapuntal writing that, even
in a romantic age, the objectivity of technique – with its associated distan-
cing – could also be claimed, and vaunted, when occasion demanded. Put
crassly, counterpoint contributed to the image of the 'complete musician'.
In slow tempi fugal writing may convey an ambience of religious thrall,
whereas rapid fugues might project a sense of compositional flair, of daring. Both aspects lend, in their own manner, emotional and philosophical
weight to the result. Furthermore, representation of 'Bach' by means of
fugal and canonic devices has consistently reinforced an idealized, heuristic representation of counterpoint akin to scaling the Olympian heights of
compositional technique. (Given Stravinsky's intense spiritual pilgrimage
in the 1920s one might more appropriately re-locate these heights to Mount

Athos for, despite the efforts of Jacques Maritain, Stravinsky returned to the bosom of Eastern Orthodoxy.) One might speculate as to the manner that this spiritual dilemma contributed to his sense of rightness – righteousness, even – in returning so blatantly to contrapuntal forms in his early neoclassical output. For many reasons, Stravinsky would have welcomed his place alongside Bach on the concert programme, of which Wiener's recital is but an early example.

Performances of Bach's music, particularly for keyboard, had become increasingly in vogue in the post-war years, a tendency that reflected the theories and compositions (particularly the transcriptions) of Ferruccio Busoni. However, Busoni's journey started much earlier and from a philosophical/literary provenance quite alien to the *esprit nouveau* of the Parisian scene. Busoni rooted his aesthetics in the Germanic philosophical tradition of Nietzsche and Schopenhauer. He founded his concept of *Einheit* – crediting the universal source of all music to an eternal harmony – in Goethe, from whom he borrowed the three criteria that formed the basis of his declared *junge Klassizität* ['young classicism']. Besides *Einheit* itself, Busoni elevated the renunciation of subjectivity in his music and its titles – a tactic of objectivization already observed in Stravinsky's elimination of descriptive titles by 1922 and *Les Cinq Doigts*. Busoni had also named melody as a fundamental element of *junge Klassizität*, although by employing this term he intended to re-invest music with a historical balance between vertical (i.e. harmonic) progressions and the horizontal (i.e. counterpoint). As he explained: 'With "young classicism" I further include the definite departure from what is thematic and the apprehension again of melody – not in the sense of a pleasing motive in a pleasing instrumentation but as the ruler of all voices, all impulses, as the bearer of the idea and the begetter of harmony, in short: the most highly developed (not the most complicated) polyphony.'[138] Busoni was less moved by post-war cynicism as by a historical (and very German) sense that his 'new classic art' would prove enduring and represent 'the definite creation that is to come' – a curious parallel to Schoenberg's own dream that, by dodecaphonic means, he too held the key for the next hundred years. Yet, momentarily, Stravinsky crossed paths with Busoni (at least with his polyphony) at a 1923 performance of the *Sechs Stücke zur Pflege des polyphonischen Spiels*. In correspondence with Ansermet, Stravinsky expressed admiration for the first piece of this set,[139] whose arpeggio-figurations may (or may not) find a parallel in the third movement of the *Sonate*. Messing suggests that 'the aesthetic premises that underlay the methods of both composers [reveal] contemporary and even sympathetic developments'.[140] Yet, however much the methods of one composer reflected those of the other, their aesthetics would remain divided by a wide cultural abyss. Stravinsky's engagement with Bach would be more pragmatic. Besides his aura of religiosity (an aspect that would have left Busoni unmoved) and his reputation as the supreme master of contrapuntal forms, Bach signified even more to Stravinsky for the way his keyboard works embrace both art and pedagogy. His inventions and fugues are useful; they serve a purpose *and* they are good music. Above all, they transmit a sense of control. Andriessen and Schönberger comment that 'the thing that Bach recognised in Vivaldi is the same thing that Stravinsky recognised in Bach – himself'.[141] Alternatively, Stravinsky created 'Bach' – as Herzen accused Turgenev of creating Rudin – 'in biblical fashion, after his own image and likeness … He is [Bach] the Second, plus a lot of philosophical jargon!'[142] At least, Stravinsky may have aspired to Bach's status of composer and holy craftsman in the perceived objectivity of his instrumental works. Extended passages for the soloist in the Piano Concerto suggest that 'Bach' is well represented via Stravinsky's meandering three-part counterpoint: the flowing lines in the first movement, especially those managed in two voices by the right hand, are particularly reminiscent of the keyboard writing in the first of the 'Three-Part Inventions': Sinfonia no. 1 in C major BWV 787 (1723). Such an idiom, Bach informs us on his title page, was fully intended to teach 'lovers of the clavier to play cleanly in two [and three] voices'. Also, as an additional goal, this music would enable eager learners to acquire 'a strong foretaste of composition'. This confirmation of Bach's engagement with keyboard tuition (within the wider context of musical education) is pertinent to Stravinsky's own methodological leanings, for both composers evidently revelled in the clavier's specific challenges. Indeed, both wrote didactic music for their children. Like Bach, Stravinsky was stimulated by the dual identity, dual function of keyboard music as art and as pedagogy.

His *cri de coeur* in *Poetics*, 'We must take up cudgels … in order to defend music and its principles', carries with it a proud personal endorsement, 'just as I defend them in a different way in my compositions'.[143] And Stravinsky gives a clear indication of where to find this music and these principles: in fugal writing. 'Let us take the best example: the fugue, a pure form in which the music means nothing outside itself. Doesn't the fugue imply the composer's submission to the rules? And is it not within those strictures that he finds the full flowering of his freedom as a creator?'[144] While formal musical education in the West has long based itself on the rudiments of harmony and counterpoint, Russia's belated slant on this tradition was the obsessive relationship to the fugue, cultivated (as has already been noted) by certain nineteenth-century composers, particularly Rimsky-Korsakov and Lyadov, who rank amongst Stravinsky's most profound influences. In their view, fugue was the ultimate role model, providing the composer (every composer) with a paradigm that was to be reflected much later in Stravinsky's admiration for musical laws and in his grateful acceptance of all sorts of practical and formal strictures. Yet the musical work cannot emerge from the rule book alone. For Stravinsky, the fugue also functions as the tap which regulates his creative flow. In addition (and crucially) it is a pure form: i.e. by signifying 'nothing outside itself' fugue is a symbol of emotional neutrality. It is precisely through his own invention-like pianism that Stravinsky reciprocated Bach's didactic spirit.[145]

With regard to counterpoint, Stravinsky's earliest terms of reference date from his first attempts at composition, for he became aware of counterpoint at the very moment of his discovery of musical theory. Stravinsky obtained his own 'manual' in 1900, one recalls, before attending his first theory lesson with Akimenko (in November 1901). This initiative enabled Stravinsky to claim imitative counterpoint *as his own* and as a starting point from which he would build all manner of musical structures. Long into the future he would re-claim counterpoint in his reading of models – starting with Lyadov, Rimsky-Korsakov and Tchaikovsky, and ending with Schoenberg, Krenek and Webern. He would come to subsume dodecaphonic counterpoint in the serial works having, it might be argued, first 'misread' this many years earlier via *Pierrot lunaire*. Thus, as Bloom would have it, 'the strong poet attains a heightened individuality through a radical re-vision of tradition'.[146]

Stravinsky's autobiographical account of his youth supports this reading. It also gives an indication of the extent to which he was regularly to call upon counterpoint to ignite the creative spark. He evidently identified and took pleasure in the processes of musical construction when this is based upon the laws of counterpoint. Therein can be viewed another dormant seed of Stravinsky's mature neoclassicism. The clear alienation of the subject, identified with much music of the modernist project, was thus an intrinsic element of Stravinsky's 'anxieties', and dates from his own musical beginnings. Stravinsky reveals, via his reminiscences, a certain contradiction between the freedoms of empiricism and a dependence on formulae much as Rimsky-Korsakov had experienced mid-career, decades before. Nevertheless, Stravinsky was able 'to extract from [this whole experience] the concepts of modelling and systematic, methodical work combined with a readiness to experiment and accept unexpected outcomes'. However, Walsh's claim that 'the formulae … would in due course be abandoned, or drastically re-interpreted' must be re-examined.[147] Sketches held at the archive in Basel illustrate how Stravinsky incorporated *pal'tserazvitiye* material into his compositional experiments to the extent, even, of using this as the very foundation of ambitious musical architecture. The outcome, viewed across the neoclassical canon, has been criticized for being un-pianistic.[148] Yet this technical 'shortcoming' derives in large part from Stravinsky's desire to re-visit characteristics of eighteenth-century keyboard counterpoint. Prominent amongst these are finger independence, equality between the hands, textural transparency (without the use of the sustaining pedal) and a sense of intellectual rigour. This latter is fundamental to reading Stravinsky's brand of objectivity, deriving as it does from his single-minded defence of music's principles. These, as he was early to recognize, are best found within the emotional neutrality of counterpoint; and neutrality is a (negative) quality inherent to the piano above all musical instruments.

There are, of course, degrees of neutrality within the domain of counterpoint; there is no 'one neutrality'. Neither was Bach's the only, or even predominant, manifestation of counterpoint in Stravinsky's field of vision; Beethoven's was another. Adam Ockleford's study of the third-movement fugue in Beethoven's op. 110 sets out to consider 'its intended expressive import'.[149] His conclusions cast light on the oft-suggested Beethovenian aspect to Stravinsky's piano fugues first proposed by Lourié with regard to the *Sonate*.[150] Ockleford proposes that there is a correlation between the level of emotional neutrality and the degree of contrapuntal complexity – whether, for example, the fugue subject is stated in its original form or inverted. If inverted, the degree of 'expressive neutrality' in the fugue subject is perceptibly greater. The initial statement of Beethoven's fugue (which appears early in the third movement) is characterized by an 'extra-operative factor' described by Ockleford as a 'connotation of vocal fugues by J. S. Bach'. Its 'aesthetic response/narrative effect' is credited with 'serenity ... imbued with ... assurance and spirituality'. However, the *inversion* of the subject has the effect of *neutralizing* the degree of expressivity perceived in its original statement.[151] Thus, the extra-operative factor of the inversion is assessed by Ockleford as 'not necessarily a connotation of a *vocal* fugue', i.e. its connotation is more instrumental. Furthermore, the aesthetic response/narrative effect of the inversion reveals the 'domination of structure over content' while articulating an 'effect of expressive neutrality'.[152]

Ockleford's study of Beethoven points up issues of wider relevance to Stravinsky's neoclassicism, particularly concerning the relationship between fugue (or counterpoint) and objectivity. The 'domination of structure' – Stravinsky's term for this is 'form' – may indeed contribute to the 'neutralizing of expression'. Extending his argument Ockleford proposes, even, that the degree of emotional neutrality of a musical passage is proportional to the extent with which the composer gives priority to structure over content. Here, already, are valid reasons why Stravinsky embraced a contrapuntal idiom: it not only provided him with inherently neutral material with which to construct his musical objects, it also provided him with the means with which to distance his 'subject'. More effectively still, Stravinsky's engagement with counterpoint and fugal devices neutralized the expressive functions of composer *and* performer, transforming them both into artisans, craftsmen, skilful technicians. This union is perhaps most perfectly realized in the final movements to the *Sonate* and the *Concerto for Two Solo Pianos*, whose fugue subjects are, respectively, augmented and inverted.

'Art is by its essence constructive', Stravinsky declared in *Poetics* with the unwritten but clear understanding that it was thus, also, that a composer revealed himself as a true craftsman and his works were justified.[153] It became Stravinsky's yardstick by which he measured other composers. For example, the music of Benjamin Britten disappointed him, and no work more so than the *War Requiem* (1960/1), for displaying 'an absence of real counterpoint'.[154] Conversely Elliott Carter's linear complexity, particularly in the Double Concerto for Harpsichord and Piano (1961), led him to echo Schumann's hype over Brahms: 'There, the word is out. A masterpiece by an American composer.'[155] Such was his life-long embodiment of contrapuntal writing and thought that, four decades after Wiener's *Sonate pour piano/Goldberg Variations* recital, Stravinsky's powers of judgement with regard to other composers were still defined by his perception of their ability, or inability, to write the one thing that mattered to him. By counterpoint's emotionally frugal, yet technically demanding, terms of reference did he recognize the stamp of a good artisan.

It is clear from Stravinsky's varied utterances that his pursuit of 'objectivity' was sustained by a belief in those processes which, of necessity, act behind and within composition and performance. His compositions (particularly the neoclassical works) may therefore be understood, also, as portraits of the process of their musical construction, as music about music – indeed, as musical processes about musical processes. Even the phrase 'the music itself' may be more profitably re-phrased, in this same vein, as 'the musical process itself'. In the spirit of such re-labelling, these re-considerations of Stravinsky's neoclassicism aim to nuance those receptions with which it has been viewed to date. Yet Stravinsky's attraction to the piano as a source of intriguing musical figurations, inspired by the fingers, is not limited to such passing or superficial engagement as this would suggest. Stravinsky made clear his preference for the continuous, fluid aspects of life and work – for the act of composing over the finished result, for thinking over understanding ('to understand is to bring to an end').[156] What engaged Stravinsky's interest, evidently, was the process by which his choices were made, and he observed this acutely in the act(s) of composing and rehearsal. Both of these labours are grounded in processes of trial and error, resulting in patterns of varied repetition. Indeed, certain works – *Les Cinq Doigts* and *Piano-Rag-Music*, for example – appear to have been conceived as portrayals of these same repetitive and hesitant, self-correcting steps that characterize the evolutionary processes of musical development. This was a dialectic that appealed to Stravinsky's ear for its balance between continuity and finality – between construction, de(con)struction, and re-construction.

Inherently inexpressive too is the exhaustive discourse of piano study, as proclaimed by its literature and traditions. There is much to suggest that Stravinsky built fundamental aspects of his neoclassicism upon his practical knowledge of two methodologies in particular, those of Leschetizky (1902–3) and Philipp (1908).[157] His familiarity with these volumes contributed to the formulation of his aesthetic of objectivity by asserting a pragmatic, intellectualized methodology essential to music's performance in terms of 'execution'. Upon their common ground he could effectively justify a single neoclassical currency to encompass composition *and* performance. He expressed this philosophy in terms of defending music's principles 'just as I defend them in a different way in my compositions'.[158] Such is the pedagogical undertone to his actions – in print or music – the instant we sense his defensiveness we read this signal as a neoclassical utterance. Yet, how consistent was Stravinsky himself when it came to his own performances? His recordings from the 1920s point to intriguing inconsistencies: however spartan the published scores and however 'inexpressive' the composer's declared aims, Stravinsky the pianist was not averse to lending his own performances a recognizably romantic tone-quality, incorporating gestures that clearly derive from the nineteenth-century Russian piano tradition.[159] In his published texts and musical scores Stravinsky was more dependable in conveying the *Octuor*'s message about the musical object. Even in the ghost-written *Poetics* 'the composer himself' reveals his subtler aims on this subject, and it is through the re-interpretation of these strategies that a fresh opportunity can be seized to re-evaluate Stravinsky's ideologies. To this end, the discussions which ensue (in Chapter 3) seek to position Stravinsky's piano centre stage within his neoclassically resonating works.

A reluctant disciple

One further aspect of Stravinsky's neoclassicism merits re-consideration in this context. This concerns the complex relationship with his teacher of instrumentation; for Stravinsky's stylistic swerve in the 1920s and the even more astonishing embrace of serialism in the 1950s find their parallel in Rimsky-Korsakov's own creative meanderings. Indeed, there are several other 'symmetries' of relevance. Firstly, Rimsky's earliest musical tastes were formulated (as were Stravinsky's) under the influence of a piano teacher of forceful personality who combined a profound respect for Bach with a passion for Russian opera. (So too was the experience of Rimsky's teacher Balakirev, whose early mentor, the pianist Karl Eisrich, introduced him to Glinka's songs and operas.)[160] At the age of fifteen Rimsky-Korsakov began to study the piano with Théodore Canille,[161] from whom he learned 'that *Ruslan and Lyudmila* really was the best opera in the world [and] that Glinka was a supreme genius! Until then I had felt it intuitively; now I heard it from a real musician! He acquainted me with Glinka's *Prince Kholmsky*,[162] *A Night in Madrid*[163] some of Bach's fugues, Beethoven's Quartet in E-flat major (op. 127), Schumann's compositions, and many other things.'[164] Significantly for Rimsky-Korsakov (with potential repercussions for Stravinsky) it was evidently not incompatible under Canille's mantel to relish a patriotic and subjective fervour for Glinka whilst acquiring a working knowledge of Bach's more objective repertoire for keyboard.

During the 1870s Rimsky developed a fierce interest in the eighteenth century, promoting concert performances of Handel and Bach, and imposing the intellectual demands of counterpoint exercises upon his pupils,[165] as well as immersing himself in the study of fugue as a compositional tool for his own use. Initially this bore fruit in some piano solos, then in works for a variety of unusual 'low art' ensembles including male-voice choir, female-voice choir and wind quintet (with piano). Rimsky also incorporated fugal writing into standard, more culturally elevated genres. The Allegretto scherzando from his Sextet for Strings (1876), for example, is a six-part fugue culminating in a double-fugue with imitation at the tenth.[166] As a dedicated teacher he could not fail to pass on his enthusiasm to his pupils. During the summer of 1878 Rimsky-Korsakov combined with Lyadov to compose a fugue every day over two months – a feat which apparently drew praise from Tchaikovsky. (Anecdotes surrounding this extraordinary venture may well have contributed to Stravinsky forming such a positive impression of Lyadov.)[167] However, Rimsky's technical ingenuities did not meet with universal approval. Balakirev accused him of putting the Russian composer 'in the kitchen' while reporting that 'the Roman' (a literal translation of *Rimskiyi*) had not been 'sitting with folded hands; he has written sixty-one fugues (!!!) and a dozen or so canons. I won't comment. *De Mortuis...*'.[168] Borodin declared that 'Korskinka is fussing about ... writing all sorts of counterpoints, learning and teaching all sorts of musical tricks'.[169] A week later he claims to have seen 'thirty-six fugues and sixteen canons'. After his death, Rimsky's tough stance met with a degree of approbation. Writing in 1916, Montagu-Nathan expresses admiration for his determination, through self-learning, to acquire an unusually elevated degree of academic competence: Rimsky-Korsakov

> never tired of referring to the technical deficiencies of [Russia's nationalist] advocates ... [In response, he] addressed himself to an arduous course of technical study, from which he eventually emerged with so great a mastery as to arouse the envy of the most experienced and respected composer of his day, Tchaikovsky. Henceforth Nationalism was to be free of the stigma of being advocated by dilettanti – its future was assured. The naval officer had become a musician at whose technical attainments none could cavil.[170]

It is difficult to assess the impact that these goings-on might have had on the young Stravinsky – even in the form of reminiscence, for this took place long before he came to receive tuition from Rimsky-Korsakov. Taruskin argues that Rimsky's academicism derives from the fact that he was himself 'innocent of academic training. He therefore embarked upon a heroic program of belated self-education that estranged him from his former circle and left him in command of a superlative technique he spent the rest of his life imparting to others, beginning with Aleksandr Glazunov and Anatoly Lyadov and ending with Igor Stravinsky.'[171] Stravinsky's super-valuation of counterpoint was, therefore, a very Rimskian sentiment.

Stravinsky's pianistic and instrumental works of the 1920s led, via *Apollo*, to a fully staged and sung enactment of his mature neoclassicism in *Oedipus rex* (1927). Rimsky-Korsakov's equivalent search for historical distance in epic and/or classical myth finds its first expression in *Servilia* (1900–1), a 'melodrama of ancient Rome, complete with senators, centurions and persecuted Christians'.[172] Stravinsky's incongruous setting of his Greek tragedy *in Latin* finds its precedent in Rimsky's own generic 'classicism' and lack of authenticity: *Servilia* reveals a similarly broad-brush approach to the Ancient World for, as the composer explains: 'the ensemble of the banqueting Romans ... [was] rigorously sustained by me *in Greek modes*'.[173] He proceeds to describe the vocal quintet at the end of Act III in terms that, again, are intended to display his erudition:[174] '[Its] beginning, enunciated in canonic form, [is] not inferior to similar forms of *The Tsar's Bride* in its sonorousness and its delicacy of part-writing.'[175] As an intensification of Rimsky's (neo)classical ideals via the dramatic exploration of early civilizations, *Servilia* led to further works that explore this overtly non-Russian, non-nationalist topic, as his interest extended from Rome to Ancient Greece. In 1901 Rimsky-Korsakov began composition of *Nausicaa*, which opens with a prelude for female voices and orchestra. That same year he

completed *Iz Gomera* (*From Homer*) to a text extracted from the *Odyssey* –
as a 'prelude-cantata' for female soloists (soprano, mezzo-soprano and
contralto), female chorus and orchestra. A definitively non-Russian and
internationalist attitude can be identified in Rimsky's 'neoclassical' canon,
though Stravinskian literature has so far directed but a faint torchlight on
this intriguing subject. Stravinsky's 'simultaneous opposite' to Rimsky's
consistent evocation of Antiquity via female soloists and a female chorus is
to follow the conventions of Greek theatre more authentically – i.e. by dark-
ening the sonority of *Oedipus rex* via the virtual exclusion of female voices:
Stravinsky's opera-oratorio is scored for a *male* speaker, a *male* cast (with
the exception of Jocasta) and a chorus of tenors and basses.

Stravinsky's vigorous dismissal of his Petersburgian heritage – in
Chroniques de ma vie and via his later *Conversations* – belies, surely, the
profound admiration he had nurtured *at the time* for 'that illustrious composer'.[176] As the young composer of twenty-five wrote to his teacher in
1907, 'Mentally, I am making a low bow to you, dear Nikolay Andreyevich,
twice'.[177] Dostoyevsky puts the same phrase into the mouth of Svidrigailov
in *Crime and Punishment*, so helping non-Russians to understand the significance of bowing as a bone fide gesture of enormous respect: 'And before
I forget [he instructs Sonya] please tell Mr Razumikhin that I bow to him.
Put it in just those words: say, "Arkady Ivanovich Svidrigailov bows to you."
Be sure to get it right'.[178] Further evidence of Stravinsky's erstwhile opinion
of Rimsky-Korsakov is revealed in this same letter, in which the (mature)
student's indebtedness is conveyed with touching intensity, that 'believe me,
I will never find those words of sincerest gratitude that might express it to
a sufficient degree'.[179]

The manifold and varied range of experiences and attitudes that were
shared by Rimsky-Korsakov and Stravinsky is too close, too pervasive to
be merely coincidental, as this accumulation of these commonalities would
suggest (in no particular order): (1) their shared claim upon 'restraint' as
being indispensable to artistic freedom; (2) their harsh dismissal of former
colleagues and friends – whether Kuchkist or Belyayevets – under the
accusation of amateurism and dilettantism; (3) their debt to former piano
teachers; (4) their entry ticket to a life of music via an early attraction to
A Life for the Tsar (and the *Spanish Overtures*), leading to (5) a life-long
adoration of both Glinka and Tchaikovsky; (6) their early acquaintance of
Bach's (keyboard) fugues, leading to (7) a life-long reverence towards, and
engagement with, counterpoint (used, both, as a compositional tool and as
a benchmark against which other composers are measured); (8) their 'habit
of self-contradiction', *pace* Walsh; (9) their 'desire to modify previous expressions of gratitude', *pace* Taruskin; (10) their shared view of autobiography as

'chronicles'; (11) their artistic and personal 'crisis', mid-life (in their forties); (12) their public dismissal of, and private dependence upon, improvisation; (13) their shared ridicule by fellow composers or (worse) by *mauvais bergers* (as Stravinsky called them, i.e. otherwise loyal biographers) for their pursuit of contrapuntal procedures;[180] (14) their extension beyond strictly 'neoclassical' horizons to embrace the ancient classical civilizations of Rome and Greece; (15) their habit of deploying more than one pair of spectacles at once (for strictly practical reasons), regardless of contemporary dictates of fashion or appearance;[181] (16) their shared view of the agency of 'making', by which the craft of instrumentation is a fundamental element of the creative process (it was a Rimskian model that Stravinsky was to deny only briefly) – this primary compositional consanguinity encapsulates the extraordinary bond between these two composers; and (17) their proud sense of Russianness – i.e. by their lives and through their compositions they believed themselves to be *true* Russians at heart; indeed, more truly Russian than other apparently Russian composers of apparently 'Russian' works. In the end, such close 'genetic matching' via (to borrow from Frank Kermode) 'the cumulative impact of number'[182] – across such a swathe of examples (creative, aesthetic, educational, behavioural) – surely vindicates Myaskovsky's graphic, somewhat visceral observation (in 1912) that 'Stravinsky's exceptional, buoyant talent is flesh of [Rimsky-Korsakov's] own flesh, blood of his own blood.'[183]

These 'symmetries' prompt questions beyond the sphere of ideas, in 'the music itself'. Kenneth Gloag has expanded upon the view that 'the innovative radical modernism of [*The Rite*] has to be seen to emerge from a background that includes Stravinsky's Russian inheritance, which sustained its own problematic relationship with convention and tradition'.[184] Central to Stravinsky's 'problem', I maintain, is his suppressed yet outstanding debt to his Rimskian ancestry. Central to *our* problem is the realization of the extent to which Stravinsky was successful in concealing (from us) how profoundly Rimskian was his own set of Russian traditions of neoclassicism. For example, Stravinsky's claim upon contrapuntal procedures – particularly in his instrumental, pianistic works – is an 'attitude' entirely consistent with Rimsky-Korsakov's disapproval of 'raw emotionality and anything improvisational'.[185] In this light, Stravinsky's rejection of the extempore – his *brozheniye slukha* ('fermentation of the ear'), as Smirnov calls it[186] – in favour of a more intellectual approach to creativity is a narrative which calls for re-telling from the perspective of Rimsky-Korsakov's own 'return to Bach' in the 1870s. (Indeed, Stravinsky's submission to 'Apollo's demands' should be re-examined for signs of a previously unsuspected dialogue with his Rimskian past.) Half a century later Stravinsky was to stir the embers of this same infatuation. By then, however, his identity as a phenomenon without a history (*pace* Walsh)[187] would render the admission of such a 'debt' quite impossible. Nevertheless, it is time to revise our view of Rimsky-Korsakov as (merely) that 'aristocrat of the kingdom of sound' and of Stravinsky as his embittered 'former' disciple. Furthermore, those Russian traditions perceived as having nourished music's modernism must also be re-considered to accommodate Rimsky-Korsakov's neglected impact upon Stravinsky's neoclassical restoration (*pace* Adorno) and even, though to a lesser degree, his serial progress.

Thus can Stravinsky's re-invention as a neoclassicist be interpreted, also, as 'no more' than the natural fulfilment of a historically embedded trait of Russian musical thought exemplified most notably by Rimsky-Korsakov. Stravinsky's neoclassicism may appear to purge his musical idiom of Russian nationalist colour – and he certainly made great efforts to portray his new classicism in that light – yet his internationalism can be understood, equally, as a thoroughly Petersburgian vision; for the projection of Russia into Europe 'has always been the *raison d'être* of St Petersburg'.[188] Indeed, one might argue that the very process of being educated musically within that specifically Rimskian context entailed an adoption of neoclassical values. In Stravinsky's particular case, therefore, Becoming a neoclassicist was a natural sequel to Becoming a Russian musician. Re-appraisal of Stravinsky's roots suggests that it was during the years of his musical apprenticeship in St Petersburg that he initially formulated those pianistic, methodological attitudes which were to impact so decisively upon his neoclassical works. Therefore, it is to the manner of these works' construction that our scrutiny now turns. In the following pages attention will focus on certain key manuscripts. Therein lie further signs of Stravinsky's renewed or, indeed, continuing interest in *pal'tserazvitiye* and of his pragmatic engagement with its creative possibilities. We proceed to address these concerns via a moment discovered in the archive material of the *Sonate pour piano*.

3   Stravinsky's piano workshop

Fingering as compositional process

Sonate pour piano
The Five Fingers
Concerto for Piano and Wind Instruments
Symphony of Psalms

The insertion of fingerings into a musical score is traditionally the concern of the publisher.[1] Composers, i.e. those with a creative role in society, on the other hand (or so Stefan George would have us believe), breathe air *von anderen Planeten*,[2] which would explain why Robert Craft should declare in a tone of cautious surprise that 'to compare the sketch and published score of the [*Sonate*] is to discover that piano fingerings were a part of the composing process, though Stravinsky might remove them later as a builder does his scaffolding'.[3] Indeed, fingerings abound in Stravinsky's sketches, fair copy and personally corrected proofs of this work.[4] Yet, it is wise to issue a caveat. There is no reason why the presence of fingerings in the sketches of a piano work should prove, necessarily, that this is 'part of [Stravinsky's] composing *process*'. He may have jotted down some fingering for an awkward passage in order to prevent his concentration from being broken by digital ineptness or hesitation. My task, therefore, has been to examine this 'scaffolding' and ascertain if it is, in fact, part of the edifice – much as the plumbing and electrical conduits exposed on the walls and ceilings of the Centre Georges Pompidou (in Place Igor Strawinsky) form an intrinsic element of its acclaimed architectural vision. If this were indeed the case, then one would need to take Stravinsky's fingerings into account analytically.

The *Sonate* was composed over eleven weeks between 4 August and 21 October 1924, these being the dates inscribed on the first and last pages of the sketches. I wish to examine just one of the thirteen musical ideas to which Stravinsky appended specific fingering at the moment of their first annotation. However, my analysis begins not on 4 August but four months earlier, on 13 April, when Stravinsky – significantly, perhaps – took time out from the urgent business of completing his Piano Concerto

Fig. 3.1 Stravinsky, sketch for *Sonate pour piano* (Biarritz, 13 April 1924). See also *Strawinsky: Sein Nachlass, sein Bild* (Basel: Kunstmuseum Basel; Paul Sacher Stiftung, 1984), pp. 102–3.

(finished a week later and given its first performance within a month) in order to write down the opening to a movement for piano solo he subtitled 'Preludio' (Figure 3.1).[5] This primordial sketch of the *Sonate* first movement is remarkable for many reasons, not least for so accurately anticipating the finished score. The autograph in ink is Stravinsky's original script

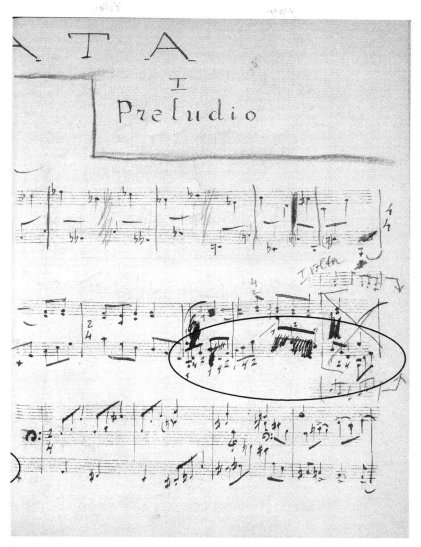

Fig. 3.1 (*cont.*)

and consists of three pages comprising thirty-two bars of music. Clearly visible on the right-hand page (circled) are fingerings in the left hand, also in ink. (The fainter writing *in pencil*, including fingerings for the right hand, is the work of later revision, probably from early August.) It *is* surprising, as Craft writes, that fingering should be present at all in sketches – even more so in this autograph that pre-dates the sketches proper by four months. These are contexts, surely, when one imagines the composer to be solely concerned with musical composition – with 'getting the notes onto paper'. Stravinsky's purpose here is certainly not editorial for he does not append fingerings (as would an editor) to suggest *to others* a solution to a difficult passage. The first two lines of the 'Preludio' certainly *do* present difficulties for the sight-reader and performer alike. In response to this, Albert Spalding – the celebrated violinist and editor who prepared the *Sonate* for publication – judged these opening bars to merit no fewer than sixty-four fingerings. The composer is no editor and offers none. Instead, Stravinsky is concerned with the arpeggio accompaniment in the left hand for which he indicates a fingering – 5,4,2,1 – to a figure which presents comparatively little technical challenge. Nor would any self-respecting pianist require that this fingering be indicated five times in succession. Once would surely suffice. Not unexpectedly, Spalding does not consider this passage to require any fingerings at all.

Looking ahead, the cadence at the conclusion of this phrase (Figure 3.1, left-hand page, final bar) might suggest Stravinsky's role to be editorial after all. Upon closer examination, however, one realizes that his fingering of 1,2,3 for the left hand, far from facilitating performance, makes for an unusually wide stretch of a fifth between thumb and index finger where more practical alternatives are readily available. Yet by indicating this fingering, Stravinsky is committed to revert to the already favoured 5,4,2,1 hand position for the final arpeggio.

Any suggestion that these markings are indicative of creative intent would need to be supported by evidence that these fingerings accompany their associated musical ideas at every stage of the compositional process just as consistently as the notes themselves. Table 3.1 illustrates how Stravinsky fingers the left-hand passage in Figure 3.1 on its journey from initial sketch to publication in the summer of 1925 – initially by Edition Russe de Musique and subsequently by Hawkes & Son. One may observe how the 5,4,2,1 fingering was consistently indicated for this figure – by Stravinsky, though not by either publisher.

Stravinsky, then, did *not* dispense with his fingerings 'as a builder does his scaffolding', neither here nor in another twelve passages which can, likewise, be traced with comparable fidelity through all compositional and editorial stages.[6] The 5,4,2,1 fingering is identified with this figure at its conception and it remained central to Stravinsky's experience of this material in performance. But if such markings were not designed to be 'merely' editorial in the conventional sense, i.e. if they were not primarily intended to facilitate performance or to accelerate the learning process, then what can Stravinsky's insistence on these fingerings possibly signify? And where might one encounter other such manifestations?

Table 3.1

(a) Sonate pour piano, **first movement. Left-hand fingering indicated by Stravinsky for bb. 18–21 (shown in chronological order):**

---

13 April 1924 – 'SONATA I Preludio', sketch:
>   **5,4,2,1,4,2,1,4,2,1,2,4,1,2,4 … 1,2,3**

4 August 1924 – *Sonate* sketchbook:
>   **5,4,2,1,4,2,1,4,2,1,2,4,1,2,5,4,2,1**

24 October 1924 – *Sonate* fair copy:
>   **5,4,2,1,4,2,1,4,2,1,2,4,1,2,5,4,2,1**

May 1925 – *Sonate* 1st edn, ed. A. Spalding (Edition Russe de Musique):[*]
>   *no fingering indicated*

May 1925 – Stravinsky's own copy of the *Sonate* 1st edn, inscribed 'Mai 1925. Exemplaire corrigé avec mes doigtés – I. Str.'('May 1925. Copy corrected with my fingerings – I. Str.'):
>   **5,4,2,1,4,2,1,4,2,1,2,4,1,2,5,4,2,1**

June 1925 – *Sonate* 2nd edn, ed. A. Spalding (Hawkes & Son):
>   *no fingering indicated*

(b) Sonate pour piano, **first movement. Left-hand fingering indicated by Stravinsky for bb. 26–30:**

May 1925 – Stravinsky's own copy of the *Sonate* 1st edn, inscribed 'Mai 1925. Exemplaire corrigé avec mes doigtés – I. Str.':
>   **5,4,2,1,4,2,1,4,2,1,2,4,1,2,4,5,4,2,4 … 5,4,2**

June 1925 – *Sonate* 2nd edn, ed. A. Spalding (Hawkes & Son):
>   *no fingering indicated*

---

[*] Stravinsky, *Sonata, Piano Solo*, ed. Albert Spalding (London: Hawkes & Son, 1925). This is the edition that has remained in print to this day.

The autograph material for *Les Cinq Doigts* (1920/1) also contains fingering of appropriately editorial nature. At the head of every movement and each principal section Stravinsky indicates the exact hand position and its location on the keyboard. As befits the author of this overtly didactic work, Stravinsky seeks, in the final movement, to develop the independence of the third and fourth fingers of the left hand through triadic alternation of the 5,4,2 and the 5,3,1 hand-positions.[7] If the music deviates from this in the slightest the composer indicates appropriate fingerings (Example 3.1).

Between this and the *Sonate* there may be a bridge that links the clearly pedagogic intent of the appropriately titled *The Five Fingers* to the, as yet, ill-defined (possibly creative) process in the later work. A transitional, certainly extraordinary example of Stravinskian fingering may also be

Ex. 3.1 Stravinsky, *Les Cinq Doigts* (1920/1), VIII. Pesante, bb. 19–25 – with the composer's (published) fingerings.

observed in the fair copy of the Piano Concerto. Stravinsky appears to be engaged here in a concentrated outburst of meticulous fingering annotations (Example 3.2). As an isolated manifestation, in a score almost devoid of markings of any kind, it is quite remarkable. One may observe how the 5,4,2,1 pattern (here in the right hand) is marked eight times in succession.[8] In fact the previous ten bars, although un-fingered (five are visible in this example), also employ this identical hand position a further twenty times consecutively.[9]

A particularly intriguing detail is to be observed in the passage that Stravinsky *has* marked: this contains uncomfortably wide leaps between the second and fifth fingers of more than an octave, but these too are made to conform to the one hand position – despite the extreme awkwardness of this at speed and the ready availability of alternatives. There are even two occasions (Example 3.2, one bar before Fig. 37) when Stravinsky – although noted, memorably by Picasso, for his large hands – recognizes the danger of these out-size stretches and proposes an effective, if simple diagrammatic symbol – a diagonal line – as warning.[10] At all costs, it seems, the pattern must be maintained even when the pianist is more likely to play the correct notes by finding his or her own solution. Fingering (as a technical element) is no longer merely the means to a musical end; rather, the music has become a means to a technical objective. By devising a passage of twenty-eight consecutive applications of the same (essentially uncomfortable) hand position,

Ex. 3.2 Stravinsky, *Concert pour piano et instruments à vent* (1923/4), 1st
movement, Figs. 36–7 – with the composer's fingerings.

Stravinsky might be accused of enjoying the composition of technical exercises with the zeal of Clementi, Czerny, Henselt, Kalkbrenner, Leschetizky
or Philipp. Perhaps Stravinsky's effort to compose a soloist's part worthy of
the genre led him to resource the available literature of piano tutors and
studies. He cannot have been insensitive to the prospect that comparisons
would be drawn between his new concerto and those of fellow Russian
composer/pianists Prokofiev and Rakhmaninov.[11]

One might conjecture that, consistent with his recent aesthetical pronouncements – 'Some Ideas about My *Octuor*' was published in January
1924 – Stravinsky now sought a pianistic idiom free of nineteenth-century
rhetoric while guaranteeing an equivalent degree of technical difficulty. His
possible aim was to mould the soloist's material not on the flashing octave
displays and massive chords of the virtuoso but on the contrapuntal rigour
of piano methods and *études*, on the literature of the musical draftsman
immersed in the intimate technical challenges of piano study, persistent
and proud of his feats of digital endurance.[12]

The opening to the final movement of the *Sonate*, however, may serve
as a more reliable witness. Here we find a two-part fugue whose subject is

born of that fundamental 5,4,2,1 left-hand position. There is no need to add fingerings this time; the fingers have 'got their way' and Stravinsky has promoted his digital aerobics from accompaniment and passage-work to primary thematic material. Furthermore, not only does the movement unfold musically – with a sense of thematic/harmonic evolution and textural contrast – there is also a technical evolution. If the fugue subject initially resembles an 'exercise for the left hand', this soon leads to material that ratchets up what Soulima Stravinsky referred to as 'technicity'[13] by exploiting an additional challenge: the rapid overlapping of the fifth finger by the fourth: see bar 6 in Example 3.3a (the circled fingerings are Stravinsky's). There are other moments, too, where this is clearly implied – for example, in the second half of b. 2 and in b. 8; suggested fingerings are shown in squares.

Continuing with the piano method analogy, one might then expect to progress to a test of augmented difficulty – intended to develop these overlapping skills – now at the upper extremity of the left hand, between the thumb and second finger. Indeed, this *is* to be found later in the movement, as illustrated in Example 3.3b (b. 78 – with Stravinsky's own fingerings circled; and b. 79 – with implied fingerings in squares). Both these challenges – the fourth finger overlapping the fifth and the index finger overlapping the thumb – are later combined by Stravinsky in bb. 84–5 (the final two bars of Example 3.3b).

Charles Joseph declares 'it is impossible to miss [Stravinsky's] reliance on Philipp's exercises as useful models' in order to justify what he refers to as 'Stravinsky's unique compositional approach to the keyboard'.[14] Not only does Joseph assert that entire passages in *Capriccio* are 'virtually lifted' from Czerny's op. 337, he also declares that '[o]ne of the great underestimates in Stravinsky scholarship is of just how important these pianistic, tactile models were in shaping the composer's writing during [this] period'.[15] But Joseph has a different agenda. He attributes those pianistic textural figurations in non-pianistic *Apollo* merely to 'the anatomy of the composer's unusually large hands'. There is clearly more to it than that. Indeed, in his study of the partnership between Stravinsky and Balanchine Joseph does recognize the important role of the piano in their artistic journey. Their neoclassical ballets were founded not only upon their makers' common ethnicity; their mutual dependence upon the piano's objective filter is more than a curious coincidence, however difficult this will be to evaluate as a creative 'referent'. But Joseph's allusion to hands is not far off the mark; any study of Stravinsky's pianistic psychology must handle the enigmatic question of physicality – a broad and imprecise concept which may be seen, like so many issues that surround Stravinsky's pianism, to originate in St Petersburg in the half-light of Rubinstein's legacy and in the full glare of

Ex. 3.3 Stravinsky, *Sonate pour piano* (1924), 3rd movement:
(a) bb. 1–8; with the composer's fingerings (circled) and the author's suggested
fingerings (in squares).

(b) bb. 77–85

Leschetizky's. Once in France (and America), Stravinsky's twenty-year
dependence on the drills of Isidor Philipp suggests that there was more to
finger-stretching (to cite, again, Soulima's recollections of his father) than
just keeping his 'paint-brushes' clean. Stravinsky had developed a unique
mode of working, i.e. a pianistic mode of thinking that could slide between
piano practice and musical composition via an inter-textuality based upon

the concept of process. Stravinsky's feat – a combination of digital and intellectual endurance – may yet be seen to address Kofi Agawu's premise that 'musical composition is re-composition … [something] simply inconceivable outside a specific pedagogical tradition.'[16] Heinrich Schenker, surely voicing the opinion of many, wrote: 'A musical person, having reached a certain level, does not need to practise in the sense of finger exercises and etudes; such practising only leads back to these very exercises, to these very etudes – a world not worth reaching.'[17] In vigorous response, one may observe in the examples cited above that Stravinsky's fingering is an indicator of musical and gestural significance – a determinant, even, of compositional process. Furthermore, his adaptation of a singularly pianistic attitude to his visualization of sound may be seen to link his (neoclassical) instrumental canon to *le domaine de la chorégraphie*. These topics carry wide-ranging implications in the broader context of Stravinsky scholarship, indicating the path to a re-evaluation of the composer's 'objective' aesthetic and his views on performance. In 'Some Ideas about My *Octuor*' Stravinsky wrote that he did not 'conceive nor feel … true emotive force except under coordinated musical sensations.'[18] Within months he was further expounding his novel aesthetic stance, this time through the medium of the piano. Immediately after completing the fair copy of the *Sonate* Stravinsky gave the first private performance of this work (in a hotel in Warsaw). His first comment, following the conclusion of the final movement, is reported to have been: 'You see, I create like this: from colour I go to the drawing. Right now I am struggling to create drawings at the expense of colour'[19] – a form of words that is strongly reminiscent of, while appearing to negate, Rimsky's phraseology of orchestration. The experience led one critic to comment that '[Stravinsky] used to walk on a rope, then a wire. Now he walks on a razor blade',[20] while the response of the Polish writer Jarosław Iwaszkiewicz is more perceptive: 'One is amazed by the unusual logic and mathematical clarity that are apparent in everything [Stravinsky] says, and most of all [in his] objectives and methods … Total awareness in all his creative work – that is what Stravinsky develops in himself and what he strives towards.'[21]

A sense of total awareness with undertones of an unusual logic is indeed suggested by the instrumental counterpoint of Stravinsky's early neoclassicism. In the specific instance of the *Sonate pour piano*, if the available edition of this work were to reproduce Stravinsky's intended fingering – and if pianists were to adhere to this as scrupulously as to the written note – they might also harness those 'coordinated musical sensations' and share the composer's 'emotive force'.[22] Bound by this digital straitjacket (like a human pianola) the performer might also more faithfully grant Stravinsky his wish that his music be executed, not interpreted.

Stravinsky's hyperbole regarding his new aesthetic – and the first compositional manifestations of this – run parallel with the launch of his equally new career as a concert pianist.[23] It is to be expected, therefore, that he should retain a pianistic attitude throughout his first neoclassical decade. Two works in particular support this view. The Piano Concerto and the *Symphony of Psalms* (and, to a lesser extent, the *Sonate*) reveal that much of the musical texture and thematic character of these works derive from stretches of passage-work resembling pianistic drills which are inscribed at the very start of the sketchbook material. (In the context of this chapter, these preliminary studies are labelled *Vorstudien* – a term borrowed from Leschetizky.) Yet the pivotal role that these little sketches provide in formulating the melodic, rhythmic and intervallic bases of these major works encourages one to elevate their status to that of a 'series', the constituent parts of which Stravinsky invested with new life and transformed into vibrant, musical (neoclassical) art. One may yet need to justify the term 'series' in referring to these preliminary studies, although the label 'sequence' can be discarded for conveying a repetitive, ascending–descending characteristic not relevant in this case. Instead, Stravinsky's interests centre upon the shifting internal composition of each group of four semiquavers, particularly when the hand and fingers rotate around a pivotal pitch or pair of pitches. Paradoxical it is, that the initial sketches of the Piano Concerto – written at a time when Stravinsky was basing key aspects of its composition on its *Vorstudien* – should coincide with Schoenberg's composition of the first fully serial movements in his *Five Piano Pieces* op. 23, *Serenade* op. 24 and *Suite for Piano* op. 25. Essential to the definition of the term 'series' is the concept and process of ordering, for the parameters of music that are being serialized must be used in strict order. Such organization is not a feature of the *Vorstudien*. However, Stravinsky's material is consistently used to define *intervallic* relationships, thereby linking this procedure with one of the chief elements in serial composition, a series being as much a set of intervals as a sequence of pitches.

Unity between the prime series, its inversion, retrograde and retrograde inversion is only aurally feasible if the intervallic relationships are maintained consistently throughout these processes of manipulation, whatever their transposition. The sound-world and the compositional process of serial music are often characterized by the motivic predominance of one kind of interval in the series. This is an important means – beyond secondary considerations such as instrumentation or dynamics – by which a serial work can establish its identity, or a serial composer's musical idiom can be distinguished from another's. A distinctive feature of Webern's serialism is the symmetry of his series; in his String Quartet op. 28 (1938) there are symmetrical relationships not only between the two hexachords of the prime series but also between the tetrachords. Stravinsky's engagement with the intervallic relationships within his *Vorstudien* is less a question of symmetry and more of *centrality* – specifically around the interval of the third: a chain of thirds in the *Sonate*, falling thirds (accented and *legato*) in the Piano Concerto, and pivotal thirds in the *Symphony*. An interval may thus be prioritized; but the other notes – constantly revolving like satellites in irregular orbit – impede the listener from perceiving anything but the most transitory form of harmonic interaction. Stravinsky's orchestral *ritornelli* at the start of the *Symphony of Psalms*, for example, are constructed from arpeggios that act on the ear as harmonies or chords in linear presentation. In succession they convey no sense of tonal (diatonic) progression. Yet, the retention of a common *interval* as the focal point of successive arpeggios/ chords provokes a subtle conflict: there emerge two simultaneous rates of harmonic change, as portrayed by the inner interval and the outer notes. As the pivotal interval at the arpeggios' centre is slower to change than the outer notes, one is able to sense the 'play' of musical procedures – of the composer engaging in a deliberate manipulation of his material. The listener is thus protected from experiencing that sense of un-musical arbitrariness which is customarily provoked by long sequences of dour pianistic drills (and is a consequence of purely technical, i.e. non-compositional, concerns). On the other hand, Stravinsky's manipulation of such drill-like figurations does lend the listening experience a sense of direction, attracting the musical ear to follow and perceive its 'thread' while it establishes its own (non-expressive) rhetoric. Stravinsky's sketches – particularly his *Vorstudien* – allow one an insight into his procedures in effecting this characteristic outcome.

In the following examples Stravinsky reveals how, from three apparently pianistic jottings, he could derive contrasting musical genres: a 'three-part invention' for piano solo (in the *Sonate*, first movement); a combination of instrumental colour with contrapuntal, pianistic virtuosity (in the Piano Concerto, first movement); and a choral hymn for the Feast of the Assumption (in the *Symphony of Psalms*, first movement). One may never know the extent to which all Stravinsky's music is essentially piano music; however, these three sketches may be seen to represent a neoclassical form of the 'tone-row'. By their methodical and ingenious transformation from 'notated improvisation' to mature composition they provided Stravinsky with the means to effect an idiom at once harmonious and desirably impersonal.

The location of these pianistic sketches at the head of the first page of their respective manuscripts – together with their careful notation and, especially, the manner of their integration into the fabric of the musical composition – illustrates the pervasive influence of Stravinsky's underlying pianistic attitude. The Piano Concerto assumes, therefore, a symbolic role being a work for piano – one that Stravinsky himself would use to deliver his neoclassical message as a 'manifesto' devised to promote the cause of his piano-generated neoclassicism. The compositions which immediately followed (*Sonate* and *Sérénade en la*) would reiterate his argument in its purest, i.e. solo-piano, form. Yet the manner in which the Concerto's vivid orchestral texture derives from such lean keyboard material is a remarkable illustration of the extent to which Stravinsky constructed large-scale classical genres – not from his 'studied' Russian pianism but 'from the wrists down', i.e. upon figurations that give every impression of having emerged almost casually from the piano itself.

Stravinsky's initial sketches are usually scribbled, hastily jotted affairs; yet he demonstrates here a particularly neat calligraphy. This would suggest that he took greater than usual care in accurately notating this source-material, aware perhaps of its potential as a point of frequent reference. Figure 3.2 shows the first page of sketches for the Concerto. At the top can be seen the *Vorstudie* under discussion. Compared with the other jottings on this and subsequent pages (which appear to have been sketched out in some haste) the top line gives the impression of having been confidently and carefully written down.[24]

The metronome mark indicated immediately below this sketch would suggest that, although the musical composition had barely started on paper, Stravinsky had already associated this semiquaver flow with a specific tempo (crotchet = 104) which would become the indication for the completed first-movement Allegro.[25] In order to trace the intricate manner with which Stravinsky based a large amount of the melodic and rhythmic material of this movement on his series it is useful, firstly, to identify its constituent parts (Example 3.4a).

The first three bars (Example 3.4a) seem to have particularly interested the composer. By labelling four melodic/rhythmic shapes one may trace their translation to the finished score and witness the diversity with which Stravinsky transforms his material. From motif *x* Stravinsky derives the principal theme of the Allegro, played initially by the trumpet 'on G' (with woodwind doublings) at Fig. 10. The theme is constructed almost uniquely from this five-note scale, a more quintessential piano figuration being hard to contemplate. Deriving from the very physical properties of the hand, the five-note scale may be regarded as more elemental still than the octave scale (which is its extension). It is the very kernel from which all piano playing emanates. Stravinsky was to admit his fascination with Czerny during

Fig. 3.2 Stravinsky, sketches for *Concert pour piano et instruments à vent* (1923/4): the first page of sketches.

Ex. 3.4 Stravinsky, *Concert pour piano et instruments à vent*: (a) sketch, bb. 1–4;

the process of preparing for his debut as a concert pianist in the following terms: 'I began … the loosening of my fingers by playing a lot of Czerny exercises, which was not only very useful but also gave me keen musical pleasure.'[26] The five-finger envelope is (inevitably) the basis upon which, for example, Czerny's preliminary *40 Daily Exercises* op. 337 and his advanced volume *Die Kunst der Fingerfertigkeit* op. 740 are founded. (Joseph, one recalls, has even suggested a direct relationship between Czerny and the Concerto).[27] By alternating the statement of the 'five-finger theme' between strong and weak beats, the composer creates variation from unity by which means the music acquires its characteristic *Synkopespiel*, this dance-like quality permeating the whole movement, through the ingenuity of its rhythmical counterpoint. An early and typical example of this may be observed in the bars prior to the trumpet entry. Here, the theme is anticipated in the upper woodwinds. The five-note scale in semiquavers is also presented in quavers (in the bassoon and II/IV horns) on alternately strong and weak beats. One may understand this simultaneous augmentation as a deliberate act of expressive neutralization, a moment where the sophistication of the contrapuntal interplay (*pace* Ockleford) prioritizes the music's structure over its content (at Fig. 9 in the score), whereas at the ensuing trumpet statement of the main theme (at Fig. 10) the orchestral texture is devoid of such contrapuntal ingenuity, so the balance of content over structure is restored. A similar instance of expressive neutralization – again through the deployment of greater contrapuntal sophistication – occurs in the third movement of the *Sonate*, in this case by inversion.[28] Such an example of inverted counterpoint is rare in Stravinsky's neoclassical works. The late serial works, though, abound in this characteristically dodecaphonic procedure, in anticipation of which this reading of the Piano Concerto's initial entry as an 'embryonic series' is surely enhanced. It is indeed paradoxical, given the 'Schoenberg/Stravinsky polemic', that such procedures should be employed in a neoclassical context.

With reference to the material in Examples 3.4a and b, it is possible to observe Stravinsky's construction methods as he transforms the three component motifs of this figuration (labelled *x*, *y* and *z*) with ever greater

Ex. 3.4 (*cont.*) (b) first movement, bb. 55–7.

ingenuity. An unimaginative, if 'adequately' classical way of varying the articulation (in Example 3.4a) would be to divide each group of four notes into pairs, i.e., two *legato* notes followed by two *staccato* notes – this being a formula particularly favoured by woodwind instruments. A less conventional, marginally more complicated though infinitely more interesting step (for Stravinsky) was to place the slurred pair in the centre of the group of four. By virtue of this gentle dislocation Stravinsky exposes the musical 'interest' of the falling third (motif *z*), further enhancing its presence through *legato/staccato* differentiation. This phraseology not only leads to the upper note appearing more accented than the remainder, it encourages the ear to separate this *legato* pair of notes from its context. Motifs *x*, *y* and *z* make a significant contribution to the first movement's thematic, rhythmic and textural material – with implications, even, for its instrumentation. Example 3.4b illustrates how one passage, typical of the movement's texture, engages in such motivic re-cycling. Here, the falling thirds (motif *z*) are prominently accented by the piano and further highlighted by the upper woodwind. Meanwhile, the soloist's four-note *gruppetti* (motif *y*) are presented simultaneously in quaver augmentation by first and third horns (on the strong beat) and by first trumpet with first trombone (on the weak beat).

In the light of Stravinsky's comments (in *Chroniques*) acknowledging the stimulus of his fingers,[29] one might concede that the composer has deliberately and enthusiastically re-activated his youthful skills of improvisation at the service of a revitalized pianistic attitude. These skills are now harnessed, in the composer's maturity, to the production of neoclassical works. It is a significant step. Now, through considerable craft, 'micro' piano figurations are transformed into 'macro' instrumental composition. The ingenuity with which Stravinsky constructed sophisticated orchestral textures from improvisatory sketches of such apparent simplicity would suggest that this was no mere fascination with the piano. He clearly viewed this instrument as much more than a compositional aid or a convenient work environment (although it also fulfilled these functions). With its help Stravinsky could now construct an entire Allegro movement whose *matière sonore* is but the barest pianistic thread re-worked into orchestral textures. The completeness, fertility and economy of this re-cycling process must have been particularly satisfying for this newly self-styled artisan-musician.

It was a working method that Stravinsky was to maintain over the coming years. The *Sonate* sketchbook (August–October 1924) displays a similar pianistic 'series' on the first page, dated '4 August' (in Russian), though its implications for the final score are restricted to textural, never thematic, essentials (Figure 3.3, circled).[30] These linked thirds – a figuration that is

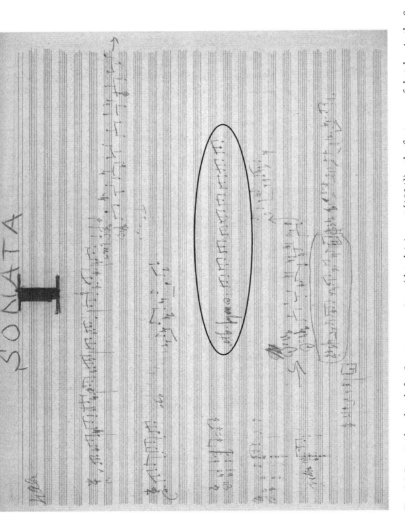

Fig. 3.3 Stravinsky, sketch for *Sonate pour piano* (dated 4 August [1924]) – the first page of sketches in the *Sonate* sketchbook, held at the Paul Sacher Stiftung, Basel. On the cover Stravinsky has drawn a very florid title: 'SONATE'. The first page, inside, is titled: 'SONATA – I'. Given the rudimentary state of the sketches on this page, one might question the date given in *Strawinsky: Sein Nachlass, sein Bild* (p. 100) for the relatively advanced sketch material on '13 April': see Figure 3.1.

Ex. 3.5 Stravinsky, *Sonate pour piano* (Edition Russe de Musique, 1925), 1st movement, bb. 143–5.

rooted in technical literature – are first deployed in the right hand as an inner voice, later as a bass-line. Example 3.5 shows their final presentation towards the end of the first movement. The circled accents in the first two bars indicate the markings which Stravinsky wrote in his own proof-copy of the first edition, although this revision was not adopted in the published score. The printed accents mirror the hemiola of the left-hand descent. However, Stravinsky's hand-written alteration provokes a marked increase in rhythmical tension and may indicate an alternative pattern that he tested in practice (although did not apply in his recordings).

The *Symphony of Psalms* provides an even more significant illustration of an orchestral composition constructed from these same procedures, confirming that fully seven years after the Piano Concerto Stravinsky continued to base his compositional process on *Vorstudien* – that is, on pianistic exercise models. Furthermore, the stature of the *Symphony of Psalms* within Stravinsky's canon, as a neoclassical icon of the highest maturity, derives from this being not only a symphony (his first since the *Probestück* of 1907) but also a work that is 'not merely choral, but severely, ritualistically sacred'.[31] Stravinsky began composition of its first movement by carefully notating – in a manner consistent with the sketches to the Concerto and *Sonate* – a single line of pianistic passage-work (Figure 3.4). This is situated near the top of the first page of sketches for the opening movement.[32] The first two annotations (circle 1) present brief arabesques formed from compact, pianistic five-finger shapes. In the third system of the page, however, this figuration is greatly extended (circle 2), forming a *Vorstudie* which contains scalic and intervallic 'cells' from which the entire first movement will be constructed. In fact, judging by the plethora of *ritornello* material that covers the rest of this first page, it appears that the *Vorstudie* has propelled the composer into immediate action. (Once again, Stravinsky's pianistic

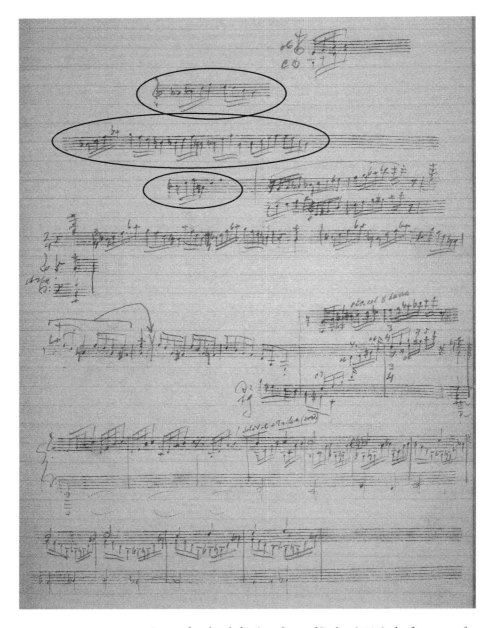

Fig. 3.4 Stravinsky, sketch for *Symphony of Psalms* (1930): the first page of sketches.

'drill' takes on the role of a neoclassical 'tone-row'.) Below this (circle 3) there is indication already of a creative response: Stravinsky's first sketch arising from the series toys with retaining another minor third (D and F) at the centre of this extended *ritornello*.

Merest fragment as this is, Figure 3.4 (circle 3) illustrates how Stravinsky embarked upon the compositional path by altering the pattern of notes for metrical variety. (This little adjustment evokes the practice of experimentation he adopted in early childhood, as he would later claim: 'As soon as I could reach the piano I tried to pick out the intervals that I had heard, and in the process found other intervals that I liked better, which already made me a composer.')[33] Stravinsky's re-working (circle 3) of his 'series' (circle 2) suggests he was attracted to, and was actively considering, a sub-division of the original four-note units into hemiolae of three-note units. This is a possibility which presents itself effortlessly the moment that the material is viewed as piano music, i.e. with the index finger on the first note.[34] Although Stravinsky did not find room to explore the implications of this in the busy *ritornelli* of the first movement, he employed hemiolae as a central element of the third movement's musical syntax. The passage at Fig. 2 in the final movement ('Laudate Eum in firmamento virtutis Ejus') shows groups of three widely spaced crotchets within a choral texture in 4/4. This measured syncopation is transformed at Fig. 3 ('Tempo: minim = 80 in 4', '*sf sub, p e stacc.*') where it re-appears full of rhythmic energy, the use of wide intervals giving way to step-wise motion in the double-basses (and, later, cellos) while remaining faithful to the original pattern of ascending units of three notes. At the serene climax to the movement (Fig. 22: *Molto meno mosso; p subito e ben cantabile*), the relationship between registers is inverted in another clear demonstration of the composer choosing to augment the degree of compositional ingenuity by stages. Now the three-note pattern, previously the counter-rhythm, becomes the main tempo and is sung by the chorus to the text 'Laudate Eum in cymbalis'. The ascending three-note shape (fundamental to the original hemiola) is presented in parallel – in its 'essence'– by the fourth trumpet. Against this the bass-line (timpani, harp and pianos) carries the four-note pattern for forty-two bars. When employed in slow tempi, the hemiola – derived from the merest pianistic 'noodle'[35] – makes a fundamental contribution to the ritual aspect of these passages and to that memorable sense of spirituality which the *Symphony of Psalms* as a whole conveys.

The pianistic formulae which act as the basis to the Concerto (and, to a lesser extent, the *Sonate*) derive from habits acquired using established didactic methods. The *Vorstudien* for this pair of piano works may reflect Stravinsky's self-confessed familiarity with Czerny, but the preliminary study for the *Symphony of Psalms* suggests another methodo-logical provenance. Its chromaticism, its angular and wholly arpeggiated (rather than scalic) flow, its sense of working within five-finger 'envelopes' while exploring permutations around a pivotal interval – these traces of *pal'tserazvitiye* all point to the piano-training materials of Theodor Leschetizky. Stravinsky would certainly have been acquainted with such exercises as a young piano student in St Petersburg, where Leschetizky – together with Anton Rubinstein – had established the pianistic traditions of the new Conservatoire. By the time Stravinsky had turned fifty he was collecting his thoughts for *Chroniques de ma vie* and could reflect upon the relative merits of his early, often conflicting experiences of the learning process. Against a background of pianistic discipline within St Petersburg's wider musical context, Stravinsky's underlying fascination with improvisa-tion should also be considered. On the one hand improvisation appears to represent the most anarchic aspect of pianism, to be in conflict with the respectably rigorous processes of method-based, regulated study. Indeed, Stravinsky was obliged to curtail his indulgence in improvisation during the years of piano study under Kashperova. Nevertheless, as he later con-firmed, he was to continue viewing improvisation as a valuable creative stimulus. From the perspective of a decade of neoclassical composition he would later recall: 'I must say that my constant work at improvisation ["as a child of nine or ten"] was not absolutely fruitless; for, on the one hand, it contributed to my better knowledge of the piano, and, on the other, it sowed the seed of musical ideas.'[36] In the pre-romantic era improvisation had been regarded as a mark of advanced musicianship, demonstrating a simultaneous capacity in performance *and* composition. Improvisation may also have formed the means by which Stravinsky's compositions remained firmly dependent upon his pianistic creativity: not just as a spon-taneous improvisatory 'art' deriving from the composer's imagination, however, but as a thoroughly practical and methodical 'science'. By uniting pedagogy, improvisation and composition under the one banner of pian-ism one may understand how Stravinsky came to respect, and resource, all three aspects of musicianship to suit his creative and aesthetic require-ments. By the manner of their construction appropriate to the origins of their raw materials, the neoclassical works thus formed the ideal comple-ment to Stravinsky's new credo of music as craft. The reception of these compositions as 'musical objects' and as iconic symbols of the neoclassical quality of objectivity was thus guaranteed.

Several reasons have been proposed as to why Stravinsky might have claimed fingering as a compositional process. Amongst these was his pursuit of formal purity, or his need for emotional neutrality in the safe knowledge that an idiom based on *pal'tserazvitiye* would be inherently inexpressive. Another reason must be Stravinsky's prioritization of objectivity. As a recently declared aesthetic goal it was too precious a concept to be lost within the conventions of the printed edition, to be trampled over by an insensitive or, worse, an oversensitive pianist. The unsuspecting, conventionally educated performer might easily miss it. This was clearly an issue when giving authorization to others to perform his neoclassical works. 'The *Concerto* risks being compromised', Stravinsky wrote in 1927, 'if incompetent or romantic hands begin to "interpret" it before undiscriminating audiences'.[37] There had to be guarantees that the executants would fully realize the composer's rigorous intentions. If the contrapuntal nature of music inhibits the subjective participation of the performer, and if (as Ockleford proposes)[38] the 'ratcheting up' of contrapuntal devices constricts still further the expressive involvement of the player, then a composer's stipulation of a determined pattern of fingerings would result in an *even* greater degree of emotional neutrality – not least, by exerting an intellectual control over the performer's every digital movement. All of these aspects suggest Stravinsky's consistent and conscious utilization of compositional and notational techniques, which, when employed in combination, were fully intended to eliminate, or at least significantly reduce, subjective interference.

Two decades after disconnecting from St Petersburg and from those dominant figures associated with the Conservatoire, Stravinsky would find himself again in a position to evaluate contrasting pianistic philosophies, this time in Paris. At such a distance he would have recognized that significant, culturally embedded aspects of French pianistic tradition reflected those utilitarian finger-based elements of Leschetizky's method. Not everyone associated with the Paris Conservatoire would agree with his denial of Rubinstein's cult of the virtuoso, yet those figures with whom he chose to associate would have immediately recognized the validity of, and emphatically endorsed, his craft-based, subject-distanced attitude to composition and pianism. From such a perspective, from within such a milieu, Rubinstein's pedagogy – that had caused Stravinsky such attrition – must now have seemed a remote and irrelevant memory. In France, Stravinsky was operating within a historically neoclassical culture where his identity as 'le bon artisan' chimed with many of the established musical figures (particularly Nadia Boulanger and Isidor Philipp) with whom he could 'dream of achieving the *beautiful* only through the categories of the *useful*'.[39]

The experience of preparing himself as a career-pianist, of applying himself to the rigorous discipline of piano practice, proved to be a fruitful opportunity to indulge his long-held fascination with those processes of musical construction upon which both performance and composition were rooted. This had become the tenor of his statements regarding the 'musical object'. Yet his decision to adopt the role of concert pianist risked undermining his whole argument. The universe of the soloist, after all, was heavily tainted with nineteenth-century notions of the romantic virtuoso, and the market-place was dominated by pianists of the Russian-German tradition. Furthermore, his decision to join the commercially driven concert circuit hardly squared with the moral tone of his neoclassical aesthetic, which had distanced his philosophical reading of music from the act of (others') performance. It was to take many years – arguably, the rest of Stravinsky's life – for these two ideologies to re-align and for the equally valid, arguably 'nobler' professional role of the objective executant – the performer-as-messenger – to be fully understood, accepted and valued. In the early 1920s, however, a concert pianist's qualities were still defined by his interpretations, and performance was still regarded as an intensely subjective art. By entering that same congregation Stravinsky would renounce, it seems, his 'sacrifice to Apollo'; he was now at risk of losing credibility as an apostle of neoclassicism in the floodwaters of his apparent surrender to Dionysus. Only by re-defining the role of the concert pianist within the terms of his new aesthetic would his 'instinctive logic' be regarded, also, as consistent.

The Piano Concerto as neoclassical *project*, i.e. as a work that incorporated composition *and* performance, may thus be seen as a deliberate and bold attempt on Stravinsky's part to implement, in practical terms, the message of his manifesto. In May 1924 he became, in effect, the executant of 'Some Ideas about My *Octuor*' for piano and orchestra'. This marriage of the practical with the theoretical – a union that brought to a head several conflicting aspects of Stravinsky's cultural pasts – suggests a determination to become a pianist on his *own* terms, in defiance of his Petersburgian heritage. His early neoclassicism can then be seen as a reaction against the cultural impositions and expectations of his Russian 'formation'. The piano had long been a practical tool for Stravinsky; but at the moment of his re-invention as a neoclassical pianist it took on a combative function. As weapon and shield the piano ensured he was well armed in his confrontation with the present (and future) musical environment while, also, it bolstered his defences against those criticisms directed at his neoclassical venture. So effective was his new strategy that once he had picked up the piano he put down the pen. There was to be no further pamphleteering for over a decade; his concerts and his pursuit of a legacy in recordings were now his manifestos. Stravinsky effectively guaranteed his future career as a composer by his pianistic initiatives. Furthermore, as a result of confronting his own musical origins – and by re-employing practical musicianship at the service of creativity and ideology – Stravinsky effectively re-invented pianism itself, investing this art-form with new responsibilities that would eventually be reflected in modernist and post-modernist reception. Stravinsky's role in imparting a Russianness to twentieth-century music is now acknowledged. His other massive achievement was in guiding performers, critics and scholars – and the wider musical community – towards a more respectful, objective, *composer*-centred orientation. This must also be regarded as a significant part of his legacy.

Before arriving at a re-definition of Stravinsky's neoclassical scores (and a re-appraisal of his neoclassical utterances) in the light of his creative engagement with pianistic pedagogy, it is necessary to re-examine his pianistic development. However, it is impossible to proceed on the basis of perceived similarities to the didactic material upon which this claim is made without first examining Leschetizky's method and the context from which it emerged. Thereafter it will be possible to construct an image of the mature Stravinsky as a fledgling keyboard professional drawing upon his pianistic heritage. The aesthetic gamble he took in becoming a concert pianist may then be understood as a calculated risk, for it was founded upon a vital truth: by rooting his neoclassical scores in didactic stock, the path to executing appropriately non-expressive and impersonal performances was more secure.

A Leschetizkian route to pianism

Stravinsky clearly indicated – in *Chroniques* and via the more acerbic moments of his dialogues with Craft – that Kashperova's artistic vision was strongly coloured by the memory of Rubinstein. ('Pianists are often exaggeratedly proud of their pedagogical pedigrees – as if musical talent were passed on by apostolic succession', as Kenneth Hamilton has warned,[40] and one must be wary of such hagiographic tendencies.) Stravinsky's case is supported by the evidence of Kashperova's only published memoirs, two-thirds of which – that is, twenty-one of its thirty pages – are given over to 'Recollections of Anton Grigor'yevich Rubinstein'.[41] Yet, Kashperova's approach to piano technique and its study (singled out for unqualified praise by Stravinsky) appears to have been based upon a more objective orientation. If it is possible to speak of a pianistic tradition upon which Kashperova based her teaching of technique, one must acknowledge that the art of pianism in late-nineteenth-century St Petersburg carried the imprint of several notable virtuosi of international reputation (besides Rubinstein) who contributed, also, to the establishment of a strong pedagogic tradition in the city. Adolph von Henselt (1814–89) came to Russia in 1838 to begin a forty-year teaching career based in St Petersburg; Theodor Leschetizky (1830–1915) co-founded the Conservatoire with Rubinstein, bringing to this institution during the first fifteen years of its existence his renowned specialization in matters of piano technique. Following Leschetizky's return to Vienna in 1879 the Conservatoire was directed from 1881 to 1885 by Vassily Ilyich Safonov (1852–1918), a Leschetizky disciple whose long line of distinguished pupils at the Moscow Conservatoire would include Aleksandr Skryabin, and Josef and Rosina Lhevinne. Following Safonov's departure – and coinciding with Kashperova's passage through the Conservatoire – Rubinstein returned to St Petersburg and directed the piano department until his death in 1894.

Of those celebrities who laid the foundations of St Petersburg's pianistic tradition, Leschetizky was the first to commit his method to print, albeit via trusted amanuenses. His publications are also chronologically the nearest to Kashperova's period of study at the Conservatoire, and to Stravinsky's period of study with Kashperova. (Safonov's *Novaya formula* and its English translation, *New Formula for the Piano Teacher and the Piano Student*, were both published in 1915.) Neither Henselt nor Rubinstein published piano methods. One is drawn, therefore, to place considerable weight upon Malwine Brée's *The Groundwork of the Leschetizky Method* and Marie Prentner's *The Leschetizky Method*. A study of these methods will enable one to glimpse something of the context within which Stravinsky acquired notions of pianism – and the means to pianistic artifice – on a professional level. The publication date of these volumes (1902–3) confirms that the methods developed by Leschetizky during his long career (of which his sojourn in St Petersburg was a significant, intensely didactic interlude) were contemporaneous with the period when Stravinsky studied with Kashperova. The Leschetizky method would, thus, have been considered both up to date and time-honoured – i.e. relevant for the growing market of young pianists, while being based upon the author's considerable experience. Given the respect historically afforded to foreign, western European culture by Russian society – as exemplified by Rubinstein's invitation to Leschetizky to develop within the Conservatoire a piano school to rival those of other European capitals[42] – one might argue that piano tuition in turn-of-the-century St Petersburg still carried familiar traces of Leschetizky's well-respected teaching methods. Furthermore, there is greater likelihood of this occurring within the community of Conservatoire-trained piano teachers who circulated amongst St Petersburg's musical elite. For such as these – and for Kashperova in particular – the use of Leschetizkian methods would have carried potent associations, not only with the Conservatoire's valued traditions but also, and by this affiliation, with the irresistible imprimatur of Anton Grigor'yevich himself.

Robert Philip, in his discussion of early piano recordings, warns of the dangers of reading too much of the nineteenth-century teacher in the twentieth-century pupil's performance style. Such is the desire, for example, to glimpse how Liszt might have played, it is a tempting though ultimately an imprecise formula that tries to eavesdrop on the *Abbé* via the recordings of, say, Frederick Lamond. 'Pupil–teacher relationships are very varied', writes Philip, 'and recordings do not reveal a simple pattern of influences. This is hardly surprising. No pianist, before or after the invention of the gramophone, made their reputations by playing exactly like their teachers, or even as their teachers instructed.'[43] With regard to concerts and recordings this is a valid point. However, one may also argue that pianists – while unwilling to imitate their teachers' mannerisms in *performance* – are more inclined in *technical* matters to follow guidelines and rituals deemed essential by their piano tutors for the advancement of their technique – i.e. to ground their daily workshop of training and preparation in procedures recommended to them during the laborious, though ultimately successful, process of their own pianistic 'formation'. It is, therefore, not unreasonable to propose that such tried and tested routines – incorporating both formal methodologies and informal tricks and shortcuts – represent for pupil-pianists a continuation of those practical working habits imparted by their teachers and adopted, on an individual basis, according to their effectiveness. One can only surmise that in St Petersburg – and for sound historical reasons – much of Leschetizky's methodology would have served as a foundation upon which piano teachers, aware of his close association with the Conservatoire, would have constructed their own approach to teaching piano technique.

Can one use such notions of a pedagogical tradition and its dissemination as a critical tool with which to examine Stravinsky's pianistic evolution? I argue that one can, and propose a re-interpretation of his early musical development from a Leschetizkian perspective that points up its relevance to Stravinsky's mature (especially neoclassical) working methods and attitudes.

How Leschetizky's teaching became synonymous with a national tradition can be traced through certain disciplines that became firmly inculcated into the learning and performance of pianists in Russia, during and following Leschetizky's professional duties in St Petersburg. For example, the prior visualization of the precise effect and sound required *before* actually playing is a technique that can be identified in many of Russia's finest performers and teachers, and well into the twentieth century. Rosina Lhevinne was famed for her constant exhortation: 'You imagine the sound you wish to produce, and then you produce it.'[44] Her husband Josef Lhevinne even published on this very subject, with 'Good Tone Is Born in the Player's Mind' (1923).[45] The Lhevinnes were among the distinguished line of musicians, including Skryabin, who were taught by Safonov at the Moscow Conservatoire. Considered one of the finest piano teachers the St Petersburg Conservatoire had produced, Safonov was a pupil of Leschetizky and a personal friend of Anton Rubinstein. His *New Formula* reveals the influence of both mentors. From Leschetizky he acquired a keen, practical interest in the minutiae of pedagogy based on the underlying principle of hand extension – devising, in Lhevinne's words, 'exercises in five-finger patterns, double notes, rhythmic scales, and chords [which have] a four-fold objective: finger independence, evenness in touch, dexterity, and tonal beauty'.[46] He also maintained the Petersburgian approach to chord playing – encouraged by both Leschetizky and Rubinstein – that was based on accurate and sensitive anticipation, guided by a striving towards the production of a vividness of tone: 'Unless a special effect of roughness is intended … the chord must, so to speak, be hidden in the closed hand, which opens, falling from above for the necessary position, just at the moment of striking the keyboard. This means that the chord must be ready in the thought of the player before the hand opens.'[47]

Isabelle Vengerova was another Leschetizky pupil to offer an insight into the manner with which several traits of her teacher were maintained during her long career – as professor in St Petersburg (1906–23) and at the Curtis Institute, Philadephia (1924–47) – and faithfully passed on to her pupils.[48] From research carried out at the Vengerova archives during the Soviet era, pianist Vitaly Neumann writes of her

> pedagogical emphasis [which] by inference [reveals much about the] Russian teaching of her day … Her influence on her students was profound. She creatively elaborated the pedagogical principles of her teachers Leschetizky and Annette Essipova, but introduced also her individual characteristics. The position of the hands, which Vengerova regarded as most important in piano technique, was characterised by the following: (1) The elbows to be kept away from the torso, (2) The wrists to be held with complete freedom, (3) The fingers to maintain a curved position with strength and precision.[49]

Yet, there is nothing particularly novel in Vengerova's emphasis – little, that is, that cannot be traced to Leschetizky's teachings. This reading is supported by Jacob Lateiner – a Vengerova pupil in Philadelphia – who summarizes her concerns as 'a singing sound and a fine legato … the need of playing deeply into the keys with strong fingers, a flexible wrist which all of her students incorporated into their technique'.[50] Lateiner's evidence also indicates the manner with which Leschetizky organized his 'School' – both in St Petersburg and, later, in Vienna – when he writes: 'Before working with [Vengerova], each one [of us] had to go through a period of intensive technical drill'.[51] The importance that Vengerova attached to digital technique, and her insistence that students acquire this to an adequate level before being admitted to her class, are features of Leschetizky's own work-pattern. Furthermore, they add weight to the evidence presented in those two Leschetizky methods published during his later years. Despite his famed *cri de guerre* ('No Method!') and his reputation for allowing his most advanced pupils considerable artistic liberty, Leschetizky did elaborate a complex and individual method for technical development at every level.[52] He also demanded that this be followed by all aspiring pupils. It is clear from biographical evidence, as well as from the Preface to Brée's volume, *The Groundwork of the Leschetizky Method*, that it was common practice for a teaching assistant, or *Vorbereiter*, to work with students at this preparatory stage specifically to supervise their technical development along the lines that Leschetizky indicated. Schnabel remarks that 'nearly 1,800 students' were taught by Leschetizky over the years.[53] Such a swarm may well have passed through his corridors; however only a select group, one would suspect, actually entered 'the emperor's throne room' to impress, and be impressed by, the great man himself.

Following the publication of his method on both sides of the Atlantic, Leschetizky could only enlarge upon the practice that he had followed all his professional life. In 1909 he ceded in an interview to Edwin Hughes (a former pupil and *Vorbereiter*) that: 'Of course, in the beginning I have a method. A knowledge of correct hand position and of the many different qualities of touch which I use and which give a never-ending variety to the tone must be learned before one can go very far. The fingers must have an unyielding firmness and the wrist, at the same time, an easy pliability'.[54] Such are the elements consistent with all of the comments and individual concerns of those celebrated Russian pianists who learned directly or indirectly from Leschetizky – and who passed these same fundamental priorities on to their pupils. As Gerig comments, 'all seem to have gone through elementary five-finger exercises. Then scales, arpeggios, chords and octave work followed'.[55] A glance at the published material may suggest this – though not the order with which these elements are developed. What differentiates Leschetizky's approach is its foundation upon the chord. Indeed, work on chords and hand positions – though *not* five-finger exercises, as one might expect – is the gateway to both Brée's and Prentner's accounts of Leschetizky's teaching. The entire evolutionary process, from rudimentary beginnings to advanced questions of tonal production, is founded instead upon chords. These not only create exercises for the fingers, more fundamentally still they determine the correct hand position – which, for Leschetizky, was a flattish hand with acutely rounded finger-tips, guided by flexible arms and wrists.[56]

The correct preparation of chords – both in the hand and in the mind – has been identified already as a feature of Leschetizky's legacy. It was, in fact, nothing less than the foundation-stone to his entire approach. As he once admitted to his biographer Ethel Newcomb: 'If I had a method it would be based upon the mental delineation of a chord.'[57] In the Leschetizky literature chords are, indeed, the basis to all drills. Thereby hangs his particular innovation. Pianoforte methods from the early nineteenth century, still in vogue when Leschetizky launched his own teaching career, rarely concern themselves with chords in the context of technical groundwork. Consistent with their historical position between the eras of the harpsichord and the piano they promote finger agility, principally through scales and arpeggios. This is true, for example, of Pleyel and Dussek's *Méthode pour le pianoforte* and also of Clementi's *Introduction to the Art of Playing on the Piano Forte*.[58] That this latter volume formed the basis to Chopin's own pianistic drilling – and, one surmises, was also recommended to *his* pupils, Julius Schulhoff included – is confirmed by information written by hand into a copy of the *2nd Pt. of Clementi's Introduction to the Art of Playing on the Piano Forte*.[59] The volume in question was presented originally to the English composer 'Wm. Horsley Esq.re [1774–1858] with Mr. Clementi's best comp.ts'. This autographed copy then passed into the hands of 'Sophie Horsley, 11, Sheffield Terrace, Kensington, W.', and it is in her hand on the inside cover of this volume that one learns of 'Chopin's favourite Scale Exercises page 26, 30, 40, 50, 82, 88, 92, 98, 102, 118'. Such detail suggests that Miss Horsley was privy to inside knowledge which could well have been obtained from Chopin himself – as his pupil – when he lived briefly London in 1848, or from a dependable third party.[60] None of these exercises concerns chords or arpeggios. Apart from one example (an exercise of a mere ten bars in parallel thirds and sixths)[61] all this material is based on scales. Unsurprising, perhaps, is the emphasis on extreme velocity: eight of the ten exercises are marked Allegro or faster. Noteworthy in this regard are those marked Allegrissimo, Prestissimo and Allegro vivacissimo – all characterized by contrary-motion scales with wide separation between the hands to the outermost reaches of the keyboard. Thus one surmises that finger velocity, based on finger-technique, was evidently much prized well into the nineteenth century despite the combined innovations, on the one hand, of Beethoven, Schumann, and Liszt and, on the other, of Broadwood, Erard and Pleyel.

It is from the testimony of the above-mentioned pianists – Josef and Rosina Lhevinne, Safonov, Essipova, Vengerova, as well as Benno Moiseiwitsch and Paderewski Schnabel – and their disciples, that one may re-construct the attitudes and teaching methods of Stravinsky's own teacher, Kashperova, and identify her too as an heir to the Leschetizky tradition. Of particular interest is the period following Kashperova's graduation, when she remained in St Petersburg making her name through an energetic combination of teaching, composition and performance, for it was at this time that she taught Stravinsky. Vengerova writes of this equivalent point in her own early career: 'Music takes up eleven hours of my day, and I sometimes feel very tired. I have 45 students of whom 20 are at the Conservatory, and 25 are private'[62] – evidence of what Gerig terms 'the great industry of the Russian pianist.'[63] There is no reason to doubt that Kashperova was a product of this same mould. It may not be far-fetched to assume that she also passed through such rigorous training herself, and would likewise have insisted that her own pupils obtain a similarly thorough technical foundation.

While demonstrating Leschetizky's unique emphasis on chords (and their derivatives, the broken chord and arpeggio), the two methods published by Brée and Prentner also give prominent attention to muscular extension through constant exhortations to stretch the gap between the fingers – a process whose combined effect leads to a widening of the span of the hand. This is considered an essential step towards achieving equality between all the fingers; and to achieve this goal the pupil must develop clear visual memorization of the hand position required for each chord and to prepare for this in the air, in advance. Brée explains how Leschetizky's fundamental concept, the mental delineation of chords, is to be accomplished: 'The hand must already catch the shape of each new chord in the air … By dint of practice, the hand finally learns to prepare the chord rightly at sight of the notes – to recognize its physiognomy, as it were.'[64] In Brée's volume this visualization of the chord is supported by the inclusion of (as the title page proudly announces) 'forty-seven illustrative cuts of Leschetizky's hand' (Figure 3.5).[65] Most notably, twenty-five of these illustrations of Leschetizky's right hand are employed to demonstrate a particular sequence of chords, the aforementioned *Accordgruppe*.[66] Indeed, it is upon this chord-sequence that the whole *Groundwork* is based. The *Accordgruppe* is a sequence of four-note and five-note chords to be used as the matrix for all broken-chord and arpeggio exercises.

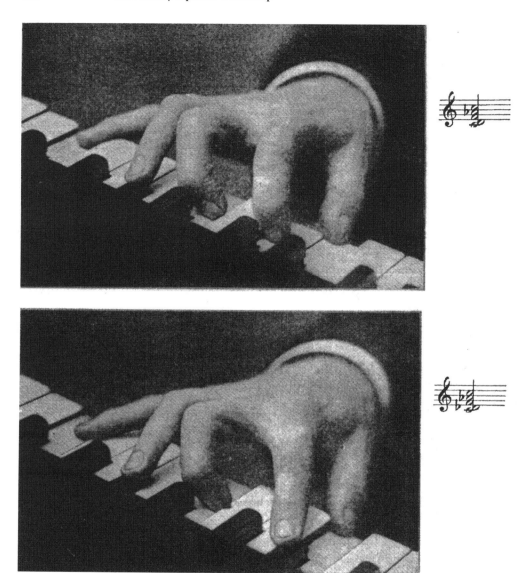

Fig. 3.5 Malwine Brée, *The Groundwork of the Leschetizky Method* (1902): excerpt from Chapter 16, 'Chords', illustrating how each chord of the *Accordgruppe* should be practised – i.e. firstly 'within the octave as an arpeggio, later as a suite of arpeggios'.

Variety within this chordal sequence is created by gradually altering the combination of the internal notes while the outer notes of the
octave-envelope remain fixed. The pupil is instructed to extend and overlap this pattern later as a 'Suite of Arpeggios' combining parallel and contrary motion. After two octaves in parallel ascent the left hand descends,
later ascending to coincide with the right hand's descent from its highest
extension. The left then changes direction so that the final two octaves are
played, once again, with both hands in parallel motion.[67] The same choreography is required for the 'Scale of Scales', which passes through all major
and minor keys. Over four octaves the two hands again alternate parallel
and contrary motion within the course of each key and mode (including,
as a final flourish, the chromatic scale).[68] Both appendices – the 'Suite of
Arpeggios' and the 'Scale of Scales' – are 'intended to be played through
without a break ... The Scale of Scales, in particular, requires great endurance [...] Play these exercises through once every day'.[69] I am indebted to
the Moscow Conservatoire-trained pianist Olena Shvetsova-van-Eker for a
demonstration of contemporary practice routines. Evidently, Russian traditions of teaching and practising these fundamentals of piano technique are
based closely on the manner that Leschetizky's pupils Brée and Prentner
advocated a century ago; the choreography of parallel and contrary motion
within the 'Suite of Arpeggios' and the 'Scale of Scales' is identical. This is
surely a testimony to the longevity of Leschetizky's influence upon Russian
pianism. It would be a fair assumption to state that this and other details
of piano technique were first introduced by Leschetizky, not in Vienna in
1902, but in St Petersburg during his tenure at the Conservatoire between
1862 and 1879. Stravinsky's sense of pianism was also, undoubtedly, formulated within this same context and tradition.

Prentner's volume was published two months later than Brée's and shares
many details with it, as one would expect, particularly as Leschetizky
declares his confidence in its author in a fulsome testimonial.[70] Significantly,
broad swathes of both volumes are based upon the sequence of chords indicated by the *Accordgruppe* (Prentner's term), such as hand position, chord
playing, broken chords, arpeggios and 'the recognition of the hand's physiognomy'.[71] Brée's illustrative cuts find no graphic equivalent in Prentner but
the sequence of chords which forms the musical substance of this pictorial
section is amplified in the latter publication. While, in Brée, the *Accordgruppe*
comprises twenty-six chords (Example 3.6a),[72] Prentner's thirty-four chords
allow for a more gradual and thorough transition through the sequence
(Example 3.6b).[73] It is clearly fundamental to the construction of a piano
technique along the lines advocated by Leschetizky.

Ex. 3.6a Malwine Brée, *The Groundwork of the Leschetizky Method* (1902): excerpt from Chapter 16, 'Chords'.

Ex. 3.6b Marie Prentner, *The Leschetizky Method* (1903): excerpt from Chapter 6, 'The Chord' – the *Accordgruppe*.

The similarity of these sequences must confirm that they reflect the same educational aims and derive, authentically (despite Gerig's misgivings) from the same source – Leschetizky himself. Brée's decision to display Leschetizky's own hand (in close-up, across twelve and a half pages), shaping each chord in the *Accordgruppe*, reflects the importance given in this tradition to correct hand position. His assistants must have given considerable attention to developing in their pupils a keen awareness of this: evidently, there was a correct position for *each* chord, involving control of the wrist, the hand, the curvature of the fingers and the exact location on the key where the notes should be depressed. These positions were then to be held, repeated and memorized until they could be anticipated in the air (in that intersection of physicality and concentration labelled by Leschetizky 'mental delineation'). Such detailed focus on the physiognomy of the hand is surely reflected in Kashperova's comments that reveal her concern that each pianist should become physically aware of the exact nature of their own hands. It was, indeed, an exact science.

Both disciples indicate how Leschetizky translated these chords into one-octave (later, multi-octave) arpeggios. Prentner has no recourse to illustrations in this section, but via a greater use of musical examples she may be considered more didactic than her colleague. Prentner's reading is also the more structured of the two, illustrating every slight modification by which, with the alteration of just one note at a time, this one-octave 'seed' is eventually transformed into flowing four-octave arpeggio-sequences that combine both parallel and contrary motion. Furthermore, she also indicates the stages required for the descending left hand, while Brée's illustrations are restricted to showing the right hand ascending. This would suggest nevertheless that, when combined, the fundamental relationship between the hands, according to Leschetizky, is contrary motion. Beside its role in developing finger-dexterity, the *Accordgruppe* is also to be used as the basis for finger-strengthening and hand extension. Here Prentner offers a panoply of Leschetizky's most challenging drills based on rapid arpeggiated chords, ascending and descending, plus a section of progressively more demanding permutations where one or more notes are held down during the exercise. Her final word on the application of the *Accordgruppe* carries far-reaching consequences: 'This group of chords is to be transposed into all keys. Exercises of great value for the flexibility of the fingers can be made out of them.'[74] This somewhat chilling instruction is clearly directed more at piano teachers than pupils. The precise means that Kashperova employed to develop the young Stravinsky's technique must certainly have related to, if not directly derived from, the methods employed in her training during her recent years at the Conservatoire. There is every reason to suppose, therefore, that she employed Leschetizkian models such as these. Reminders to transpose the *Accordgruppe* exercises to all keys reflect the thoroughness and effort that both parties were expected to invest. The educational policies by which Leschetizky is represented in these two volumes are of undoubted relevance to the further understanding of Stravinsky's relationship with the piano. The twin-foundations to Leschetizky's teaching method (the chord/arpeggio *Accordgruppe* and the physiognomy of the hand) explain much about Stravinsky's response to piano technique. His engagement with this particular brand of pianism spanned the years from his early encounter with such techniques in St Petersburg, to their later re-working within a series of compositions whose characteristics were eventually labelled 'neo-classical', and beyond, very possibly, to the late serial works.

As the eighteen-year-old Stravinsky implied (in his 1900 letter to his parents, referred to earlier)[75] his study with Kashperova undoubtedly stimulated his awareness of, and respect for, *pal'tserazvitiye*, i.e. pianistic exercises. Only six months after initiating lessons with Kashperova Stravinsky had evidently become aware of a higher responsibility towards piano study. His correspondence would clearly suggest that he can now differentiate between holiday piano playing of the kind enjoyed on the dacha's upright in Ustilug and the serious business of piano practice on the grand piano at Kryukov Canal. As if to emphasize the contrast between these two universes the Russian word for 'piano' employed by Stravinsky in his correspondence on the subject is not the usual term *pianino* or *forte-piano*. (This means upright piano and is used in this sense by Varunts, for example, in his caption to the photo referred to earlier – see p.269n90 – of Yuri, Ekaterina and Igor Stravinsky gathered around the dacha piano at Ustilug.) Instead, Stravinsky employs the French-derived *royal'* – a term which invariably refers to a grand, or concert instrument. In this early example of his celebrated lexicographical sensitivity Stravinsky is clearly communicating to his parents the seriousness of his pianistic intentions. He does not mean the usual *playing around* at the piano (for which he already had a certain reputation). The holidays are over, he is back in St Petersburg and tomorrow he will re-engage with an established practice routine. This is a small but significant indication of musical maturity in this late developer. Under the influence of Mlle Kashperova, 'playing the piano' now signified dedication to the development of his technique according to *pal'tserazvivatel'nïkh* [*zanyatii*] ('finger-development [exercises]'), i.e. five-finger exercises specifically programmed by his teacher and which required his responsible application. At least, Stravinsky respected the need for them. From Kashperova he learned not only the knowledge of how to acquire an advanced piano technique; equally importantly, she also taught him the mental discipline of practising the long hours necessary to maintain it. One may surmise that it was this exceptionally solid foundation that provided Stravinsky with the professional footing upon which he was able to prepare for his professional debut twenty years later.[76]

Stravinsky, with his penchant for improvising and an awakening interest in the rudiments of music, would surely have been intrigued by the musical 'anarchy' that exercises of the *Accordgruppe* variety present. Diatonically and developmentally the sequence is 'non-sense' and without equivalent in musical literature. It appears to confound the rudiments of music, particularly those laws of harmony and related traditions of 'musical sense' that govern, for example, the tasteful balance of phrase-lengths. Yet such meanderings can hardly be classified as errors when part of improvisation or harmless experimentation. According to musical theory Leschetizky's *Accordgruppe*, for example, could only be represented in print in the form of an exercise; for technical drills (not being performed publicly) are considered outside the jurisdiction of musical laws. They are just too far removed from the true art of music which, by contrast, *is* performed and must therefore be subject to artful critique concerning taste, style, interpretation and related issues of *musikalisches Geschmack*. Yet here, in the finger-development exercise, is a form of music devoid of style, not critiqued for its taste (nor even for lack of it) and where the question of its 'interpretation' is plainly irrelevant. This music can only be executed – either correctly or incorrectly. Yet, it is not entirely without interest, even when judged on musical terms. When executed well, it is not devoid of impact and can be appreciated by both performer and listener; however, its musicality is defined by the limits of its musical 'sense', which is perceived as existing somewhere outside the force field of history's diatonic conventions. Put bluntly, piano methods are not considered to be music at all, though they are *the means to music*. As such, pedagogic drills represent the raw materials of the pianist's craft. For Stravinsky, pianism was a craft he relished. And his enthusiastic portrayal of composition as (another) one of music's crafts, under the banner of neo-classicism, may well be attributed to his respect for the processes of pianism that he became acquainted with during his years with Kashperova. For a composer who preferred the processes of creation to admiring the finished result, the workshop of piano study and his engagement with its materials would have undoubtedly lent the graft of practice a creative edge.

Besides the principal function of these techniques as piano practice, this arpeggio-based form of study would certainly have stimulated Stravinsky's compositional ear as well, in other poignant respects. Writing from personal experience the present author can affirm that the experience of playing these drills in the manner indicated, i.e. with constantly varying dynamic gradations between *crescendos* and *diminuendos*, does give the musical ear a sensation of sonorous and physical energy. And within this shimmering, jangling sound-world, the ear inevitably follows the movement of those notes that change, one at a time and from one pattern to the next, as if they were forming an inner voice. It is inevitable that the moving notes are perceived more clearly – as in the foreground of an image or as a sculptured inscription, carved in relief. Furthermore, by repeating this sequence of chords and arpeggios on a daily basis – and by subjecting the *Accordgruppe* to transposition – it no longer appears to be devoid of harmonic progression. It establishes its own musical logic. The sheer habit of repetition acclimatizes the ear, encouraging it to lend this odd progression a sense of normality such that, if one omits the smallest part, one's ear is immediately disturbed as if the fingers had played a wrong note. Likewise, an accurate rendering of the arpeggios, in order, provides a pleasing sense of correctness equivalent to the smooth performance of a diatonic harmonic progression. Perhaps this is due to our view of the *Accordgruppe* from the perspective of the twenty-first century, yet one cannot but suspect that the capacity of familiarity to breed a sense of order and normality is indeed limitless.

As Leschetizky's *Accordgruppe* unfolds, the constant adjustment from one pattern to the next, by one or two notes at a time, conveys subtle variations in the degree of consonance and dissonance. These shifting harmonic fields, as Prentner advises, are not to be understood as progressions with a linear tonal logic. It is precisely this lack of 'goal-orientation' that links the *Accordgruppe* to a characteristic of Stravinsky's future compositional style. Writing in 1947, White observed such a characteristic in the latter part of *Hymne*, the opening movement of the *Sérénade*: '[This] provides a good example of how Stravinsky may take a straightforward arpeggio accompaniment proceeding in waves and, by careful manipulation of the inner parts – sometimes accelerating, sometimes retarding the natural note changes – succeed in endowing a simple harmonic device with all sorts of contrapuntal implications.'[77] White's observation could serve as a description of exercises from Leschetizky's *Accordgruppe* method, for he notes with accuracy the 'contrapuntal implications' that arise from 'manipulation of the inner parts'. Prior to the *Sérénade* instances of what Taruskin refers to as 'musical mobiles' positively abound in the music of the Swiss years, a characteristic example of which is the set of *Detskiye pesenki* (*Trois histoires pour enfants*) of 1920. The accompaniment to the first song, 'Tilim-bom' (as already observed), is particularly notable for its centripetal revolutions reminiscent of the broken-chord drills of the pianist at practice.[78]

That Stravinsky was intensely attracted to 'waves of arpeggios' as early as 1914 would be confirmed by Edwin Evans 'one Sunday morning' in the summer of that year, and in a most surprising way:

> Stravinsky and I took a taxi and, roaming around the deserted City of London, came upon St Paul's Cathedral just as the bells were pealing. Stravinsky stopped the cab, and listened intently to the 'changes', taking occasional notes on the back of an envelope. He was most enthusiastic about the inexhaustible variety of the sequences in which he claimed to hear the most wonderful music.[79]

Stravinsky's annotations are accompanied by his own caption which reads: 'The bells of St Paul's in London. Astonishingly beautiful counterpoint such as I have never heard in my life' (Figure 3.6).[80] The use of the term 'counterpoint' is interesting. Craft understandably interprets this as indicating that Stravinsky was hearing cross-rhythms from the simultaneous pealing from more than one church – 'Wren's churches'. I would argue, however, that Stravinsky was attracted to this recital of 'changes' out of joyous *recognition* – this, mingled with the impact of hearing an example of the uniquely varied and melodic tradition of English bell-ringing 'such as I have never heard in my life'. His reaction was of someone unexpectedly meeting an old

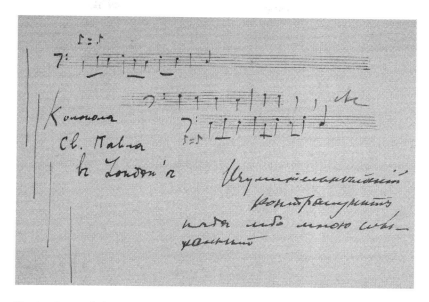

Fig. 3.6 Stravinsky's annotation of the peals of St Paul's Cathedral, London (June 1914), held at the Paul Sacher Stiftung, Basel.

friend in the street who (without his foreknowledge) had been released from distant incarceration… Such was Stravinsky's long and secret acquaintance with this music in the solitary confinement of his piano practice. Within earshot of St Paul's he marvelled at (to use Evans's term) an 'inexhaustible variety of … sequences' which evoked those labyrinthine resonances that had for so long intrigued him but which had remained captive within the inner ear of his musical imagination.

The composer's reference to counterpoint in his caption is also an accurate description of what happens when rendering sequences of arpeggios at the piano in similarly interminable cycles, as in the *Accordgruppe*. Indeed, there is much in common between Wren's peal of bells and Leschetizky's piano keyboard – these two diverse 'instruments' whose repertoires consist of 'ringing the changes'. Furthermore, both Wren's peal and Leschetizky's piano are restricted in their permutations by their confinement to a limited number of pitches, within a restricted 'envelope'. Their respective renditions are performed for the benefit, primarily, of the executants themselves and also share the characteristic of unfolding over a considerable time-frame and in a pre-conceived, thorough plan of execution. Neither do they follow a goal-oriented progression of harmonies. They offer no beginning and no end, but present a continuum wherein there is no arrival, no perfect cadence nor even much sense of finality. The peal of bells and the *Accordgruppe* can only stop when the permutations are complete (or when, as is more common, the rendition breaks down for technical reasons).[81] However, the most fundamental of all their commonalities is their paradox: that sense of inertia at the heart of what, on the surface, transmits great energy. This is derived from the fact that, although the peals and 'sequences' have their own rigorous logic, this appears quite arbitrary compared with harmonic progressions born of the tonal universe. Both 'musics' move agitatedly, but go nowhere. As such, they are the paradigm of the musical mobile by which image Taruskin chooses to explain the Stravinskian trope of immobility – in Russian, *nepodvizhnost'*.

Stravinsky was certainly receptive to the finer effects of syncopation and accent produced by the shifting patterns of inner notes within finger-drills, whether their provenance was Czerny, Leschetizky, Philipp or Stravinsky. Unevenness of volume is more pronounced in a church peal than on the piano owing to the lack of rhythmic precision at the moment of change – even in the hands of experienced ringers – and owing to the varying timbres of the bells. Those with sensitive musical antennae can easily distinguish these small imperfections; thus, the overall texture is experienced in such a manner that these minute variations of rhythm or pitch are identified, indeed welcomed as moments of special interest – as *moments musicaux*. The intensity of Stravinsky's reaction would be well accounted for in the context of his intimate acquaintance with literature designed also, and specifically, to explore the subtle and constant permutation of notes through dedicated, daily repetition. For, as the Brée and Prentner methods make abundantly clear, piano technique taught in the Leschetizky School was grounded upon the intricate adjustment of the five fingers often with the purpose of extending the span of each hand.[82] Looking ahead to Stravinsky's later output – particularly, his neoclassical and serial scores – it is this syntax of permutation that underpins much of the musical fabric as experienced, for example, in the subtle inter-relationship between pitches, rhythms, accents and restrictive harmonic fields.

Taruskin's nepodvizhnost' *re-considered*

In *Stravinsky and the Russian Traditions* Taruskin names *nepodvizhnost'* ('immobility') as one of three 'solid Turanian virtues' which, together with *drobnost'* ('sum-of-parts') and *uproshcheniye* ('simplification'), are 'qualities inimical to the linear, harmony-driven temporality of Western classical music'.[83] Furthermore, in his concluding remarks – after more than 1,600 pages of persuasive reasoning – he declares that this triumvirate of

Stravinsky's most essential characteristics 'informs his mature works from first to last with rare authenticity and constancy'.[84] It may seem churlish to quarrel with this thesis which underpins such an extensively researched evaluation of Stravinsky's music. Still, the plain fact is – and Taruskin himself shows full awareness of this[85]– the three Russian terms upon which his case is founded represent concepts that have been imposed upon Stravinsky's music. *Nepodvizhnost'*, for example, is a label inspired originally by the 'ostinato-driven music' of *The Rite of Spring* and is particularly applicable to 'the vamping pieces of the Swiss decade'.[86] It is certainly this, though (again) it was not the composer himself who identified and baptized the concept. The reservations I have with all three Turanian 'qualities' are rooted in their lack of authentic cohesion, however conveniently they may be applied to Stravinsky's music and despite the impressive chronology of their application. In the case of *nepodvizhnost'* the greater problem lies with the tendency to illustrate this term via pictorial or otherwise folkloric baggage, for this distracts attention from its essentially musical quality. This misrepresentation then colours the very prose which ought, more appropriately, to be concerned with the concept's objectivity – thus has one such reading of the *Three Pieces for String Quartet* (1914) clearly affected the musicological commentary. Ansermet's programme note for the first London performance (in 1919) declares that the first movement represents 'a group of peasants singing and dancing against the monotonous background of the steppes'.[87] Such imagery leads Taruskin to his own cultural-climatic associations: '[The] piece develops … the rhythmic *nepodvizhnost'*, [that is] the *frozen* immobility created in *The Rite* by the use of ostinati. Here [in the first movement of the string quartet] there are two *frozen* levels.'[88] This sensory association then diverges from musical reality and analytical objectivity still further by indulging in a thoroughly graphic, even decorative, choice of terminology: 'The result is what we have called a mobile … The "musical mobile" was an important stylistic resource throughout the Swiss years and beyond.'[89] Identified, somewhat confusingly, as 'the most immobile pieces' of all are the *Trois pièces faciles*, the *Tsvetochniy Val's*, the 'Figaro' Waltz and 'several of the *Cinq pièces faciles*' – a judgement based on their similarity as 'wind-up toy automata' constructed upon 'a single ostinato for the duration'.

Within this notion of immobility, *nepodvizhnost'* now must accommodate both 'the musical mobile' (from which springs an image of gently rotating baubles) and 'the genre of toy "automata"' (which, to some, may suggest jerky, robotic movements). Yet despite the argument that the most immobile pieces include the *Cinq pièces faciles*, 'the genre of the automata [is] not "coexistive" with that of the "easy" or children's pieces'.[90] Is one to understand, then, that the difference between the infantile genre with its single ostinato and the 'art' genre – of which the first movement of the String Quartet (with its 'multiplicity of hypostatized ostinati')[91] is cited as a prime example – is this very 'multiplicity'? The importance of addressing this question cannot be understated when Robert Craft is moved to declare that 'the *Trois pièces faciles* are [no less than] landmarks in Stravinsky's art, which cannot be said of the national songs and dances of the *Cinq [pièces faciles]*'.[92] Whatever the rationale behind Taruskin's segregation he admits that the String Quartet's first movement 'carries the device to extremes'. While one broadly comprehends his point, the case is not enhanced by a less-than-clear comparison between 'devices' from which there are now four possibilities to choose: the musical mobile, the genre of (toy) automata, hypostatized ostinati and *nepodvizhnost'*. Taruskin relates them to the 'Augures printaniers' and 'Cercles mystérieux' of *The Rite* (and, indirectly, to the *garmoshka* music in *Petrushka*), yet not one of these terms adequately appertains to all the contexts that he wishes to illustrate. He further credits *nepodvizhnost'* with being an 'important stylistic resource' within and well beyond the Swiss decade, citing the 'Petit concert' from *Histoire du soldat* (1918), the coda to the finale of *Pulcinella* (1919/20), the 'Russian Maiden's Song' from *Mavra* (1921/2) and the *Requiem Canticles* (1965–6). Despite the yawning gap of four decades between the two latter works it is still an attractive proposition: no matter the compositional idiom, Stravinsky's entire output – from the great ballets to the serial works – is interwoven with three Turanian threads. Indeed, once *nepodvizhnost'* has been traced backwards 'to the *vesnyanki* and *petrivki* of the immemorial agrarian calendar'[93] the theory can be seen to encapsulate most perfectly a study that otherwise illuminates 'newly available archival source materials and … a wealth of Russian documents linguistically inaccessible to most Western musicologists'[94] in what is, in every other regard, a model of generous and rational musicological research. However, I would gladly exchange four constructed (and conflicting) terms[95] for *one* that has been endorsed by the composer himself and which unifies the aforementioned devices by a single and, importantly, purely musical concept. For this reason I propose the addition of *pal'tserazvitiye* to the Stravinskian lexis, awkward linguistic construct as this may at first appear to non-Russian speakers. Through re-consideration of the composer's youth and his pianistic origins, Stravinsky's own term *pal'tserazvitiye* more accurately reflects his life-long interest in the two creative processes of composition and piano practice as 'the means to music'. So potent and yet so humble was this musical/gestural seed that the mature composer never adequately acknowledged his debt, effectively erasing its traces from (his version of) the sands of time.

'Philipp' and Balanchine

> It is important to devote some practice on a daily basis to finger gymnastics.
>
> Isidor Philipp, *Exercices journaliers* (1897)

As we know from the testimony of Otto Klemperer,[96] Stravinsky sought guidance from Isidor Philipp in the earliest days of his career as a concert pianist.[97] Philipp's methods, based on classical finger-technique, must have seemed an endorsement of many of Stravinsky's long-held views. It was an encounter that had a primary, practical goal; but working with Philipp must also have reinforced an awareness of the fundamental notion of musical process, which Stravinsky would have experienced again from within a learning environment. By simultaneously composing and practising the Piano Concerto he would have been reminded how educational procedures are creative in a way comparable to the clear-headed and deliberate act of compositional craft. Both proceed on the basis of gradual innovation, repetition, evaluation and selection. Together they take a progressive, constructive path towards attaining their objectives. Such a reading would confirm Agawu's viewpoint, cited earlier, that musical composition as re-composition is best understood within the ambit of musical pedagogy, where originality is subservient to the goal of technical perfection.[98] In a didactic framework transcription, arrangement, improvisation, imitation and the synthesis of pre-existing material are all considered to be forms of originality and encouraged as a matter of course. Kashperova and the St Petersburg tradition (as exemplified in Leschetizky) now encountered in Paris another great European piano tradition through the *grand personnage* of Philipp, who was for a short time Stravinsky's private teacher. There can be little doubt that Koussevitsky's suggestion – made in the autumn of 1923 – that Stravinsky himself should premiere the Piano Concerto in Paris the following spring was the spur for the composer to seek pianistic guidance of the highest order. Following his auspicious debut in May 1924, Stravinsky required someone who could supervise every aspect of his preparations for the greater challenge of maintaining a level of pianism – and a professional attitude – to cope with repeated performances of this new work. It was to be his first return to the piano pupil's bench for over two decades.

Stravinsky could have confidence that his new teacher – whose reputation as a specialist in piano technique and as a voluminous author of pedagogical literature was second to none at that time – would concern himself with pianistic issues rather than stylistic or interpretative questions. Henry Bellamann confirms that 'the greater part of what constitutes [Philipp's] essential teaching is the result of restless and endless experimentation, during which he quite simply discovered *what would work, and work quickly*'[99] – an invaluable gift of perception, and most useful given Stravinsky's predicament. Stravinsky would also have been favourably inclined towards Philipp's aesthetic sympathies of *clarté*, *simplicité* and *précision*, those French virtues particularly associated with the late sonatas of Debussy, *musicien français*, and with those of Philipp's life-long mentor and friend, Saint-Saëns.

Stravinsky's omission adequately to acknowledge his debt to Philipp must, one assumes, be due to sensitivity that given the celebrity status of the composer it would have been inconsistent to have portrayed himself as anything less than the master of all he purveyed – much less to be seen as a student, still, of an instrument for which he was writing compositions in an idiom that might be taken as a concession to his pianistic shortcomings.[100] It would therefore have been paramount for Stravinsky that any course of piano tuition at this stage in his career be conducted with the utmost discretion.[101] For this reason, perhaps, Stravinsky made no reference to Philipp in his *Autobiography* beyond a brief comment concerning the benefits that young American pianists would undoubtedly have gained from studying in Paris with Nadia Boulanger and with Philipp, to whom he refers as 'invaluable teachers … eminent masters'.[102] It is very possible that Stravinsky arrived at the door of Isidor Philipp on the recommendation of Nadia Boulanger. They were colleagues on the faculty of the Franco-American Conservatory which had opened at Fontainebleau in 1921, and Philipp had been a close friend of the Boulanger family for a considerable time. Leonie Rosenstiel's biography *Nadia Boulanger: A Life in Music* carries a photograph (dated 1907) showing a well-attended garden party at the home of the pianist Raoul Pugno.[103] Nadia Boulanger's Russian-born mother Raissa – whose husband had been a former winner of the Prix de Rome[104] – is seen standing beside Isidor Philipp. Although Philipp was on the jury of the Paris Conservatoire which had voted, in 1909, against Boulanger's application to become professor of piano accompaniment,[105] by 1921 they were working alongside each other at Fontainebleau. According to Rosenstiel, Philipp's stature was a major draw for the new intake of American students: 'He had built a great reputation in the States for his articles on piano technique and interpretation in *Etude* magazine as well as for his performances.'[106] If Stravinsky had sought Boulanger's advice – as is likely – on where to turn for help, one may easily comprehend the context, and reasons, behind her recommendation that he should approach Philipp. It is, then, not through Stravinsky himself but through others – and almost forty years after the event – that one learns of his course of tuition with Philipp at this crucial time. Otto Klemperer, interviewed in 1961 by the Zurich journal *Die Tat*, reveals that 'at a mature age Igor Stravinsky took piano lessons from Isidor

Philipp in Paris'.[107] Klemperer's credentials as a reliable witness are not to be doubted, for it was under his baton that Stravinsky performed the Piano Concerto in Wiesbaden in 1925, on the occasion that elicited the oft-quoted anecdote concerning the manner with which the composer admonished the conductor at the first rehearsal for too expressive a rendering of the Largo introduction. As Klemperer was later to recall: 'I did the orchestral introduction a little too romantically and Stravinsky said, "No, no. You must think of Savonarola." Then I understood.'[108] Walsh supports the view that Stravinsky admired Klemperer and 'liked his respectful and painstaking attitude to new music, in contrast to the lordly conservatism of most German conductors'.[109] Such was the mutual respect between them that Klemperer won the right to conduct the Berlin premiere of the Concerto in 1929 – with Stravinsky as soloist – and programmed the work with *Les Noces* and *Apollo*, the latter completed only the previous year. Mutual admiration generates a spirit of trust and a freer exchange of private disclosures than is normal between those whose acquaintance is more distant. There is, therefore, good reason to have faith in Klemperer's word, even to believe that he was informed by Stravinsky himself of his studies with Philipp.

Vera Stravinsky and Robert Craft, who cite Klemperer in 1978, confirm the profound impact of the composer's association with Philipp stating that Stravinsky based his whole piano-training ritual upon a key Philipp text for more than two decades subsequent to this initial and possibly sole course of lessons. 'In fact', they write, 'Stravinsky took lessons from Philipp in 1924 before playing the Piano Concerto, and during the next twenty-two years practised exercises from Philipp's *Complete School of Technic for the Pianoforte* (Philadelphia: Theodore Presser, 1908)'.[110] One must take note of such testimony, for there are no other individuals who shared and witnessed Stravinsky's domestic rituals so closely or for so long. However convincing the case may be that Kashperova was accustomed to advocating Leschetizky's materials and practice techniques in her tutelage of the young Stravinsky, it must remain a matter of informed conjecture. By contrast, here is clear evidence of Stravinsky's adoption of Philipp's didactic literature as the basis to his piano technique throughout his fifteen-year concert career and beyond. How much more relevant and revelatory, therefore, might Stravinsky's intimate association be with the methods of this iconic representative of the French school of pianism? And how would this collaboration impact on the construction of Stravinsky's neoclassical idiom and the desire to create his own performance tradition?

Joseph's claim regarding the importance of Philipp's method as a 'guiding influence of [Stravinsky's] piano writing',[111] and his affirmation that 'one of the great underestimates in Stravinsky scholarship is of just how important these pianistic, tactile models were in shaping the composer's writing during this period',[112] can only be supported in the light of the above research into Stravinsky's heritage from his earlier phases of pianistic education. Joseph bases his observations upon parallels (which, unfortunately, he refrains from drawing) between annotations in the composer's copy of the *Complete School* and the pianistic writing in Stravinsky's works of the early 1920s:

> Those familiar with the *Piano Concerto*, and the slightly later *Sonata* and *Sérénade en la*, will immediately understand: it is impossible to miss their reliance on Philipp's exercises as useful models. Many of the compositional sketches for these works reveal that Stravinsky experimented with various fingerings for certain sections that are similar to those found in his copy of Philipp's manual. Much of the idiosyncratic passage work of Stravinsky's piano writing in the 1920s owes greatly to Philipp's influence.[113]

Czerny is credited with providing 'a clear pianistic model' for *Capriccio* (1929, revised 1949), as Joseph declares that this work 'virtually lifts passages from Czerny that the composer studied and marked. And, like Philipp's exercises, several of Czerny's *études* (all bearing the composer's notations) had provided Stravinsky with an important compositional prototype for the earlier *Concerto for Piano and Winds* in 1923.'[114] Joseph's tantalizing contribution implies that Stravinsky's long-guarded fascination with aspects of piano study impacted on his creative work too. There is no doubt that there are passages in *Capriccio* that resemble extracts from a pianist's practice-hour, whether or not they can be traced (as Joseph proposes) directly to specific, published methods. A particularly idiosyncratic aspect of Stravinsky's piano writing in these neoclassical works is the use of wide intervals and leaps in the left hand. There is scant precedence for this, either in musical literature or in drills and studies of a technical purpose, beyond the studies of Henselt (already commented on above, p. 20). This was, evidently, a sonority that appealed to Stravinsky; and, owing to his own wide hand-stretch, it was one that he could manage better than most. He was surely aware, too, that other pianists would find this a truly virtuosic element, its inclusion justified in *concertante* works. However, the right hand does betray, on occasion, a pattern to its melodic *ritornello* traceable directly to the workshop of piano study. In Example 3.7 Stravinsky underscores thematic material in the winds with passage-work that gives every impression of being based on technical exercises of a wide variety. Rising and falling scales – transposed, step-by-step, in the manner of a pianist rattling through the keys – lead into an extended exploitation of chromatic runs and melodic ('linked') thirds to produce a result that resembles, as it were, a 'concert-paraphrase on Czerny'.

Ex. 3.7 Stravinsky, *Capriccio*, 1st movement, Figs. 14 and 15.

Ex. 3.7 (*cont.*)

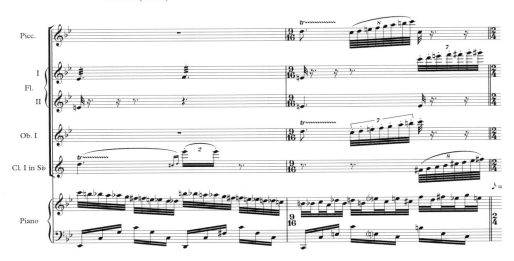

Whether this passage suggests the hand of Czerny alone is debatable, for the student of Philipp's *Complete School* is also well served with material of this nature. In a sense such conjecture is unnecessary; Stravinsky was perfectly capable of devising or improvising such material to suit his need. The point is, surely, that such passage-work – shared between the soloist and the orchestral instruments – fulfilled pianistic *and* compositional functions: the music sounds like an *étude* and the performer appears to be enacting, momentarily, the efforts of a pianist-at-work. It is a 'pedagogical instant' similar to so many presented, for example, by the *Symphony of Psalms* (to be discussed later).[115] This great work – consistent with Stravinsky's neoclassical idiom – can also, on occasion, give the distinct impression of being, on paper, a mere compositional exercise, and in performance an orchestra-in-rehearsal – a 'sectional' at half-speed. Such references demonstrate that dual aspect of Stravinsky's neoclassicism: while the performer in Stravinsky rehearses the music, the composer in Stravinsky – to borrow a term from Christopher Small – 'musicks', i.e. portrays the rehearsal.[116]

Further insight into the pianistic philosophy to which Stravinsky may be seen to have so fully committed himself can be obtained by comparing the approaches of other French pedagogues of the period: Marguerite Long, with whom Philipp had much in common, and Alfred Cortot, whose manner of teaching may be viewed as the antithesis of the Long/Philipp/Stravinsky approach. Long's own publications – particularly those that recall her personal experiences 'at the piano with' Fauré, Debussy and Ravel – would suggest that her principal contribution was to recent French repertoire. Yet her editorial interests lay in the eighteenth century and in Mendelssohn – Long edited the complete Mozart Sonatas and four Piano Concertos (nos. 20, 23, 24 and 27) as well as the complete *Songs without Words*. Her pupils testify to the importance she gave to technique in her lessons. Many are the references to identical priorities in Philipp's teaching approach, including the development of finger-technique (i.e. without weight from the arms or shoulders), clear articulation, sparing use of the pedal, the *jeu perlé* – and total respect for the composer's score. Gaby Casadesus confirms that she was 'a very good teacher for clear finger technique. We did a lot of Hanon, Czerny, and Clementi and it all had to be memorized.' Jeanne-Marie Darré recalls Long's preference for certain technical material: 'I remember we did a great deal of technique … Like Philipp, she taught technique basically from the knuckle and wrist. For me, Philipp was an extension of Long's technical outlook, and I got even more from him.'[117]

Nicole Henriot-Schweitzer's recollections confirm the similarity of approach between Long and Philipp where several details and attitudes would have met with Stravinsky's approval, particularly their 'great respect for the score'.[118] Long's aversion to the pedal was echoed by Philipp, and in this Stravinsky would have recalled his own childhood experiences at the hands of Kashperova: 'Long did not have a very sophisticated idea of pedalling. She used to say "The pedal is for hiding problems."'[119] Henriot-Schweitzer goes on to confirm (with Darré) that Philipp was even more forceful a personality (in his quiet way): 'I would say that [Long's] technical ideas could always be used as a base – unlike the technique that Philipp taught, which had to be taken entirely or not at all.'[120] Stravinsky's commitment to Philipp's *Complete Technic* over the next two decades would confirm this view.

Gabriel Tacchino offers a particularly clear indication of how the Long/Philipp approach contrasted with other current piano trends when he states: 'Her technique was the opposite of the Russian school – not much weight, not much sound.'[121] Yet Marguerite Long was surely not alone in recognizing the qualities in other national methods; Philipp too would have been alert to the boldly differing characteristics of the young pianists trained in Moscow and St Petersburg who were travelling to the West with increasing frequency to enter piano competitions, or to form part of the buoyant circle of touring, recital-giving virtuosi.[122] However, and despite obvious respect for the Russian pianists, if anything was to tax Philipp's famed good nature it was the sight of a pupil crossing the line to the enemy camp. His pupil Paul Loyonnet subsequently studied with Martinus Sieveking,[123] a leading disciple of Leschetizky – a move which for a French pianist was most unusual. Loyonnet recalled: 'Philipp never forgave me for it. Many years later, when

I asked for a re-conciliation [*sic*] with him, he refused.'[124] Quite clearly then, at the time Stravinsky studied with Philipp there was still a distinct national identification within the various trends of French pianism.

The Long/Philipp model was not the sole voice of French pianism. Cortot approached piano teaching from the perspective of his all-round musicianship – between 1898 and 1901 he had worked at Bayreuth as choral coach, later assistant to Mottl and Richter.[125] His wide experience of music beyond the limitations of the piano repertoire belies the reputation of his Chopin editions. His pupils recall how he imparted an inspirational example, drawing upon his immense musical personality. Marthe Morhange-Motchance called this 'artistic teaching', declaring that 'he threw us straight into a bath of music, forming our taste and enthusiasm for all things beautiful. His teaching was a mixture of pianism, aesthetics, and history. He opened a whole generation of French pianists to new ways of thinking about music, ways that went far beyond *the usual considerations of good fingers and good rhythm*.'[126] Gaby Casadesus identifies these wider interests amongst others within the French camp: 'Many people associate [the "French school"] with Madame Long and Isidor Philipp. But there were other ways of playing here – think of Cortot, Risler, Lazare-Lévy, and Blanche Selva ... Another great French pianist who was different from Long and Philipp was Francis Planté, a really wonderful Chopin player.'[127] Yet despite their differences, the elder statesmen of piano tuition working in Paris in the 1920s would have recognized their common provenance in Chopin, many of whose characteristics – including agile finger-pianism, restrained sensitivity and modest volume – had been transmitted to them, directly or indirectly, via Chopin's pupil Georges Mathias. Casadesus goes so far as to comment on how 'Philipp used the same diminished seventh chord as the basis for his exercises as Chopin used for some of his.'[128] References to Philipp inevitably concern questions of technique, Gaby Casadesus revealing that she and her husband (Robert Casadesus) both employed Philipp exercises in their own teaching 'if a student needs some stretching' – a comment which suggests a further and specific reason why Stravinsky, with his long-standing engagement with *pal'tserazvitiye*, would have deemed Philipp's brand of technical orientation most useful, if not essential, to his urgent need for pianistic fortification. Stravinsky would have recognized the fundamental correctness of a teacher whose reputation was founded on technique and on modes of practice that reinforced the importance of finger-stretching through chords and their arpeggio derivatives – i.e. those very elements of Kashperova's teaching that he had come to value above all others. Indeed, one suspects that these were the only elements of piano teaching that interested him. Stravinsky's practical sense would have diverted him away from a teacher

Ex. 3.8 Isidor Philipp, *Exercices pratiques (Introduction aux exercices journaliers)* op. 9, p. 290.

who might have wished to discuss the interpretation of other composers' music, and he would clearly not have wished to discuss the 'interpretation' of his own.[129] By approaching Philipp, Stravinsky clearly sought to build a piano technique adequate not only for one performance, but for an entire career – and he was prepared, patiently, to assemble his technique upon the scaffolding of Philipp's construction manual.

Two characteristically Philippian traits – revealed both in print and from reports of his private lessons – demonstrate his didactic philosophy, and suggest how such techniques were of interest to Stravinsky in mirroring his own compositional concerns. Philipp advocates transposing every exercise into all the keys *while using the same fingering*.[130] This recalls the section of the Piano Concerto noted earlier, where Stravinsky indicates his own fingering for the passage in an unchanging use of 5,4,2,1 regardless of this pattern's appropriateness to the pianist's comfort – or so it seems.[131] While Philipp may be inflexible with regards to the fingering, he constantly exhorts the student to experiment rhythmically according to specific indications (as with 'Rythmes: 7/8' in Example 3.8), or through the use of accents variously placed on different degrees of the drill. Philipp had built his reputation upon this very aspect which, as far back as 1897, he had claimed as his 'system of accent displacement and rhythmic modification'.[132]

Such was the association of Philipp's name with this technique, the Introduction to the *Complete School* states that it 'need scarcely be added

Ex. 3.9 Isidor Philipp, *Complete School of Technic for the Piano* (1908), from 'Exercises in Velocity', p. 8.

that, carrying out M. Philipp's ideas, the rhythmic system is to be used in the preparatory practice of all passages occurring in etudes and piano pieces'.[133] Stravinsky may have been interested, from a compositional angle, in Philipp's characteristic instruction to the pianist to enrich his practice with such rhythmic and accent variants. This is typical of Philipp's method and can be traced throughout his canon, as for example in the 'Exercises in Velocity' from the *Complete School of Technic* (Example 3.9).[134] Such a didactic work-out may have appealed to Stravinsky as a sonority that wears its permutations 'on its sleeve', in a demonstration of deliberate musical construction. An illustration of this can be seen (and heard) in the second movement of the *Symphony of Psalms*. The fugue subject in its original form is presented in even note-values. Thereafter Stravinsky alters his subject rhythmically 'in the Philippian manner' – for example, at the movement's *fortissimo* climax where three rhythmical variants are presented simultan-eously (Fig. 14): in the lower strings (doubled in the woodwinds and brass), in the timpani part and in the chorus. Prior to this *tutti* material Stravinsky presents a more lyrical, melodic version of the subject, on trombone (Fig. 13), while anticipating the subsequent Philippian dotted rhythms. The phrase illustrates once more the central elements of the movement in com-bination: i.e. contrapuntal, imitative woodwinds (followed in the next bar by a further entry of this same figure, on the horn) while the low-register instruments hold a(nother) pedal point.

Ex. 3.10 Isidor Philipp, *Complete School of Technic for the Piano*: excerpt from 'Chords', p. 98.

Other technical challenges explored by Philipp – for example, the extended and rapid *ritornello*, and inordinately widely spaced chords – appear to reflect Stravinskian imprints.[135] They would certainly have resonated with the composer, familiar with Russian models of pedagogy, as he addressed his daily practice. Particularly Leschetizkian is Philipp's employment of the chord-sequence. The *Complete School* contains an intriguing 'version' – *en format réduit* – of the *Accordgruppe* in the form of a six-chord pattern. Upon this sequence there is launched, as with Leschetizky, a gradually expanding series of broken chords and arpeggios, ascending and descending, to be transposed through the twelve degrees of the chromatic scale. Their familiar aim is to develop the extension of the hand and independence of the fingers, and to afford 'perfect preparation for shaping the hands to chord positions' (Example 3.10).[136]

In line with the Philippian tradition of 'rhythmic modification', the pupil is encouraged to experiment with the rhythm and continually vary other parameters. For example, Philipp recommends positioning the left hand two octaves lower than the right, as well as practising this and all exercises with and without the pedal. Stravinsky would have recognized these, too, as familiar concepts reflecting his own acquired values. Of particular relevance would have been his engagement with exercises (such as those discussed) that provided the 'means to piano technique' whilst *also* suggesting the 'means to musical composition'. Within the confines of Stravinsky's music studio the dual-manifestations of his neoclassicism – performance and composition – would have been well served during the two decades he spent religiously adhering to Philipp's routines. By the time he formulated his Harvard lectures he could write with the confidence of experience: 'My freedom [is] so much the greater and more meaningful the more narrowly I limit my field of action and the more I surround myself with obstacles.'[137] He appears to refer, in this passage, to *compositional* limits and the creative stimulus he derived from them. While one is tempted to read into this text an anticipation of Stravinsky's adoption of the greater compositional rigours of serialism, it may be more reasonable to understand this as a reference to past experience. Within the next decade his neoclassical chapter and his career as a concert pianist both drew to a close – a 'coincidence' that suggests that the one may indeed have nourished the other. After all, Stravinsky could have championed his serial music too from the soap-box of the piano stool, but he never did. The Septet and *Movements* could have provided him with pamphleteering opportunities – just as the *Sonate*, *Sérénade*, Piano Concerto and *Capriccio* had done in the past. He could have followed Second Viennese tradition by writing his first serial essays for piano solo and then, even, surpassed Schoenberg's example by performing (and recording) these compositions *himself*, but he did not.[138] The demands of maintaining a career as a concert pianist do not diminish with age, and by his seventies no-one could begrudge Stravinsky a permanent shuffle across to the conductor's rostrum or (with increasing enthusiasm) to Balanchine's dance studio.

Philipp can hardly be recognized as an artistic collaborator. There is not enough endorsement of this idea from Stravinsky himself to warrant awarding Philipp this title; nor is the interface between Philipp's method and Stravinsky's art nearly scientific enough. Nevertheless, 'Philipp' – as a model of pianistic discipline – must have represented a significant part of that referent of commodity, the piano, which Stravinsky mined during the years of neoclassical output. And Stravinsky would confirm his engagement with 'the benefits of artifice'[139] through his extended embrace of the *Complete School*. 'Philipp' offered him the raw materials for his daily rituals from whose limitations and constraints emerged performances and compositions of complete artistic freedom. Stravinsky's evident respect for Czerny and Philipp – and 'Kashperova/Leschetizky' – indicates that he read into these culturally diverse figures a commonality that transcended their dissimilarities. Much as Rimsky-Korsakov was drawn to the hieratic nature of counterpoint, Stravinsky also recognized in such methods

timeless qualities of the musical art that remain constant – regardless
of changes in idiom, aesthetics or any cultural-historical-geographica
l ambience. One may deduce that these pedagogues represented important role models through whom Stravinsky could access pre-romantic,
eighteenth-century paradigms of discipline ('order') and emotional
restraint ('objectivity'), while bypassing issues of style, musical character
and narrative. However, bonds such as these (formed via methodology) –
while important to a composer's daily work – do not necessarily qualify
as creative partnerships. Stravinsky certainly did not regard them as such.
Kashperova, one might say, he damned with faint praise; Czerny, at least,
he admired as a 'remarkable teacher' and a 'thoroughbred musician' without claiming him as any sort of meaningful (potentially artistic) point of
reference. Janet Mills, researching into pupil perceptions of conservatoire
teaching, has written of 'the tendency of musicians to focus on their teachers' foibles'.[140] One might read Stravinsky's behaviour in a similar light.
By never making public the nature of his debt to Philipp he was merely
exemplifying the lamentable, but archetypal, disrespect of a student for his
instrumental teacher.

Compared to 'Philipp', George Balanchine is the epitome of a true collaborator and Stravinsky acknowledged his importance to him throughout their long and productive association. He was, after all, a composer
too – of movement. Apart from Diaghilev there is hardly a more significant influence upon Stravinsky's output. Balanchine is credited with leading Stravinsky back to the theatre and to the composition of ballet scores
after his disenchantment with the Ballets Russes.[141] Their partnership over
four decades – from *Apollon musagète* in 1928 to *Requiem Canticles* in
1968 – resulted in several productions that have become iconic representa-
tions of the neoclassical arts as a whole. Particularly after his emigration
to the United States, Stravinsky could elaborate his aesthetic via musical
scores that were mirrored in Balanchine's 'abstract, non-anecdotal choreography'.[142] Theirs was a perfect match in the creation of artistic objects, for
the closeness of their understanding was quite remarkable and based upon
mutual respect. Stravinsky's knowledge of dance (and ability to demonstrate
the gestures he required) was balanced by Balanchine's considerable musicianship (extending well beyond his pianism, to arrangement and original
composition).[143] Both were talented improvisers (and clowns) on the studio
floor and at the piano. Furthermore, they shared a host of aesthetic and
practical traits. Balanchine also welcomed the constraints of a new commission (and all manner of 'limitations') as a liberating force; he wished
his choreographies to be transmitted, not interpreted ('Simply dance the

steps'); and he found the process of constructing a new ballet more reward-
ing than the finished result ('God creates, I assemble'). Like Stravinsky, he
considered creation to be a process, viewing the end result as something of
a by-product. Balanchine possessed an extraordinary sense of space, both
visual and aural, encouraging his dancers to 'see the music' while he would
extend this art to 'touching the sounds' as well – via the piano. Joseph has
written of Balanchine's 'spatial and temporal equipoise' with which, like
Stravinsky, he could understand 'the visual rhythms of a structure, like an
architect does, and … match them convincingly with underlying aural patterns'.[144] Stravinsky was later to comment that to see Balanchine's choreography of *Movements* 'is to hear the music with one's eyes', adding, with an
awareness of the unique and precious nature of their collaboration, 'this
visual hearing has been a greater revelation *to me*, I think, than to anyone
else'.[145]

At the very core of this partnership was the piano, for both Stravinsky and
Balanchine used the instrument as a functional tool with which to stimu-
late the imagination and work with those ideas. Just as, for Stravinsky, the
piano was a 'means to music', it was also, for Balanchine, a 'means to choreography'. Both were alert to the creative possibilities that tactile exploration
of the keyboard could uncover. Balanchine would respond to 'the interior
configuration of music – by touch, not just by sound'.[146] In short, he too considered his fingers to be inspirational. Metaphorically, the piano was at the
centre of all ballet rehearsals. Balanchine would arrive, place his metronome
on the piano and set Stravinsky's tempo with the rehearsal pianist. During
the session he would often return to the piano to run through the score
himself or, according to Joseph, in order to allow his visual imagination
to feed into the aural patterns through this physical contact with the notes
themselves: 'His dancers not only remember Balanchine playing the piano,
they remember him "noodling" … that is, letting his fingers roam freely
over whatever thoughts came to mind. In the process, the sounds seemed to
inspire choreographic setting of the lines or chords he hit upon.'[147] Musical
mechanics fascinated him; he found time to continue his studies of musical
theory and enjoyed devouring musical scores, excited (it seems) by the
intricacies of musical composition.[148] Clearly, Balanchine understood much
of music's machinations and would have appreciated Stravinsky's practical,
constructivist approach to musical work regarding their projects as processes, combinations and formulations building towards a finished product.
They clearly relished the journey – such that their understanding has been
described as 'a shared artistic belief, a mutually embraced ethnicity, a bind-
ing aesthetic, a methodical approach to creativity, a blending of pragmatism
and idealism and a veneration of classical order and structure'.[149] Recalling

his conversations with Soulima, Joseph ventures to equate Balanchine's creative 'noodlings' at the piano with Stravinsky's daily search for 'fingerprints … intently testing one chord after another, sometimes altering the spacing of a chord slightly … It was these subtleties that Balanchine understood, and understood not only instinctively but from the standpoint of a musician conversant with the fundamental principles of voice-leading.'[150]

Evidently, both men worked by raising structures one step, one note at a time. They accepted that gradual processes of selection and elimination were fundamental to the realization of a truly well-made object. It was, above all, a route free from hasty and emotional response, but guided by a clarity and deliberation that valued each unit of sound and each unit of movement. Furthermore, it valued the manner with which these elements were combined. A. S. Eddington has written, from a scientific stance, of our tendency to overlook the crucial element of interconnectivity: 'We often think that when we have completed our study of *one* we know all about *two*, because "two" is "one and one". We forget that we still have to make a study of "and".'[151] From an artistic stance, one might argue similarly that our perception of meaning (in this ultimately abstract sphere) depends to a significant degree on the connections, the in-between – upon our reading of that dynamic linking of concepts and thoughts to visual or aural outcomes. It is of vital importance and characterizes (our understanding of) the very act of creation. While we may recognize and later recall certain 'moments', our deeper appreciation is stimulated by an awareness of the whole as a series of processes, whether successfully realized or denied. This engagement with fluidity, it can be argued, even resides at the heart of our perception of the (immobile) plastic arts; our reading of painting and sculpture is also largely defined by our ability to make sense of line and 'movement' – and to recognize when these are being affirmed or frustrated. Connectivity is part of the illusion of experience that must be skilfully constructed in order to succeed. For Balanchine, as Suzanne Farrell recalled, 'dancing did not reside in the pose but within the *transitions*', adding: 'The act of getting from one step to another, and from one place to another, *is* the dancing.'[152] For both Balanchine and Stravinsky, preoccupied with the methodical processes of artistic object-building, the most useful means of winkling out the 'and' on a daily basis was via physical contact with the piano keyboard. While Balanchine, master choreographer, fed his creative work on musical stimulus, Stravinsky, master composer, fed his upon a diet of calisthenics – corporeal, but mainly digital.

While Balanchine could impress with his musical talents, Stravinsky too could charm (in social situations) and illustrate (in the professional context, in the rehearsal studio) with his ability to strike a pose, to dance a step, to move choreographically. Balanchine praised Stravinsky's intimate knowledge of dance as greater than any other composer he had worked with. Stravinsky did indeed maintain a close engagement with his own body. Not only did he keep his fingers in shape (just as Kashperova had encouraged him to value his hands), he regularly practised gymnastics, particularly before concert appearances.[153] The act of musical performance was nourished and invigorated by physical preparation of the whole bodily frame. At one time Stravinsky even programmed into his domestic routine a daily hour of sunbathing, presumably for the toning benefits to his musculature and for his general health. Physicality was a fundamental aspect of Stravinsky's way of life for many years – especially on tour – even into his sixties. In 1948 he was still exercising, as William King reported: 'With a little encouragement [Stravinsky will] stand on his head to demonstrate one of the ways he keeps physically fit. "A brief head-stand", he says, "rests the head and clears the brain". It's something he picked up from a Yogi. And no day passes without a quarter-hour of calisthenics.'[154]

Stravinsky always maintained that, during his earliest years in St Petersburg, the theatre and the ballet had been higher priorities than music. Later, during the painful decay of relations with the Rimsky-Korsakov family, he would elevate this private infatuation with dance to the level of an aesthetic statement. In the context, he was writing in defence of Diaghilev's achievements and his own part in them, but the greater significance of his remarks lies in their anticipation of his own, life-long commitment to physicality. A letter to Vladimir Rimsky-Korsakov (written in 1911) makes clear his early appreciation of dance's classical, indeed, neoclassical virtues through being concerned essentially with itself: 'The only form of scenic art that sets itself, as its cornerstone, the *tasks of beauty*, and *nothing else*, is ballet.'[155] This remarkable statement surely begs the question: what form of *non*-scenic art, then, shares this same corner-stone? From every indication thus far – obtained via scores, sketches and references made by Stravinsky (alone or via the hand of others) – it is clear that he greatly valued instrumental music too. Owing to its central role as a vehicle for his neoclassical idiom, piano literature might be proposed as the answer to this conundrum. Instrumental music, then, is non-scenic art's 'ballet', and the piano is the best-equipped instrument to address the task of beauty. That beauty should be a 'task' at all is already – in 1911 (the year of Stravinsky's letter on this subject) – a precociously neoclassical attitude. And it was through the piano that Stravinsky sought his musical solutions regardless of the work's eventual genre or instrumentation. The finished result was of less concern than the act of assembly; and however the final product was wrapped and displayed on the shelf the assembly line passed through the fingers to the piano keyboard and back again. There is no need here to elaborate (with Roger Shattuck) about how it is 'obvious [that] Stravinsky composed with his whole body'.[156] However, as for the triumvirate relationship between Stravinsky, the piano, and the manner whereby aspects of visual and aural space are addressed through the composer's heightened sense of music's physicality – this *can* usefully be addressed.

One must be careful not to generalize about the external manifestation of Stravinsky's works or, worse, about his mannerisms on the concert stage. Yet, by reading certain Stravinskian fingerprints (pianistic patterns) in terms of finger/hand *choreography* one is left with the indelible sense that the central tenets of this composer's neoclassical aesthetics are founded upon movement.[157] Stravinsky understood movement as a path to beauty – his affirmation to Vladimir Rimsky-Korsakov makes this association clear. And as Stravinsky's career led him in and out of the theatre, away from narrative dance (Ballets Russes) and back to dance via abstract choreography (Balanchine), one may observe that, whatever the context, his path to creativity remained faithful to a physical engagement with music's patterning – and could, in specific situations, even depend upon this. That this path should be nourished by his respect for, and utilization of, piano methods would suggest that his constructivist approach both pre-dated and post-dated the neoclassical works. Furthermore, his claim on *pal'tserazvitiye* and the workshop of piano study as a means to (his) music can be seen, also, to embrace a choreographer's sense of space and time. His physical engagement with music's patterning is measurable.

There is a certain irony in the fact that, in attempting to liberate his neoclassical music from any stylistic reverberations from his past, Stravinsky may have succeeded merely in replacing one Russianism with another.[158] In the light of Taruskin's thematic comparisons – between, for example, the Piano Concerto and Tchaikovsky's Fifth Symphony[159] – Stravinsky's tactic served to disguise his Russian nostalgia only temporarily. Yet, while musical scholarship may have caught up with him in this regard, the impact of Stravinsky's new idiom upon his contemporaries led them to seek answers in terms of his stylistic nostalgia while the composer, as it were, 're-organized his pedagogical workshop' in terms of constructions and objects. Such paradoxes lie at the heart of Stravinsky's neoclassicism; and the friction between gestures of control and of theatricality were part of that common experience by which Stravinsky and Balanchine were drawn into fruitful partnership.

'Exaudi orationem meam': pedagogy applied

Writing of the piano as Stravinsky's compositional 'fulcrum', Charles Joseph observes that 'such a grossly stated observation as "Stravinsky composed at the piano" may be a deceptively subsumptive epitome that actually conceals more than it informs'.[160] What initiatives, though, have been taken since these words were published to unravel this deceptive subsumption? The Sacher Stiftung has coordinated some significant work. In addition to offering access to the Stravinsky archive (and guarding it for posterity) the Foundation has endorsed a series of pronouncements (*Mitteilungen*) which present research topics undertaken by visiting scholars. Interest in pianistic issues, however, has been scarce. With regard to his compositional processes, neither Gretchen Horlacher's analysis (1999) of the sketches of ('and superimposition in') *Symphony of Psalms* nor Lynne Rogers' more performance-oriented view of 'varied repetition' (1994) takes the debate to Stravinsky's piano.[161] Put bluntly, the cautious arguments of these authors – and of Joseph in his texts published since 1983 – are hindered by inadequate consideration of Stravinsky's attitude to pianism. Without consideration of the pedagogical origin of Stravinsky's creative process, little more than superficial and conjectural comment on pianistic influence is possible. An informed analysis that addresses the composer's attitude to the piano as a constructive facilitator of neoclassical objectivity is altogether more problematic.

Earlier it was suggested that Stravinsky's 'composed fingerings' could shed light on his pianistic attitude to neoclassicism. Yet how did Stravinsky's pianistic attitude contribute to the greater neoclassical structures? Study of the manuscripts (above, pp. 143–7) has demonstrated that the Piano Concerto was founded upon pianistic materials from its very inception, this moment coinciding with the composer's enthusiastic immersion in the routines and processes of piano study. That there was the profoundest interface, on a metaphysical level, between *pal'tserazvitiye* and Stravinsky's finest neoclassical works may now be addressed via the *Symphony of Psalms*. Stravinsky's authentic expression of religiosity, to paraphrase Ernest Ansermet,[162] has already been viewed from the perspective of earlier works: for example, as a demonstration of block-like thinking (as in *Symphonies of Wind Instruments*);[163] or as a religious, non-narrative ritual (in contrast to *The Rite of Spring* and *Les Noces*);[164] or – in its closing bars – as an illustration of *uproshcheniye*, Taruskin's concept of 'simplification', (as in *Symphonies of Wind Instruments* and *Les Noces*).[165] Stravinsky's *own* account of his intentions with regard to the *Symphony of Psalms* also places this work in the context of a precedent. Significantly, however, his point of reference is the *Sonate pour piano*:

> As in the case of my *Sonate*, I wanted to create *an organic whole* without conforming to the various models adopted by custom … I also had under consideration *the sound material* with which *to build my edifice*. My idea was that my symphony should be a work of *great contrapuntal development* … I finally decided on a choral and instrumental ensemble in which the *two elements* should be on an *equal footing*, neither of them out-weighing the other. In this instance, my point of view as to the mutual relationship of the vocal and instrumental sections coincided with that of *the masters of contrapuntal music*, who also treated them as equals.[166]

This testimony raises several key issues. By placing these compositional and aesthetic intentions under the umbrella of the *Sonate*, Stravinsky is drawing attention to that phase of his early neoclassicism when he was moved to proclaim the rigorous tenets of his manifesto, 'Some Ideas about My *Octuor*', through every element of his professional activity. The composition, concert performances and recordings of the *Sonate* indicate that, at the time, Stravinsky regarded this work as fundamental in establishing his new idiom. The view from the autobiography – and one must assume that this accurately reflected the composer's attitude during the recent composition of the *Symphony of Psalms* – suggests that the *Sonate* carried associations for Stravinsky of the keenest, most idealized neoclassical spirit, whose successful 'execution' as a score represented a particularly refined distillation of his neoclassical aesthetic. The Piano Concerto was conceived before 'Some Ideas about my *Octuor*'; the *Sonate*, therefore, as the first work to be composed following its publication, emerges with unrivalled immediacy to Stravinsky's theories. Through the hand of Walter Nouvel, Stravinsky is declaring that in his conception of the *Symphony of Psalms* he had consciously revisited the *Sonate*, regarding it as a point of reference – as a model, even, of how to access and apply those original principles. It would therefore be a relevant line of enquiry to observe the pianistic inferences within this later work as a manifestation of self-reference and as a return to fundamental neoclassical ideals. Such a process of self-exploration might suggest that there was also a personal, existential aspect to Stravinsky's objective presentation of religiosity. I propose, however, to observe the *Symphony of Psalms* from the perspective of those processes of study already discussed – as a further, shining example of the transformation of *pal'tserazvitiye* into neoclassical artwork.

In this sense, the first movement offers a singular concentration of study-based materials which reflect the composer's interest in the organic processes behind the act of creation – regardless of whether this creative energy is directed towards the manuscript paper or the piano keyboard. The outcome invites a reading of this psalm-setting, therefore, as both 'compositional exercise' and as *étude*. The following case-study is restricted to observations concerning the first movement of the *Symphony of Psalms* and will address the issue of Stravinsky's pianistic attitude by re-considering elements in the score in terms of those pedagogic disciplines most relevant to composition and performance. These elements comprise: the index-finger-over-thumb overlap (as *étude*), progressive extension (as *étude*), varied articulation (as both *étude* and compositional exercise), the 'organic whole' (as compositional exercise), the musical stutter (as *étude* and compositional exercise – in fact, as a process of refinement essential to both piano practice and to composition), the tonic pedal (as both compositional exercise and *Accordgruppe*) and mono-thematicism (as compositional exercise under the same terms as the Bachian Invention). Parameters of compositional competence find their equivalent in the diverse incarnations of pianistic 'good practice'. Together, they contribute to the construction of this neoclassical object. Stravinsky calls upon them all, as he puts it, to 'build his edifice'.

That the *Symphony of Psalms* lists two pianos in its instrumentation is already an indication of the pianistic attitude behind this composition, although they never occupy the spotlight. However, their presence is constantly felt, if not actually heard, as the first movement especially is impregnated with a distinctly pianistic inflection in the writing for all sections of the orchestra. The opening bars already evoke Leschetizky's *Accordgruppe* in several respects. The oboe–bassoon duet consists of a series of arpeggios characterized by their similarly constant and subtle variation. In addition, these arpeggios also operate within or with reference to an 'envelope' which, by its compression, suggests the span of the pianist's hand. Harmonically, too, this *ritornello* is an echo of the *Accordgruppe* in its denial of any diatonic goal-orientation, while also reflecting its pianistic model in the predilection for diminished and augmented triads and for chords of the seventh. Stravinsky's neoclassical response mirrors several of these characteristics, although the *ritornello*'s own permutations of endurance do not transpose, modulate nor otherwise 'lead anywhere', but are merely exchanged as one musical block replaces another. The outcome is a presentation of musical 'events', their rhetoric defined not by any symphonic or ritual narrative but by the interplay of musical elements. However, the identification of this opening *ritornello* as a reading of the *Accordgruppe* lies not merely in superficial resemblances to sonority and rhetoric. There is a fundamentally pianistic shape to the *gruppetti* from which the *ritornello* is made.

Index-finger-over-thumb overlap

Foremost amongst pianistic shapes inherent to this *ritornello* is the index-finger-over-thumb overlap. This pianistic manoeuvre was cited (in Chapter 2, pp. 79–82) as the paradigm for the longevity of certain pianistic patterns across several decades of Stravinsky's output. It has also been observed (above, pp. 137–9) contributing to the technical difficulty that Stravinsky progressively introduces into the third movement of the *Sonate*. The same technical knot is now revisited in the *Symphony of Psalms* where it provides the basis for much of the orchestral material. The opening woodwind *ritornello* barely disguises its origins, fitting comfortably 'under the pianist's hand' as a sequence of five-finger envelopes in the form of ascending and descending arpeggios. It is a reasonable assumption that this passage was not only written at Stravinsky's piano[167] but was also derived from it: each *gruppetto* can be managed one-handed, and comfortably so (Example 3.11a). However, the repetition of the thumb (from B to B♭ across the bar-line) *is* an issue: it is both incompatible with the *legato* indication and un-pianistic. If the orchestral passage is to be read as fundamentally *pianistic* – as evidence of how Stravinsky's pianism has been absorbed into his mature neoclassical idiom – a truly pianistic solution must be found. In order to respect the composer's wish for one *legato* phrase comprising these five *gruppetti*, fingering is therefore required that prevents the thumb from being employed twice in succession. An appropriate solution for this is for the index finger to overlap the thumb wherever required. This would also impact upon the first note of the phrase. This B♭ would now 'be played' with the index finger to preserve the desired *legato*, and for reasons of consistency and ease of performance – and (to perpetuate this fiction for a moment longer) to facilitate the pianist's memorization of this passage (Example 3.11b).

In this way we may speculate on how the composer arrived at his solution. By slipping this instrumental line into a pianistic (five-finger) envelope we can more clearly sense how Stravinsky made his compositional choices by way of 'a tactile model' as Joseph has suggested.[168] Throughout the score the index-finger-over-thumb manoeuvre offers a template with which Stravinsky can formulate his *ritornello* as an 'instrumental transcription' of piano music. Indeed, the passage immediately following the oboe–bassoon duet (i.e. Fig. 2 to Fig. 4) 'reverts to' piano music – two-piano music, in fact – in a 'demonstration' of how to execute this material. The

Ex. 3.11 Stravinsky, *Symphony of Psalms* (1930), 1st movement, bb. 1–3, with suggested piano fingerings.

first movement's *ritornello* music is thus confirmed by two pianists as essentially *pal'tserazvitiye*.[169]

Progressive extension

The process of rehearsing is another rhetorical gesture from Stravinsky's 'workshop of study' that he chooses on occasion to portray in the score of the *Symphony of Psalms*. One may observe phrases of 'progressive difficulty' suggesting a step-by-step addition of greater challenges for the player. This issue, too, was first observed in the current chapter, (p. 138) and read as an organic aspect of the *Sonate*'s last movement, being illustrative of the gradually increasing technical difficulty that this movement presents. It was observed that the technique required for the fourth-finger-over-fifth overlap (a manoeuvre vital to playing the fugue subject) at the start was later applied to the other extremity of the hand via the index-finger-over-thumb overlap. The concept of technical extension, via a drill that is developed through ever longer phrase-lengths, refers to the fundamental gradation of the learning process and of musical rehearsal. In the *Symphony of Psalms*' first movement it is particularly associated with the figuration played by the oboes (at Fig. 5) that White refers to as 'interlinked thirds'.[170] This passage demonstrates, in quavers, then in semiquavers and finally in semiquaver sextuplets, a gradual extension of phrase-lengths and pace (and technical difficulty) – like a well-devised practice routine. In fact, the very opening of the *Symphony* is an exemplary illustration of phraseology based upon this same notion of 'progressive extension'. The opening oboe–bassoon duet is structured according to a pattern of increasing phrase-lengths: five *gruppetti*, then six, then ten, while the two pianos extend this 'exercise' still further in an unbroken sequence of twenty-two semiquaver arpeggios.[171]

Varied articulation

The issue of varied articulation – specifically, the employment of simultaneous *legato* and *staccato* – is a regular feature of Stravinsky's music. Noted already in the F♯ minor Sonata, the Octet, the Piano Concerto and the *Sonate*, it has been recognized as a neoclassical imprint that reflects 'good pedagogic practice' and is a reference to that practice. However, this quirk of instrumentation has never been as clearly portrayed in its pianistic guise as it is in the *Symphony of Psalms*. Yet, fundamentally, the *jeu d'articulation* in this work is subtly different from that employed in the first movement of the *Sonate*. There, the relationship between right and left hand, i.e. between *legato* melody and *staccato* accompaniment, is fundamental to the musical argument: in the coda the two hands not only play in unison, but their articulation also 'agrees' – first, *staccato*, then *legato* – as they present a joint rendition of the final ascending, diminished seventh, arpeggios. The narrative of the *Sonate* is thus driven by the articulation. However, in *Symphony of Psalms* the varied articulation *is* the narrative; the *jeu d'articulation* has become the very currency of its idiom.

Stravinsky makes this manifestly clear in the following three contexts. For example, the instrumental passage which leads into the altos' first entry ('Exaude orationem meam, Domine') juxtaposes three layers of articulation: *legato*, non-*legato* and *staccato*.[172] Such a 'compositional exercise in varied articulation' is employed again in the two climactic *tutti* declamations. At the first these (Fig. 9) the orchestral layers are constructed from a combination of four articulations – *legato*, non-*legato*, *staccato* and *marcatissimo* – in ever subtler combinations, superimpositions and fragmentations.[173] This passage returns *fortissimo* at Fig. 12 with *seven* varieties of articulation; indeed, every orchestral and choral part is now marked with accents. Thus the *jeu d'articulation* is affected, too, by the notion of 'progressive extension' (Example 3.12).

The step-wise increase in dynamics and in textural volume throughout the movement is matched by a correspondingly progressive addition of new articulations until this parameter, too, reaches its maximum complexity. In complete contrast, Stravinsky's sound-material for the chorus provides a slow pulse – here (Fig. 12) and in the previous *tutti* (Fig. 9) – over which the instrumental layering, in diminished note-values, can be more clearly perceived. The aural experience cannot fail to communicate to the listener a 'precise sonorous image' of that (multi-storey) edifice which the composer has built. This impression is reinforced by reference to the score. Whereas the *Symphonies of Wind Instruments* juxtaposes its block-materials in a chronological (horizontal) format, the *Symphony of Psalms* presents its block-materials as superimpositions, as *vertical* construction. Stravinsky is constantly rearranging his material, formed predominantly from three contrasting but well-matched elements: the pedal point, the *ritornello* and the two-note chant. These are combined in much the same manner as the soloist's part in the first movement of the Piano Concerto is constructed from three linear strands. Seven years on, Stravinsky is still working with musical layering but has now added to his repertoire that 'counterpoint of elements' which he had first announced in 'Some Ideas about My *Octuor*'. As he wrote then and still held to be true, 'Form, in my music, derives from counterpoint. I consider counterpoint as the only means through which the attention of the composer is concentrated on purely musical questions. Its elements also lend themselves perfectly to an architectural construction.'[174] In the intervening years he had developed the art of counterpoint-by-articulation.

Ex. 3.12 Stravinsky, *Symphony of Psalms*, 1st movement, bb. 65–7 (Fig. 12).

The *Symphony of Psalms* thus combines two compositional techniques fundamental to his recent past: block-construction, as in the *Symphonies of Wind Instruments*, and counterpoint, as in the neoclassical piano works. In the *Symphony of Psalms* the 'sound materials' (pedal point, *ritornello* and chant) are treated contrapuntally and freely exchanged between the low, middle and high registers of the orchestral texture. Stravinsky's 'form' is no longer determined merely by 'the play of movements and volumes' *alone* (as he had affirmed in 'Some Ideas about My *Octuor*'). His architectural approach to composition is now combined with linear and constructionist concerns, these latter derived from *pal'tserazvitiye* (including issues of articulation) and from Stravinsky's view of counterpoint as, essentially, a pianistic discipline.

The *tutti* moments in the *Symphony of Psalms* present the first movement's most complex textures. At the height of his neoclassical maturity, however, he preferred to construct his orchestral climaxes through the demonstration of academic technique and relatively rudimentary choices in terms of orchestration. That Stravinsky shunned such opportunities to indulge his acknowledged gift for instrumentation reflects his embrace of neoclassicism's down-to-earth ideology and mundane requirements with regard to notation. In years past, Stravinsky's skill as a musical draftsman must have given him immense satisfaction, both tactile and aesthetic, especially when writing out his completed orchestral scores for the publisher. Stravinsky's reputation as a brilliant orchestrator has always been enhanced by the visual impact of his impressive musical handwriting.[175] We know that Stravinsky took great pride in his own beautifully handwritten scores. How, then, at the moment of writing out the *tutti* in Example 3.12 by hand, did he justify such choices to himself? How did he compare the experience with memories of the finesse and instrumental colour of his earlier ballet scores? Compared with *The Rite*, for example, such layering in the *Symphony of Psalms* resembles little more than a student's exercise. Such was his declared aim – to 'create drawings at the expense of colour'; to exclude nuances; and to make music out of the play of volumes, tempos and objective elements – this must have been exactly what Stravinsky was intending. Not since the *Sonate* had he so faithfully set to music his neoclassical manifesto. A decade after 'Some Ideas about My *Octuor*' Stravinsky was still prioritizing objectivity and the construction of musical objects.

Simultaneous diminution as a contrapuntal device had already been used by Stravinsky in *Sonate* (the third movement) and *Sérénade* (Rondoletto). Stravinsky would use this academic device again on several occasions, notably in another biblical work, *Babel* (1944). Here, the ground-bass from the introduction is subjected to variation and inversion, and combined with itself in diminution. Such domination of structure over content would rate highly on Ockleford's hierarchy of those compositional techniques which articulate an 'effect of expressive neutrality'.[176] However, compared with the brickwork neatly stacked in the *tutti* passages of *Symphony of Psalms*, *Babel*'s musical elements appear recklessly ornamental.[177] This contrast supports the central proposal: that the first movement of the *Symphony of Psalms* represented for Stravinsky an ideological demonstration of music as an inherently non-expressive craft – its ideal representation, in fact, of this fundamental neoclassical plank. The tools which Stravinsky uses to convey this signification draw upon two sources: the 'performance *étude*' and the 'compositional exercise'. In terms of the latter, the movement self-consciously displays academic compositional devices. On this basis, the first movement of the *Symphony of Psalms* should be read as an 'Appendix (1930)' to his Manifesto (1924) for it is an archetype of the composer's most extreme form of neoclassical construction.

The pedal point

As 'compositional exercise' this movement engages with another key aspect of Leschetizky's method: the pedal note. From the first bar, Stravinsky's unchanging *tutti* chord obliges the listener to perceive the woodwind *ritornello* in relation to its tonal centre on E. (While the pedal note is not literally sustained, the harmonic sense of its insistence, if not the musical effect, is that of a tonic pedal.) Most of Leschetizky's drilling exercises for one hand are balanced by a pedal note in the other. Stravinsky's allusion to pianistic training is particularly transparent in the opening section (prior to the choral entry); yet the function of this introductory material is not merely preparatory. Such is the constant pull towards a pedal note throughout the movement, one may regard Part I of *Symphony of Psalms* as an elaborate synthesis of that paradigm of Leschetizkian drill exercises, the *Accordgruppe* – over an E rather than a C pedal.

The effect of the pedal note, as it underpins the waves of intervallic permutations, is to provide a sense of harmonic reference to balance the non-diatonic nature of the arpeggio sequence, whose function is not musical, but non-musical and technical. Prentner recognized the harmonic infrastructure of the *Accordgruppe* by providing it with a figured bass.[178] This would suggest that the left hand should hold down a bass note, octaves even, throughout the right-hand drill, thus forming a tonic pedal; similarly,

Ex. 3.13 Stravinsky, *Sonate pour piano*, 3rd movement, bb. 89–93 – with suggested fingerings.

when the exercise is inverted, the right hand should provide an upper pedal note (or octave) to balance the left hand's execution of the *Accordgruppe*.[179] The impact of the chord that opens the *Symphony of Psalms* reverberates throughout the first movement: at its two climactic declamations, for example, it is the chorus which provides a tonic pedal as a basis to the instrumental *ritornelli*.[180] Furthermore, the sense of harmonic stasis that the frequent use of the two-note chant creates is comparable to the musical consequence of the one-note pedal which (due to its narrow, usually semitonal oscillation) it so closely resembles. Effectively, the entire movement is unified by this musical device.

In countless drills by Czerny, and in didactic literature generally, it is common to regard one or other finger as the focus of varied repetitions for the sake of developing agility and endurance. The musical effect is of a pedal point created by the constant repetition of the upper or lower note.[181] Most commonly the thumb or the fifth finger will secure the 'pedal' while the other fingers remain free to develop their agility. Isidor Philipp refers to this technique as *note tenue*.[182] It provides a useful basis, or equivalent in pedagogic terms, for the versions presented in the *Sonate* and *Symphony* (Example 3.13).[183] This passage in crotchets is a further example of Stravinsky's 'studied' (slowed-down) approach to compositional technique that unites the last movement of the *Sonate* with the first movement of the *Symphony of Psalms*. Both refer to the eighteenth-century contrapuntal model and to pianistic exercise drills.[184] This particular combination – of an upper pedal over a two-note oscillation – may also be observed, for example, in the *Symphony* at 'Remitte mihi', where the altos secure a pedal B over an oscillating tenor-line of E–F.[185]

Ex. 3.14 Stravinsky, *Symphony of Psalms*, 1st movement, bb. 1–3.

'An organic whole'

It is not only in those grand moments that the first movement of the *Symphony of Psalms* presents its correctness as a well-executed compositional exercise; there are many subtleties of academicism to be found in the score's intricacies. For example, the first verse of the psalm 'Exaudi orationem meam, Domine' is set to an oscillating chant, E–F–F–E (Fig. 4), derived from the preceding horn and solo cello material: sounding B–C–C–B (written for horn as: F♯–G–G–F♯) at bb. 4–6 of Fig. 2. The outline of this 'first theme' bears close motivic comparison with the left-hand material of piano 1 stated immediately beforehand: E–F–E (Fig. 2, bb. 1–5). This slowly oscillating bass-line can itself be traced to the very opening bars of the *Symphony*, where the root of each oboe–bassoon *gruppetto* also outlines this semitonal 'chant': B♭–B–B–B♭–(B) (Example 3.14).

Having formed the outline of the movement's principal theme, Stravinsky's two-note 'pedal' recurs at several points throughout the movement.[186] Such uniformity of melodic material, whose steady step-wise movement is reflected in the other choral parts, is consistent with the composer's declared wish 'to create an organic whole'.[187] A semitonal relationship is also the basis to Leschetizky's *Accordgruppe* which rises inexorably through twelve steps underpinned by pedal notes. Stravinsky's organic application of this fundamental platform of *pal'tserazvitiye* to the *Symphony of Psalms*, whether consciously or subconsciously, is an illustration of the completeness with which he had synthesized these constructive, pedagogical processes into his mature neoclassicism.

The oscillation between two notes is intrinsic to the musical fabric of the *Symphony of Psalms* and reflects the composer's own observations on this subject. Referring to the vocal line of *Elegy for J. F. K.*, Stravinsky commented on the alternation of D and E as 'two reiterated notes [which] are the melodic-rhythmic stutter characteristic of my speech from *Les Noces* to the *Concerto in D*, and earlier and later as well – a lifelong affliction, in fact'.[188] Van den Toorn has observed this oscillation 'reaching into every crevice of melodic, rhythmic, formal, or pitch-relational matter'.[189] Straus, in his search for 'affective meaning', concludes that Stravinsky's musical stutter is often to be 'associated with grief' while its specific meaning is 'always shaped by the local music context'.[190] The religious nature of the *Symphony of Psalms* would suggest that the work emerges from the composer's recent re-conversion to Russian Orthodoxy. 'It is incontestable', writes Glenn Watkins, 'that the dual experience of *Pater noster* (1926) and *Oedipus* (1926–27) led Stravinsky directly to the composition of the *Symphony of Psalms* (1930)'.[191] *Oedipus rex* had revealed to Stravinsky the advantages of writing in Latin as a fixed and supranational language,[192] but musically the *Symphony of Psalms* owes little to the earlier work. On the other hand *Pater noster* – which would remain in Church Slavonic (*Otche nash*) until its re-publication in Latin in 1949 – did provide Stravinsky with a musical as well as religious source. Taruskin has demonstrated that 'the soprano part [of *Otche nash*] is modelled loosely on the traditional Orthodox chant melody for the Lord's Prayer',[193] whilst Walsh observes that 'almost everything hinges on one or two melodic intervals and figures, reiterated over and over again in such unvarying patterns that a kind of sublime monotony emerges as the controlling idea'.[194] Such descriptions of the *Symphony of Psalms* also serve well for Stravinsky's a cappella setting of *Otche nash* (the Lord's Prayer) and *Simvol' Verï* (the Creed).[195] The symphony's omnipresent two-note chant and its predilection for resting upon a pedal point may well be a reflection of Orthodox tropes, particularly its melodic simplicity and associated harmonic stasis. Stravinsky's performance indications for the Creed printed at the head of the score and in **bold** (in the Russian edition) clearly bear the hallmark of the composer's aesthetic consistency: '**Tutte le ♪ equale. Tutto molto metrico, non forte, non espressivo**'. (Was Stravinsky alerting choir conductors, particularly those of the Anglican cathedral tradition, *not* to indulge in their customary fluidity by directing this work in the manner of responses or psalms, i.e. in speech-rhythm?) The *Symphony*'s energetic *ritornello*, however, reflects a quite different and Catholic aspect of Stravinsky's sense of spirituality – one that is closely related to Maritain's celebration of 'the spiritual conditions of a labour that is *honest*'.[196]

Viewed from the *Symphony of Psalms* the hermeneutic origins of Stravinsky's two-note stutter also lie, surely, in his pianistic processes – specifically, in the step-wise shift of the *Accordgruppe*'s bass-line. One may easily envisage how an industrious and imaginative pupil (gifted, as was Stravinsky, with the ability to improvise and with an eagerness to experiment) would have been captivated by this shift upwards. The anarchy of wildly ranging harmonies conflicts with the tonic pedal in an improvisatory manner (distantly) reminiscent of Bach's C major Prelude from Book II of 'The 48'. Eventually the *Accordgruppe* reaches its momentary resolution before veering upwards a semitone. It is a moment which, despite its open-endedness, provides a sense of achievement, if not of finality. Above all it brings aural relief (after such a long period in the same 'key') and a fleeting cessation of harmonic aimlessness. It is but a short step for the young pianist (or adult composer) to take – either intentionally or in error – but the impact of raising or lowering the pedal note whilst the wave of arpeggios is in progress would provide a welcome change of sonority. Not least of the potential benefits of moving the pedal note up and down during the *Accordgruppe* is to give the otherwise interminable arpeggios a sense of phrasing; it is almost an instinctive reaction for a musician to seek ways of enhancing an otherwise dour working atmosphere.[197] The *Symphony of Psalms*, foremost among several neoclassical examples, demonstrates the creativity of the work-driven interface between the two identities which make up the composer/pianist. It is only through the private ritual of pianoforte study and its relevance to Stravinsky's (equally private) compositional process that one can appreciate how much he drew strength from the texts and act of pianistic apprenticeship. Their integration into Stravinsky's mature neoclassicism cannot be better exemplified than in his setting of the closing verses of the 150th Psalm: the spirituality of musical creation is celebrated through music that 'seems to float in defiance of tonal and rhythmic gravity'[198] in a union of Orthodoxy, Catholicism and plain *pal'tserazvitiye*.

Stravinsky still took pride in considering himself a craftsman – to borrow from Hogarth, in being an 'industrious 'prentice'.[199] Now in his High Neoclassicism Stravinsky was affirming that this remained, more than ever, a vital plank of his ideology. He could rely on the pedagogic basis of his sound materials to ensure the complete objectivity of their result. The first movement of the *Symphony of Psalms* is possibly Stravinsky's finest work of musical craft in this regard for the unity, in Cingria's phrase, of its 'lyrical expression and composition'.[200] With an ear to the *Symphony of Psalms* Ansermet observed how this work 'expresses the religiosity of others – of the imaginary choir of which the actual singing choir is an *analagon*: but it must be agreed that the expression of this religiosity is absolutely authentic'.[201] 'Stravinsky's piano' guaranteed the composer proof of that authenticity. The final chapter now pursues the application of Stravinsky's time-honoured, piano-derived craft to his last neoclassical works and, even, to his serial output before arriving at some remarkable, yet not altogether unexpected, conclusions.

4   Departures and homecomings

Serial neoclassicism

Duo concertant

Concerto for Two Solo Pianos

Violin Concerto

Symphony in Three Movements

Lied ohne Name für Zwei Fagotten

The Rake's Progress

Duo concertant *(1931/1932)*

> What triumphs are the 'Cantilène', 'Eglogue I' and 'Eglogue II'! This is music at once succulent, learned and slow, meaty and profound. No-one else could have written it. One has to transform oneself into a crystal bird to understand such a dish.
>
> From an undated letter to Stravinsky
> from Charles-Albert Cingria.[1]

Following the composition of the *Symphony of Psalms* Stravinsky wrote two works for the violinist Samuel Dushkin: the Violin Concerto (1931) and the *Duo concertant* (1931/2) for violin and piano. According to Stravinsky this latter work was 'closely connected' to the writings of Charles-Albert Cingria,[2] whom the composer describes as 'an author of rare sagacity and deep originality. Our work had a great deal in common.'[3] The 'views, tastes and ideas' which Stravinsky had shared with the Swiss writer since their first meeting in 1914 'not only still existed [two decades later] but seemed to have grown' over time. They would continue to meet regularly at concerts and rehearsals (for example, Cingria would be invited to the premiere of *The Rake's Progress* in Venice in 1951)[4] and corresponded regularly until Cingria's passing in 1954. With regard, specifically, to the *Duo concertant*, Stravinsky notes in *Chroniques* that there were 'coincidences' between Cingria's recent work and his own.[5] Stravinsky's memory was fresh from having read the Swiss author's 'remarkable *Petrarch*', which was published in December 1932, five months after *Duo concertant* was completed.[6] In fact it was Cingria who first planted the seed of an underlying connection between the two works. Following his attendance at the French premiere of the work on 8 December 1932, Cingria sent a postcard to the composer enthusiastically expressing a sense of personal identification with the slow movements (to which he refers, somewhat curiously, by the collective term 'l'adagio'):[7] 'This was [pure] Petrarch, [indeed] you are his equal. The result was so good … I am still quite overcome by it!'[8] Cingria then inserts an enigmatic and poetic verse reflecting, perhaps, an Alpine subconsciousness or, possibly, a specific memory that he wished to share with Stravinsky: 'Des arbres secs rouges sur de la neige' ('Dry, red trees on the snow'). A note squeezed into the margin reads: '*Petrarch* is now out. I'll send you a copy from Lausanne.' Judging, therefore, from this chronology there can be no suggestion of 'influence upon' Stravinsky's work; but rather this duo of Swiss neoclassicists recognized that they were in poetical–philosophical alignment at that precise moment and, as old friends, derived much satisfaction from this connection. Cingria reported to his brother (in a letter written on Christmas Day 1932) that the Stravinskys were enormously interested in his book, 'Igor above all', because 'he was at that very same point in his art'.[9] The timing and nature of this intriguing parallel only confirm Stravinsky's assertion of a decade earlier, that he follows in his art 'an instinctive logic and [does] not formulate its theory in any other way than *ex post facto*'.[10]

But to what Cingrian ideas was Stravinsky referring that his current work had thrown so sharply into relief? 'Lyricism cannot exist without rules' is the phrase cited by Stravinsky in his autobiography, and which he underlined in his personal copy of *Pétrarque*.[11] (Stravinsky's choice of quotation sheds light on the issue of the composer-as-craftsman.) Cingria continues: 'It is essential that [rules] should be strict … What does not exist everywhere is lyrical expression and composition. To achieve that, apprenticeship to a trade is necessary.'[12] But no easy path is proposed. Stravinsky's written reply to Cingria's exhortation is categorical: 'Your comment on lyricism is perfectly on target, so much so that one is tempted to turn it into a generalization to be applied to all art forms.'[13] Lyrical art, therefore, will also be constructed via craft, and it too must be ingenious and difficult. Stravinsky finds his position reflected 'with the utmost appropriateness' in Cingria's text; and, whilst the context is *Duo concertant*, Stravinsky makes it clear that he had been experiencing 'more than ever … the advantage of a rigorous discipline which gives a taste for the craft and the satisfaction of being able to apply it – and more particularly in work of a lyrical character'.[14] Furthermore (and 'more than ever'), such a disciplined attitude will, to a significant extent, determine his imminent, supremely pianistic constructions. The *Concerto for Two Solo Pianos* (1931/5), the *Sonata for Two Pianos*

(1943/4) and, in an orchestral context, the *Symphony in Three Movements* (1942/5) maintain the traditions of Stravinsky's neoclassical pianism. The 'lyricism' of the chamber works especially is prone to an unremittingly methodological idiom *in extremis* and reflects a degree of objective crafts-manship that Stravinsky attributes to (of all composers) Tchaikovsky, who desired to be like 'the most illustrious masters … an artisan, just as a shoe-maker is'.[15] Initiating this new phase, the *Duo concertant* owes its origin to a long-held dissatisfaction:

> After the *Violin Concerto*, which is orchestral as well as instrumental,[16]
> I continued my researches in the domain of the violin and turned to its
> function in the chamber-music ensemble. For many years I had taken
> no pleasure in the blend of strings struck in the piano with strings set in
> vibration with the bow. In order to reconcile myself to this instrumental
> combination, I was compelled to turn to the minimum of instruments, that
> is to say, only two, in which I saw the possibility of solving the instrumental
> and acoustic problem presented by the strings of the piano and those of the
> violin.[17]

Perhaps this tussle derives from that old Russian chestnut, the orchestral piano, and from Stravinsky's dilemma in *Petrushka* outlined earlier (see Chapter 1, pp. 65–70). Stravinsky's answer to this problem is to reduce the volume of strings to a single violin and elevate the piano from its traditional role as an accompanying instrument to that of a fully *concertante* soloist. In the final solution both performers display an appropriately neoclassical, i.e. technical, aspect to their virtuosity in equal measure.

Stravinsky's 'researches' were undoubtedly facilitated by his long-standing engagement with the craft of piano writing and his employment of (now familiar) tools, from piano methodology to contrapuntal devices. Behind the mask of those evocative titles which characterize the *Duo concertant* ('Cantilène', 'Eglogue', 'Dithyrambe') – with their self-conscious allusion to medieval and, even, Virgilian poetry – lies a musical formula notable for a pedagogical consistency that is entirely in agreement with Stravinsky's neoclassical idiom. For example, the notion of 'progressive extension' (observed in the context of the *Symphony of Psalms*) is taken, in the Gigue, to exhaustive extremes: the movement's thirteen pages of unrelenting and breathless energy demand a level of endurance to rival methodology's most sadistic (and the practice studio's most masochistic) ordeals. Its cen-tral section (in 2/4) provides a particularly blatant example of Stravinsky's didactic single-mindedness. Here, the violin part offers a veritable *étude* on double-stopped thirds (marked *piano*) consisting of an unbroken chain of ninety-one such tasks. The keyboard element of this *étude de concert en doubles notes* (to borrow a title from Philipp)[18] is also restricted in design and dynamic: the piano emulates the violin's trial of endurance via 200 rapid and angular semiquavers (marked *pianissimo possibile*). Furthermore, and recalling Leschetizky's and Philipp's preferred arrangement, the pianist's hands operate in parallel, two octaves apart throughout. The Gigue's prolixity has not been without its critics, particularly at closer proximity to the work's emergence than our own. Writing in 1947, Walter White describes the movement as 'perhaps the only one of Stravinsky's fast movements to merit the epithet "boring" ... the cascade of notes poured forth by violin and piano seems to lack significance and becomes in the end an almost meaningless babble'.[19] Certainly, the music's flow may confound one's expectation of pastoral lyricism and sense of ordered concision. However, within the broad sweep of Stravinsky's neoclassicism (incorporating its considerable technicity as well as its objectivity), the Gigue of 1932 presents itself as a perfectly logical and beautifully constructed point on the same curve as (much earlier) the *Sonate pour piano* of 1924 with its energized (double-octave) jig-like introduction, and (much later) 'The Owl and the Pussy-Cat' of 1966 with its slow-motion (double-octave) 'jig-in-rehearsal'.[20] Slow down the former and quicken the latter, and their blood-relationship becomes very apparent.

Perhaps the most symptomatic of the connections between *Pétrarque* and *Duo concertant* is one that Stravinsky omitted to mention at all: namely, Cingria's quotation from a 'Canzone italiana per organo' by Adriano Banchieri.[21] In its mellifluous step-wise wove it bears an uncanny resemblance to 'Dithyrambe', particularly to its central section without bar-lines. Here, Stravinsky appears to be striving for a pastoral blend of (violin) ornamentation and (piano) counterpoint such as might evoke, on the one hand, the formal requirements of Dante's *canzoni* and, on the other, Petrarch's flexibilities which were to lead towards a more expressive, 'poetic' form of Italian verse. (White conveys the tension between these emotional–technical extremes admirably in his description of 'Dithyrambe' as an 'exalted threnody'.)[22] If Stravinsky had been looking for a pre-baroque justification for his fusion of contrapuntal discipline with lyrical intent, he could have done no better than explore (with Cingria) the path by which the instrumental sonata had evolved via the *canzone da sonar* from transcriptions of Italian vocal *canzonette*, with their scalic part-writing and equally characteristic, brief (and delightful) moments of imitation (Example 4.1a).[23]

In the second movement, 'Eglogue I', Stravinsky can be observed resourcing his *own* distant pre-history. The opening *perpetuum mobile* recalls the scurrying ostinato from the 'Wet-Nurses' Dance' in *Petrushka* (which also

Ex. 4.1a Adriano Banchieri, 'Canzone italiana per organo', opening, as quoted by Charles-Albert Cingria (1932).

Ex. 4.1b Stravinsky, *Duo concertant* (1931/2), 'Dithyrambe', line 2.

happens to be rooted on G/A) and, even, the obstinately contained five-finger envelope in *Tarantella* – by way of countless such examples already observed in the child's-world and neoclassical repertoires. A comparison of metronome indications in *Duo concertant* exposes a characteristically neo-classical concern for didacticism. While the 'Wet-Nurses' Dance' is marked crotchet = 116–20, 'Eglogue I' has 76–80. This slower tempo suggests an attitude of deliberation and of 'study'. One might argue that performances of this movement should take this into consideration and portray, in its opening lines, a sense of constructive process (Example 4.2). This sugges-tion of 'reduced-speed' representation not only recalls our earlier reading of the *Symphony of Psalms* as both 'compositional exercise' and *étude*, but it also anticipates a similar device in *The Rake's Progress*, to be discussed in due course.

The most intriguing feature of *Duo concertant*, however, may reside in the paradox of its instrumentation – an aspect of composition so often used by Stravinsky either to reinforce or to deny his Russian, specific-ally Rimskian, education. From the start of 'Cantilène' the violin (an instrument whose standard technique, with the bow, favours the use of repeated notes) performs rapid arpeggios, whilst the piano (for whom arpeggios are standard fare, especially when divided between the hands) is given repeated notes, which represents one of the instrument's most advanced technical challenges. In its extended attention to such uncom-fortable demands this opening movement sets the tone for the whole work, whose thin patina of cultured dialogue (according to the con-ventions of chamber music) conceals a didactic spirit that may appear unconventional at first but is, in fact, entirely consistent with Stravinsky's embrace of *pal'tserazvitiye*. The latest edition of, or variation upon, this traditional neoclassical 'test' is declared openly in the very first bars of *Duo concertant*. I do not refer to the violin's exploratory snatches – 'arpeggio arabesques' as White has described these shapes when allud-ing to the opening of *Symphony of Psalms*. Rather, it is the piano's nervy tremolo that catches the ear from the outset of this supposed 'Cantilena' and will continue to unsettle both texture and mood throughout the first movement. Unfamiliar as this sonority may appear, such a rapid – indeed, insistent – pulse is not without precedent as a Stravinskian trope of energy (vitality) wherever there is an interest to convey motor energy to the exclusion of emotional energy. A notable precursor of such object-ive dynamism can be observed in *Petrushka*: in the strident and vigorous links on timpani (F♯) and side-drum (without snares) that interrupt the performance.[24] On three occasions the listener is held momentarily in rapt attention; but there is no ratcheting-up of the emotions despite the

Ex. 4.2 Stravinsky, *Duo concertant*, 'Eglogue I', opening.

Eglogue I

ominous alarm-call that lies behind the apparent frivolity of pantomime and circus. (For does not the drum-roll also signify a dark premonition of the leading protagonist's eventual 'execution'?) Rather, compared to the action that precedes and follows each link, the repeated-note interruption represents a mere hiatus in the emotional narrative. In other words, despite the percussive vigour of these passages, one's emotional response is more likely to be unmoved – and this coolness may be attributed to the immutably repetitive nature of these *tremoli misurati*. As an aside, it is interesting to note – in *Baika* (*Reynard*), for instance, or *Rag-Time*, or in the earlier versions of *Svadebka* – that Stravinsky's cimbalom parts are similarly characterized by repeated-note sonorities that explore the natural idiom of this family of instruments. Stravinsky's youth spent on the Gulf of Finland and his honeymoon in that country (at the time still a Grand Duchy of Imperial Russia) may suggest familiarity with the *kantele*. His close association with Rimsky-Korsakov – whose appreciation of *gusli* culture is encapsulated in his portrait of the twelfth-century *guslyar* Sadko (after whom Rimsky's tone-poem and opera-*bïlina* are named)[25] – may have been a factor. Similarly, Stravinsky's later collaboration with the eminent Russianist N. K. Roerich could also have stimulated Stravinsky's interest in the sonority and 'instrumentation' of the *gusli*, one the most ancient of Russian stringed instruments of the box zither or psaltery type.[26]

The heightened significance of the repeated-note 'sign' in *Duo concertant* resides in the manner of its absorption into the neoclassical syntax. Indeed, it becomes the epitome of objective energy and, as vitality devoid of emotional energy, may be understood as the *ne plus ultra* of Stravinsky's neoclassical *ritornello* idiom. The dispersions of the Rondoletto (in *Sérénade en la*) and the Gigue (in *Duo concertant*) are thereby distilled into this one-note essence: a concentration, in its purest form, of the eighteenth-century toccata spirit whereby the virtuoso improvisations that would normally range across wide intervals (indeed, over the entire keyboard) are now compacted into the most restrictive of non-intervals, i.e. onto this *one note* the full pianistic arsenal is now pinpointed.[27] A visual analogy would be of the elegantly revolving ballerina or ice-skater who, by suddenly drawing her limbs into her body, transforms her measured *fouetté en tournant* into a full-blown (yet curiously static) *pirouette*. The spectator may be spellbound momentarily by the intensity of the spinning figure (just as the listener is transfixed by *Petrushka*'s percussive links) but the narrative of the dance – and any sense of movement (from which one more clearly identifies a message of corporeal expressivity) – is only resumed when the ballerina emerges, arms outstretched, from her whirling immobility.

Duo concertant is an unusual representative of a rarefied genre, though Stravinsky may have found a useful precedent in the catalogue of a composer for whom he had often expressed admiration. Weber's *Grand duo concertant* op. 48, for clarinet and piano (1815/16), displays a similarly egalitarian distribution of concerto-level virtuosity between the two performers. In Stravinsky's version the curious imbalance between the duration and weight of its five movements further impedes its acceptance as concert repertoire, though less, surely, than its doubly uncomfortable technicity. This is regrettable, for the *Duo concertant* and, indeed, the work to be considered next, may be ranked amongst Stravinsky's finest though most neglected chamber compositions.

Concerto for Two Solo Pianos *(1931/1935)*

> On the evidence of [this] music, [Stravinsky] has confidence only in himself and in his prodigious technique, and thus realizes in the aesthetic domain a sort of 'pelagianism'.
>
> Boris de Schloezer, from a concert review published in *Vendredi* (1 July 1938)

In the above epigraph Stravinsky is accused of likening himself to Pelagius. The implication is that the *Concerto for Two Solo Pianos* serves principally as a means for Stravinsky to earn his salvation, and that by its dour hammerings and contrapuntal rigidity he would pay for his sins… To anticipate de Schloezer's equally bitter criticism of the Concerto in E♭, 'Dumbarton Oaks' (1937/8): 'he must obey the diabolical dialectic of his evolution'.[28] As far as pianists are concerned, *Duo concertant* may be viewed as a preliminary study for the even greater challenges of the aptly named *Concerto for Two Solo Pianos* (1931/5). Here, rapidly repeating notes form an intrinsic element of this work's tour de force. Not only is this emotionless energy central to the concerto's virtuosic dimension as performance, but Stravinsky incorporates repeated-note elements into the construction material to particularly striking effect in the four-part fugue that concludes the work, which, if de Schloezer is to be believed, would represent Stravinsky's bid for redemption-by-counterpoint.

The notion of Igor Stravinsky deliberately writing virtuoso piano music should not strike one as incongruous. In his pre-concert talk delivered at the premiere of the *Concerto for Two Solo Pianos* Stravinsky confessed to being a veteran of this romantic procedure: 'It was in the summer of

1921 that I wrote my transcription of [*Trois mouvements de*] *Pétrouchka*. My intention was to give piano virtuosi a work … to show off their technique';[29] and this same intention was behind the *Four Studies* of 1908. With regard to the *Concerto for Two Solo Pianos* Stravinsky took the opportunity to clarify his long-standing view of the concerto genre, of which he now had four examples in his catalogue, in terms of *l'ancienne formule*: namely the Piano Concerto, *Capriccio*, the Violin Concerto and the *Concerto for Two Solo Pianos*. His declared affinity with the concerto grosso enabled him to justify his conception of this new work as a match between equal rivals where the absence of an accompanying role, i.e. the omnipresence of two solo performers, called for a composition of an essentially contrapuntal nature.[30] This fascination with *le concours concertant* would eventually lead Stravinsky to transfer this instrumental formula to the stage, in *Agon* (1953/7), via a dramatic narrative combining French courtly dance with ancient Greek competition. Supported by that much-vaunted mélange of neoclassicism and duodecimal patterning, this ballet 'magically coheres' (to borrow from Jonathan D. Kramer)[31] *also* by framing its representation of ancient Greek contest within a counterpoint of relationships wherein the twelve dancers interact through varying degrees of rivalry (and affinity) within an overall context (and structure) of equal importance. Not only the music of *Agon*, therefore, but also its choreography (important aspects of which Stravinsky himself devised during the work's composition) is rooted in the original concept of concerto and in the 'rôle called *concertant*'. For, as Stravinsky had already made clear in the context of the *Concerto for Two Solo Pianos*, the term concerto 'derives from the Italian word *concertare*, which means *compete*, [that is] participate in a contest, in a match'.[32]

The notion of 'struggle', thus evoked, is not inconsistent with that aspect of *pal'tserazvitiye* which concerns the mental and physical effort of the learning process particularly, of course, in the field of (Stravinsky's) arduous piano practice – an observation which may provide the key to the continuing employment of that *ur*-objective element, the repeated note (already observed in *Duo concertant*). This sonority is developed further in the *Concerto for Two Solo Pianos* and the *Sonata for Two Pianos* (1943/4). Stravinsky's regular use of Philipp's *Complete School of Technic* in order to maintain his finger-technique might suggest a pedagogical origin to this curiously inclement drilling. (One suspects that it was this above all other aspects of the work that provoked Boris de Schloezer to write, above, with such a tangible sense of frustration and disappointment.)[33] The several instances of repeated-note textures in these latter works for two pianos – when considered alongside the composer's inevitable immersion in matters pianistic throughout the process of their composition – would support

Ex. 4.3a Isidor Philipp, *Complete School of Technic for the Piano*, 'Linked Trills' exercise, p. 107.

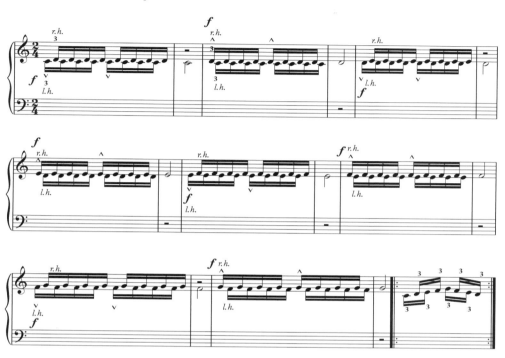

the view that this particular element derives from Stravinsky's familiarity with the set of exercises entitled 'Linked Trills' which form part of Philipp's method (Example 4.3a). Whereas, it must be noted, Stravinsky's tremoli are on one note and Philipp's linked trills are on two, their affinity is sealed by their shared technique: both require the rapid and skilful alternation of two hands utilizing the *same* finger from each in order to generate this virtuosic, mechanistic, supremely inexpressive (therefore ideally objective) 'music'. In this regard, Stravinsky's linked tremoli (as they surely deserve to be christened) present the most extreme manifestation of *pal'tserazvitiye* in Stravinsky's neoclassical output (Example 4.3b). In contrast, a decade after the rapid-fire power of the *Concerto*, the *Sonata for Two Pianos* presents a more conciliatory application of this pianistic knot (Example 4.3c): the latter's first movement reveals a more lyrical, more gesturally expressive foil to the former work's 'pedagogical' astringency. Stravinsky's ingenious solution (Example 4.3c) might even have been derived from the final bar of Philipp's

Ex. 4.3b Stravinsky, *Concerto for Two Solo Pianos* (1931/5), 4th movement, 'Preludio e Fuga', bb. 1–8.

Ex. 4.3c Stravinsky, *Sonata for Two Pianos* (1943/4), 1st movement, 'Moderato', bb. 14–16.

exercise, which similarly presents a scalic, i.e. quasi-melodic, expansion of the linked trill, while maintaining its mono-digital fingering and quicksilver hand exchange.

Performers of the *Concerto for Two Solo Pianos* already gain an insight into the direction that Stravinsky's intellect is moving when, in Variation III, they are asked to identify – and find some way of communicating to the listener – the subtleties of the composer's thematic thread as it is divided (somewhat idealistically) between the two players. The intricacies of such proto-serial obfuscation augment throughout this variation according to neoclassical/didactic patterns of 'progressive extension'. Whether or not Stravinsky imagined that listeners to the *Concerto* could realistically perceive these subtleties, the very presence of these ley lines criss-crossing the score (linking the soloists' four hands) would suggest that it was important to the composer that *someone* notice his architectural ingenuity. Inevitably, and by design, the two pianist-performers are offered this privilege in the first instance (Example 4.4).

It comes as no surprise that such extreme manifestations of *pal'tserazvitiye*, as noted in the first and third movements, should lead to a finale which extends these elements within a contrapuntal rubric that is also, in its turn, taken to extremes. Contrapuntal organization via the manifestation of linear order receives its most rigorous treatment in 'Preludio e Fuga'. The 'Fuga a 4 voci' is underpinned by tremoli which, owing to the elevated dynamics of this section (ranging from *mezzoforte* to *fortissimo*), significantly enhance the dual effects of energy and virtuosity whilst, also, shaking any trace of subjectivity or *lyrisme* off the expressive map. Upon its return (at 'Lo stesso tempo della Fuga nell'inversione') Stravinsky inverts the theme in a deliberate ratcheting-up of compositional academicism. Paradoxically, though, at this second statement he employs a 'melodic' variant of the linked tremolo (snatches of which will re-appear, as described above, in the *Sonata for Two Pianos*). Stravinsky thus forms an ostinato that would sit comfortably within the covers of *Petrushka*. (The juxtaposition of 'baroque' inverted fugue subject and 'Russian' counter-subject creates an intriguing impression.) By opting for a *piano* dynamic at the outset of this second wave of fugal entries Stravinsky draws attention, *sotto voce*, to the erudition of his compositional technique. For it is as if, by creating his own 'Contrapunctus inversus a 4', Stravinsky wished *sub rosa* to share with us an act of homage to *The Art of Fugue*, Bach's own testimonial to the musical/cerebral rigours of a passing era. The employment of *two* pianofortes in this concerto (without any other acoustic distractions) enabled Stravinsky to indulge his neoclassical interests with twice the focus, and so give full rein to a sophisticated matrix of those same contrapuntal devices which the use of this instrument had

Ex. 4.4 Stravinsky, *Concerto for Two Solo Pianos*, Variation III, bb. 18–20.

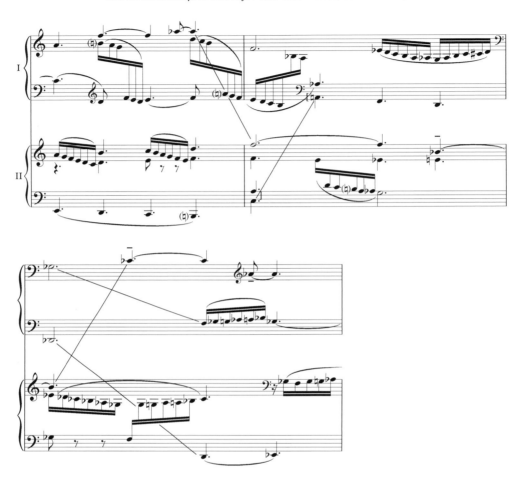

generated so often in the past. Now, though, he could call upon the added assistance of rapidly repeating notes to act as a novel and highly effective guarantor of objectivity. Stravinsky's judicious application of repeated-note material considerably negated the expressive 'effect' of the concerto's calculated virtuosity via the most acidulous and imaginative application of *pal'tserazvitiye* of any work considered thus far.

Symphony in Three Movements *(1942/1945)*

Some may consider that the *Symphony in C* (1938/40) represents the summit of Stravinsky's achievements in symphonic form, wherein the independent character of each movement is moulded formally into the one 'circle of symphonic experience'.[34] Certainly, the *Symphony in Three Movements* presents something of a problematic response to this arch-classical genre, not least because of its disparate 'sources'.[35] A composer of such practical nous as Stravinsky – especially one whose creative outlook has for so long been modelled upon the archetypal craftsmen of the eighteenth century (and earlier) – might well view the recycling of musical ideas in this manner as a practical and thoroughly classical (indeed, somewhat gratifying) aspect of musical composition. What *is* surprising – for it represents a complete denial of the neoclassical credo – is Stravinsky's later declaration concerning the images behind this work: specifically, the wartime documentary footage of 'scorched-earth tactics in China' (in the first movement), of 'goose-stepping soldiers' (at the opening of the third movement) and 'the rise of the Allies' (from the exposition of the fugue to the coda).[36] The term of endearment used in the title of Vera Stravinsky's diary ('Bubushkin') suggests that the composer was an eternal complainer, even of the little things in life.[37] Such disclosures relating to Stravinsky's extra-musical sources provide confirmation of his inevitable and understandably profound sensitivity to the violence of war. However, his admission to having written the *Symphony* in response to such stimuli compromises Stravinsky's whole neoclassical creed, that music is by its very nature powerless to *express* anything at all (*Chroniques*, 1935). His misdemeanour is hardly exonerated by his belated attempt to portray the earlier comments as 'simply a way of saying that music was supra-personal and supra-real' (*Expositions and Developments*, 1962). Furthermore, by viewing the *Concerto for Two Solo Pianos* as a prelude to the *concertante* role of the piano in the *Symphony in Three Movements*, one is drawn ineluctably to regard the statements made during his pre-concert talk (before the premiere of the *Concerto*) as infinitely more reliable – especially with regard to the special stimulus he sensed when writing for piano:

> Why not love music for itself, just as one loves a work of art, for the beauty of its painting, design and form? Why not just accept music as having its own value, independent of feelings and images which, by analogy, it may be able to evoke but only by distorting the listener's perception? Music needs no additive. It is sufficient unto itself.[38]

The *Symphony in Three Movements* might, then, be more profitably and more accurately defined (with *Duo concertant* – cf.p.207) as a solution to the instrumental and acoustic problem represented in the outer movements by the 'blend of strings struck in the piano with strings set in vibration with the bow'. The addition of a *concertante* harp (in the second and third movements) would suggest that Stravinsky was interested in widening the scope of his solution by coopting a third method of string sound-production: plucking. The debate over the work's title – incorporating the composer's apparent preference for *Three Symphonic Movements* over Nadia Boulanger's *Symphonie concertante* – merely distracts from the work's burlesque aspect in the tradition of that other *concertante* piano work, *Petrushka* (a 'Burlesque in four scenes'). Rather, the *Symphony* is perfectly consistent with Stravinsky's understanding of *l'ancienne formule* via the concerto grosso and the *principe du concours*. Furthermore, the harp (in partnership with the flute) may be seen as an emblem of the Cingrian ideal of ordered lyricism – to be continued in *Orpheus* (1947). In this latter work the harp enacts a prominent role as timbre and as a metaphor for an ancient form of eclogic (or, in the Stravinskian orthography, 'eglogic') classicism.[39]

Notwithstanding those stylistic disparities which are exposed to full view on the surface, the inner syntax of the *Symphony in Three Movements* is unified by a common pedagogical environment within which the piano material and those attitudes that are embodied in the spirit of *pal'tserazvitiye* play a central and cohesive role. Evidence that Stravinsky's attention at this time continued to be fully attuned to didactic goals – as a foil for undesirable subjectivity on the part of the performer – can be found via two contrasting devices and locations: (1) in the fluent part-writing of the *Sonata for Two Pianos* (1943/4), already noted; and (2) in the studied technicity of the *Elégie* (1944), a modest, yet revelatory 'two-part invention' for solo viola (or violin). Recalling the composer's stubborn adherence to certain fingerings in the *Sonate*, the Piano Concerto and, even, the Valse transcription (as discussed in earlier chapters), the 'assembly instructions' which accompany the fully edited score of *Elégie* clearly state: 'The fingerings have been chosen with a view to underlining the counterpoint, and not for technical facility.'[40] Stravinsky was still making the connection between pedagogy and art. Contrary to editorial conventions, Stravinsky designed his fingerings – as so often before – as a means to achieve an artistic result, not primarily to make life easier for the performer. His ground rules ensure that the work (as a 'task') is infused with technical priorities more commonly found in studies, exercises and drills than in a concert-piece. Once again, Stravinsky incorporates the rigours of pedagogy into his artistic vision, though here, in *Elégie*, he makes a rare intrusion into the technical orbit of an instrument other than the piano. Stravinsky had discussed the violin writing of his *Concerto* (1931) with Samuel Dushkin throughout its composition, and the violinist is duly credited in the score. One therefore assumes that such discussions continued with *Duo concertant* and the violin-and-piano transcriptions made for their many shared recital tours. By 1944 Stravinsky was well able to apply that didactic aspect of his neoclassicism – already a familiar trait in his piano works – to the demands of a solo polyphonic work for viola. Furthermore, *Elégie* witnesses Stravinsky avoiding virtuosity in its romantic, nineteenth-century sense by resourcing timeless laws of technique to re-create (his) 'neoclassical virtuosity'.

This reading is supported by the employment of several contrasting modes of piano writing in the *Symphony in Three Movements*. On the one hand, fluid contrapuntal textures recall the Piano Concerto, particularly its first movement Allegro. On this basis, the *Symphony* might appear to represent little advance on well-established Stravinskian neoclassical practice. However, whilst the 1924 concerto was fashioned with a preponderance of three-part counterpoint, the 1944 symphony will, on occasion, extend the technique briefly to encompass four-part writing (as in the first movement, Figs. 45–6 – the texture reverting to three parts at Figs. 46–7). Such 'progressive extension' – familiar from earlier discussions of the *Sonate* (last movement) and the *Symphony of Psalms* (first movement) – bears witness to Stravinsky's consistency across the wide chronological divide. Here are three piano parts written over a twenty-one-year span (1924/30/45) that are connected by a common thread of singularly neoclassical constructivism.

Another methodological and thoroughly pianistic issue is surely at the source of, arguably, the most innovative piano writing in the *Symphony in Three Movements*: the passage in the first movement where chords are rapidly exchanged between the hands, from right to left, in brilliant flashes of sound over a stuttering ostinato in the strings (initially at Fig. 7). Here, Stravinsky has drawn upon the lexicon of piano methodology by way of virtuous (timeless) exercises, combining these with heroic snatches of nineteenth-century romanticism – e.g. brilliant octave-exchanges between the hands, such as one might term 'Lisztian cascades'. These contrasting tropes are merged into another manifestation of Stravinskian 'neoclassical virtuosity' whose origin and focus is its technicity. This memorable passage offers a sense of energy, which – in the manner of the repeated-note trope viewed in *Petrushka*, *Duo concertant* and the *Concerto for Two Solo Pianos* – does not, however, convey any emotional excitement. Similarly, the piano 'cascades' in the *Symphony* fail to elicit from us any such romantic response. This is principally due to their limited envelope and their circular (non-directional) ostinato-repetitions (Example 4.5a). Rather, they relate to the workshop of piano practice and thus portray a work-in-progress by means of the efforts of a 'pianist-in-progress', executing with valiant perseverance a purely technical exercise.

During his twenty-year engagement with the pedagogy of Philipp, Stravinsky may have become acquainted with an earlier set of his piano studies, his *Exercices pratiques* (*Introduction aux exercices journaliers*) of

Ex. 4.5a Stravinsky, *Symphony in Three Movements* (1942/5); 1st movement, Figs. 9–10.

Ex. 4.5b Stravinsky, Violin Concerto in D (1931); reduction by the composer for violin and piano, 4th movement, 'Capriccio', bb. 16–21.

1897. The eighth drill within this volume is marked 'Très lent et fort (du poignet)'. It aims to strengthen the wrists in a manner that is not covered in the later *Complete School* (1908). For this reason one can only speculate whether Stravinsky knew of this publication. (Philipp's studies were readily available for much of the past century in Europe and America. The *Complete School* remains in print to this day in its original edition.) Alternatively, or additionally, Philipp himself may have passed on such an exercise to his distinguished pupil as preparation for Stravinsky's anticipated series of performances of the Piano Concerto – a demanding work full of rapid chords and octaves requiring advanced wrist-technique, forearm strength and considerable stamina. According to Philipp's well-established *système de modification rythmique* all his exercises should be varied in speed, accent and rhythm as a matter of course. The full technical potential of the *exercice pratique* in question, therefore, although marked 'très lent', would be explored by adapting the raw material according to several well-established modifications: for example (1) by playing at the extremes of tempo (from very slow to very fast); or (2) in groups of two or more chords; or (3) by altering the regularity of these dense chords, for example into dotted patterns or triplets; or (4) with octave displacement. Whether or not the fast exchange of hands, which is the hallmark of this notable passage in the *Symphony in Three Movements*, derives from Philipp alone (or at all), Stravinsky is undoubtedly resourcing the literature and gestures of piano methodology as he has done on so many occasions.

The Violin Concerto – or, more precisely, Stravinsky's labours to produce a piano reduction from the full score of this work – may also provide a clue to understanding this memorable passage. It was a crafting task he undertook in parallel with the concerto's creation. In the process of translating certain figurations from orchestra to keyboard he might well have registered an attraction to the particular energy generated by such irregularly metred chordal cascades – alternating in the main (as in the *Symphony*) between pairs and single chords. Stravinsky may have stored that resultant sonority in his aural memory. The passage occurs on three occasions during the final movement ('Capriccio') of the Violin Concerto.[41] Although, in this context, it lacks the ostinato accompaniment which will underpin the equivalent passage in the first movement of the *Symphony in Three Movements*, the lower register of the texture is similarly knitted, as it were, with the aid of a vamping bass-line. The similitude of these cascades in both works is noticeable when the concerto material is played in its original, string/orchestral guise; but it is particularly striking when heard (and played) in the version made by Stravinsky himself for violin and piano (Example 4.5b).[42] Furthermore, one must consider the implications of Stravinsky composing this string material originally *at the piano*, for this would suggest a two-way or circular journey. If this passage was composed at the piano (as is assumed) then, at the moment Stravinsky formulated his piano reduction (so-called), the 'string' cascades were in fact reverting to their original state as piano music. From the process of modelling the reduction upon his original sketches for the *Concerto* Stravinsky may, therefore, have noted the pianistic possibilities inherent in this texture and developed these during the composition of the *Symphony*.

In his later pronouncements Stravinsky was to suggest that his initial concept of the first of the *Symphony*'s three movements was as a concerto for orchestra. However, when Alexandre Tansman paid the composer a visit in 1942 he came away with the impression that Stravinsky was working on an orchestral movement 'with a piano concertant'.[43] There is no reason to doubt either testimony, even in an otherwise unremarkable transitional passage (at Fig. 70). This concerns a brief interlude which emerges from a veritable barrage of rhythmical poundings, *tutti* and *forte fortissimo* (*fff*).[44] The contrasting material which ensues (from Fig. 70) is for woodwind and piano, gently oscillating in *legato*, before it is gradually transformed via strings and brass into another rhythmically animated episode. It is this aimlessly rocking interlude, however, that betrays both an orchestral and, ultimately, a pianistic foundation.[45] The material is based on classic string tropes from *Apollo* ('Naissance d'Apollon', starting at Fig. 13), which, in turn, are re-workings (by doubling its note-values) of *ur*-neoclassical piano-practice gestures that Stravinsky first employs in the final movement of the *Sonate* (at bb. 53–63).

Other manifestations of *pal'tserazvitiye* abound in the music of this period. For example, such *legato/staccato* simultaneity between hands and registers (which was identified as a typical sonority of Stravinskian neo-classicism as far back as the Piano Concerto) continues to prove useful in the *Ebony Concerto* (1945/6), Stravinsky's tribute to Woody Herman and his celebrated big band.[46] Regarding this work, Walsh has commented that Stravinsky 'cunningly [adapted] the rhythmic-ostinato style of [his] neo-classicism to the jazz clichés he had picked up from Herman's records'.[47] One should recall, however, that the practice of juxtaposing extremes of articulation pre-dates even Stravinsky's earliest neoclassical years. The F♯ minor Sonata, particularly the varied treatment of the first movement's second theme,[48] reveals a precocious fascination with this texture. Spurred on by Kashperova's diktat to avoid the sustaining pedal, Stravinsky evidently relished turning this singularly pianistic challenge to his creative advantage. As we have seen, he employed this device on several occasions throughout his long career.

Whatever the difficulties in defining the *Symphony in Three Movements* as a whole, the first movement represents a clear and consistent represen-tation of Stravinsky's core neoclassical parameters: particularly those that relate to, and derive from, the use of the piano as both metaphor and frame of reference. In fact, the use of this instrument in simultaneous and oppos-ing articulations (*legato/staccato*) seems to have provoked the composer to re-awaken his erstwhile partiality for the woodwind as an ideally 'objective' co-vehicle for neoclassical utterances – displaying a degree of interest not seen in his scores since the early 1920s. Specifically, the passage between Figs. 76 and 82 presents something of the 'essence' of this sonority. Here one can observe three strata which confirm a lineage of traditional neoclassical values, as represented by *pal'tserazvitiye* and by the use of woodwind: (1) the *concertante* piano part consists of an ingenious 'play' of *legato* and *stac-cato* articulations. This is combined with and accompanies two bassoons (marked *forte*). (2) Representing the strings, the violins and violas offer merely a distant commentary (marked *piano*) which is based on inexpres-sive or, to borrow from Ortega, 'dehumanized' snatches of repeated notes which form a 'reminiscence' of piano material heard at the start of this pas-sage (at Fig. 76). The third stratum concerns (3) the notable entry of a pair of bassoons *soli* (at the third bar of Fig. 81), which reminds the listener of Stravinsky's former bias for woodwinds.

Within the aural universe of wind instruments, the particular sonority provided by two bassoons has something of a distinguished pedigree as far as Stravinsky's instrumentation is concerned. The Octet, for example, offers this double-act exceptional status. From their trills in the opening bars of the work to the finale's extensive preamble, the pair of bassoons are granted regular prominence. Their contribution to the Variations movement is particularly virtuosic and original. If one is sympathetic to Taruskin's view (that the premiere of the Octet marked the 'official' start of Stravinskian neoclassicism)[49] then it follows that this historically significant launch was founded upon the basis of this unusual sonority. However, in the context of the *Symphony in Three Movements* Stravinsky's brief exposure of bassoons in the final movement may have a different significance entirely. It is an intriguing possibility that Stravinsky may have wished to re-visit his earlier duet, *Lied ohne Name für zwei Fagotten* (*Song without a Name for two Bassoons*), penned in 1918 but never published in the composer's lifetime (Figure 4.1). White states that this work 'was sketched out in 1918'.[50] In fact, the manuscript, held in Basel, is as flawless and neat as any Stravinskian *Reinschrift*.[51] Stylistically, this miniature for double-reeds relates to the extreme *nepodvizhnost'* posture of the piano solo 'Valse pour les enfants' (1917/22), whose composition straddles that of *Lied ohne Name*. The use of a treble clef for the high register rather than a tenor clef (the more usual custom for bassoon-writing) further emphasizes the work's relation to other piano solo material of that ilk. In its unusual instrumentation and complete absence of agogic markings *Lied ohne Name* reflects Stravinsky's increasing confidence in wind instruments to provide an ideally cold and 'less vague' sonority for his emerging objective idiom.[52] It is a demonstration of the extraordinary trajectory that Stravinsky's neoclassicism has travelled (effectively a total role-reversal) that, in the passage from the *Symphony* under review, it is the body of strings that maintains the most inexpressive line, while the bassoons – in complete contrast to *Lied ohne Name* – must now respond to notation that is full of agogic indications of emotional intent. Their 'duet' (at Fig. 82) is even, though this is hardly credible, marked *espressivo*.

While such an inverted sense of instrumentation may occasionally reveal a radical departure from standard neoclassical policy, the final movement of the *Symphony* – in particular, its *alla breve* fugue (two bars before Fig. 170) – serves as a timely reminder that Stravinsky still believed in the conventional appropriateness of imitative counterpoint to reinforce the objectivity of his major neoclassical statements. Indeed, the oscillating character of this fugue subject alludes to other thematic material by Stravinsky: for example, the lower contour of the inverted fugue subject at the conclusion of the *Concerto for Two Solo Pianos* ('Lo stesso tempo della Fuga nell'inversione'). There may even be passing reference to Rimsky-Korsakov's opera *The Legend of the Invisible City of Kitezh* (premiered in 1907), for which the young Stravinsky was enrolled by his teacher to assist with the orchestration. The start of the male-voice chorus 'O toute puissante souveraine des cieux' (cited in Rimsky's *Treatise on Orchestration* with the libretto translated into French)

Fig. 4.1 Stravinsky, *Lied ohne Name für Zwei Fagotten* (1918), complete. Stravinsky has signed his neat copy of this work using a form of script described by Taruskin as 'an archaistic calligraphy modelled on the pre-Petrine Slavic alphabet – that is, the true old-Bulgarian *kirillitsa*, the alphabet of SS. Cyril

outlines this same oscillation, doubled in the woodwind.[53] A more likely allusion, however, given the chant-like outline of the fugue subject, is to the opening chorus of the *Symphony of Psalms*. Whereas in this latter work the oscillation is semitonal, it is based in the *Symphony* upon the whole tone. Devoid of any specific textual association, it now forms the basis for an expressively 'minimal' motif – never chromatic, but entirely consistent with the step-wise relationships that characterize the motivic material of the *Symphony* as a whole. The latter half of the fugue subject expands from its initial oscillation (upon the interval of the second) to adopt a more melodic contour via its use of wide-ranging intervals. This might suggest a parallel expansion of expressive effect across the fugue exposition; however, the predominance of (major and minor) sevenths and ninths – intervals which are equivalent, by inversion, to (minor and major) seconds – guarantees that the fugue subject, initially at least, conveys a predominantly ascetic mood. In wider context amid the tumult of the final movement, the fugue may be heard as a momentary and drastic call-to-neoclassical-arms: 'No, no, you must [still] think of Savonarola!' The subsequent *agitato* charge for the line demonstrates, to borrow from Goubault, Stravinsky's 'extreme enthusiasm' at news of the Allied victory.[54] As if to emphasize the orthodox neoclassical intent that lies behind this fugal section, its exposition is characterized by the gradual addition of wind instruments to the original *concertante* pair of piano and harp: i.e. the trombone plays at the start, then, between Figs. 174 and 178, bassoons take up the fugue and clarinets the countersubject. The entry of the strings is sporadic, their more expressive/subjective sonority introduced hesitantly: firstly via isolated pizzicato notes (more rhythmic in their effect than contrapuntal), then with fragmentary arco phrases. Eventually the whole five-part string orchestra present their version of the fugue subject (Figs. 178–81) in their own terms: lyrical, chromatic, increasingly intense and expressive, decreasingly articulated and objective. The old neoclassical (indeed, Rimskian) dichotomies are alive and well, it seems.

The concluding section, marked 'Agitato ma sempre l'istesso tempo', effectively sets in motion the energetic pulse which will drive the movement to its resounding conclusion. Yet, Stravinsky does not relinquish all notion of contrapuntal discipline. The harp part reveals a complex web of invertible counterpoint reflecting established, indeed conservative, Viennese/Schoenbergian practice: Stravinsky appears to treat the fugue subject as a micro-series (P0) ripe for proto-serial manipulation (Figs.

Caption for Fig. 4.1 (*cont.*)
and Methodius', introduced to Russia in the tenth century (Taruskin, *Stravinsky and the Russian Traditions*, p. 1130).

182/3). The harp proceeds to combine the retrograde of the 'series' (R0) with its retrograde inversion (RI). The procedure is not strict but the composer is clearly absorbed with the possibilities of tightly organized invertible counterpoint. It would be going too far to suggest that Stravinsky is here anticipating his own dodecaphonic future. The signs are, however, that he is beginning to cross that same paradoxical bridge between neoclassicism and serialism that Schoenberg traversed twenty years earlier when he resolved to couch his first strictly twelve-tone works in terms of eighteenth-century genres, via the 'classical' *Serenade* op. 24 (1920/3) and the 'baroque' *Suite for Piano* op. 25 (1921/3). Indeed, the *Serenade* offers a particularly intriguing parallel with Stravinsky's neoclassical enchantment with Petrarch, for its fourth movement is a setting of 'Far potess' io vendetta di colei'.[55] According to Christophe Calame, Cingria's *Pétrarque* is a meditation upon the end of the 'Dark Ages' and the beginnings of Modernity.[56] Cingria cites Bartoli in his defence of the great Italian poet: 'With him an era vanishes and the first modern man appears on the horizon.'[57] Seven centuries later and from their different perspectives, Schoenberg and Stravinsky sought to advance their latest modernist projections upon the very same foundation. At first glance Petrarch's impact on twentieth-century music would appear to have resulted in two opposing outcomes. Yet all the while, as Stravinsky's later adoption of serialism would confirm, these two composers had always shared a singular fascination: namely, 'composition with intervals'. Their regard for Arezzo's greatest son (born in 1304) may also represent another underestimated point of unity. Schoenberg (in his *Serenade*) employed the ancient timbres of guitar and mandolin to aid his Petrarchan flight into dodecaphonism. Despite his use of exclusively modern instruments, Stravinsky (in *Duo concertant*) would also justify his antique form of neoclassicism by its fundamental affinity, via Cingria, with Petrarch.

The final pages of the *Symphony in Three Movements* present something quite unique in Stravinsky's music: a chronological pageant of historical style. Aside from the fugue, which registers its presence so strikingly, the principal device used by the composer to characterize this fly-past of musical idioms is articulation – that musical parameter which has been shown so often to derive from his pianistic workshop. Stravinsky's adaptations of the fugue subject represent an exemplary demonstration in the use of varying articulations to evoke musical style. In such expert hands articulation can also convey to the listener a clear message as to the music's (inexpressive) objectivity or its (expressive) subjectivity. Quite simply, Stravinsky alters the articulation of the fugue subject according to the ever-evolving musical setting, in the following manner: at the start of the *alla breve* fugue (Fig. 170), i.e. at the moment of blandest neoclassical objectivity, there is maximum definition between the extremes of *legato* and *staccato*. Although the piano is given the dominant role in the presentation of the fugue, Stravinsky has added a pre-statement on trombone, an instrument of relatively imprecise attack. (The sketches indicate that the inclusion of this passage on the trombone was a late decision.) Evidently Stravinsky was alert to the risk, by using this instrument, of losing the desired clarity of articulation at the start. He therefore notated the opening notes of the trombone part as *staccato* quavers (separated by rests) in an attempt to emulate the 'ideal' clarity of the ensuing piano statement. However, at the entry of the harp (Fig. 172) the clear-cut enunciation of the opening becomes nuanced by the natural resonance of this instrument and the resultant sonority is 'warmed' by this softening of articulation. This 'harp version' of the fugue subject reflects a greater sense of expressivity also by its subtle rhythmic adaptation: the first note is now altered from a crotchet to a minim. The contribution of the piano to the harp's statement is notable too for its nuanced sonority: the marking *una corda* recalls the use of this device in *Petrushka* where (it was claimed in Chapter 1, pp. 67–8) the composer was deliberately evoking an eighteenth-century, pseudo-*clavier* sonority by means of a less resonant timbre. If one reads the initial trombone/piano statement of the fugue as its most antique sonority, then, by comparison subsequent presentations of this material can be heard as projecting a more recent, more expressive musical idiom with each statement. By such instrumentation the original 'pure' neoclassical sonority of the outset is further nuanced, its academic clarity replaced by a more artistic intent with a tangible effect upon its diminishing sense of 'objectivity'. In the final passage leading into the return of the Agitato (Figs. 178–82), *legato* has now become the all-pervasive articulation and the harp's rhythmic variant of the fugue subject (with a minim as its first note) now dominates, contributing to the smooth and sustained texture. The musical flow becomes ever more characterized by long phrases, sonorous four- and five-part string textures, wide melodic intervals, chromaticism of inner parts, and expressive dynamics (*crescendo*, *sforzando*, *marcato*). Even the piano part is transformed, now offering (Figs. 179–81) a lush, almost Brahmsian dimension to the orchestral sonority.

One might well pause amid this romantic landscape and recall Stravinsky's protest at the disastrous premiere of the *Symphonies of Wind Instruments* in 1921. 'The radical misunderstanding', so the composer explained, 'was that an attempt was made to impose an external pathos on the music'.[58] Truly, over the intervening twenty-four years Stravinsky had formulated an entirely different understanding of the term 'neoclassicism' – for his new

music written under this old banner could now fully embrace several layers of 'external pathos'. Viewed as a whole, the *Symphony*'s chronological
cortège may have set off to the ancient call of the sackbut (represented by
this instrument's heir, the trombone); but, in fact, the entire procession was
aided and abetted throughout by 'Stravinsky's piano', which fulfilled a crucial role in guiding the musical discourse forwards to 1945. Milan Kundera
views Stravinsky's whole output in such terms: 'In [his] work, European
music recalled its thousand-year history; that was its final dream before
setting out for an eternal dreamless sleep.'[59] Articulation, that *ur*-pianistic
parameter and essence of *pal'tserazvitiye*, is the language in which this historical pageant is couched. Alternatively, if one prefers to read the final
pages of this work as a commemoration of the Allied triumph then the
foregoing procession may also be heard as a respectful march-past cele-
brating the long legacy of western musical culture in defence of which that
nightmarish conflict was fought.

There is, however, another interpretation to which the present author
lends a sympathetic ear. (Was it not Paul Valéry who called poetry a sustained hesitation between sound and sense?) This concerns the hesitant
two-note fugue subject in its two variants, for trombone-and-piano and for
harp as characterized, respectively, by a crotchet-first-note (Fig. 170) and
a minim-first-note (Fig. 172). Could this possibly derive from a rhythmic
play *al roverscio* upon the Italian *canzona* and its characteristic opening
rhythm – as revealed, for example, in the Banchieri excerpt cited by Cingria
(Example 4.1a)? Intriguingly, the second of Stravinsky's *Two Sacred Songs* –
transcribed in 1968 from the *Spanisches Liederbuch* of Hugo Wolf – is also
permeated with a rhythmic pattern (crotchet–crotchet–minim–crotchet)
identical to that of the fugue in the final movement of *Symphony in Three
Movements*. A particularly notable passage may be observed in 'Wunden
trägst du, mein Geliebter ...' (bb. 19–22) where this rhythm *al modo di canzona* occurs three times in succession to the text: 'An den Wunden muß ich
sterben, weil ich dich geliebt so heiß'. White has commented that, according to Craft, 'Stravinsky made this instrumentation [of *Two Sacred Songs*]
because he wanted to say something about death and felt that he could not
compose anything of his own.'[60] This is indeed a curious remark about the
composer of *Requiem Canticles* (1966). Wolf's setting might have attracted
Stravinsky not only for its sombre topic, but also for the rhythmic characteristics of its thematic material, which may well have carried positive
associations for the composer. Yet, in *Symphony in Three Movements*, it is
articulation more than any other parameter that is the real currency of the
last movement's fugal *fantasia concertante*, this beautifully contrived *étude
d'articulation*. And the piano, with a natural capacity to vary its touch by

subtle shades of articulation (of which the contrast between *legato* and *staccato* is at the heart of all its methodologies) is its playful catalyst.

It is, of course, the pianistic/methodological foundation to Stravinsky's neoclassicism that differentiates his aesthetic so fundamentally from Schoenberg's preoccupation with pitch organization. Nowhere is this more clearly illustrated than in Stravinsky's loyalty to the minutiae of keyboard performance, its challenges (great and small), and its laborious but very necessary practicalities. Before addressing Stravinsky's serial works it is instructive to view the panorama of Stravinsky's neoclassical output in retrospect. From this, one observes that the epitome of *pal'tserazvitiye* resides in the pianistic conundrum of articulation and its partner in practice, fingering. In many ways the final-movement fugue of the *Symphony in Three Movements* – and its cautiously measured phraseology – encapsulates the essence of Stravinsky's life-long engagement, regardless of the musical idiom, with such a seemingly banal issue as the contrast between music's subtle gradations of *legato* and *staccato*. This fundamental drill (so elementary in its demand upon the pianist) has grown throughout Stravinsky's career from specific and isolated examples into a generalized idiomatic device. Thus, articulation informs the whole of this composer's neoclassicism. Such momentary focus on pure digital coordination leads inevitably into a hiatus of repetitions and oscillations which have contributed, in their impact upon the otherwise forward motion of the music's narrative, to their being understood and labelled according to such familiar terminology as *nepodvizhnost'*, 'stuttering' or just plain ostinato. Yet these terms, while they are undoubtedly appropriate to a degree, merely reflect one's reception of such aural manipulations. They do not address the origins of this phenomenon and so cannot adequately reveal its true identity or meaning. It is as if, for example, one merely recognized the perfect cadence for its effect of finality, rather than understanding it as the result of a process of harmony and voice-leading grounded in music's rudiments, out of which its function emerges ('is constructed') and, ultimately, makes sense. Certainly, the dubious status of the *Symphony in Three Movements* as something of a *tertium quid* is emphatically contradicted when one considers the fistful of pianistic consistencies that form a convincing demonstration of integrity – owing, principally, to an underlying and tangible unity between material and method. Despite the distractions of Stravinsky's 'war programme' – which might suggest to the unwary some sort of documentary soundtrack or twentieth-century equivalent to Beethoven's *Battle of Vittoria* or Tchaikovsky's *1812* – it is, rather, the work's profound indebtedness to the composer's personal campaign waged at the piano which persuades the more attentive listener of the solidly neoclassical credentials which lie at the heart of the *Symphony in Three Movements* – that enigmatic partner to the more 'truly symphonic', apparently more objective (and 'Great') *Symphony in C*.

The Rake's Progress *(1948/1951)*

'Can a composer re-use the past and at the same time move in a forward direction?' Stravinsky asked in 1964, and immediately responded: 'Regardless of the answer (which is "yes"), this academic question did not trouble me during the composition [of *The Rake's Progress*] ... If the opera contains imitations, however – especially of Mozart, as has been said – I will gladly allow the charge if I may thereby release people from the argument and bring them to the music.'[61] Stravinsky's comments, written more than a decade after completing *The Rake*, confirm his belief in neoclassicism as a force for musical and aesthetic progress. Yet, he continues, 'I am not concerned with the future of my opera. I ask for it only a measure of present justice.' This would best be achieved, he proposes, by bringing audiences to *The Rake's Progress* – that is, to 'the music' and away from the wider debate that the opera had provoked. Stravinsky considered it important that the listener should submit individually to the full musical and emotive impact of the work – this, at a time when the composer had fully adopted the framework of serialism as his latest constructive re-invention. This appeal on behalf of the score and its much-admired libretto was made following Stravinsky's re-appraisal of his earlier polemic surrounding the supposed incapacity of music to 'express anything at all'. By 1962 Stravinsky preferred to re-draw his argument by saying, simply, that music was 'supra-personal' and 'supra-real'. As an illustration of these super-powers *The Rake* is, *pace* Cingria, the epitome of lyricism-underpinned-by-rules.

The opera presents a musical narrative which alternately interweaves and unpicks the mannerist conventions of eighteenth-century diatonicism,[62] revealing another side to Stravinsky's neoclassicism from that *retour à Bach* which, according to Charles Koechlin, represents an art-form that is neat, vigorous, non-descriptive and even non-expressive.[63] And within the covers of this *faux*-naive tale *The Rake*'s darkest and therefore (inevitably) most expressive passages portray Tom Rakewell's psychological decline at the hands of Nick Shadow. Such tension is particularly marked in the graveyard scene (Act III, scene 2: 'Well, then' ... 'My heart is wild with fear'). This duet-*scena* takes the form, apparently, of a *recitativo secco*; that is, the two singers are accompanied solely by a keyboard continuo. It is the longest passage in the opera when the comforting sonority of the classical orchestra is absent (Example 4.6 offers merely the opening of this scene). In *Poetics* Stravinsky

Ex. 4.6 Stravinsky, *The Rake's Progress* (1948/51), Act III, scene 2, bb. 1–9.

had summoned the aid of Verdi (via Roland-Manuel) in his citation of that admirable injunction: 'Let us return to old times and that will be progress.'[64] Truly, as Paul Griffiths reminds us, the most startling single aspect of *The Rake*'s neoclassical instrumentation is Stravinsky's 'resurrected convention' of the harpsichord (his only previous interest being part of an early, orchestral version of *Svadebka*).[65] In this scene the desiccated sonority of the harpsichord is used 'to portray a musical quicksand in which Tom tries in vain to find his footing'.[66] Yet, despite this almost unbearable psychological load, it seems that rarely has a continuo been so unresponsive to the sentiment and the inflections of the vocal line. The rigidity of the accompaniment calls into question its very identity as a recitative or an operatic 'number'. Is this not, rather, an art song (for voice(s) and piano accompaniment) interposed within the pages of an operatic/orchestral score? And is not the keyboard material formulated out of an extreme spirit of irony from the expressionless, technical kit of piano methodology, i.e. from the coordinated, calibrated and self-consciously deliberate ritual of practising arpeggios 'by key'? The neoclassical complexion of this duet is provided by the blatant clash of tonalities – D major–F♯ minor; F major–F♯ minor; G major–G♯ minor[67] – that serve to illustrate the mental disintegration of the hero's humanity and the ascendancy of the villain's heartless 'mechanistic' manipulation. Its objective attitude is derived from the manner of its construction – i.e. this passage, patiently built upon the sliding re-positioning of the hands between pairs of neighbouring chords, is surely grounded in the pianistic drills of methods immemorial. And there is another significant connection with *pal'tserazvitiye*. In the manner that these triadic arpeggios pivot upon one or more common tones – often the third degree of the scale – they vividly resemble the interminable intricacies of Leschetizky's *Accordgruppe*, now dutifully applied to both hands. Its new adaptation, so long after Stravinsky's apprenticeship in St Petersburg, is not so much a reflection on his 'extraordinary memory' but, rather, it is evidence that such pianistic configurations – whether based 'officially' in Leschetizky and Philipp or (less formally) in Stravinsky's daily routine of piano studies and intervallic explorations – remained a living ritual throughout his career.

The epilogue to *The Rake* – when the cast come out of character and remove their wigs – is indeed a rude awakening. Yet the extraordinary duet that precedes it (above) reveals, in a far subtler manner, the shocking ingenuity of Stravinsky's 'cunning engine'.[68] With the full palette of orchestral and dramatic resources at his disposal, the composer opted instead to resurrect the present in terms of the past via a more extreme route, even, than the epilogue's dramatic trick. In his response to W. H. Auden's (and Chester Kallman's) verses – their 'beautiful gift', as Stravinsky famously described their libretto[69] – the composer chose to re-visit a very personal and elemental place: namely, the piano workshop of his daily creativity.[70] Rakewell's malfunctioning Reason is mirrored in the music's apparent 'wrong-ness', in the apparent dysfunction of its syntax. Drained of intellectual competence and the capacity for rational response, the opera's protagonist is restricted (like the digital drills against which his pathetic responses are set) to deliberate and laboured efforts. Tom's psychological unravelling is 'portrayed' by the accompaniment's return to the basics of five-finger practice, where cognitive engagement is limited and where self-expression is similarly minimal. It turns out, then, that Stravinsky's continuo performs its function to perfection. Far from being unresponsive it is in fact hyper-sensitive to Tom's predicament to which it responds with graphic and uncomfortable realism.

As in so many previous contexts, Stravinsky found that the most appropriate vocabulary for *The Rake*'s particular psycho-denouement was the supremely neoclassical resource of the piano, its exercises and the minutiae of repeating and subtly varying revolutions, each note and interval weighed, measured and recycled. (Indeed, how much more revelatory and effective would it be to hear this scene, indeed the whole opera, performed with a piano rather than a harpsichord – an option that the composer himself suggests in the full score?)[71] Yet, it is not only by way of its syntax that this duet alludes to earlier manifestations of Stravinsky's piano-derived neoclassicism. This is also evoked by its rhetoric, sounding like a slowed-down drill or a study in practising mode. Thus, this 'art song accompaniment' – anchored in those hand-formulated figurations of *pal'tserazvitiye* – neatly conforms to the most rigorous models of Stravinskian objectivity. Notation, too, plays its part. The metronome indication (quaver = 69) would suggest a measured pulse, yet the movement's notation in semiquavers is consistent with other Stravinskian *ritornelli* previously considered: for example, in the *Sonate* (final movement), the *Sérénade* ('Rondoletto'), *Duo concertant* ('Eglogue I', 'Gigue') and the *Concerto for Two Solo Pianos* ('Con moto'). In all of these contexts Stravinsky's tempi are based on the crotchet-pulse rather than the duet's quaver-pulse. It is precisely this slow quaver-pulse which most firmly communicates a practice-rhetoric. One only has to play the duet 'up to speed' – for example, at double-speed (crotchet = 69) as its semiquaver notation implies – to recognize the strongly characterized *ritornello*-nature of its material and how this duet-accompaniment (apparently at half-speed and in workshop mode) achieves its decadent, psychologically unsettling effect.

There are many levels on which this music provides intriguing parallels with earlier manifestations of *pal'tserazvitiye*. Such deliberate, intellectually driven and gradual manipulation of arpeggio patterns is at the very essence of pedagogical routine. So, too, the emphasis on mental rigour whereby the *gruppetti*, although not unfamiliar or difficult in themselves, are made more challenging because of their journey via unfamiliar, uncomfortable combinations. Furthermore, there is that unmistakable element of endurance – mental endurance, in this case, more than physical – so characteristic of *pal'tserazvitiye* and which has often been observed, particularly in the 'over-long' *ritornelli* of earlier neoclassical piano parts. Thus, in this aspect too, *The Rake's Progress* displays that characteristically Stravinskian blend of constancy and evolution of which the graveyard scene is, in so many senses, a supreme illustration. The following discussion will focus on Stravinsky's serial transformation in the 1950s and the continuing relevance of pianism to his creative continuum. For, as we shall see, it was from Stravinsky's loyalty to his pianistic roots that those initial forays into twelve-tone composition remained indubitably Stravinskian in spite of the radical change of idiom and concomitant swerve of aesthetic. Owing to his faithfulness to the means of production – both at and out of the piano – Stravinsky's late music is equally representative of his long and varied career. Far from denying the validity of his previous output, the serial works are merely a continuance (as Herzen would phrase it) of Stravinsky's Russian and neoclassical past(s).

Neoclassical serialism

Septet

Movements for Piano and Orchestra – and beyond …

Septet (1952/1953)

Stravinsky's engagement with pianism as a source of creative energy has now been traced over half a century: from the embryonic *Tarantella* of 1898 – that is, pre-dating even competent notation – to *The Rake's Progress* of 1951. The habit and manner of this engagement with the piano persisted into his late serial phase. Stravinsky's practice of deriving the intervallic bases of his newest compositions from aspects of *pal'tserazvitiye* – justifying their validity within the reassuring stock of pianistic groundwork – was maintained until well after his career as a concert pianist was over and he had re-invented himself as a serialist. Its impact can be heard in many of Stravinsky's late works of which the Septet (1953) is an early example (Example 4.7). In common with Stravinsky's canon of neoclassical piano works, the Septet also features a certain academicism. This is apparent from the very opening bars, and takes several forms: (1) through the simultaneous augmentation, by the bassoon, of the clarinet's opening theme; and (2) even more so via the inversion of

Ex. 4.7 Stravinsky, Septet (1952/3), 1st movement, bb. 1–5.

this theme in augmentation, by the horn (bb. 1–5). Furthermore, (3) the
'technicity' of the piano writing is demonstrated by the four-fold use of
the index-finger-over-thumb overlap in the left hand (bb. 3–4; it is almost
a direct quotation from the last movement of the *Sonate pour piano* and
refers, more distantly, to the left-hand figuration noted in 'Les Canards,
les cignes, les oies …').[72] All this confirms that Stravinsky's engagement
with *pal'tserazvitiye* – in its dual manifestation as compositional exercise
and pianistic study – continued hale and hearty beyond the strictly neoclassical context.

Two anecdotes taken from Stravinsky's 'late phase' serve to illustrate
this very point. Milton Babbitt relates how, during the composition of
Movements, Stravinsky was keen to impress upon his inner circle – which
on that occasion (at the Gladstone Hotel, London in late December 1958)
comprised Mrs Stravinsky, Robert Craft and Babbitt himself – just how
devoutly he followed a serial plan: '[Stravinsky] suddenly bolted out of
the room in his robe, waving a page of manuscript paper, smiling broadly
that pixie-like smile, and shouting: "I found a mistake, and the right note
sounds so much better."'[73] Nine years later, having successfully established
his credentials as a serial composer, Stravinsky could admit his preferred
allegiance to and dependence upon his feelings. He preferred to trust
'my musical glands above the fool-proofing of my musical flight charts,
though I realize that the flight charts are formed in part by these same
glands. [Furthermore] I think the tendency which seeks to attribute every
factor in a musical composition to a punch-card master plan could con-
strict the "free" options of the ear.'[74] In another of Stravinsky's conversations with Robert Craft, the composer speaks openly about the source
which, like the Fontaine de Vaucluse, supplies him with his 'free options'
in an ever-dependable flow: 'I continue [however] to believe in my taste
buds and to follow the logic of my ear, quaint expression which will seem
even quainter when I add that I require as much hearing at the piano as
ever before.'[75] Even when viewed from a serial perspective, such vocabulary – to speak of the 'logic of my ear' – is, of course, entirely consistent with the objective tenets of Stravinsky's never-ending neoclassicism
and with those notions of process that are firmly embedded in the rigorous methods of pianistic/academic construction. I make no apology for
reiterating these fundamental connections, for it is instructive to discern
how faithfully Stravinsky's creative consistencies (especially those which
relate to *pal'tserazvitiye*) were retained through the late serial works, and
in a manner which (as Turgenev would say) is 'already familiar to my
tolerant readers'.[76]

Movements for Piano and Orchestra *(1958/1959) – and beyond ...*

There are many reasons for including a commentary on *Movements* in the present study, not least of which is the obvious point that this work represents Stravinsky's last demonstration of his abiding interest in *concertante* piano relationships, both overtly or covertly solistic, within the context of instrumental/orchestral sonorities. As such, it extends and concludes Stravinsky's series of concerti for piano which have taken a variety of forms: from within the orchestral body (in *Petrushka* and *Symphony in Three Movements*) in a nineteenth-century sense, to the neoclassical Declaration (1st edition) that is the Piano Concerto, to an eighteenth-century re-enactment of the *ripieno–concertino* relationship (as in *Capriccio*), and via Stravinsky's absorption of both piano concerto and piano duo elements in the one wholly (extreme) pianistic manifesto that is the *Concerto for Two Solo Pianos*. In *Movements*, and with great originality, Stravinsky re-invents his abiding fascination with the concerto grosso by treating the soloist as an equal partner within a constantly changing instrumental context. It is a refined and transparent score characterized by the intimate, chamber-music quality of its subtly varying sonorities. That Stravinsky should later admit that 'I now see [it] as the corner-stone of my later work'[77] encourages one to view *Movements* as a dodecaphonic parallel to the Piano Concerto which, in its turn, may be described as the corner-stone of the composer's piano-derived neoclassicism. Having already explored the processes of construction with which Stravinsky built the earlier work, it is intriguing to observe once again how he draws upon similarly solid pianistic foundations thirty-five years on. It is a surprising parallel that is recognized by Joseph Straus mid-analysis, as he pauses to contemplate Stravinsky's paradoxical reliance on the piano even for the late music, and 'particularly ... when working towards a central, generating idea'.[78] Straus reinforces his point by citing Stravinsky's first set of *Conversations* with Robert Craft (recorded between 1958 and 1959), which coincided exactly with the composition of *Movements*:

> I begin work by relating intervals rhythmically. This exploration of possibilities is always conducted at the piano. Only after I have established my melodic or harmonic relationships do I pass to composition. Composition is a later expansion and organization of material ... When my main theme has been decided I know on general lines what kind of musical material it will require. I start to look for this material, sometimes playing old masters (to put myself in motion), sometimes starting directly to improvise rhythmic units on a provisional row of notes (which can become a final row). I thus form my building material.[79]

Stravinsky's relaxed admission to composing at the piano is, surely, no longer remarkable – even though, by the late 1950s, the business of creation now concerns the supposedly cerebral or pre-composed aspect of serial construction. His comments also reveal that neither has he abandoned those other methods upon which he has always depended to set himself in motion, namely improvisation and 'the old masters'. Alluding to Theodore Stravinsky's description of his father's need to be close to music as sound, Straus writes that 'even when the music seems most abstract, most reliant on intricate pre-compositional schemes, Stravinsky always worked out the details at the piano, in constant physical contact with the tactile and acoustical realities of the sounds he was writing'.[80]

It goes without saying that Stravinsky's reference, above, to his 'building material' is entirely consistent with a life-long attitude to composition as, essentially, a constructive process; or, as Volker Scherliess has described it in the context of 'classicist composition', Stravinsky continues to indulge in 'the playful manipulation of musical elements'.[81] *Movements* is remarkable, too, for other familiar avenues taken by Stravinsky as he fashioned a personalized re-invention of serial composition. With regard to the latter – specifically, Stravinsky's adaptation via Krenek of rotational arrays – there is no need at this juncture to plough over well-tilled ground. Rather, it is towards other less-explored aspects of Stravinsky's serial architecture that our concerns are directed. It is noteworthy, for example, to view the similarity between the piano writing in *Movements* and that of neoclassical precedents. Despite the obvious syntactical contrast between idioms there is, nevertheless, a tendency in *Movements* for the piano material to revolve around repeated notes (involving, on occasion, their exchange between hands), and contrastingly 'expressive' triplet phraseology. The resultant texture 'refers' to the first movement of the *Sonate pour piano*, particularly its introductory bars. In that context, the triplet flow of quavers is also characterized by the inclusion of repeated notes which, at speed, must be deftly articulated via the rapid exchange of hands. One recalls how this passage was written down immediately upon Stravinsky's return to Paris from his March 1924 visit to Spain – despite the urgency of needing to complete the Piano Concerto. This would suggest that the composer was indeed smitten by those flamenco guitar gestures he had witnessed during his recent trip – despite later, vehement denials.[82] By extension, the guitar-like nature of the piano instrumentation in *Movements* is further evidenced through the occasional and rapid reiteration of notes.[83] This is hardly a serial characteristic, but one that conforms naturally to both guitar and piano writing. It also contributes to a reading of common parentage between such outwardly diverse creations as the *Sonate* and *Movements*.

The piano writing in *Movements* is also notable for its discretion. Here, in contrast to the Piano Concerto and *Capriccio*, Stravinsky avoids a brazenly romantic projection of the soloist; rather, the pianist is portrayed as a chamber musician. *Movements* confirms Stravinsky's continuing preference for an eighteenth-century approach to instrumentation that favours an egalitarian (more musical, more collaborative, more 'crafted') relationship between *all* the participants. He has even taken pains to diminish the role of the piano when, as the sketches reveal, his initial impulse had been to write more extensively for the soloist. Such recycling of pianistic elements as orchestral material (already commented upon in several earlier works) can also be observed in *Movements*. A prominent instance of this occurs in a passage featuring two flutes (bb. 175–9) which, in its measured 'notated acceleration', recalls Bartók's 'night-music' – as in the central movement of the Fifth String Quartet (1934), *Music for Strings, Percussion and Celesta* (1936) and *Concerto for Orchestra* (1943/5). Yet Stravinsky's own nattering effect upon a single note (to borrow from Taruskin)[84] propels the music forwards in a manner quite unlike Bartók's nocturnal call, for the latter is characterized by its immediate reversal – i.e. the whole phrase is formed from the diminution then augmentation of its note-values, in mirror-image. However, in the context of *Movements* its greater significance is in the manner with which Stravinsky devised this initially as a pianistic idea, although he subsequently transferred this cumulative rhythm to other instruments. Perhaps the composer felt that the outcome as piano music was too rhetorical and that this gesture cast the pianist too blatantly in the role of the overwrought nineteenth-century soloist? In common with so many works, the sketches for *Movements* are well equipped to reveal the composer's original intentions particularly with regard to his keyboard-oriented experimentations. To cite Susannah Tucker: 'The documents that record the explorations of style and technique that took place during the "slow climb through the 1950s" are indeed fertile ground for study; it is from the twin currents of evolution and constancy, reflected so resourcefully in Stravinsky's sketches, that the proto-serial and serial masterpieces of the 1950s derive their potency and their individuality'.[85] Stravinsky's sketches clearly reveal that he conceived the passage in question initially for the piano, as the indication for the sustaining pedal confirms (Figure 4.2).

The finished score offers this passage to an instrumental quintet of two flutes and three cellos (Example 4.8). The pseudo-*accelerando* becomes the anacrusis to a flamboyant passage for the soloist, the last moment of pianistic bravura in the whole work. (Significantly, the springboard for this pianistic elaboration is an abrupt *sf f* impulse from the piano's traditional

Fig. 4.2 Stravinsky, sketch for *Movements for Piano and Orchestra* (1958/9).

Ex. 4.8 Stravinsky, *Movements for Piano and Orchestra*, 5th movement, bb. 175–9.

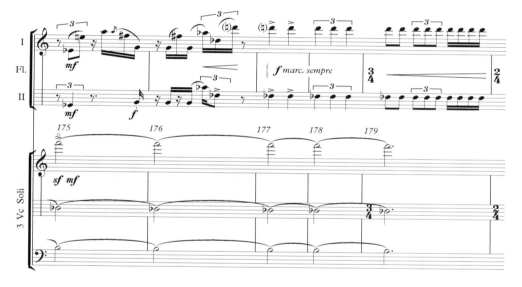

partner, the harp.) The individuality of Stravinsky's repeating note – which is treated so differently to Bartók's – may be observed in the way in which this gesture is incorporated within a rich textural palette. The piano's expansive solo (bb. 180–3) reaches its climax in a rapid and *fortissimo* presentation of repeated notes which, this time, are retained in the piano part. Stravinsky's sketches reveal that this whole phrase was initially intended for the piano alone. Yet the finished score confirms that he later decided to reinforce this energetic chatter by sharing it with the piano's 'partners', harp and celesta. The whole passage culminates in a *sforzando* note-repetition in the strings, from which point tensions are rapidly unwound in ever more fragmentary presentation. By way of brief snatches from harp, celesta and solo strings, this work *for piano and orchestra* emits its final breath via an exchange between a quartet of chamber musicians: harp, piano, violoncello and double-bass. The piano does not have the last word, but contributes discreetly to the briefest of orchestral codas.

The prominent role of the harp throughout *Movements 'for Piano'* is not insignificant when viewed in the context of Stravinsky's on-going relationship with that old Russian art of instrumentation. Stravinsky's neoclassical portfolio, especially *Symphony in Three Movements*, suggests both a restorative view of the harp – which would lead to its ultra-classical, pictorial deployment in *Orpheus* (1947) – and a progressive use of the piano, leading to the serial abstraction of the late music, aptly described by Straus as 'a willed, adventurous voyage of compositional exploration'.[86] It is, then, quite a paradox that this bold foray into serialism should have been accompanied by something of a retreat into the cosiest of timbristic reassurances such as the pairing of harp with piano provided. At the close, it is essentially a dialogue between the piano and the harp (coloured by other instruments) that concludes the narrative. Their union in Stravinsky's Russian works, especially *Petrushka*, has already been extensively noted. Indeed, their collaboration in the final movement of the *Symphony in Three Movements* can now be viewed as the opening gesture to a final twenty-year chapter in which the proximity of these two instruments is gradually enhanced until such point as they merge in perfect unity and in perfect unison.

In *A Sermon, a Narrative and a Prayer* (1960/1) the harp and the piano are quite literally one: in this work's concluding movement ('A Prayer: From Thomas Dekker') they not only double the same material but share a single stave marked 'arpa & piano'. By 1965 Stravinsky could not deny the intimacy with which he now viewed this instrumental hybrid. In a programme note (dated 11 March 1965) intended for the premiere of *Variations (Aldous Huxley in Memoriam)* he wrote that 'percussion instruments are not used, but their position is occupied by the piano and harp which appear as a couple (married)'.[87] This somewhat simplistic view of what one might term the *harpiano* will lead, a year later, to the absolute transparency of the accompaniment to 'The Owl and the Pussy-Cat' (Example 4.9).[88] The piano accompaniment is derived from and largely restricted to the 'pure concept' of unison, for the most part at a respectable distance of two octaves (what else!), *pace* Leschetizky and Philipp (who else!).[89] In *Themes and Conclusions* Stravinsky, now established as a serial composer, defines the 'sense' upon which his setting of 'non-sense' is rooted in terms

Ex. 4.9 Stravinsky, 'The Owl and the Pussy-Cat' (1965/6), opening.

of 'group[s] of pitches … a syncopated canonic voice [and a] double mirror'. Yet, in the same breath, Stravinsky the piano-craftsman also concedes that 'octaves are peculiarly pianistic. No other instrument produces them so well',[90] which might explain why the late serial music resonates with this usually forbidden sonority. The octave and its inevitable mirroring between the two hands is, of course, implicit in every scale, arpeggio, drill and technical exercise ever devised for the piano – with its fundamental aim of even-handed parity. Specifically, its two-octave spacing may be traced directly to the opening bars of the *Sonate pour piano*. There, intriguingly, forty years earlier, Stravinsky traces a proto-dodecaphonic line just as neoclassically serial as his angular yet lyrical piano accompaniment to 'The Owl and the Pussy-Cat' is serially neoclassical. Both textures owe their compositional gestalt to the digital permutations of *Accordgruppe*-like patterning. Stravinsky's setting of the Edward Lear nonsense poem was penned between 1965 and 1966. That Stravinsky should have remained, at the age of eighty-three, creatively bound to (and amused and stimulated by) the bare physicality of *pal'tserazvitiye* is a testimony to the enduring power of this default attraction.

'Stravinsky's piano' remained a versatile and practical tool, a limitless resource of intervals and sonorities. By his own admission it remained a vital support as he evolved his idiosyncratic, hexachordal response to the challenges of composing in twelve tones. Babbitt, in his contribution to *A Composers' Memorial* in 1971, shared with his readers 'the private words of our great colleague' and arrived at the conclusion that 'Stravinsky, in the last decade of his creative life, learned what Schoenberg knew through-out most of his creative life: how it feels to have the history of music leave you ahead.'[91] Stravinsky's own sense of advantage (if this were the case) may have derived from that inexhaustible font of intervals provided by his piano. It was a well-spring that remained forever dependable and adapt-able and, despite its distant provenance in Stravinsky's Russian past, it proved unashamedly inspirational regardless of style or aesthetic. Boris de Schloezer wrote in 1928 of Stravinsky's 'faculty for renewal' and, with regard to *Apollo*, that 'the work reveals to us its author's secret, this thirst for renunciation, his need for purity and serenity'.[92] It is a description that might also be applied to *Movements* which, as Walsh reminds us, may well have been set in motion by the composer's encounter with Stockhausen's *Klavierstücke* (I, II, III and V).[93] There may be a more Gallic connection, however.

Stravinsky's deployment of rotating arrays, and the subtle, kaleido-scopic adjustments to his instrumentation (revolving 'around' the solo piano), tempt one to draw distant associations between *Movements* and Debussy. One recalls that this old master had already been honoured twice by Stravinsky: with the dedication of *Zvezdoliki* (1911/12) and with that notable *tombeau*, the *Symphonies of Wind Instruments* (1920).[94] The transparency of texture that characterizes *Movements* is also to be found in Debussy's *Mouvement*, from the first set of *Images pour piano* (1905). Although Stravinsky never referred explicitly to this work, Debussy's solo with its lightly shimmering ostinati is in many ways a perfect illustra-tion of (a rapidly revolving form of) *nepodvizhnost'*, despite the strongly directioned diatonicism of this *perpetuum mobile*. Stravinsky's *Movements* operates at an altogether different pace, of course, and inhabits a diamet-rically contrasted aesthetic. (In fact, the work's title is more likely to reflect Stravinsky's desire to show himself just as capable as the next young seri-alist of affixing labels – such as 'Piano Piece' or *Klavierstück* – instead of titles. 'Movements' is just as defiantly non-descriptive.) Just how often had Stravinsky admitted his fascination with the 'different rhythmic episodes [that can be] dictated by the fingers themselves'! It was in connection with *Piano-Rag-Music* (1919) that he had first acknowledged in print (in 1935)

the generative support provided him by his digits – his *grands inspirateurs.*
Over time, this touching relationship proved its longevity, even retaining
its authority through the 1950s and 1960s. Viewed within the context of
Stravinsky's various cycles of renewal the piano represented a powerful
metaphor that denoted, above all, 'well-crafted composition'. It also set
him in motion via familiar tactile processes towards every next stage of his
'willed and adventurous voyage'.

Although Stravinsky would declare (citing Baudelaire) that he preferred
a music box to a nightingale,[95] his sympathetic treatment of *both* elements
in his opera *The Nightingale* (1908–14) would suggest that the composer
acknowledged early his enchantment with these two seemingly irreconcilable elements. It was an attraction that would remain constant over the
next five decades. Which might explain why Stravinsky, perhaps more than
any other serial composer, was so keen to justify them both especially in
the context of this prickly defence of twelve-tone composition: 'Yesterday's
non-starter [Stravinsky's term for those who resist serial music] opposed
the substitution of an "arbitrary order" (those Draconian twelve-tone
laws!) for a "natural gravitational system", as if both the arbitrary and the
natural were not equally artificial and composed.'[96] For Daniel Albright
'this is what Stravinsky's music is all about: the deep equivalence of the
natural and the artificial. At the centre of his dramatic imagination is the
desire to juxtapose in a single work two competing systems – one of which
seems natural, tasteful, approved alike by Man and God, the other of which
seems artificial, abhorrent, devilish – and to subvert these distinctions as
best he can.'[97] One might question the term 'system' when applying this
argument to *pal'tserazvitiye*, but Albright's reading of Stravinsky's 'sub-
version of distinctions' is well judged. *Pal'tserazvitiye* is certainly a mode
of musical organization firmly rooted in gravitational relationships. In
Stravinsky's hands it proved itself, time and again, to be the most natural
and useful adjunct to his creative flow – even in the final works. It was
regarding this newly acquired serial voice that he famously commented:
'Though [musical form] may be mathematical, the composer must not
seek mathematical formulae', citing Ortega to support his carefully crafted
argument: 'Musical form is mathematical because it is ideal, whether it is
"an image of memory or a construction of ours".'[98] Stravinsky's engagement
with *pal'tserazvitiye* – for its physicality and its inherent atonality – may
provide a key to our understanding of this conundrum. While injecting
a sense of motor energy to the rotational rigours of serial composition,
pal'tserazvitiye's extra-tonal qualities complemented Stravinsky's unique
reading of twelve-tone mechanics. The result was a musical form 'ideal'

in its unique combination of mathematical construction and finger-digital memory. As such, the serial works confirm Scott Goddard's view of the composer (already commented upon) – as expressed in his 1936 review of the *Autobiography* in *Music & Letters*.[99] Stravinsky continued to value the past 'as a depository of doctrine'. Specifically, his own distant past continued to inform his musical present to the very end.

Conclusions

As you were, clarifying for us
Those sublimated notions
That have no place … in futile conversations
But only in rehearsing the right sounds
For your elliptical meanings
Which now belong to us, Père Igor
Luciano Berio, 'Adieu' (1971)[1]

I agree with you. Art must be clever [*astucieux*] and difficult.
Igor Stravinsky, letter of 28 December 1932
to Charles-Albert Cingria[2]

Let us return for a moment to the scene described in the Introduction: of Stravinsky energetically re-engaging with *Das wohltemperierte Klavier*. Such spirit in his eighty-seventh year, such desire to overcome his frailties, to check out from his *hôtel-Dieu* and 'make his own arrangements'. Those admirable qualities aside, it still makes surprising reading (with due allowance for the composer's age and state of health) that, at the end of the E minor Fugue, Stravinsky should inscribe the following note: 'All dynamix after Czerny's "piano solo". Well Tempered Clavichord. Igor Stravinsky, April 14 1969.' Every detail of Stravinsky's punctuation and orthography is here reproduced exactly as it is in the manuscript.[3] He was working from Czerny's edition, of course, which was then (as now) widely in circulation. Yet, even so, Stravinsky's choice of terminology is still unexpected: 'Czerny's "piano solo"'? This cannot be an error or an aberration; nor was it Stravinsky's habit to insert witticisms in his sketches for his own or for posterity's amusement. This is something quite different. For this phrase to flow from Stravinsky's pencil, for such a notion even to enter his consciousness … what *was* he thinking? Was he so appreciative of Czerny's 'arrangement'? Did he perhaps interpret Czerny's thick layers of editing (via dynamics, phrasing, metronome markings etc.) as a precedent which gave him licence to make his *own* re-creation of Bach's original, carrying the process of transformation a stage further by adding another (Stravinskian) layer? In his autobiography Stravinsky informs us that he had 'always admired Czerny, not only as a remarkable teacher but also as a thoroughbred musician'.[4] When writing of *Pulcinella*, Stravinsky expresses the nature of his

role – 'breathing new life into [Pergolesi's] scattered fragments'[5] – in terms
of respect and love. One might borrow the same argument, by substituting
this composer's name, when considering the present dilemma: 'Should my
line of action with regard to [Czerny and Bach] be dominated by my love or
by my respect for [this] music? In order to create there must be a dynamic
force, and what force is more potent than love? To me it seems that to ask
the question is to answer it.'[6] For the contributions that Bach and Czerny
had made in their different ways to Stravinsky's career as composer and
pianist, he had every reason to love and to respect them both.[7] It is tempting
to read in Stravinsky's 'misnomer' recognition that his path to composition
had indeed been inextricably bound to counterpoint – as he had proposed
in his autobiography – and that his path to counterpoint (as constructed
composition) had been similarly bound to his experience of keyboard technique (as constructed pianism).

It is remarkable, and undeniably touching, to view the great composer
sharpen his pencils even at that 'late hour' and set to work. (Although
Stravinsky would survive for a further two years, he surely believed, as
did his close family and associates, that these were, very possibly, his final
moments.) As so many composers before him, Mozart amongst them,
Stravinsky sought to re-activate his musical antennae by diligently and rev-
erentially copying out those sinuous contrapuntal threads. It is a mark of
Bach's extraordinary qualities that musicians find themselves receptive to the
healing benefits that immersion in this literature provides. By re-enacting
Bach's processes, one's skills and functions (both digital and intellectual) are
invigorated by such intimacy with 'pure and radiant counterpoint'. It would
appear that health-giving properties of particularly impressive powers are
to be found in keyboard counterpoint that is 'by' Bach *and* Czerny. Above
all, one may view Stravinsky's last musical act as conclusive evidence that, in
the words of Ivan Goncharov, he 'carried the vessel of life to the end without
spilling a single drop'.[8]

In 1983 Joseph brought his important study on Stravinsky and the piano
to an eloquent conclusion with the affirmation that, 'even now, it is clear
that the significance of this association is as vital a part of his legacy as any.
As such, surely it warrants a higher distinction than history has heretofore
adjudged.'[9] If the pretext for this volume had been confined to those questions outlined in Chapter 3 my task would have been limited to accommodating Stravinsky's fingerings within the performance tradition of his piano
works. However, from such a reductive treatment alone little would have
been accomplished in evaluating the true import of 'this association' and
its place in Stravinsky's legacy. From the broader considerations that have
been addressed it has become apparent that the *Sonate* sketches must be

read as part of a far more complex equation – one that unites several aspects of Stravinsky's experience from his earliest contact with music (improvised or studied) to the mature neoclassical work and beyond. Through its ill-defined, but contextually measurable effect upon Stravinsky's 'attitude', to the generative spark of his creative response, this relationship with the piano occupies the core of his very being as a composer. From the perspective of these 'Conclusions', at least, one may vigorously endorse Joseph's assessment while reflecting upon certain readings of Stravinsky that are nuanced by the foregoing discussion.

Firstly, it has become clear that some Stravinsky editions urgently require revision. Joseph has written on this subject in another context:

> How much of *Orpheus* as we hear it today is as Stravinsky intended it to be heard fifty years ago, since the scores in many cases remain inaccurate? … Accents are added [by the composer] … pauses inserted … and numerous other refinements are made that still go unrealized in contemporary performances … a bassoon trill is extended … the composer altered several pitches … but the changes never made it into print … The original published score does not include Stravinsky's handwritten addendum.[10]

Joseph's indignation is directed at *practical* issues such as misprints or questions of balance, the majority of Stravinsky's errata having been 'performance-tested, resulting from the composer's making immediate adjustments' based on his experience in rehearsal.[11] How much more vital it is, surely, to consider *compositional* elements intrinsic to the very fabric of this music and its performance! New editions of the piano works would need to take account of Stravinsky's agogic and technical markings, including his idiosyncratic fingerings, for this information must be considered as part of Stravinsky's artistic concept. It should never have been edited out.[12] What was regarded as offering Stravinsky and 'the public' helpful if conventional assistance, one can now see – as in the case of the *Sonate*, *Sérénade* and the Piano Concerto – to be an act of utter, if unintentional disrespect to all parties. The nineteenth century has long been fertile soil for 'authentic' performance research; it is surely appropriate, as modernism too recedes into history, to include within Stravinsky studies the contribution of musicologists and practitioners specialized in historical performance practice.

A consideration of Stravinsky's fingerings and of the performance issues that arise from a methodology-derived reading of this literature would gain much from such insight. Sandra Rosenblum – in her observations concerning the varied functions of classical piano technique – confirms that certain composers would indicate fingering for 'musical', i.e. *non-technical*, purposes as a matter of course: 'A significant number of fingerings relate more to musical than to technical considerations and, of these, the preferred fingering is not always the easiest.' In Rosenblum's opinion these 'musical purposes' may quite legitimately concern themselves with the psychological state of the performer, for the classical composer might also take this into consideration as a determinant of considerable relevance to the music's resultant execution:[13] 'The fingerings chosen are likely to affect the sounds produced, if not in a concrete manner – such as enhancing some particular articulation or accentuation – then on the more intangible level of the way the player feels about and projects the notes.' Rosenblum adds that, from around 1793, Beethoven demonstrated 'an early interest in the relationship of fingering to interpretation and sound quality, and [in] experimentation with novel fingerings that would put the player in a new psychological as well as physical relationship to tone production'.[14] In response to Stravinsky's demand that music's translation into plastic terms 'requires exactitude and beauty'[15] one might well ask: what more accurate means could there be to achieve this than for the composer to indicate a pre-composed plan for each finger, just as the dancer's every gesture follows a precise and pre-defined choreography? There remains much to explore within the more intangible levels of Stravinsky's aesthetics.

In a project of this kind, which on occasion may yield to conjecture of a 'musico-psycho-archaeological' nature (to adapt a term of Roger Shattuck's),[16] one is constantly aware of others' concerns and possible scepticism. Points addressed, regardless of the vividness of their context, still needed to be verified in the music itself (rather than depend exclusively on the sources for their credibility) if one is not to fall into the pit of non-academic speculation. Martha Hyde warns against 'squabbling about first sightings'.[17] Yet the question of chronology has not been the sole issue. Stravinsky's formulation of notated musical works out of improvised piano-drills clearly does not start with *Tarantella* nor end with 'The Owl and the Pussy-cat'. The *fortepianicheskiy slog* ['pianistic morphology'], as one might call it, was an intrinsic element of Igor Stravinsky. In this light, such plundering of sketches and scores with which this study has concerned itself would support the view that the piano, its pedagogy and its workshop should be considered amongst those Russian traditions upon which Stravinsky constructed his life's work. The contrasting stylistic phases of his output can now be viewed in the context of his underlying engagement with pianism. Particularly relevant is Stravinsky's identification with musical processes, and how the methods of piano study and its raw materials would come to symbolize his views on musical craft and fuel their application to compositional ends. Both aspects of this 'honest labour' are central to his ideology, regardless of the genre or idiom of the finished 'object'. Stravinsky's return to the Orthodox faith (of his childhood) was accompanied by his return to the pianistic rigours of his youth; and he used them both as a foundation upon which to re-construct his creative initiative and to provide the tranquillity and sense of permanence he needed amid a geographically, domestically and emotionally transient life. As Theodore Stravinsky has written, 'All his life, wherever he might be, he always surrounded himself with his own atmosphere.'[18] Stravinsky's Russian enculturation, therefore, also needs to be re-assessed.

Improvisation as a creative source was clearly linked to his enjoyment of rehearsal and his claim on its concomitant repetitions and inspirational accidents. In this light, one might profitably review Stravinsky's reading of jazz and his early contact with American music. In addition to *Pribaoutki*, *Renard* and the courtiers' material in *The Nightingale*, Stravinsky's rag music, especially *Piano-Rag-Music* (1919), may now be seen to reflect V. E. Meyerhold's fairground *grotesk* with its stumbles, slides, stops and starts. On a gestural level all of these deal with those intriguing patterns which, together, portray music *in rehearsal* through a celebration of creativity's essential processes. Just as Meyerhold extracted from his street-farces the fundamentals of movement, so Stravinsky (and Bartók before him) saw through the exteriors of folklore – its sonority and rhetoric – to reveal the fundamentals of musical production. Stravinsky was to refer admiringly to G. K. Chesterton's definition: that revolution 'in the true sense of the word, was the movement of an object in motion that described a closed curve, and thus always returned to the point from where it had started'.[19]

Stravinsky's early neoclassical scores – from the domestic duets to the piano solos and *concertante* works – all respond to a Meyerholdian, biomechanical reading. The tri-partite structure of Meyerhold's *étude* is a metaphor for Stravinsky's concern for music's physicality, its creative release through his compositions, and its innate tendency for revolution ('in the true sense of the word'). Firstly, *otkaz* (literally 'refusal', but intended as a gestural preparation or pretext for action) may be understood as Stravinsky's intellectualized or finger-derived starting point. In this context *otkaz* can denote Stravinsky's pianistic 'attitude'. Secondly, *posil'* (from the verb 'to send') corresponds to the 'parcelling up' of Stravinsky's material in intriguing and demanding patterns guided by the pedagogical spirit (and 'letter') of *pal'tserazvitiye*, as a volitional reflex. And, finally, *tochka* – literally 'full-stop', in the sense of arrival, outcome, goal, i.e. the object(ive) triumphantly constructed. In the Meyerholdian *étude* this 'end' is merely an apparent termination, for *tochka* is but a moment of rest.[20] Inherent in its concept is the act of looking back (in the *étude* known as 'Throwing the Stone', the actor's final movement is to glance over the shoulder) as a preparation for beginning again.[21] *Otkaz, posil', tochka … ad gustum, ad infinitum.* The implication for creativity is clear: action and process are cycles of never-ending affirmation and negation, combining both energy and reflection. Stravinsky's entire compositional life cycle can be read in similar terms. His re-inventions, as surges of renewal, were made possible through repeated access to the foundations of his working methods and through an unwavering ability to formulate objects of any shape and consistency (or musical idiom) out of the limitless minutiae of music's syntax. The piano gave Stravinsky access to this facility. Whatever crisis that the man and the composer (to engage with Maritain's partition) should face, the piano 'called upon' Stravinsky to look back over his shoulder as a preparation for taking the next step. His piano showed him the way out and a way forward – and it never let him down.

From the perspective of tracing a work's 'origins', Hyde's theory of imitation (incorporating eclectic, reverential and dialectic forms of imitation) might usefully be expanded to take into account Stravinsky's assimilation of the piano as a referent of imitative response and, in the process, review the whole question of stylistic imitation. In addition, a qualification to this theory might be negotiated via the sub-category of 'heuristic imitation', should Hyde be persuaded to recognize Stravinsky's accommodation of *pal'tserazvitiye* as a form of eclectic imitation characterized by a 'deeper engagement with the past'.[22] As a further consequence of this, Taruskin's treasure-house of Russian Traditions – now embracing pianistic-pedagogic enculturation, as discussed – would need to expand further in order to accommodate Rimsky-Korsakov's hitherto unappreciated impact on Stravinsky's post-Russian scores. These essentially pianistic processes also indicate the path to comprehending Stravinsky's transition from 'rough theatre' genres to neoclassicism. The objectivity of the latter is to be found in Stravinsky's (and Balanchine's) 'misreading' of constructivist gesture: as 'strong poets' they effected a radical revision of the Meyerholdian tradition – which was itself a radical revision of both *commedia dell'arte* and eastern, non-European, traditions. And out of this experience they attained their 'heightened individuality'. While Adorno viewed neoclassicism as regressive and authoritarian, Stravinsky demonstrated that it could be both empowering and transformative. Far from being a non-ideology, it was a celebration of music's ability to liberate itself through processes of renewal. As an illustration of this *Les Noces* (and its four pianos) enabled Stravinsky to escape from the nostalgic, Eurasian landscape into an objective, neoclassical workshop. *Pulcinella* was a revelation, as the composer would later admit. However, it was with his hands on the piano that Stravinsky found his true moment of epiphany, although this he never admitted – except through this music. As Stravinsky gradually compiled a neoclassical canon he (re-)discovered 'the right tool for the job'. This may even have been a factor – musically and psychologically – in Stravinsky's permanence in the West. Without this pianistic 'attitude' his nostalgia for the Russia of his imagination – revealed in his use of liturgical Slavonic calligraphy in his Eurasian scores – might have led him homeward-bound in advance, even, of Prokofiev. But the piano enabled him to re-launch, to construct a new musical identity strong enough to overcome his decadent association with the Ballets Russes. The ability to ground this and future transitions on the piano would impact his every step thereafter, from his return to ballet (on his own terms) in France, to his eventual adoption of serial techniques (again, on his own terms) in America. The piano was a vital life-force for Stravinsky, essential to his personal and professional identity – to his 'creative swerve', as Taruskin calls it – and to the 'great stripdown from *kult'ura* to *stikhaya*' ('the cultural to the elemental') that coloured the rest of his career.[23] Remaining loyal to his trusty helper, Stravinsky could re-work his patterns over and again, improvising, transposing, transcribing, feeling and hearing his way forward. In the words of André Gide: 'He is perpetually forming, un-forming, re-forming himself. One thinks one has grasped him … Proteus! He takes the shape of what he loves.'[24]

Stravinsky's engagement with this instrument as a tool of composition will continue to provide an absorbing subject for research. No longer is it an adequate response merely to account for certain orchestral motifs by the fact that they may 'lie under the fingers'. Neither can Stravinsky's idiosyncratic form of writing for the piano continue to be viewed disrespectfully for being un-pianistic – despite its most inhospitable challenges – when its morphology, gesture and 'technicity' derive from that literature to which pianism and pianists owe their very existence. After all, one might ask, should *études* be considered un-pianistic because they are awkward to play – deliberately so, in most cases – or because they fulfil a didactic purpose? Future study of this topic could usefully address the correlation between art and education, and consider the implications for both whenever their paths cross. The great *concert-études* may aspire to the condition of musical art just as Stravinsky's neoclassical concert-works, one might argue, aspire to the condition of the technically useful study.

Yet Stravinsky's intimate, symbiotic relationship with the piano differs from that of other recognized *étude* composers (such as Chopin or Liszt – both admired for the pianistic quality of their writing, however great the demands of performance). 'Stravinsky's piano' was more than a musical instrument for the access it provided to improvisation which, since childhood, had been his preferred stimulus to creativity. The process of 'making' immersed him in an intricate web of intervallic relationships and in the shimmering sonorities of their exploration, repetition and transposition. On a daily basis this experience kept him in touch with the *materia prima* of music which he could mould with his fingers on the keys before taking up his composer's pencil. Stravinsky's manuscripts frequently reveal a 'gap' in the written progression between early sketches and the final result, suggesting that the intervening stages of the compositional process were resolved at the piano, then written down virtually complete. (Samuel Dushkin comments on early rehearsals of the *Duo concertant* when Stravinsky played without a score, the piano part already committed to memory and at his fingertips.) Processes conducted at the piano clearly contributed to his formulation of those aspects of his neoclassical aesthetic that relate to objectivity, to craft and to the inherent inexpressivity of the musical 'object'. Through this reciprocal filter he could extract only that material which his musical ear required. The patterns of *pal'tserazvitiye* may also be understood, then, as patterns of resistance. By denying access to idiom, nationality, colour and, above all, *style*, the piano (through the filter of *pal'tserazvitiye*) aided Stravinsky in formulating, dispassionately, his musical objectivity.

The de-mystification of musical creation ('inspiration') is central to Stravinsky's artistic posture, and this, too, requires reassessment. Owing to certain statements he made in 1923, and continually defended thereafter, Stravinsky is widely understood (and quoted) as a composer thoroughly grounded in the technique and aesthetic of 'making' music. His ideologies should now also be read as products of his creative engagement with pianism, and no longer labelled 'made at the piano' but 'hand-made *of* the piano'. On this basis, the question of stylistic modelling also requires revision. Stravinsky's neoclassicism, for example, had less to do with a modernism that accommodated innovation and tradition than we had thought; neither had it much to do with Pergolesi, Beethoven, Weber or Tchaikovsky – and much less with 'old Bach'. Stravinsky's self-diagnosis of 'a rare form of kleptomania' surely understates the singularity of his condition which might more accurately be described as chronic self-referentiality. When Stravinsky viewed his 'models' he only saw items (musical materials 'in operation' and interacting) identifiable as being a part of his *own* home. As in Milan Kundera's metaphor, 'he lingered in each room of that mansion, touched every corner, stroked every piece of furniture'.[25] He was there to collect them for they were already a familiar part of his intellectual archive, of his private reference library derived from that infinitely renewable (and infinitely invigorating) pianistic universe, *pal'tserazvitiye*. This represented for him a 'collection' which he would patiently amass throughout his musical life. It was, in fact, produced *from* his musical life. In response to Taruskin's question 'Back to Whom?' there can therefore be but one answer: back to Stravinsky.[26] Far from there being an *Oedipal* (Bloomian) relationship with his ancestors, the focus of Stravinsky's 'anxiety' might more accurately be described as narcissistic. Above all, Stravinsky's concerns were less cultural and stylistic than technical. Did he not, for example, admire Beethoven's *Grosse Fuge* for being 'pure, interval music and I love it above any other'?[27] Neither was Stravinsky's adoption of eighteenth-century instrumental texture due to a reverence of past composers. Rather, it was the opposite: he showed interest in past composers because of the means they provided him of gaining access to eighteenth-century instrumental textures.

Stravinsky's legacy in the recording studio confirms this: his solo piano recordings of the 1920s and early 1930s reveal a 'classicism' born of the unlikely marriage between the concert grand of St Petersburg and the harpsichord of Paris. In his initial recordings of the *Sonate* and the *Sérénade* Stravinsky attains the transparency of a *claveciniste* by avoiding the use of the sustaining pedal. However, the contrapuntal equilibrium of his performances, i.e. any semblance of eighteenth-century style, is compromised by a forcefully projected 'nineteenth-century' right hand – specifically, by his pursuit of a singing melody through the constant pinging of his romantic, virtuoso's fifth finger. This is particularly noticeable in his rendition of the faster music of the two solo works – the *ritornello* movements – and also in his version (without orchestra) of the first movement of the Piano Concerto.[28]

Stravinsky's attempt to establish a performing legacy for his music was also, therefore, subject to that same self-referentiality.[29] Future initiatives to construct a performance tradition for Stravinsky's neoclassical works will need to recognize that it is not sufficient to impose 'authentic' eighteenth-century rhetoric, for example, upon those overtly 'Baroque' *ritornelli*. The signposts which the composer meticulously laid out for posterity indicate that he understood these contrapuntal textures from his *own* perspective. To present Stravinsky's counterpoint as a union of equal parts is to deny its Stravinskian identity. While he emphatically rejected the Rubinstein model, Stravinsky's neoclassical ideology did not embrace the restoration of pre-romantic aesthetics or modes of performance as its replacement. As a composer rather than a musicologist, Stravinsky's impulse was always to create. (Recalling Herzen's description of Turgenev, neither was Stravinsky a pamphleteer, but an artist.)[30] However, while the basis of these new textures might embrace linear models, his focus on order and discipline did not preclude the restoration of 'the melodic smile'[31] through his meticulous and ringing performances. Accordingly, Stravinsky's recordings present these neo-Baroque textures within recent pianistic traditions and one should not mistake the absence of pedal for musicological correctness. This was, rather, another weapon of his neoclassical armoury for which he was deeply indebted to his pianistic formation in St Petersburg. Concomitant with the idiomatic outcome was the technical application required of the pianist in order to execute this feat. To perform an entire movement without the sustaining pedal – as Stravinsky so often demands – requires the performer also to adopt a *physical* engagement with the task, much as the *étude* literature derives technical virtue from its musical restrictions. Therein lies the neoclassical paradox: for all Stravinsky's concern with self-negation and order, his 'objects' invariably and memorably achieve a re-evaluation of expression that favours the thinking body and the choreographic imagination – 'visual hearing' he called it[32] – while possessing 'the order and sense of limits that allow reason and feeling to fuse'.[33] He constructed all his neoclassical legacies from in to out – in other words, upon his own experience. Despite Apollo's demands, Stravinsky could not deny himself an intense response to music. His concern for discipline and technique was never intended to be more than the means to guaranteeing the integrity of the final result. Music's grace, while never called into question, drew but a thin veil over Stravinsky's Dionysian response – projected via the experience 'of others'. As Ansermet might phrase this, Stravinsky's piano music expresses the sensibility of the imaginary performer of which the actual performer is an *analogon*: 'but it must be agreed that [Stravinsky's] expression of this [sensibility] is absolutely authentic'.[34]

Alastair Williams' description of music as 'encrypted subjectivity, even as a carrier of ideology'[35] chimes admirably with Stravinsky's non-expressive neoclassicism – viewing this as an apparently subject-distanced ideology, though one that is also firmly encrypted within a fusion of several intensely held convictions and interests. These include pedagogy, choreography, objectivity and spirituality, even – all of which were re-formulated within the atelier of pianism's processes. For decades following his re-invention as a concert pianist Stravinsky shared the piano stool with 'Philipp'; the neoclassical project and his international persona were nourished by immersion in musical literature that is the epitome of passionless neutrality. It was a daily reminder not, actively, to pursue feeling or emotion but – citing Boris de Schloezer's apt summary of *Symphonies of Wind Instruments* – to strive for an art that 'attains grace infallibly by its force and by its perfection'.[36]

In his study of revolutionaries in Russian literature Richard Freeborn assesses the qualities of Pasternak's hero, Dr Yuri Zhivago, to be three-fold: his unique transforming role, his need to do something useful and his poetic vision.[37] Stravinsky, multi-tasker extraordinaire, mirrors this same multiple heritage. His uniqueness may be measured by the manner in which he combined these same qualities with his concern for the piano as a radical, i.e. original, source of musical creation. Marguerite Long observed that 'it is not our mind which moves our fingers, but our fingers and their almost conscious movements which set our mind in motion'.[38] It is a sentiment that echoes Stravinsky's own. And how well it encapsulates the simplicity and the mystery of that inimitable and richly productive identification with the piano keyboard which lies, most notably, behind his neoclassical achievements – monuments of restrained sensibility and extraordinary beauty. If, as Richard Taruskin famously claimed, Stravinsky was the 'very stem' of twentieth-century music,[39] then his piano also related to that world, though not by just any angle: it was at the very root.

Notes

Acknowledgements

1 A. S. Pushkin (1799–1837), *Trud* (1830), in Aleksandr Pushkin, *Eugene Onegin: A Novel in Verse*, trans. Vladimir Nabokov (1956), 2 vols., Vol. II. *Commentary and Index* (Princeton: Princeton University Press, 1990), Part 2, p. 384. The opening lines of the poem read: 'Come is the moment I craved: my work of / long years is completed. / Why, then, this sense of woe / secretly harrowing me? / Having my high task performed, do I stand as / a useless day labourer / Stands, with his wages received, foreign / to all other toil?'

Introduction

1 Photographs by Dominique Cibiel; in Vera Stravinsky and Robert Craft, *Stravinsky in Pictures and Documents* (New York: Simon and Schuster, 1978), p. 488; and Stephen Walsh, *Stravinsky: The Second Exile. France and America 1934–1971* (London: Jonathan Cape, 2006), opposite p. 493.

2 Walsh, *Stravinsky: The Second Exile*, p. 546.

3 Stravinsky's arrangements from Bach's *Das wohltemperierte Klavier* comprise four works: from Book I, the Prelude and Fugue in E minor and B minor; and from Book II, the Prelude and Fugue in C♯ minor and D minor. See V. Stravinsky and Craft, *Stravinsky in Pictures and Documents*, pp. 489–90. Stravinsky's personal copy of Bach's score and his transcriptions (in pencil) are held at the Paul Sacher Stiftung, Basel.

4 Universal Edition UE5 presents the two books of Bach's opus in one volume.

5 V. Stravinsky and Craft, *Stravinsky in Pictures and Documents*, p. 490.

6 Nikolay Vasilievich Gogol (1809–1852), *Dead Souls* (1842), trans. Robert A. Maguire (London: Penguin, 2004), pp. 299–300.

7 From Act III, scene 2. Libretto by W. H. Auden and Chester Kallman (1951).

8 Walsh, *Stravinsky: The Second Exile*, p. 546.

9 Igor Stravinsky, 'Quelques mots de mes dernières oeuvres', *Muzyka* 1.1 (1924), 15–17 (p. 14).

10 Walsh supplements this account by demonstrating that Stravinsky's 'official studies in theory' began (when he was nineteen) in November 1901 with F. S. Akimenko and continued from April 1902 with V. P. Kalafati. They 'taught strict technique and made Igor do weekly exercises' that, according to the composer, 'covered chorale harmonization, species counterpoint, writing in two and three parts, and fugue'. Stephen Walsh, *Stravinsky: A Creative Spring. Russia and France 1882–1934* (London: Pimlico, 2002), pp. 58, 564n38.

11 Anatoly Konstantinovich Lyadov (1855–1914) also wrote *Three Canons* – in G major, C minor and F major – in 1894, published two years later. His last composition was *12 Canons on a Cantus Firmus* (1914). Stravinsky was to praise him, almost uniquely amongst the Russian connections of his youth, as 'the most progressive of the musicians of his generation'. Igor Stravinsky and Robert Craft, *Memories and Commentaries* (London: Faber and Faber, 1960), p. 63. It would be mere speculation to suggest that this represented some form of recognition of Lyadov's engagement with counterpoint at an impressionable time.

12 Igor Stravinsky, *An Autobiography (1903–1934)* (London; New York: Marion Boyars, 1990), pp. 14–15 – written by the composer originally in French (with the assistance of Walter Nouvel) and published in Paris in 1935 as *Chroniques de ma vie*. The following year this emerged in English translation under the title *An Autobiography* (New York: W. W. Norton, 1936). The Introduction to the 1990 edition states: '[*An Autobiography*] covers [Stravinsky's] career as a composer from the early Piano Sonata in F sharp minor (1903/4) to *Persephone* (1933/4).'

13 'In two places he wrote notes below the range of the violins and violas.' V. Stravinsky and Craft, *Stravinsky in Pictures and Documents*, p. 490.

14 *Ibid.*, p. 489.

15 In his 'Foreword' to Edward E. Lowinsky, *Tonality and Atonality in Sixteenth-Century Music* (New York: Da Capo Press, 1961), pp. vii–ix Stravinsky writes (p. ix) that the 'subject matter of [this] study is for me perhaps the most exciting in the history of music'.

16 Stravinsky, *An Autobiography (1903–1934)*, p. 15.

17 Luciano Berio, 'Adieu', in *Stravinsky (1882–1971): A Composers' Memorial*, special double issue of *Perspectives of New Music* 9.2, 10.1 (1971), 129–30.

18 Stravinsky, *An Autobiography (1903–1934)*, p. 15.

19 *Ibid.*, p. 5.

20 See the photo of Stravinsky '[i]n his studio at 1260 North Wetherly Drive, *c.* 1963', in Walsh, *Stravinsky: The Second Exile*, between pp. 492 and 493.

21 Stravinsky, *An Autobiography (1903–1934)*, p. 5.

22 Stravinsky's copy of Philipp's *Complete School of Technic for the Piano* (held at the Paul Sacher Stiftung, Basel) reveals the following dates: 'Sept 19' (p. 18), 'Sept 26' (p. 19), 'Oct 14' (p. 60), 'Oct 17' (p. 52). I am grateful to Dr Ulrich Mosch for his confirmation that these are in Stravinsky's hand, and for his informed suggestion that they refer to the autumn of 1924 when Stravinsky enjoyed a break from touring the Piano Concerto around European cities. His visits to Paris during this interval would have provided him with the opportunity to make contact with Philipp. This brief series of lessons (four, possibly more) would also have coincided exactly with the composition of the *Sonate*.

23 'Some Ideas about My *Octuor*' was printed in the January 1924 edition of the Brooklyn monthly, *The Arts*. Igor Stravinsky, 'Some Ideas about My *Octuor*', in Eric Walter White, *Stravinsky: The Composer and His Works* (London: Faber and Faber, 1966), Appendix A2, pp. 574–7.

24 From anon., *Igor Stravinsky*, Miniature Essays (London; Geneva: J. & W. Chester, 1925). It is possible that the author is Eric Walter White.

25 Stravinsky, *An Autobiography (1903–1934)*, p. 14.

26 Charles M. Joseph, *Stravinsky Remembered* (New Haven; London: Yale University Press, 2001), p. 91; Joseph's writings – which also include *Stravinsky and the Piano* (Ann Arbor: UMI Research Press, 1983); *Stravinsky Inside Out* (New Haven; London: Yale University Press, 2001); and *Stravinsky and Balanchine: A Journey of Invention* (New Haven; London: Yale University Press, 2002) – must be considered the principal body of reference on this subject.

27 Joseph, *Stravinsky Remembered*, p. 91.

28 Eric Walter White, *Stravinsky's Sacrifice to Apollo* (London: Leonard and Virginia Woolf, 1930), p. 104. He appears to be referring to the passage beginning at b. 26. This features material that Stravinsky commented upon very favourably – following an informal recital in a Warsaw hotel – delighted, apparently, with its unintentional resemblance to Mozart and (by varying its metre) to Johann Strauss. As reported by Jarosław Iwaszkiewicz in *Wiadomosci literackie (Warsawa)* 46 (1924), in Viktor Varunts, *Igor Stravinsky: Publitsist i sobesednik* (Moscow: Sovetskiy Kompositor, 1988), p. 47.

29 Eric Walter White, *Stravinsky: The Composer and His Works* (London; Boston, MA: Faber and Faber, 1966), p. 326.

30 'It follows that [Stravinsky's] abilities and limitations as a pianist are also imprinted on his piano works, for while he was not obliged to solve every conducting problem in his orchestral scores – conductors can and do leave orchestras to their own devices – he *had* to play his *Sonata*, his *Serenade*, and his *Concerto*.' V. Stravinsky and Craft, *Stravinsky in Pictures and Documents*, p. 215.

31 Richard Taruskin, *Stravinsky and the Russian Traditions: A Biography of the Works through 'Mavra'* (Oxford: Oxford University Press, 1996), p. 1608. It is a reference made without the impartiality of quotation marks.

32 Scott Messing, *Neoclassicism in Music: From the Genesis of the Concept through the Schoenberg/Stravinsky Polemic* (Ann Arbor: UMI Research Press, 1988), p. 154.

33 Taruskin, *Stravinsky and the Russian Traditions*, p. 1607.

34 Alexis Roland-Manuel, 'La Quinzaine musicale: L'Octuor d'Igor Stravinsky', *L'Eclair* (29 October 1923), 3, quoted in Messing, *Neoclassicism in Music*, pp. 132–3.

1 Becoming a Russian musician

1 Walsh, *Stravinsky: A Creative Spring*, p. 53.

2 Alexander Ivanovich Herzen (1812–70), *Childhood, Youth and Exile* (1853), trans. J. D. Duff (Oxford: Oxford University Press, 1994 [1923]), p. 50.

3 *Ibid.*

4 'A lad led off the singing, a strapping, broad-shouldered fellow … in a voice pure and resonant that brought forth the opening notes of the song as if from

a nightingale's throat; five others took it up, six more carried it further, and out it poured, boundless as Rus' … and Chichikov himself felt like a true Russian' (Gogol, *Dead Souls*, p. 341).

5 Robert Craft, *Stravinsky: Chronicle of a Friendship*, rev. and expanded edn (Nashville; London: Vanderbilt University Press, 1994), p. 328 (emphasis added).

6 "'Europe's sun rises in Perm." Or so goes the old saying in this city, perched on the continent's easternmost rim.' From Sjeng Scheijen, *Diaghilev: A Life*, trans. Jane Hedley-Prole and S. J. Leinbach (London: Profile, 2009), p. 19.

7 Stravinsky's last visit to St Petersburg was 4–7 October 1912. The Stravinsky family's permanent residence – at 66 Kryukov Canal – was a few hundred yards from the Maryinsky Theatre. There the composer's father, Fyodor Ignatyevich Stravinsky (1843–1902), 'had a leading [role] in which he was particularly admired by the Petersburg public. He was a very well-known artist in his day. He had a beautiful voice and an amazing technique, acquired in studying by the Italian method at the St Petersburg Conservatoire, in addition to great dramatic talent – a rare attribute among opera singers at that time.' Igor Stravinsky, *An Autobiography (1903–1934)*, p. 6.

8 Philip V. Bohlman, 'Ontologies of Music', in *Rethinking Music*, ed. Nicholas Cook and Mark Everist (Oxford: Oxford University Press, 2001), pp. 17–34 (p. 18).

9 Joseph Brodsky, 'A Guide to a Renamed City', in *Less than One: Selected Essays* (1986), cited in Orlando Figes, *Natasha's Dance: A Cultural History of Russia* (London: Allen Lane; Penguin, 2002), p. 6.

10 Andrei Bely (1880–1934), *Petersburg* (1916), trans. Robert A. Maguire and John E. Malmstad (London: Penguin, 1983), p. 2.

11 Figes, *Natasha's Dance*, p. 151. In his Commentary to *Eugene Onegin* (1964) Vladimir Nabokov refers to Moscow as Russia's dowager duchess.

12 From the Prologue to Aleksandr Sergeyevich Pushkin, *Ruslan and Lyudmila* (1817–20), in *The Garnett Book of Russian Verse: A Treasury of Russian Poets from 1730 to 1996*, ed. Donald Rayfield with Jeremy Hicks, Olga Makarova and Anna Pilkington (London: Garnett Press, 2000), p. 66.

13 Robert A. Maguire and John E. Malmstad, 'Translators' Introduction' to Bely, *Petersburg*, pp. vii–xxi (p. vii).

14 Cited, with additions, in Figes, *Natasha's Dance*, p. 5.

15 From A. S. Pushkin, *The Bronze Horseman*, in Rayfield *et al.*, *The Garnett Book of Russian Verse*, p. 104.

16 Cited in Stuart R. Grover, 'The World of Art Movement in Russia', *Russian Review* 32.1 (1973), 28–42 (p. 34).

17 Figes, *Natasha's Dance*, p. 211.

18 Sergey Ivanovich Taneyev (1856–1913) taught composition at the Moscow Conservatoire and was also a distinguished performer, taking over Nikolay Rubinstein's piano class when the latter died in March 1881. Taneyev was interested in a wide range of intellectual pursuits, his vocal compositions

including settings of Esperanto. His reputation as an influential teacher rests with the testimony of his distinguished pupils, who included Skryabin, Lyapunov, Glière and Rakhmaninov.

19 Oskar von Riemann, *Rachmaninoff's Recollections as Told to Oskar von Riemann* (London: George Allen & Unwin, 1934), p. 64.

20 Ivan Glebov (the *nom de plume* of Boris Asaf'yev), 'Pathways into the Future', in *Melos*, Book II (1918), in Stuart Campbell (ed. and trans.), *Russians on Russian Music, 1880–1917: An Anthology* (Cambridge: Cambridge University Press, 2003), p. 250.

21 S. I. Taneyev, *Podvizhnoy kontrapunkt strogovo pis'ma* (Leipzig; Moscow, 1909), translated into English as *Invertible Counterpoint in the Strict Style* (Wellesley, MA: Branden, 1962); *Ucheniye o kanone* [*The study of canon*], ed. V. M. Belyayev (Moscow, 1929).

22 Von Riemann, *Rachmaninoff's Recollections*, p. 69. (Rakhmaninov passed this exam. Skryabin failed.)

23 Taruskin, *Stravinsky and the Russian Traditions*, p. 187.

24 Igor Stravinsky, '*The Sleeping Beauty*', trans. Edwin Evans (open letter to Serge Diaghilev reprinted from *The Times* of 18 October 1921), in Eric Walter White, *Stravinsky: The Composer and His Works* (London: Faber and Faber, 1966), Appendix A1, pp. 573–4 (p. 573).

25 *Ibid.*, p. 574 (emphasis added). Jennifer Homans – *Apollo's Angels: A History of Ballet* (London: Granta, 2010), p. 550 – writes persuasively of *Beauty* residing 'in the imagination of Diaghilev and Stravinsky as they clung to their … fast-receding past'.

26 From Pushkin, *The Bronze Horseman*, p. 66.

27 Herzen, *Who Is to Blame?* (1845–6), trans. Margaret Wettlin (Moscow: Progress Publishers, 1978), pp. 135–6.

28 Stravinsky, *An Autobiography (1903–1934)*, p. 6.

29 Gerald Abraham, 'Nikolay Andreyevich Rimsky-Korsakov', in *The New Grove Dictionary of Music and Musicians*, 20 vols., Vol. XVI, ed. Stanley Sadie (London: Macmillan, 1980), pp. 26–41 (p. 27).

30 Cf. Robert Craft: 'The *Conversation* books, unlike the ghosted *Poétique musicale* and *Chroniques de ma vie*, the pamphlets on Pushkin and Diaghilev, are the only published writings attributed to Stravinsky that are actually "by him" in the sense of fidelity and substance of his thoughts. The language, unavoidably, is very largely mine.' From the Preface to Stravinsky and Craft, *Memories and Commentaries*, p. xiii. Cf. Taruskin: '[T]he voice that speaks to us from the Stravinsky/Craft books – and especially the first of them, *Conversations with Igor Stravinsky* (1959) – was, in an indirect but important sense, as much the creation of Pierre Souvtchinsky as the voice that had spoken two decades earlier out of the *Poétique musicale*.' Taruskin, *Stravinsky and the Russian Traditions*, p. 4.

31 Fyodor Stepanovich Akimenko (1876–1945).

32 Vasily Pavlovich Kalafati (1869–1942).

33 From *I. F. Stravinskiy: Stat'i i materialï*, ed. L. S. Dyachkova with B. M. Yarustovsky (Moscow: Sovetskiy Kompositor, 1973), pp. 444–5, quoted in V. Stravinsky and Craft, *Stravinsky in Pictures and Documents*, pp. 21–2.

34 Taruskin, *Stravinsky and the Russian Traditions*, pp. 95–6 (emphasis added).

35 Walsh, *Stravinsky: A Creative Spring*, p. 26.

36 Varunts (ed.), *I. F. Stravinskiy: Perepiska s russkimi korrespondentami* (1977), Vol. I, p. 51. Information given in Walsh, *Stravinsky: A Creative Spring*, p. 26.

37 Walsh, *Stravinsky: A Creative Spring*, p. 557n50.

38 The exact date of termination of this long course of lessons is also a question of some disagreement: Taruskin opts for March 1899, Walsh for April (Taruskin, *Stravinsky and the Russian Traditions*, p. 96; Walsh, *Stravinsky: A Creative Spring*, p. 52). Despite such minor inconsistencies it is established that Stravinsky enjoyed a considerable period of regular piano tuition at this time.

39 Felix Mendelssohn(-Bartholdy) (1809–47), Piano Concerto in G minor op. 25 (1831). 'The concerto … bears some resemblance to the fantasia form: the first two movements run together and the finale is improvisatory in style.' Karl-Heinz Köhler, 'Felix Mendelssohn(-Bartholdy)', in Sadie, *New Grove Dictionary*, Vol. XII, p. 149.

40 Stravinsky and Craft, *Memories and Commentaries*, pp. 25–6.

41 Dyachkova (ed.), *I. F. Stravinskiy: Stat'i i materialï*, p. 496.

42 'Over his first piano teacher, Alexandra Petrovna Snyetkova (… the daughter of a Mariyinsky Theatre violinist) we need not tarry.' Taruskin, *Stravinsky and the Russian Traditions*, p. 95.

43 Varunts (ed.), *I. F. Stravinskiy: Perepiska s russkimi korrespondentami*, cited in Walsh, *Stravinsky: A Creative Spring*, p. 563n9.

44 John A. Sloboda, 'Musical Learning and Development', in *The Musical Mind: The Cognitive Psychology of Music* (Oxford: Clarendon Press, 1985), pp. 194–238. Enculturation, he writes, covers the period roughly from birth up to the middle years of childhood, although in Stravinsky's case this may be qualified by his upbringing in the household of a professional singer and his close proximity to, and familiarity with, the Maryinsky Theatre and its productions. Such experiences would have made him ahead of his years when compared to a more typical child within a non-musical family. Nevertheless, Sloboda defines enculturation as a 'universally-experienced set of experiences and responses'.

45 A. N. Whitehead, *The Organisation of Thought* (London: Williams and Northgate, 1917).

46 Sloboda, 'Musical Learning and Development', p. 195.

47 Resourcing several established lines of study with emphasis on the work of Piaget and Chomsky, Sloboda acknowledges a particular debt to N. Chomsky, *Syntactic Structures* (The Hague: Mouton, 1957); *Aspects of the Theory of Syntax* (Cambridge, MA: MIT Press, 1965); and *Language and Mind* (New York: Harcourt Brace Jovanovich, 1968). Sloboda, *The Musical Mind*, especially Chapter 2: 'Music, Language and Meaning'.

48 Sloboda, 'Musical Learning and Development', p. 196.

49 Such a claim can draw only limited support from research: in her study into conservatoire teaching Janet Mills laments that the impact of the academy professor has not yet been widely researched. Nevertheless, she asserts that performer-teachers fulfil 'a [crucial] role within the culture of Western classical music'; they 'have influenced and continue to influence' this culture. Janet Mills, 'Working in Music: The Conservatoire Professor', *British Journal of Music Education* 21.2 (2004), 179–98 (p. 183).

50 Dyachkova (ed.), *I. F. Stravinskiy: Stat'i i materialï*, p. 496.

51 Walsh, *Stravinsky: A Creative Spring*, p. 53.

52 Taruskin, *Stravinsky and the Russian Traditions*, p. 96.

53 Walsh, *Stravinsky: A Creative Spring*, p. 53.

54 Stravinsky, *An Autobiography (1903–1934)*, pp. 12–13. The impact not only of Rubinstein's teaching but of his death on 20 November 1894 – during Kashperova's final year at the Conservatoire – may explain why she appeared to Stravinsky to be 'obsessed by her adoration for her illustrious master'. Stravinsky was twelve years old when he filed past Rubinstein's coffin. His memories of that occasion are amongst the most vividly recollected episodes of his childhood: '[Kashperova] talked endlessly about her teacher, Anton Rubinstein; I was attentive to this because I had seen Rubinstein in his coffin and could not forget this memory … Rubinstein was white, but with a thick black mane. The body was in full dress, as if for a concert, and the hands were folded over a cross.' Stravinsky and Craft, *Memories and Commentaries*, p. 33.

55 Taruskin, *Stravinsky and the Russian Traditions*, p. 96: a reference to Stravinsky, *An Autobiography* (1936), p. 13.

56 Yastrebtsev reports that, according to Rimsky-Korsakov, Solovyov 'loved her very much as a talented pupil and used to call her Snegurochka ['Snow Maiden']'. Taruskin, *Stravinsky and the Russian Traditions*, pp. 96–7.

57 Igor Stravinsky, *Chronicle of My Life* (London: Victor Gollancz, 1936), p. 27; *An Autobiography* (1936), p. 13. Edward Garden confirms that Anton Rubinstein was deeply antipathetic to Wagner and his music. It is possible, therefore, that such an admiring disciple of his as L. A. Kashperova would also be anti-Wagner. Edward Garden, 'Anton Rubinstein', in Sadie, *The New Grove Dictionary*, Vol. XVI, pp. 297–300 (p. 298).

58 Stravinsky and Craft, *Memories and Commentaries*, p. 25.

59 *Ibid.*, p. 26.

60 Stravinsky, *Chronicle of My Life*, p. 27; *An Autobiography (1903–1934)*, p. 13.

61 Stravinsky and Craft, *Memories and Commentaries*, pp. 25–6, from the section 'Teachers'. Walsh offers sympathetic insight into the reasons behind this vitriolic response.

> [T]he late memoir of Kashperova fits a pattern which is to recur. Stravinsky, with his lack of self-assurance, was much more likely to respect disciplined

teaching at that stage than to rebel ostentatiously against it, even if it went against the grain. All the evidence of his relations with his father in his last years is that he loyally accepted a tight regime … Something comparable will happen later with Rimsky-Korsakov and (for a time) Diaghilev, to look no further into the future. But the image of rebellion suited the aging Stravinsky who wanted to distance himself from the narrow rules and petty preoccupations of provincial St Petersburg and from the insecure young man who accepted this village green as if it were the whole planet. He wanted, rather, to be thought of as a free spirit, a phenomenon without a history. (Walsh, *Stravinsky: A Creative Spring*, p. 53)

62 Stravinsky and Craft, *Memories and Commentaries*, pp. 25–6.

63 Walsh, *Stravinsky: A Creative Spring*, p. 53.

64 Edith J. Hipkins, *How Chopin Played (Notes of A. J. Hipkins)* (London: J. M. Dent, 1937), p. 5.

65 Edward Dannreuther, 'Henselt', in Sadie, *The New Grove Dictionary*, Vol. VIII, p. 489.

66 Sergey Rakhmaninov quoted in Catherine Drinker Bowen, *Free Artist: The Story of Anton and Nicholas Rubinstein* (New York: Random House, 1939), pp. 291–2, quoted in Reginald R. Gerig, *Famous Pianists and Their Technique* (New York: Robert B. Luce, 1974), p. 294.

67 Wilhelm von Lenz (1808–83), *The Great Piano Virtuosos of Our Time from Personal Acquaintance*, trans. Madeleine R. Baker (New York: Da Capo Press, 1973 [1899]), p. 143.

68 *Ibid.*, p. 168n20.

69 Dannreuther, 'Henselt'.

70 Oscar Bie, *Das Klavier und seine Meister* (1898), translated into English as *A History of the Pianoforte and Pianoforte Players*, trans. and rev. E. E. Kellett and E. W. Naylor (New York: Da Capo Press, 1966 [1899]), pp. 295–6.

71 Josef Hofmann, *Piano Playing with Piano Questions Answered by Josef Hofmann* (Philadelphia: Theodore Presser, 1920), p. 60; quoted in Gerig, *Famous Pianists and Their Technique*, p. 295.

72 Bie, *A History of the Pianoforte*, pp. 296–7.

73 *Ibid.*, p. 298.

74 Kenneth Hamilton, 'The Virtuoso Tradition', in *The Cambridge Companion to the Piano*, ed. David Rowland (Cambridge: Cambridge University Press, 1998), pp. 57–74 (p. 69).

75 *Ibid.*, pp. 72–3.

76 *Ibid.*, p. 69.

77 *Ibid.*, pp. 69–70.

78 Ives and Grainger were rare examples of composers who experimented with incorporating the stylistic vagaries of Romantic performance practice into their notation. As Hamilton observes: '[The late nineteenth-century] obsession with a singing tone was … no doubt the chief stimulus for what Percy Grainger

(1882–1961) described as a "harped" or highly arpeggiated piano style. The most detailed attempt to notate this manner of playing is Grainger's own *Rosenkavalier Ramble* where the individual voicing of each chord, and the speed of the spread, is meticulously indicated.' See *ibid.*

79 Malwine Brée, *The Groundwork of the Leschetizky Method: Issued with His Approval by His Assistant Malwine Brée with Forty-Seven Illustrative Cuts of Leschetizky's Hand*, trans. Th. Baker (New York: G. Schirmer, 1902), p. 69.

80 Igor Stravinsky, Concerto in D for Violin and Orchestra (1931); from the fourth movement, 'Capriccio' (Fig. 116).

81 Taruskin, *Stravinsky and the Russian Traditions*, pp. 113–38.

82 Stravinsky, '*The Sleeping Beauty*', p. 573. This was, of course, written before Stravinsky had assumed his pianistic career and formalized the bond between his neoclassicism and the (neoclassical) piano.

83 Stravinsky, *An Autobiography (1903–1934)*, p.13.

84 Stravinsky and Craft, *Memories and Commentaries*, p.33.

85 Alfred Cortot, *La Musique française de piano, troisième série* (Paris: Presses Universitaires de France, 1944), p. 150. Cortot's ambivalence is further illustrated in his contribution to the special Stravinsky edition of *La Revue musicale*. While praising the Piano Concerto for its vitality 'from the first page to the last', he also refers to this work, a page earlier, as the first of a series of (neoclassical) compositions for piano that displays a sense of what he calls *création destructive*. Alfred Cortot, 'Igor Strawinsky, le piano et les pianistes', *La Revue musicale* 20.191, special issue on Igor Stravinsky (May–June 1939), 24–68 (pp. 23–4, 263–4).

86 I am indebted to Peter Hill for pointing out that Rubinstein was later to modify his views on Stravinsky's 'intractability'. To cite Rubinstein's biographer Harvey Sachs: 'In later years [Rubinstein] said that Stravinsky had told him to make whatever changes he saw fit in order to render [the *Three Movements from Petrushka* (1921)] playable without having to "retard the dynamic progress of the piece". For years his playing of this retouched arrangement brought him great success in many countries.' Harvey Sachs, *Arthur Rubinstein: A Life* (London: Phoenix, 1997), p. 199. Sachs is referring to the relevant passage in Arthur Rubinstein, *My Many Years* (New York: Knopf, 1980), p. 138. Nevertheless, with regard to Stravinsky's latest neoclassical works (as opposed to arrangements of earlier 'Russian' repertoire), the composer did indeed demand *exécution*, i.e. utter self-abnegation in the transmission of his scores. This was, after all, one of the prime reasons for his determination to provide a legacy of recordings – an interest that derived from the earliest years of his neoclassical (pianistic) production.

87 Walsh writes: 'The tarantella … was first described and quoted by Smirnov (*Tvorcheskoye formirovaniye* [Leningrad, Muzika, 1970], pp. 26–7). See also Igor Stravinsky's letter of 22 April 1899 (OS) to M. E. Osten-Saken, [Varunts,] *Perepiska s russkimi korrespondentami* [Vol. I], pp. 64–5. Osten-Saken was a classmate

of Stravinsky's at the Gurevich school.' Walsh, *Stravinsky: A Creative Spring*, p. 561n72. Smirnov's observations have formed the basis for subsequent references (including the present study).

88 Valeriy Smirnov, *Tvorcheskoye formirovaniye I. F. Stravinskovo* (Leningrad: Muzïka, 1970), pp. 26–7.

89 Varunts, *I. F. Stravinskiy: Perepiska s russkimi korrespondentami*, Vol. I; L. Kutateladze and A. Gozenpude (eds.), *F. Stravinsky: Stat'i, pis'ma, vospominaniya* (Leningrad: Muzïka, 1972). This latter volume contains ten letters – unpublished in English – written by Stravinsky to his parents between 8 July 1899 and 27 July 1901.

90 'It is the sort of piece every thirteen-year-old piano student writes, only Stravinsky wrote it at sixteen.' Taruskin, *Stravinskiy and the Russian Traditions*, p. 95.

91 Igor Stravinsky, letter of 28 July 1893 from Pechisky to his parents in Bad Homburg, in Varunts, *I. F. Stravinsky: Perepiska s russkimi korrespondentami*, Vol. I, pp. 41–2, quoted in Walsh, *Stravinsky: A Creative Spring*, p. 40.

92 Igor Stravinsky, letter of 13 March 1908, in Dyachkova (ed.) *I. F. Stravinskiy: Stat'i i materialï*, p. 444.

93 See photo, captioned 'Igor at the piano, with Catherine and Yuri Stravinsky, Ustilug, 1910 (?)', in Varunts, *I. F. Stravinskiy: Perepiska s russkimi korrespondentami*.

94 Taruskin, *Stravinsky and the Russian Traditions*, p. 95.

95 Smirnov, *Tvorcheskoye formirovaniye I. F. Stravinskovo*, pp. 26–7; the problems of notation in the second part are, for Smirnov, of secondary importance compared to the evidence of Stravinsky's 'harmonic fantasy'. This 'fermentation of the ear' (*brozheniye slukha*) is attributed to similar enharmonic procedures in Rimsky's *Sadko*, published in 1897 (the year before *Tarantella*). As Smirnov observes, 'it was in the Stravinsky library because the role of Dudka was written for his father F. Stravinsky'.

96 Stravinsky's lessons with Akimenko commenced in November 1901.

97 Such imitation of technical exercises (whether consciously employed or not) may have been recognized as such and appreciated as part of the 'turn' by Stravinsky's informal audience of family members and close friends. Such sport at the expense of piano practice can perhaps best be witnessed in Saint-Saëns' *Le Carnival des animaux: Grande fantasie zoologique* (1886). An editor's note at the start of the 'Pianistes' movement helpfully, though somewhat unnecessarily, suggests: 'Les exécutants devront imiter le jeu d'un débutant et sa gaucherie' (Paris: Durand et Cie, 1922), p. 34. Czerny's *Daily Exercises* are quoted at Fig. 4.

98 V. V. Yastrebtsev, *Rimsky-Korsakov: Vospominanya, 1886–1908*, 2 vols., ed. A. V. Ossovsky (Leningrad: Musgiz, 1959–60); abridged English translation by F. Jonas, as *Reminiscences of Rimsky-Korsakov* (New York: Columbia University Press, 1985), pp. 327–8.

99 Walsh, *Stravinsky: A Creative Spring*, p. 69.

100 Stravinsky, *An Autobiography (1903–1934)*, p. 82.

101 Stravinsky and Craft, *Memories and Commentaries*, pp. 25–6.

102 Charles M. Joseph, 'Stravinsky's Piano Scherzo (1902) in Perspective: A New Starting Point,' *Musical Quarterly* 67.1 (January 1981), 82–93.

103 Taruskin, *Stravinsky and the Russian Traditions*, p. 103.

104 Nikolay Ivanovich Richter (1879–1944).

105 *Ibid.*, pp. 102–3.

106 Ossovsky is reviewing the imminent publication of the *Songs* op. 21 (nos. 25–36), the *Variations pour le piano sur un thème de F. Chopin* op. 22 and the *10 Préludes* op. 23. Ossovsky was Associate Editor of the *Russkaya muzïkal'naya gazeta*.

107 A. V. Ossovsky, *The Word* 10, 62–5, cited in Campbell, *Russians on Russian Music, 1880–1917*, p. 177.

108 Taruskin, *Stravinsky and the Russian Traditions*, pp. 103–4.

109 N. A. Rimsky-Korsakov, *Uchebnik garmonii* [*Textbook of Harmony*] (St Petersburg, 1884–5; 2nd edn published 1886 as *Prakticheskiy uchebnik garmonii*). 'The organ point admits all chords of its own tonality and even some chords of modulatory digressions. In more extended organ points such digressions are highly appropriate.' From Nikolay Rimsky-Korsakov, *Practical Manual of Harmony*, trans. from the 12th Russian edn by Joseph Achron, ed. Nicholas Hopkins (New York: Carl Fischer, 2005), p. 66.

110 Anatoly Konstantinovich Lyadov, *Six Pieces* (1893) comprising: Prelude, Giga, Fuga, three Mazurkas.

111 Walsh provides useful clarification in *Stravinsky: A Creative Spring*, p. 562n6: 'According to Fyodor's account book, the lessons with Akimenko did not begin until November 1901, by which time Igor was at the university. But according to Smirnov, there is in the Theatrical Institute in St Petersburg a copy of Lyadov's *Canon* of 1898 inscribed "I. Stravinsky 1900".' See Smirnov, *Tvorcheskoye formirovaniye I. F. Stravinskovo*, p. 28. This is presumably the 'ordinary manual' which the composer tells us he began to study on his own when he was eighteen, in Stravinsky, *An Autobiography (1903–1934)*, p. 14.

112 See the passage starting at b. 38. Mikhail Glinka (1804–57), *Complete Works (Urtext)*, Vol. II: *For Piano*, ed. Alexander Bouzovkin and Victor Yekimovsky (Budapest: Koenemann Music, 2011), p. 33. Between 1833 and 1834 Glinka studied counterpoint and composition in Berlin with Siegfried Dehn (1799–1858). These three fugues for piano – in E♯ major (*a 3*), in A minor (*a 3*) and in D major (*a 4*) – may therefore be considered, like Stravinsky's Scherzo and Sonata in F♯ minor, student works or, even, compositional assignments written to order.

113 A. V. Ossovsky, *The Word* 10, 62–5, cited in Campbell, *Russians on Russian Music, 1880–1917*, p. 177.

114 Taruskin, *Stravinsky and the Russian Traditions*, p. 102.

115 *Ibid.*, pp. 99, 113–28.

116 Hamilton, 'The Virtuoso Tradition', p. 58; cf. Sigismond Thalberg, *L'Art du chant appliqué au piano* op. 70 (*c.* 1853).

117 Sandra P. Rosenblum, *Performance Practices in Classic Piano Music: Their Principles and Applications* (Bloomington: Indiana University Press, 1988), pp. 382–3.

118 *Ibid.*, p. 382.

119 Taruskin, *Stravinsky and the Russian Traditions*, p. 115.

120 Igor Stravinsky, letter of 3 July 1904 to Vladimir Rimsky-Korsakov, in Varunts, *I. F. Stravinsky: Perepiska s russkimi korrespondentami*, pp. 144–5, cited in Walsh, *Stravinsky: A Creative Spring*, p. 37. Rakhmaninov's Piano Concerto no. 2 in C minor was premiered in November 1901.

121 See, for example, the *Sonate* first movement (bb. 10–22); also the opening and central sections of the Adagietto.

122 Walsh, *Stravinsky: A Creative Spring*, p. 77.

123 Taruskin, *Stravinsky and the Russian Traditions*, p. 115.

124 *Ibid.*, p. 138.

125 Walsh, *Stravinsky: A Creative Spring*, p. 81.

126 Louis Andriessen and Elmer Schönberger, *The Apollonian Clockwork: On Stravinsky*, trans. Jeff Hamburg (Amsterdam: Amsterdam University Press; Amsterdam Academic Archive, 2006), pp. 29–30.

127 Stravinsky, *An Autobiography (1903–1934)*, pp. 82–3.

128 *Fireworks* had been published by Schott in 1909.

129 André Schaeffner, *Strawinsky* (Paris: Les Editions Rieder, 1931), p. 13.

130 Once again it is the polyrhythmic element that is the key to Schaeffner's reading of this work; in his view, even its emotional charge derives from this parameter. With regard to the first study, in C minor, he attributes to the three-against-two polyrhythm 'un pathétique inattendu et peut-être précurseur'. *Ibid.*, p. 13.

131 Igor Glebov, 'Pathways into the Future', Book II, in Campbell, *Russians on Russian Music, 1880–1917*, p. 241.

132 In Igor Stravinsky, *The Rite of Spring: Sketches 1911–1913* (London: Boosey & Hawkes, 1969), Appendix, p. 7. Robert Craft, author of Appendix I, 'Commentary to the Sketches', writes: 'With reference to Skryabin, I might digress to say that for me it is precisely the *lack* of any influence on Stravinsky that is perplexing, except perhaps, and very negligibly, in the piano *Etudes* and in *Zvezdoliki* [*Le Roi des étoiles*, 1911/12].'

133 Taruskin, *Stravinsky and the Russian Traditions*, p. 380.

134 'In his solitary training sessions Nijinsky took to performing the steps of a typical ballet class at an accelerated pace and with forced energy – what [Nijinska] later called "muscular drive".' Homans, *Apollo's Angels*, p. 306.

135 Taruskin, *Stravinsky and the Russian Traditions*, p. 381.

136 Schaeffner referred to these as 'études chromatiques autant que rhythmiques'. Schaeffner, *Strawinsky*, p. 13.

137 N. Ya. Myaskovsky, 'Ig. Stravinsky: Zhar-ptitsa, skazka-balet', *Music* (8 October 1911), in Campbell, *Russians on Russian Music, 1880–1917*, p. 207.

138 Schaeffner, *Strawinsky*, p. 13.

139 'The existence of [Stravinsky's] unpublished compositions became known in 1966, when Eric Walter White published the "Catalogue of Manuscripts (1904–1952) in Stravinsky's Possession" prepared by Robert Craft for Stravinsky's private use in 1954.' (See Appendix C in White, *Stravinsky: The Composer and His Works*, pp. 599–618.) Taruskin, *Stravinsky and the Russian Traditions*, p. 138.

140 Walsh, *Stravinsky: A Creative Spring*, p. 10.

141 The additional line is inserted over bb. 48–50.

142 Taruskin, *Stravinsky and the Russian Traditions*, p. 151.

143 *Ibid.*, p. 151.

144 An 'instrumental third stave' is also a feature of Stravinsky's Verlaine setting 'La Lune blanche …' (*Two Poems of Verlaine*, 1910), in bb. 4–5 and bb. 17–18. Stravinsky was to make two initial attempts at orchestrating these songs in 1910 and in 1914. He completed a version for baritone and chamber orchestra in 1951.

145 Taruskin, *Stravinsky and the Russian Traditions*, p. 150. Fyodor Ignatyevich Stravinsky died on 21 November 1902.

146 Walsh, *Stravinsky: A Creative Spring*, p. 99. The piano reduction was published by Belyayev (Leipzig) in 1908, the full score in 1913.

147 'Both works end in the key of B major with an octave B held by the strings playing tremolo, while the inner parts move towards a final resolution on the major triad.' White, *Stravinsky: The Composer and His Works*, pp. 175–6.

148 Cited in *ibid.*, p. 179.

149 *Ibid.*, p. 178.

150 See Taruskin, *Stravinsky and the Russian Traditions*, pp. 348–9.

151 Sergey Mitrofanovich Gorodetsky (1884–1967).

152 Aleksandr Sergeyevich Dargomïzhky (1813–69), *Slavonic Tarantelle* (1864–5), in *Dargomïzhky: Collected Piano Works* (Melville, NY: Belwin Mills, *c.* 1983), pp. 102–9.

153 Aleksandr Porfiryevich Borodin (1833–87), *Tarantella for One Piano, Four Hands*, ed. Joan Yarborough and Robert Cowan (New York: International Music Company, 1992).

154 See *Lyadov: Complete Piano Works* (Dover Publications). In an article to mark the composer's passing in 1914, Karatïgin comments that this work 'sounds amazingly original in the upper register of the piano, but it gains even more in the composer's own arrangement of it for two flutes, piccolo, three clarinets and metallophone (*campanelli*)'. V. G. Karatïgin, 'In Memory of A. K. Lyadov', *Apollo* (1914), nos. 6–7, cited in Campbell, *Russians on Russian Music, 1880–1917*, p. 161.

155 See Taruskin, *Stravinsky and the Russian Traditions*, pp. 364–8.

156 Yastrebtsev refers to 'Pastorale' as 'an original song, but not without strange harmonies'. Yastrebtsev, *Vospominanya*, Vol. II, p. 440, cited in Taruskin, *Stravinsky and the Russian Traditions*, p. 365.

157 For its direction away from Belyayevism, Stravinsky (claims Taruskin) 'continued to love and "recognize" ['Pastorale'] throughout his career'. Taruskin, *Stravinsky and the Russian Traditions*, p. 368.

158 *Ibid.*, pp. 364–8. See p. 366 for reproduction of a pastel by Leonid Pasternak (the poet's father) of a 'Concert by Wanda Landowska' (1907). Diaghilev is clearly discernible in the audience.

159 *Ibid.*, p. 368.

160 V. Stravinsky and Craft, *Stravinsky in Pictures and Documents*, p. 602n16.

161 Figes, *Natasha's Dance*, p. 560.

162 'Some Ideas about My *Octuor*' appeared in *The Arts* (Brooklyn, New York) in January 1924. As Walsh observes: 'It must have made bizarre reading for the magazine's American subscribers, who had as yet had no opportunity to hear a note of the Octet'; Walsh, *Stravinsky: A Creative Spring*, p. 375. However, this does not diminish the importance of the article to the composer, especially as 'according to an editorial note, this was the first article Stravinsky had ever written for publication'. Cited in White, *Stravinsky: The Composer and His Works*, p. 574.

163 Stravinsky, 'Some Ideas about My *Octuor*', p. 574.

164 *Ibid.*, p. 577.

165 'Petrograd, after all, in spite of being for a century the seat of Government, is still an artificial city. Moscow is real Russia, Russia as it was and will be.' John Reed, *Ten Days that Shook the World* (London: Penguin, 1977 [1919]), p. 221.

166 As cited in Maguire and Malmstad, 'Translators' Introduction' to Bely, *Petersburg*, p. xiv.

167 Richard Taruskin, *On Russian Music* (Berkeley; Los Angeles; London: University of California Press, 2009), p. 166. The citation is from 'The Case for Rimsky-Korsakov', first published in *Opera News* in 1992.

168 Andrey Rimsky-Korsakov, 'Chronicle of N. A. Rimsky-Korsakov's Life during the Period Not Included in *My Musical Life* (September 1906–June 1908)', in N. A. Rimsky-Korsakov, *My Musical Life* (1923), ed. Carl Van Vechten, trans. Judah A. Joffe (London; Boston, MA: Faber and Faber, 1989 [1923]), pp. 425–61 (p. 430; emphasis added). This Appendix concludes with the poignant and significant information that Rimsky-Korsakov continued to work on *Principles of Orchestration* to the very end of his life: '*June 7*: last date of jottings for *Textbook of Instrumentation* … On the night of June 7–8 [/20–1] after a brief but violent storm and downpour – the last attack of suffocation and death'. *Ibid.*, p. 461.

169 Rimsky-Korsakov began to work on this material, initially conceived as a *Treatise on Instrumentation*, in 1873.

170 Bohlman, 'Ontologies of Music', p. 21 (emphasis added).

171 N. A. Rimsky-Korsakov, *Principles of Orchestration*, ed. Maximilian Steinberg, trans. Edward Agate (New York: Dover, 1964 [1922]), p. 2: from the Preface to the 1st edn (1891; original emphasis). Page references are to the 1922 edition.

172 Rimsky-Korsakov, *Principles of Orchestration*, p. 3.

173 *Ibid.*, pp. 3–4.

174 *Ibid.*, p. 35. This extract is taken from the 'Comparison of Resonance in Orchestral Groups and Combinations of Different Tone Qualities' – the final section to Chapter 1, dated '7 [/20] June 1908'.

175 Rimsky-Korsakov, *Principles of Orchestration*, p. 16–17.

176 Maximilian Steinberg, 'Editor's Preface' (dated 'St Petersburgh [*sic*], December 1912'), in Rimsky-Korsakov, *Principles of Orchestration*, p. xii.

177 The 'Note to Table B' explains: 'The signs $>$ and $<$ are not to be mistaken for *diminuendo* and *crescendo*; they indicate how the resonance of an instrument increases or diminishes in relation to the characteristic quality of its timbre.' Rimsky-Korsakov, *Principles of Orchestration*, p. 15.

178 *Ibid.*, p. 14.

179 The closest that Rimsky-Korsakov gets to offering advice regarding timbre or expression in these other instrumental categories is in Table E, for tuned percussion. The highest three notes and lowest six (chromatic) notes of the 'glockenspiel (with keyboard)' are indicated as 'ill-sounding'; and the lowest five notes of the xylophone are marked, also in square brackets, as 'confused'. Rimsky-Korsakov, *Principles of Orchestration*, p. 31.

180 *Ibid.*, p. 19.

181 *Ibid.*, pp. 18–19.

182 *Ibid.*, p. 20.

183 Cited in White, *Stravinsky: The Composer and His Works*, p. 210.

184 'It cannot be denied that the constant use of compound timbres in pairs, in three's [*sic*] etc. eliminates characteristics of tone, and produces a dull, neutral texture, whereas the employment of simple combinations gives scope for variety in colour.' Rimsky-Korsakov, *Principles of Orchestration*, p. 35.

185 Cited in V. Stravinsky and Craft, *Stravinsky in Pictures and Documents*, p. 64.

186 Cf. *Three Japanese Lyrics* (1912–13), *Pribaoutki* (1914), *Berceuses du chat* (1915–16), *Reynard* (1915–16), *Ragtime pour onze instruments* (1918).

187 Lukas Foss, 'Thirteen Ways of Looking at Igor Stravinsky', in *Stravinsky (1882–1971): A Composers' Memorial*, 61–2.

188 Jonathan Cross, *The Stravinsky Legacy* (Cambridge: Cambridge University Press, 1998), p. 25.

189 Theodor W. Adorno, 'Vers une musique informelle', in *Quasi una fantasia: Essays on Modern Music*, trans. Rodney Livingstone (London: Verso, 1992), p. 272; cited in Cross, *The Stravinsky Legacy*, p. 25.

190 Cross, *The Stravinsky Legacy*, p. 26.

191 This seven-bar section begins at Fig. 8 in the score.

192 These recollections, from Stravinsky, *An Autobiography* (1936), and from Stravinsky and Craft, *Memories and Commentaries*, are cited in White, *Stravinsky: The Composer and His Works*, pp. 181–2.

193 Frank Kermode, *Pleasing Myself: From Beowulf to Philip Roth* (London: Penguin, 2001), p. 14. The author is referring to *Autobiographies* by W. B. Yeats.

194 Rimsky-Korsakov, *Principles of Orchestration*, pp. 126–7.

195 Fig. 125 in the (1947) score.

196 Rimsky-Korsakov, *Principles of Orchestration*, p. 30.

197 Walter Piston, *Orchestration* (London: Victor Gollancz, 1973).

198 Rimsky-Korsakov, *Principles of Orchestration*, p. 32.

199 Stravinsky, *An Autobiography (1903–1934)*, p. 21.

200 Rimsky-Korsakov, *Principles of Orchestration*, p. 2: from the Preface to the 1st edn.

201 *Fireworks* was premiered on 17 June 1908, shortly after Rimsky-Korsakov's death. Stravinsky suggests, in his *Autobiography*, that he wrote the entire work 'unseen'. However, as Rimsky 'had told me to send it to him as soon as it was ready' there can be little doubt that the pupil would have sensed his teacher looking over his shoulder and would have anticipated 'in his mind's ear' Rimsky's reaction to this new score and, even, the pianistic contour of some of its material; see White, *Stravinsky: The Composer and His Works*, p. 180.

202 Similar pianistic 'origins' may be viewed (via the application of identical piano fingerings) in the *tutti* presentation of this theme at Fig. 22.

203 Fyodor Mikhailovich Dostoyevsky (1821–81), *Crime and Punishment* (1865–6), trans. David McDuff (London: Penguin, 2003 [1991]), p. 512.

204 Stravinsky, *An Autobiography (1903–1934)*, p. 31.

205 Igor Stravinsky, *Poetics of Music in the Form of Six Lessons*, trans. Arthur Knodel and Ingold Dahl (New York: Vintage, 1956 [1947]), p. 83.

206 *Ibid.*, p. 82.

207 Pre-eminent amongst earlier pianistic models of the *Konzertstück* are Mozart's Rondo in D K. 382 and Rondo in A K. 386 (both composed in Vienna in 1782); Schubert's *Wandererfantasie* D. 760 (1822; arr. Liszt, *c.* 1851); and Schumann's Fantasie in A minor (1841), later coopted to form the first movement of his Piano Concerto (1846).

208 Malcolm MacDonald, 'Preface' to Igor Stravinsky, *Pétrouchka: Revised 1947 Version* (London: Boosey & Hawkes, 1997), p. v.

209 Paul Sacher Stiftung (PSS) 227–0611. The Sammlung Igor Strawinsky (Igor Stravinsky Collection) is housed at the Paul Sacher Stiftung in Basel and includes seven *Skizzenbücher* ('sketchbooks') which contain a large quantity of the composer's manuscript material, all of which is available for examination on microfilm.

210 This transition could be accommodated during the side drum and timpani link 'ben articulato' (Fig. 119), the pianist's arrival timed to coincide with the downbeat at the start of the Third Part, 'The Blackamoor' (Fig. 120).

211 Nikolay Yakovlevich Myaskovsky (1881–1950).

212 N. Ya. Myaskovsky, '*Petrushka*, Ballet by Igor Stravinsky', *Music* 59 (14 January 1912), 72–5, in N. Ya. Myaskovsky, *Sobraniye materialov* [*Collection of Materials*], 2nd edn., 2 vols., Vol. II (Moscow: Muzïka, 1964), pp. 41–4. Cited in Campbell, *Russians on Russian Music, 1880–1917*, p. 212.

213 Campbell, *Russians on Russian Music*, p. 211. Stravinsky's 1947 revision of *Petrushka* replaces Adagietto (quaver = 54) with Andantino (quaver = 80); in his re-organization of the rehearsal numbers, Fig. 52 becomes Fig. 102.

214 *Ibid.*, pp. 210–12.

215 *Ibid.*, p. 211.

216 *Ibid.*, p. 212.

217 'Today, 4/17 XI 1912, with a violent toothache I completed the composition of *Le Sacre du printemps*. Clarens, Châtelard Hotel.' Stravinsky, *The Rite of Spring: Sketches*, p. 96 (original in Russian).

218 Christian Goubault, *Igor Stravinsky* (Paris: Librairie Honoré Champion, 1991), pp. 157–8. White is of the opinion that a 'four-handed piano reduction was made by Stravinsky himself, probably as and when the work was being composed in 1911 and 1912 and before the orchestration was completed'; see White, *Stravinsky: The Composer and His Works*, pp. 217–18.

219 Goubault, *Igor Stravinsky*, p. 158.

220 Apart from the musicological value of this facsimile edition of 139 pages, it is also a precious testimony to Stravinsky's beautiful calligraphy even in the 'heat' of creativity – an impression enhanced by his use of coloured inks to clarify his intentions or to insert minutiae of instrumentation. The almost total absence of any crossings-out is a further cause for admiration. As a useful pointer Robert Craft assures us, in the Appendix, that the composer worked from top left to bottom right in a consistent manner.

221 Stravinsky to Nikolay Konstantinovich Roerich, from La Baule (27 July 1910): 'Please write your address legibly because I have no idea where to find you, and I have much to say about our future child'; from Ustilug (2 July 1911): 'I feel it is imperative that we see each other to decide about every detail – especially every question of staging – concerning our child'; from Clarens (6 March 1912): 'A few words about our child'. Stravinsky, *The Rite of Spring: Sketches*, Appendix, pp. 29–31.

222 *Ibid.*, Appendix, p. 32.

223 Igor Stravinsky, letter of 2 December 1912 to N. F. Findreizen, Editor of the *Russian Musical Gazette*, from the Hotel du Châtelard, Clarens, in *ibid.*

224 Igor Stravinsky, letter of 6 March 1912 to N. K. Roerich, from Clarens, in *ibid.*, Appendix, p. 31.

225 Stravinsky, letter of 2 December 1912 to Findreizen, from the Hotel du Châtelard, in *ibid.*, Appendix, p. 33.

226 Robert Craft, 'Commentary to the Sketches', in Stravinsky, *The Rite of Spring: Sketches*, Appendix, p. 17.

227 *Ibid.*, Appendix, p. 36.

228 For 'Glorification de l'élue' see *ibid.*, pp. 59 ('5 March [1912]'), p. 61 ('7 March [1912]'); for 'Danse Sacrale' see *Strawinsky: Sein Nachlass, sein Bild* (Basel: Kunstmuseum Basel; Paul Sacher Stiftung, 1984), pp. 45ff. Here, the two-stave material (in pianistic guise) awaits re-notation from quaver to semiquaver note-values; this elaborate sketch also reveals details of its eventual instrumentation. Comparisons can be drawn with the published score, Fig. 146.

229 Craft, '*The Rite of Spring*: Genesis of a Masterpiece', in Stravinsky, *The Rite of Spring: Sketches*, pp. xv–xxv (p. xxv). In a footnote to this passage Craft acknowledges that the 'trumpets play dotted rhythms at two measures before

No. 33, but this is the exception that proves the rule', an admission that has encouraged this author to propose his own views regarding *The Rite* and the (non-)piano, despite the obvious exceptions ('Glorification of the Chosen One' and 'Sacrificial Dance'), which have, also, been openly declared.

2   Becoming a neoclassicist

1 *Four Studies* op. 7 (1908). See Chapter 1, pp. 37–40.

2 As a sequence of arpeggiated chords, this 'principle' relates to the shifting harmonies at the end of *The Faun and the Shepherdess*. There, the chords change – just as, in the study, the internal fingers change.

3 Carl Czerny (1791–1857), *The Art of Finger Dexterity: Die Kunst der Fingerfertigkeit* op. 740 (699) (London: Edition Peters, 2003), pp. 25–8.

4 The first movement of the *Sonate pour piano* (1924) also illustrates this index-finger overlap on several occasions – most notably, perhaps, at bb. 122–4 in the left hand. Here, the overlapped E♭, i.e. the final note of each bar, might be more comfortably played by the right-hand thumb, but this would negate Stravinsky's delicately crafted pattern – especially memorable, in this context, for its wide intervals.

5 PSS 123–0684 reveals that Stravinsky's initial conception of the first movement, bb. 160–1, was to utilize this fingering in the right hand (descending 2,1,2, i.e. Bb, A, Ab) when he first considered that the hands would be crossed over. In the final score this material was rearranged between the hands.

6 Stravinsky, *An Autobiography (1903–1934)*, p. 82.

7 Igor Stravinsky, from 'Love Music!', in *Komsomolskaya pravda* (27 September 1962). Reprinted (trans. Sarah S. White) in White, *Stravinsky: The Composer and His Works*, p. 591.

8 Stravinsky, *An Autobiography (1903–1934)*, pp. 82–3.

9 Taruskin, *Stravinsky and the Russian Traditions*, p. 365.

10 Igor Stravinsky and Robert Craft, *Expositions and Developments* (London: Faber and Faber, 1962), cited in White, *Stravinsky: The Composer and His Works*, p. 286. Ironically, 'Pastorale' is an entirely originally composed 'Stravinsky work', *Pulcinella* 'merely' a re-composition/re-arrangement of others' 'material I had at my disposal'; see Stravinsky, *An Autobiography (1903–1934)*, p. 82.

11 Stravinsky's comment regarding his Sonata in F♯ minor.

12 Christopher Butler, *Modernism: A Very Short Introduction* (Oxford: Oxford University Press, 2010), p. 11.

13 *Ibid.*

14 Stravinsky and Craft, *Memories and Commentaries*, p. 92 (emphasis added).

15 Yevgeny Ivanovich Zamyatin (1884–1937), *We* (1920–1), trans. Clarence Brown (London: Penguin, 1993). These two citations may be found, respectively, on pp. 189 and 170.

16 Igor Stravinsky, 'Tilim-bom', *Trois histoires pour enfants* (1915–17). English version by Rosa Newmarch (1920) in the published score of Igor Stravinsky, *Trois histoires pour enfants* (J. & W. Chester, 1920), p. 3.

17 Stravinsky, 'Les Canards, les cygnes, les oies …', in *Trois histoires pour enfants*, pp. 8–9.

18 Zamyatin, *We*, pp. 168–9.

19 'March', 'Waltz' and 'Polka'.

20 'Considero minhas obras como cartas que escrevi à Posteridade, sem esperar resposta.' Museu Villa-Lobos, *Villa-Lobos, sua obra*, 2nd edn (Rio de Janeiro: MEC/DAC/Museu Villa-Lobos, 1972), p. 332.

21 An illustration of Boris Asaf'yev's ability for telling observation is the value he affords the two series of piano duets (*Three Easy Pieces*, 1914–1915; *Five Easy Pieces*, 1917) for revealing 'the shrewd and incisive intellect of a great artist. [This is music in which] no transplantation of the past can be found, but only contemporary life, with its cinematographic quality' – as paraphrased by Robert Craft, *Stravinsky: Glimpses of a Life* (London: Lime Tree, 1992), p. 261. Richard F. French's translation reads:

> All the pieces are very expressive and deeply contemporary. They do not represent a transplantation of the past into our life, but a new interpretation of the rhythmic formulas and the intonations characteristic of another epoch in the context of our energetic twentieth century, with its dynamic perception of life and obedience to the discipline of work and the steady beat of the pulse of the machine … I need not add that the construction and dynamic conception of the pieces … bear the imprint of cinematography and the jazz band. (Boris Asaf'yev, *A Book about Stravinsky*, trans. Richard F. French (Ann Arbor: UMI Research Press, 1982), pp. 102–3)

22 Taruskin, *Stravinsky and the Russian Traditions*, p. 1456.

23 See Chapter 1, pp. 25–6 and 47.

24 The title page reads: '*Paraphrases on the Theme of "Chopsticks" (1878) by* / 24 Variations et 17 petites Pièces pour Piano sur le thème favori et obligé … Dediées aux petites pianistes capables d'exécuter le thème avec un doigt de chaque main par / *A. Borodin, C. Cui, A. Liadow, N. Rimsky-Korsakov, N. Stcherbatcheff, F. Liszt / for piano*. Original version revised and edited by Alexander Tcherepnin (St Petersburg, 1880; repr. Bonn: Editions Belaieff, 1959).'

The movements include: 'Valse' (Lyadov), 'Gigue' (Lyadov), 'Fughetta on BACH' (Rimsky-Korsakov), 'Tarantella' (Rimsky-Korsakov), 'Menuetto' (Rimsky-Korsakov), 'Valse' (Cui), 'Carillon' (Rimsky-Korsakov), 'Fugue grotesque' (Rimsky-Korsakov). Gerald Abraham writes that Rimsky-Korsakov 'was so much more industrious than the rest [of the invited composers] that some of his pieces – a sonatina, a chorale (on "Ein' Feste Burg"), a "recitative *alla* Bach" and others – had to be omitted from the printed edition'. Gerald Abraham, *Rimsky-Korsakov: A Short Biography* (New York: AMS Press, 1975 [1945]), pp. 63–4.

25 PSS 0215–0622.

26 PSS 123–0285. In Stravinsky's *Reinschrift* the final bars of 'Canard' show that the note-pair a/b is fingered consistently – and 'method'-ically – as

2,3 (right hand); 3,2 (left hand); 2,3 (right hand) leading to the final chord. The published score relents from this somewhat pedantic, quasi-didactic insistence on fingers 2 and 3. This tension between fingering options is an early demonstration of the difference between an editor's performer-oriented solution and Stravinsky's composer-oriented preference. This topic will be explored in Chapter 3.

27 Igor Strawinsky, *Valse from* Histoire du soldat *for Pianoforte Solo* (London: J. & W. Chester, 1922). Stravinsky confines his piano miniature to a faithful re-creation of the first fifty-five bars of the original music (up to Fig. 16 in the study-score published by J. & W. Chester) for violin, double-bass and bassoon with decorative flourishes from 'Clarinetto in la' and 'Cornet à pistons in la'.

28 White, *Stravinsky: The Composer and His Works*, p. 267.

29 Bars 4–6 of Fig. 12 (in the miniature score).

30 As Walter Piston observes: 'To obtain a tone of very soft floating quality the [violinist] may be directed to play on the fingerboard (Fr., *sur la touche*; It., *sulla tastiera* or *sul tasto*; Ger., *am Griffbrett*).' Piston, *Orchestration*, p. 20.

31 Similarly with the final chord of the piece: the left hand plays C–G–E across a span of a tenth which Stravinsky (with his enormous hands) fingers 1,3,5. (As with *Les Cinq Doigts* one gratefully acknowledges the policy at J. & W. Chester Ltd to print Stravinsky's markings in the Valse without editorial alterations.)

32 'In these eight pieces, which are very easy, the five fingers, once on the keys, remain in the same place sometimes even for the whole length of the piece, while the left hand, which is destined to accompany the melody, executes a pattern, either harmonic or contrapuntal, of the utmost simplicity.' Stravinsky, *An Autobiography (1903–1934)*, p. 91. On stylistic grounds alone, this may explain the composer's interest in transcribing the *Soldier's Tale* Valse for the piano at this particular moment.

33 Robert Scholes, *Structuralism in Literature: An Introduction* (New Haven: Yale University Press, 1974), p. 176. I am indebted to this excellent volume for much of my argument in relation to Formalism.

34 William Wordsworth (1770–1850), Preface to *Lyrical Ballads, with Pastoral and Other Poems* (1800, 1802), cited in *The Norton Anthology of Theory and Criticism*, ed. Vincent B. Leitch (New York: W. W. Norton, 2001), p. 650. Wordsworth's early poetry and creative partnership with Samuel Taylor Coleridge resulted in the anonymous publication of *Lyrical Ballads* (1798). The second edition (1800) included a Preface in which Wordsworth declared that the book's object was 'to choose incidents and situations from common life and to relate or describe them … in a selection of language used by men … tracing in them … the primary laws of our nature' (*ibid.*).

35 Samuel Taylor Coleridge (1773–1834), co-author of the first edition of *Lyrical Ballads*, from his 'Lecture on Poetry, 12 December 1811', cited in Samuel Taylor Coleridge, *Coleridge: Selected Poems*, ed. Richard Holmes (London: HarperCollins, 1996), p. xiii.

36 Scholes, *Structuralism in Literature: An Introduction*, p. 176.

37 The Prague Linguistic Circle, also known as the Prague School, remained active in the 1920s and early 1930s. 'Leading figures included Roman Jakobson, Boris Eikenbaum [*sic*], [Nikolay] Trubetskoy, Viktor Shklovsky and [Jan] Mukařovský. They were influenced by Russian Formalism and by futurism and developed the theory of phonology, in which sounds are analysed in sets of oppositions.' J. A. Cuddon, *The Penguin Dictionary of Literary Terms and Literary Theory*, rev. C. E. Preston (London: Penguin, 1999), p. 694.

38 Cuddon, *The Penguin Dictionary of Literary Terms and Literary Theory*, p. 327.

39 *Ibid.*, p. 328.

40 Viktor Shklovsky (1893–1894) is cited in *ibid.*, pp. 327–8.

41 Igor Stravinsky, letter of 28 December 1932 to Charles-Albert Cingria, in *Charles-Albert Cingria: Correspondance avec Igor Strawinsky*, ed. Pierre-Olivier Walzer (Lausanne: Editions L'Age d'Homme, 2001), pp. 28–9. (See epigraph to *Conclusions*.)

42 Cited in Scholes, *Structuralism in Literature: An Introduction*, p. 84 (original emphasis). The rallentando which concludes the 'Rondoletto' in *Sérénade en la* (1925) is surely Stravinsky's most blatantly engineered compositional process.

43 Cited in Cuddon, *The Penguin Dictionary of Literary Terms and Literary Theory*, pp. 213–14.

44 Milton Babbitt, [untitled article], in *Stravinsky (1882–1971): A Composers' Memorial*. Special double issue of *Perspectives of New Music* 9.2, 10.1 (1971), 103–7 (p. 106).

45 Cited in White, *Stravinsky: The Composer and His Works*, p. 283.

46 *Apollon musagète* was similarly to be re-christened: the Russian form of Apollo (*Apollon*) was dropped, together with the overtly ornamental term *musagète* (reminiscent of nineteenth-century French ballet) in favour of the universal, supra-national title *Apollo*.

47 'I have written an architectonic work, not an anecdotal one.' Igor Stravinsky, 'Ce que j'ai voulu exprimer dans *Le Sacre du printemps*', *Montjoie!* 8 (29 May 1913), reproduced in *Igor Stravinsky: Le Sacre du printemps. Dossier de presse*, ed. François Lesure (Geneva: Editions Minkoff, 1980), pp. 13–15; cited in Walsh, *Stravinsky: A Creative Spring*, p. 376.

48 Figes, *Natasha's Dance*, pp. 286–7.

49 Stravinsky and Craft, *Expositions and Developments*, p. 118.

50 Rimsky-Korsakov, *Principles of Orchestration*, p. 35.

51 'The same has to be said of Mozart and Haydn', although Rimsky-Korsakov does concede that the 'gigantic figure of Beethoven stands apart'. As useful models from which to learn orchestration Rimsky-Korsakov cites 'Mendelssohn, Meyerbeer (*The Prophet*), Berlioz, Glinka, Wagner, Liszt and modern French and Russian composers'; *ibid.*, p. 4.

52 With the exception, that is, of *Fanfare for a New Theatre* (1964), which is scored for two trumpets. Dedicated to Lincoln Kirstein and George Balanchine it was

first performed on 19 April 1964, at the opening for the New York State Theater at Lincoln Center. Duration: less than 30 seconds.

53 Compared to the more distinct and melodic tone-quality of the violin, viola and violoncello, the relatively indistinct timbre of the double-bass may be considered more closely allied to that of the timpani, which Stravinsky also includes in the instrumentation of this work.

54 The scoring of *Capriccio* includes a *concertino* (violin, viola, violoncello and double-bass), which Stravinsky employs in the 'authentic' baroque manner, i.e. to provide textural contrast with the *ripieno* sonority of the full ensemble.

55 Rimsky-Korsakov, *Principles of Orchestration*, p. 35.

56 Stravinsky, *An Autobiography (1903–1934)*, p. 20.

57 As reported by Iwaszkiewicz, *Wiadomosci literackie*, p. 47. See Chapter 3, p. 140.

58 Rimsky-Korsakov, *Principles of Orchestration*, p. 2: from the Preface to the 1st edn.

59 Harry Partch, 'Bach and Temperament' (1941), in *Bitter Music: Collected Journals, Essays, Introductions and Librettos*, ed. Thomas McGeary (Urbana; Chicago: University of Illinois Press, 2000), p. 162.

60 Carl Dahlhaus, *Nineteenth-Century Music*, trans. J. Bradford Robinson (Berkeley: University of California Press, 1989 [1980]), p. 391.

61 Richard Taruskin, *The Oxford History of Western Music*, 5 vols, Vol. IV (New York: Oxford University Press, 2005), p. 447.

62 Gottfried Boehm, Ulrich Mosch and Katharina Schmidt (eds.), Foreword to *Canto d'Amore: Classicism in Modern Art and Music, 1914–1935* (London: Merrell Holberton, 1996).

63 Arnold Whittall, *Romantic Music* (London: Thames and Hudson, 1987), p. 35.

64 Cross, *The Stravinsky Legacy*, p. 178.

65 'By the early twentieth century', writes Jim Samson, 'the distance between background and foreground – between model and parody – had become large enough to generate a calculated heteronomy of style'. Jim Samson (ed.), *The Cambridge History of Nineteenth-Century Music* (Cambridge: Cambridge University Press, 2001), pp. 270–1.

66 Jean Philippe Rameau, 'Menuet', in Isidor Philipp (ed.), *L'Art pianistique: Collection de pièces célèbres des maîtres anciens et modernes. Sixième série* (Paris: Ch. Hayet, 1908), pp. 18–19.

67 G. B. Pergolèse, 'Arietta (Transcrit par S. Thalberg)', in *ibid.*, pp. 28–9.

68 José Ortega y Gasset, *The Dehumanization of Art* (1925), trans. Helene Weyl (Princeton: Princeton University Press, 1968), p. 25.

69 Jonathan Cross, 'Stravinsky's Theatres', in *The Cambridge Companion to Stravinsky*, ed. Jonathan Cross (Cambridge: Cambridge University Press, 2003), pp. 137–48 (p. 147).

70 Andriessen and Schönberger, *The Apollonian Clockwork*, p. 25.

71 A decade later *The Musical Times* published the first London review of Stravinsky's autobiography. It is, by contrast, a text that projects a less admirable,

though surely more representative, incomprehension of 'Stravinsky's dislike of expression in the ordinary sense of the term'. The author continues: '[Stravinsky] makes no allowance for the personal equation that must be a factor in all vital music performance.' Harvey Grace, 'Igor Stravinsky: *Chronicle of My Life*', *The Musical Times* 77.1120 (June 1936), p. 516. The problems of such impact histories are evident, however, as Dahlhaus has warned: Carl Dahlhaus, 'Problems of Reception History', in *Foundations of Music History* (Cambridge: Cambridge University Press, 1983), pp. 150–95.

72 Samson, *The Cambridge History of Nineteenth-Century Music*, p. 270. Samson is commenting on how the reception of earlier composers, from Palestrina to Schubert and Beethoven, 'was directly instrumental in shaping nineteenth-century styles'.

73 Cross, *The Stravinsky Legacy*, p. 14.

74 Stravinsky, *An Autobiography (1903–1934)*, p. 109.

75 Interview, Warsaw (22 November 1924), in Varunts, *Igor Stravinskiy: Publitsist i Sobesednik*, pp. 43–5.

76 Prague (24 November 1924), in *ibid.*, pp. 49–50; originally published in *Auftakt (Prag)* (November 1924), 280–2; translated from German by L. S. Tovaleva. Varunts writes: 'This fragment, taken from the article by V. Chupik … [was] published in the Czech press during the composer's visit to Prague in November 1924.'

77 Berlin (11 December 1924), in *ibid.*, pp. 52–5 (emphasis added); originally published in *Rul'* [*Russische demokratische Tageszeitung*], Berlin (11 December 1924), 4: interview by S. Levin. It may be argued that only a Slav would have it in him to mention the soul in such a context. The Russian soul, in particular, occupies a central position in Pan-Slavic culture. Stravinsky's reference may be an indication of the heightened spirituality he was experiencing at this time amid a profound dilemma of faith, before eventually re-assuming the Orthodoxy of his birth.

78 Glenn Watkins, *Pyramids at the Louvre: Music, Culture, and Collage from Stravinsky to the Postmodernists* (Cambridge, MA: Belknap Press, 1994), p. 3.

79 *Ibid.*

80 According to Stravinsky it was Serge Koussevitzky who convinced him, on a visit to his home in Biarritz in September 1923, to assume the role of soloist in the *Concerto pour piano et instruments à vent*, then at an early stage of composition. The premiere took place on 22 May 1924 (at the Paris Opéra).

81 *Trois pièces faciles*, for piano duet (1914–15): March, Waltz, Polka; *Cinq pièces faciles*, for piano duet (1916–17): Andante, Española, Balalaika, Napolitana, Galop. (London: J. & W. Chester).

82 *Les Cinq Doigts* (1920/1): 1. Andantino, 2. Allegro, 3. Allegretto, 4. Larghetto, 5. Moderato, 6. Lento, 7. Vivace, 8. Pesante (London: J. & W. Chester).

83 Andriessen and Schönberger, *The Apollonian Clockwork*, p. 43.

84 *Ibid.*, p. 61.

85 'En amateur' – one of Vassily Ivanich's choice Frenchisms in Ivan Turgenev, *Fathers and Sons*, trans. Rosemary Edmonds (London: Penguin, 1975), p. 204.

86 Grace, 'Igor Stravinsky: *Chronicle of My Life*', p. 516.

87 Kofi Agawu, 'Schubert's Sexuality: A Prescription for Analysis?', *Nineteenth-Century Music* 17.1 (Summer 1993), 79–82 (p. 81).

88 Jim Samson, *Chopin* (Oxford: Oxford University Press, 1996), p. 51.

89 Edward Dannreuther (1844–1905), 'Study' (1904), reprinted with additions in *Grove's Dictionary of Music and Musicians*, 9 vols., Vol. VIII, ed. Eric Blom (London: Macmillan, 1954), p. 156. As a professor (of composition and piano) at the Royal College of Music, and as the translator of Wagner's 'Music of the Future' (1872) – he received Wagner at his house in Orme Square, Bayswater – Dannreuther's view on the nature of music as an expressive art carries with it the 'authenticity' of both the conservatoire academic and the Romantic scholar. The greater value of the study, he writes, lies in its depiction of 'some characteristic musical sentiment, poetical scene or dramatic situation susceptible of musical interpretation or comment'.

90 Ferguson demonstrates how little this fundamental understanding of the relationship between the exercise and the artwork has changed over the years. Howard Ferguson, 'Study', in Sadie, *The New Grove Dictionary*, Vol. XVIII, p. 304.

91 Samson, *Chopin*, p. 51.

92 Igor Stravinsky, letter of 23 August 1900 from St Petersburg, to his parents staying at his Aunt Yekaterina's estate in Pechisky, in Varunts, *I. F. Stravinskiy: Perepiska s russkimi korrespondentami*, p. 88.

93 *Pal'tserazvitiye* is the nominal form of the adjective that Stravinsky employs. Varunts completes the phrase with the instrumental form of the Russian word for studies or exercises, *zanyatii*; thus Stravinsky's term, transliterated from the Russian, would read: *pal'tserazvivatel'nïkh* [*zanyatii*], from which the noun *pal'tserazvitiye* has been extracted. Walsh translates this as 'finger stretchings' in *Stravinsky: A Creative Spring*, p. 47.

94 In fact, Stravinsky's model for his concerto genre is more baroque than classical in the manner with which he incorporates the piano soloist in a *concertante* relationship with the orchestral *ripieno*. Indeed, it is the *concerto grosso* rather than the classical or romantic *concerto* that is predicated upon a collaborative, subject-distanced, *non*-virtuoso and, hence, truly *objective* working relationship between all participants.

95 *Accordgruppe* (in this orthography, i.e. not *Akkordgruppe*) would have been, therefore, the term Leschetizky himself used during his years developing the technical programme at the St Petersburg Conservatoire. The Russian language is characterized by its acquisition of German vocabulary, particularly in the fields of the arts and other imported disciplines, reflecting the dominant influence of German theory on the Russian tradition.

96 This *Accordgruppe* exercise is discussed in Chapter 3, pp. 161–5.

97   See Richard Taruskin, 'Russian Folk Melodies in "The Rite of Spring"', *Journal of the American Musicological Society* 33.3 (1980), 501–34 (p. 502).

98   According to Robert Craft, 'Stravinsky wrote approximately 1,500 words for the "Poetics of Music", but in verbal note-form: not a single sentence by him actually appears in the book of which he is the author. The 30,000-word text was written by Roland-Manuel, with assistance, in the lecture on Russian Music, from Pierre Suvchinsky.' – 'Roland-Manuel and the "Poetics of Music"', *Perspectives of New Music* 21.1–2 (1982–3), 487–505 (p. 487).

99   Taruskin, *Stravinsky and the Russian Traditions*, p. 4.

100 Stravinsky and Craft, *Memories and Commentaries*, p. xiii.

101 Joseph N. Straus, *Remaking the Past: Musical Modernism and the Influence of the Tonal Tradition* (Cambridge, MA: Harvard University Press, 1990), p. 187n2.

102 'Claude Roland-Manuel me rappelait que son père revenait épuisé de ses séjours à Sancellemoz … et la rédaction commune de la *Poétique*. Roland-Manuel avait coutume d'ajouter en souriant: "Il ne me laisse rien passer."' From the Preface to Igor Strawinsky, *Poétique musicale sous forme de six leçons*, ed. Myriam Soumagnac (Paris: Harmonique Flammarion, 2000), p. 14.

103 Stravinsky, *Poetics of Music*, p. 24.

104 *Ibid.*, pp. 24–5.

105 Strawinsky, *Poétique musicale sous forme de six leçons*, p. 78.

106 *Poétique musicale* will employ this term once again, in Chapter 4 ('Musical Typology'): 'Son souci dominant s'attache à la rectitude d'une opération *bien* conduite selon un ordre *vrai*.' Strawinsky, *Poétique musicale sous forme de six leçons*, p. 112 (original emphasis). This has been translated by Alfred Knodel and Ingold Dahl (in *Poetics of Music*) as: '[The composer's] prime concern is applied to the rightness of an operation that is performed *well*, in keeping with a *true* order.'

107 Stravinsky, *Poetics of Music*, p. 75.

108 *Ibid.*, p. 53. See Jacques Maritain, *Art et scholastique* (Paris: Art Catholique, 1920).

109 Stravinsky, *Poetics of Music*, p. 78.

110 *Ibid.* (original emphasis).

111   *Ibid.*, pp. 68–9.

112 Stravinsky, *Poetics of Music*, p. 66 (emphasis added). This reference to 'working over' suggests the repetitive aspect to piano 'drilling', particularly so in the original: 'Plus l'art est contrôlé, limité, travaillé et plus il est libre.' Strawinsky, *Poétique musicale sous forme de six leçons*, p. 105. One might dispute the translation of 'contrôlé' as controlled, in favour of inspected, monitored or tested.

113 Stravinsky, *Poetics of Music*, pp. 67–8 (emphasis added). In Chapter 4 ('Musical Typology'), Stravinsky makes it clear that while praising rules and limitations in these terms he is not yet prepared to accept the 'spirit of systematization' currently being demonstrated by 'irritating … artistic rebels, of whom Wagner offers us the most complete type'. This may, rather, be a sideswipe at Schoenberg

and the German Tradition. Stravinsky was clearly unprepared to endorse such systematization at the time of the original lecture series (and subsequent publication) of *Poetics*. One can only lament the opportunity missed years later by failing to commission from Stravinsky an expanded edition of this text, which would have reflected his subsequent adoption of serial techniques.

114 *Ibid.*, p. 37.

115 *Ibid.*, pp. 37–8.

116 *Ibid.*, p. 44.

117 Andriessen and Schönberger, *The Apollonian Clockwork*, p. 41.

118 See Chapter 3, pp. 181–2.

119 Stravinsky, *Poetics of Music*, p. 22.

120 Kenneth Silver, *Esprit de corps* (Princeton: Princeton University Press, 1989), pp. 260–1.

121 V. Stravinsky and Craft, *Stravinsky in Pictures and Documents*, p. 200.

122 Stravinsky, *Poetics of Music*, p. 39.

123 *Ibid.*, p. 40.

124 Igor Stravinsky and Robert Craft, *Dialogues and a Diary* (London: Faber and Faber, 1982), p. 24.

125 Stravinsky and Craft, *Expositions and Developments*, pp. 51–2.

126 Stravinsky, *Poetics of Music*, p. 51.

127 *Ibid.*, p. 52.

128 *Ibid.*, p. 53.

129 *Ibid.*, p. 54.

130 *Ibid.*, p. 56.

131 *Ibid.*, pp. 56–7 (emphasis added).

132 Cross, 'Stravinsky's Theatres', p. 137.

133 *Ibid.*, pp. 137–8.

134 Scott Goddard, '"Chronicle of My Life", by Igor Stravinsky', *Music & Letters* 17.3 (July 1936), 253–5 (p. 255).

135 For example: the presence of 'repeated groups of notes' in the serial music, which suggests to Straus that 'the series represent[s] a kind of apotheosis of the ostinato'. Joseph N. Straus, 'Stravinsky the Serialist', in Cross, *The Cambridge Companion to Stravinsky*, pp. 149–74 (p. 152). However, this manifestation is clearly *also* rooted in Stravinsky's unique engagement with pianism and the ritual of piano practice – in short, with *pal'tserazvitiye*.

136 Frederic Jameson, *Postmodernism; or, The Cultural Logic of Late Capitalism* (London: Verso, 1991), p. 15; it is interesting that both Stravinsky (in *Study for Pianola*) and Adams (in *Grand Pianola Music*) channelled their path towards de-personalization through this same mechanical instrument.

137 'The music [of *Apollon musagète* and the classical tale of *Orpheus*] achieves a "pure", hieratic character through its sense of control and through the use of such devices as fugue.' Cross, 'Stravinsky's Theatres', p. 147. The pianist and composer Jean Wiener [Wiéner] (1896–1982) promoted a series of so-called 'concerts salades' in Paris between 1921 and 1925 at several of the city's most prestigious

venues including the Salle Gaveau and the Théâtre des Champs Elysées. His innovative programming policy juxtaposed the avant-garde with standard repertoire, and introduced French audiences to American jazz and the 'big band'; he also included his own arrangements of ethnic musics from Latin America. Under his umbrella several works by Milhaud, Poulenc, de Falla and Stravinsky received their first performance. Wiener also programmed works for the pianola, including Stravinsky's *Study for Pianola* (1917) – which became the final movement ('Madrid') of *Four Studies for Orchestra* (1928) – and the composer's transcription of *The Rite of Spring*. Milhaud directed the French premiere of *Pierrot lunaire* during the opening season of 'Concerts Jean Wiener'.

138 Ferruccio Busoni, *Frankfurter Zeitung*, 1, quoted in Messing, *Neoclassicism in Music*, pp. 69–70.

139 Robert Craft (ed.), *Stravinsky: Selected Correspondence*, 3 vols. (London: Faber and Faber, 1982–5), Vol. I, p. 171.

140 Messing, *Neoclassicism in Music*, p. 74; he suggests that both works share affinity with a 'common model' in Bach's E minor Prelude from 'The 48'.

141 Andriessen and Schönberger, *The Apollonian Clockwork*, p. 25.

142 Alexander Herzen, *Sobraniye sochineniy v tridtsati tomakh*, 30 vols. (Moscow, 1954–66),Vol. XI, p. 359. *Rudin* (1855) is the first of Turgenev's six novels that reflect Russian life *c*. 1830–70.

143 Stravinsky, *Poetics of Music*, p. 18.

144 *Ibid.*, p. 79.

145 Regarding his father's habit of composing at the piano and his need always 'to be in direct contact with his *matière sonore*', Theodore Stravinsky has written: 'il compose, toujours au piano, par méfiance de l'abstrait' ['he always composes at the piano, being mistrustful of abstract experience/processes/concepts']. Théodore Strawinsky, *Le Message d'Igor Strawinsky* (Lausanne: Librairie F. Rouge, 1948), p. 107.

146 Harold Bloom, 'From "The Anxiety of Influence" (1973)', in Leitch (ed.), *The Norton Anthology of Theory and Criticism*, pp. 1794–805 (p. 1795).

147 Walsh, *Stravinsky: A Creative Spring*, p. 77.

148 See Eric Walter White, *Stravinsky: A Critical Survey* (London: John Lehmann, 1947); and White, *Stravinsky: The Composer and His Works*.

149 Adam Ockleford, 'Relating Musical Structure and Content to Aesthetic Response: A Model and Analysis of Beethoven's Piano Sonata Op. 110', *Journal of the Royal Musical Association* 130.1 (2005), 74–118.

150 Arthur-Vincent Lourié, 'La Sonate pour piano de Strawinsky', *La Revue musicale* 6 (1925), 100–4. Stravinsky was to confirm this work's indebtedness to Beethoven's 'instrumental side': 'All these ideas were germinating in me while I was composing my sonata and renewing my contact with Beethoven.' Stravinsky, *An Autobiography (1903–1934)*, p. 119.

151 Beethoven, Piano Sonata op. 110, 3rd movement. The inversion is presented at b. 137: 'L'istesso tempo della Fuga poi a poi di novo vivente – sempre una corda'.

152 Ockleford, 'Relating Musical Structure and Content to Aesthetic Response', p. 109, Figure 8. Ockleford cites his 'growing interest in emotion and meaning in the field of musical psychology: as Patrik Juslin and John Sloboda's recent compilation of contemporary theory and research illustrates, there now appears to be sufficient empirical evidence of direct links between musical features and affective response for these usefully to inform certain types of analysis'.

153 Stravinsky, *Poetics of Music*, pp. 12–13.

154 Igor Stravinsky and Robert Craft, *Themes and Conclusions* (New York: Knopf, 1966), pp. 13–14.

155 Stravinsky and Craft, *Dialogues and a Diary*, p. 48.

156 Craft, *Chronicle of a Friendship*, p. 263.

157 Brée, *The Groundwork of the Leschetizky Method*; and Marie Prentner, *The Leschetizky Method*, trans. M. De Kendler and A. Maddock (London: J. Curwen & Sons, 1903); Isidor Philipp, *Complete School of Technic for the Piano* (Philadelphia: Theodore Presser, 1908). It is this latter volume that Craft claims the composer used daily for over twenty years. See Chapter 3.

158 Stravinsky, *Poetics of Music*, p. 18.

159 Stravinsky's recordings are discussed further in my 'Conclusions', pp. 257–8.

160 Stravinsky's path towards the contrapuntal devices of the eighteenth century (if not also his eventual disdain for improvisation) can be traced, via Rimsky-Korsakov, to their mutual aversion to Balakirev's quixotic and opinionated spirit: 'The majority of melodies and themes were regarded [by Balakirev] as the weaker part of music', writes Rimsky-Korsakov. 'Nearly all the fundamental ideas of Beethoven's symphonies were thought weak; Chopin's melodies were considered sweet and womanish; Mendelssohn's, sour and bourgeois. However, the themes of Bach's fugues were undoubtedly held in respect.' Rimsky-Korsakov, *My Musical Life*, p. 28.

161 He is referred to in *My Musical Life* as F. A. Kanille.

162 '[A] tragedy by Kookolnik [Nestor Vasilievich Kukolnik (1809–68)] for which Glinka had composed incidental music. Tchaikovsky, by no means an indulgent critic of Glinka, says of this work: "Glinka here shows himself to be one of the greatest symphonic composers of his day. Many touches in *Prince Kholmsky* recall the brush of Beethoven."' Carl van Vechten, editorial footnote in *ibid.*, p. 15.

163 Rimsky's admission – in *ibid.*, p. 19 – that 'Glinka's *Jota Aragonesa* simply dazzled me' is mirrored in Stravinsky's account of his first trip to Iberia in 1917: 'Many of the musicians who had preceded me in visiting Spain had, on their return, put their impressions on record in works devoted to the music they heard there, Glinka having far outshone the rest with his incomparable *La Jota Aragonesa* and *Une Nuit à Madrid*.' Stravinsky, *An Autobiography (1903–1936)*, p. 69; Stravinsky's reference is to the *Capriccio brillante on the jota aragonesa* (1845), also known as the *First Spanish Overture*; and to *Recuerdos de Castilla* (1848) later expanded as *Souvenir d'une nuit d'été à Madrid* (1851), also known as the *Second Spanish Overture*.

164 Rimsky-Korsakov, *My Musical Life*, p. 15.

165 It was during this period that Rimsky-Korsakov directed the first performance in St Petersburg of the B minor Mass, whilst also inveigling his pupils at the Free High School into re-orchestrating Handel for internal concerts.

166 Rimsky-Korsakov, Sextet in A major (1876). Other examples featuring contrapuntal writing in Rimsky-Korsakov's output from this period include: *Six Fugues for Piano* op. 17 (1874); *Two 3-Part Choruses for Women's Voices* (1875); *Six Choruses without Accompaniment* (1876); *Four Variations and a Fughetta on the Theme of a Russian Song* (1875); *Three Pieces for the Piano* (n.d.); *Six Fugues for the Piano* (n.d.); Piano Quintet with Wind Instruments (1876); and *Four 3-Part Choruses for Male Voices* (1876).

167 'My recollection of Lyadov is a pleasant one … he had a gentle, agreeable, and kindly nature. Bent on clear and meticulous writing, he was very strict with his pupils and with himself, composing very little, and working slowly, and, so to speak, under a microscope.' Stravinsky, *An Autobiography (1903–1934)*, p. 18.

168 Abraham, *Rimsky-Korsakov: A Short Biography*, pp. 55–6 (original punctuation).

169 Aleksandr Borodin, letter of 15 April 1875 to Lyubov Karmalina, cited in *ibid.*, pp. 55–6.

170 M. Montagu-Nathan, *Rimsky-Korsakoff* (London: Constable, 1916), p. 9.

171 Richard Taruskin, *Defining Russia Musically* (Princeton: Princeton University Press, 1997), p. 83.

172 Abraham, *Rimsky-Korsakov: A Short Biography*, p. 109.

173 Rimsky-Korsakov, *My Musical Life*, p. 393 (emphasis added).

174 Abraham, consistently hostile towards Rimsky-Korsakov's contrapuntal leanings, views *Servilia* as the 'necessary pretext for writing colourless music. It must be admitted that [Rimsky-Korsakov] took the fullest advantage of it.' Abraham, *Rimsky-Korsakov: A Short Biography*, p. 109.

175 *The Tsar's Bride* (*Tsarskaya nevesta*) was composed in 1898 to a libretto, as with *Servilia*, by L. A. Mey. Rimsky-Korsakov, *My Musical Life*, p. 393.

176 Stravinsky, *An Autobiography (1903–1934)*, p. 15.

177 'From a letter … etc', cited by A. Rimsky-Korsakov, 'Chronicle of N. A. Rimsky-Korsakov's Life', pp. 439–40.

178 Dostoyevsky, *Crime and Punishment*, p. 597. Early-twentieth-century usage of the term can be observed in Reed, *Ten Days that Shook the World*, p. 268: 'Following were other banners; of the District Soviets – of Putilov Factory, which read: "We bow to this flag in order to create the brotherhood of all peoples!"'; and on p. 270: 'Stachkov, a dignified old peasant of the presidium of the Peasants' Congress, bowed to the four corners of the room. "I greet you with the christening of a new Russian life and freedom!"'

179 Igor Stravinsky, letter of 10 July 1907, in Dyachkova (ed.), *I. F. Stravinskiy: Stat'i i materiali*, quoted in Taruskin, *Stravinsky and the Russian Traditions*, p. 171.

180 Igor Stravinsky, 'Interview avec Serge Moreux de *L'Intransigent* pour la Radiodiffusion, Paris; 24 December 1938', in White, *Stravinsky: The Composer and His Works*, Appendix A/7, pp. 585–7 (p. 586).

181 It is a familiar part of Stravinsky's photographic legacy: the bespectacled composer, in rehearsal or listening to a playback in the recording studio, balancing an additional pair of glasses on his head. For evidence of Rimsky's similar habit of 'wearing two pairs of specs on his nose, one in front of the other' – a shared example of workman-like practicality regardless of apparent eccentricity – one must rely on the testimony of Fyodor Ivanovich Chaliapin. 'Of that period the only pleasurable recollection I have is that of meeting Rimsky-Korsakov, on the occasion of the rehearsal of *Christmas Eve* [in 1895]. It was with the greatest interest that I watched this silent, deeply reflective musician at work, his eyes hidden from view behind double spectacles.' Fyodor Ivanovich Chaliapin, *Chaliapin: An Autobiography as Told to Maxim Gorky*, ed. and trans. Nina Froud and James Hanley (London: Macmillan, 1968), pp. 118–19.

182 Kermode, *Pleasing Myself*, p. 167.

183 N. Ya. Myaskovsky, '*Petrushka*, Ballet by Igor Stravinsky', 72–5; *Sobraniye materialov*, Vol. II (1964), pp. 41–4. In Campbell, *Russians on Russian Music, 1880–1917*, p. 212.

184 Kenneth Gloag, 'Russian Rites: *Petrushka*, *The Rite of Spring* and *Les Noces*', in Cross (ed.), *The Cambridge Companion to Stravinsky*, pp. 79–97 (p. 94). Gloag reflects on the complementary observations of Whittall ('*Le Sacre* ... needs the perspective of tradition for its nature as well as its effect to be comprehended') and Taruskin ('[*The Rite*] was written out of – and not against – a tradition, and ... its stylistic innovations relate to and extend that tradition').

185 M. F. Gnesin, 'N. A. Rimskiy-Korsakov: Pedagog i chelovek', *Sovetskaya muzika* 3 (1945), p. 204, quoted in Taruskin, *Stravinsky and the Russian Traditions*, p. 171.

186 Smirnov, *Tvorcheskoye formirovaniye I. F. Stravinskovo*, p. 197.

187 Walsh, *Stravinsky: A Creative Spring*, p. 53.

188 'It was not simply Peter's "window on to Europe" – as Pushkin once described the capital – but an open doorway through which Europe entered Russia and the Russians made their entry to the world.' Figes, *Natasha's Dance*, p. 61.

3   Stravinsky's piano workshop

1 This initial section is derived from a previously published article: Graham Griffiths, 'Fingering as Compositional Process: Stravinsky's Sonata Sketchbook Revisited', *British Postgraduate Musicology Online* (May 2005), available online at www.bpmonline.org.uk/bpm7/griffiths.html (last accessed 14 August 2012).

2 See Schoenberg's George setting in his String Quartet no. 2 (1908).

3 Craft, *Stravinsky: Glimpses of a Life*, p. 329.

4 The *Reinschrift* ('fair copy'), dated 21 October 1924, is in a separate, hardbound book held in folder R 91 at the Paul Sacher Stiftung.

5 This manuscript double-page is located in a hardback sketchbook catalogued at the Paul Sacher Stiftung as 'Skizzenbuch VII'. It can be viewed on microfilm at PSS 123–0516/0517; and in *Strawinsky: Sein Nachlass, sein Bild*, p. 103.

6 For whatever reason, Stravinsky declined to insist that this considerable body of information be published along with his music. Yet, up to that point, it had clearly been important to him that these passages were always played in the same manner.

7 See also the melodic fragment that follows, where the fingering is clearly designed to stretch the gap (across the divide of a minor third) between fingers 3 and 4. The fingering is important, therefore, to the didactic purpose of this movement.

8 Stravinsky's indications begin four bars before Fig. 37 of the published score (copyright 1924 by Hawkes & Son, London, Ltd).

9 The third movement of the *Sonate pour piano* takes up this same notion. There is, however, no need for the composer/performer to provide fingerings; the persistent use of a 'set' fingering pattern is now built into the pianistic thread: see the left-hand material at bb. 26–44 (5,4,2,1,2,4), and bb. 88–94 (5,4,2,4,2,1,2,4).

10 This symbol is to be found twice in the penultimate bar between notes 2 and 3 (C♯–D), and 7 and 8 (C–C♯).

11 In the opinion of Robert Craft: 'In most types of keyboard virtuosity Stravinsky cannot be compared, for example, with Rachmaninoff, though their respective performing skills correspond to the different kinds of music that each composed.' V. Stravinsky and Craft, *Stravinsky in Pictures and Documents*, pp. 215–16. The same point could also be made in relation to the piano music of Prokofiev.

12 Parallels may be drawn, even, with Nijinsky's 'muscular drive' (commented upon earlier, p. 271n131). Stravinsky's exploitation of fundamental aspects of technique, via intensive routines, has an intriguing precedent – in general terms, in the rigorous daily preparation of every ballet dancer; more specifically in the extreme, almost masochistic, example set by Nijinsky himself.

13 As recalled by Joseph, *Stravinsky Inside Out*, p. 91.

14 Charles Joseph, *Stravinsky Remembered* (New Haven and London: Yale University Press, 2001), p. 91.

15 Ibid., p. 91.

16 Kofi Agawu, 'Schubert's Sexuality: A Prescription for Analysis?', p. 81.

17 Heinrich Schenker, *Kunst des Vortrags*; translated into English as *The Art of Performance*, ed. Heribert Esser, trans. Irene Schreier Scott (Oxford: Oxford University Press, 2000), p. 75.

18 Stravinsky, 'Some Ideas about My *Octuor*', p. 576.

19 Jaroslaw Iwaszkiewicz, *Wiadomosci Literackie (Warsawa)*, 1924, no.46; cited in Viktor Varunts (ed.), *Igor Stravinskiy – publitsist i sobesednik* (Moscow: Sovetskiy Kompozitor, 1988), p. 47.

20 *Ibid.*

21 *Ibid.*

22 Stravinsky, 'Some Ideas about My *Octuor*', p. 576.

23 A striking publicity photo of Stravinsky as concert pianist can be found in *Strawinsky: Sein Nachlass, sein Bild*, p. 119. It was taken at Studio Lipnitski, Paris, in 1929; *Capriccio* was premiered by the composer on 6 December that year.

24 PSS 220–0634.

25 Crotchet = 104 is the tempo indicated in the published score for the first-movement Allegro at Fig. 5 in the Hawkes & Son original edition (1924) and the revised edition (1960).

26 Stravinsky, *An Autobiography (1903–1934)*, p. 113.

27 'Like Philipp's exercises, several of Czerny's etudes (all bearing the composer's notations) had provided Stravinsky with an important prototype for the … *Concerto for Piano and Winds* of 1923.' Joseph, *Stravinsky Inside Out*, p. 91.

28 The statement at b. 19 is inverted in b. 117.

29 Igor Stravinsky, *Chroniques de ma vie* (Paris: Editions Denoël, 1962), p. 103; *An Autobiography (1903–1934)*, p. 82.

30 The script prior to the bass clef is the abbreviation in Russian of 'left hand'.

31 'Each of the outer movements [is] studiously inscribed to a church festival.' Walsh, *Stravinsky: A Creative Spring*, p. 493. The final page of sketches (PSS 114–0295) is signed 'I. Strawinsky, 15 Août 1930, Jour de L'Assomption de L'Eglise Romaine'.

32 PSS 114–0262.

33 Stravinsky and Craft, *Memories and Commentaries*, p. 3.

34 The first note of this fragment (circle 3) would be B♭ if this were derived from the third *gruppetto* of the line above (circle 2) – as is likely. The semitonal relationship between the two lower notes of the hemiola (B♭ and A) would be consistent with the intervallic structure of much of the work, especially in the first movement. This topic will be explored further later in the chapter, p. 201ff.

35 A term used by Nathan Milstein to describe George Balanchine's habit of 'letting his fingers roam freely over the [piano] … over whatever thoughts came to mind. In the process, the sounds seemed to inspire choreographic settings of the lines or chords he hit upon.' Joseph, *Stravinsky and Balanchine*, pp. 18, 364n30. This subject is explored further later in the chapter, pp. 201–2.

36 Stravinsky, *An Autobiography (1903–1934)*, p. 5.

37 'Try, above all, to place [the Piano Concerto] in the hands of honest pianists of the genre of Borovsky, Orlov, Marcelle Meyer …'. Igor Stravinsky, letter of 14 August 1927 to his editor, G. G. Païchadze, quoted in V. Stravinsky and Craft, *Stravinsky in Pictures and Documents*, p. 629n34.

38 Ockleford, 'Relating Musical Structure and Content to Aesthetic Response'. See Chapter 2, p. 123.

39 Stravinsky, *Poetics of Music*, p. 78 (original emphasis); *Poétique musicale*, p. 112.

40 Kenneth Hamilton, 'The Virtuoso Tradition', p. 72.

41 Leokadiya Aleksandrovna Kashperova, 'Vospominaniya', in *Muzikal'noye nasledstvo: Sborniki po Istorii Muzikal'noi Kul'tury SSSR*, Vol. II, Part II, ed. M. P. Alekseev (Moscow: Muzïka, 1962), pp. 135–68.

42 Leschetizky was Polish by birth and had acquired a considerable reputation as a pianist and conductor touring Germany, Austria and Russia.

43 Robert Philip, 'Pianists on Record in the Early Twentieth Century', in *The Cambridge Companion to the Piano*, ed. David Rowland (Cambridge: Cambridge University Press, 1998), pp. 75–95 (p. 86).

44 Winthrop Sargeant, 'The Leaves of a Tree', *The New Yorker* 38.47 (12 January 1963), p. 52.

45 Josef Lhevinne, 'Good Tone Is Born in the Player's Mind', transcribed by Harriette Brower, *The Musician* 28.7 (July 1923), 7.

46 'As an example [of Safonov's approach] a simple five-finger pattern should be practised with the following combination of fingerings between the hands.' Gerig proceeds to illustrate this via the first five notes of the scale of G, fingered for the right hand: 1,2,3,4,5 or 2,1,3,4,5 or 2,3,1,4,5 or 2,3,4,1,5 or 2,3,4,5,1. A similar pattern is shown for the left hand. Gerig, *Famous Pianists and Their Technique*, p. 296. The progressive extension of the thumb-under manoeuvre in this manner is derived from Leschetizky.

47 Vassily Safonov, *New Formula for the Piano Teacher and the Piano Student*, English edn (London: J. & W. Chester, 1915), p. 25.

48 In the United States her pupils included Samuel Barber, Lukas Foss, Jacob Lateiner, Gary Graffman and Leonard Bernstein.

49 From an unpublished article by Vitaly Neumann quoted by Gerig, *Famous Pianists and Their Technique*, pp. 312–13n17.

50 *Ibid.*, p. 313.

51 *Ibid.*

52 Still active in his seventies, Leschetizky appears to have relented and authorized two assistants to issue their accounts of his method based on their own extensive experience as his trusted *Vorbereiterinnen*.

53 Arthur Schnabel, *My Life and Music* (Gerrard's Cross: Colin Smythe, 1970), p. 124; quoted in Gerig, *Famous Pianists and Their Technique*, p. 272.

54 Edwin Hughes, 'Theodore Leschetizky on Modern Pianoforte Study', *The Etude* (April, 1909), p. 227; quoted in R. Gerig, *Famous Pianists and Their Technique*, pp. 277–8. Evidently, in the early stages there was a clear pedagogical structure defined by Leschetizky and, such are the similarities between the two published methods, this pianistic curriculum was a fundamental requirement. While Leschetizky himself may not have worked with this material in his own advanced classes, it was evidently the backbone of his assistants' orientation in the preparatory stages.

55 Gerig, *Famous Pianists and Their Technique*, p. 278.

56 One pupil, Eleanor Spencer, commented that the first joints of his fingers had been curved so firmly for so long that they stayed that way even 'if he only passes

his fingers through his hair!'. Annette Hullah, *Theodore Leschetizky* (London: John Lane; The Bodley Head, 1906), pp. 41–2, related by Gerig, *Famous Pianists and Their Technique*, p. 277. Pianists, wrote Leschetizky, must 'yield to the movements of the arms as far as necessary, as the rider yields to the movements of his horse'. Brée, *The Groundwork of the Leschetizky Method*, p. 1.

57 Ethel Newcomb, *Leschetizky as I Knew Him* (New York: Da Capo Press, 1967 [1921]), p. 127.

58 Ignaz Pleyel and Jan Ladislav Dussek, *Méthode pour le pianoforte* (Paris: Pleyel, 1797); Muzio Clementi, *Introduction to the Art of Playing on the Piano Forte* (London: Clementi, 1801).

59 This volume is held at the Music Reading Room of the Bodleian Library, Oxford.

60 It is possible that her source was Chopin's pupil Thomas Tellefsen (1823–74). There are several options as to how Sophie Horsley obtained this detailed information. She could have had lessons with Chopin, for, as Jim Samson relates: 'for a short time [in 1848] he was able to earn a small supplementary income from teaching some of the wealthy socialites of the capital', although being the daughter of a musician it is more likely that she acquired this information from musical associates. Samson explains: '[T]he truth is, Chopin was happiest when he could retreat to the company of fellow musicians, such as his former pupils Thomas Tellefsen … and Lindsay Sloper, his old friend Pauline Viardot … and his new friend Jenny Lind.' Samson, *Chopin*, p. 255. The third possibility is that she took piano lessons with Tellefsen. This Norwegian pianist 'was taught periodically by Chopin (for two years in all)' in Paris, later 'staying in London on several occasions … for concerts and teaching … He was especially admired as an interpreter of Chopin's music … and after Chopin's death also took over some of his teacher's pupils, including Jane Stirling [who had invited the composer to Scotland].' Kari Michelsen, 'Thomas Tellefsen', in *The New Grove Dictionary of Music and Musicians*, 29 vols., Vol. XXV, ed. Stanley Sadie (London: Macmillan, 2001), p. 244. Whichever reading is preferred one feels confident that the information noted in this volume of Clementi studies, concerning Chopin's mode of practice, is very likely to be accurate.

61 The exercise, 'Moderato', is located on p. 88.

62 An 'early letter to her mother' as reported by Vitaly Neumann (unpublished); quoted in Gerig, *Famous Pianists and Their Technique*, p. 312.

63 *Ibid.*

64 Brée, *The Groundwork of the Leschetizky Method*, pp. 34–5.

65 This visual aid was personally endorsed by Leschetizky in his Foreword accepting Brée's dedication. The final paragraph reads: 'Approving the illustrations of my hand as genuine and lifelike, I declare your book to be the sole authorized publication explanatory of my method, and wish it all success and popularity. With sincerest regard, (Signed) THEODOR LESCHETIZKY.' *Ibid.*, p. iv.

66 See p. 111. This term is employed in its archaic orthography as a specific reference to the term used by Prentner, for example, in the introduction to this section in her

book. This is translated in the original, bi-lingual edition as: 'The following group of chords [*Accordgruppe*], not written with any idea of harmonic progression, lends itself best to the foregoing practice through multiplicity and variety in chord "stretches" [*Accordgriffe*].' Prentner, *The Leschetizky Method*, p. 44.

67 'Suite of Arpeggios: Triads and Seventh-Chords', in Brée, *The Groundwork of the Leschetizky Method*, pp. 97–9.

68 'Scale of Scales', in *ibid.*, pp. 86–93.

69 *Ibid.*, p. 85.

70 'Marie Prentner was my pupil for a very considerable time, since then having for a number of years supported and aided me in my work, as one of my very best assistants … [with a] perfect acquaintance with my method' (in Prentner, *The Leschetizky Method*, n.p.). Despite this, Gerig dismisses Prentner's work as less than fully endorsed. Gerig, *Famous Pianists and Their Technique*, p. 280.

71 Leschetizky's fingering for the F major chord/arpeggio (right hand: C–F–A–C) is invariably 1,2,4,5. This may have a bearing on Stravinsky's predilection for this (not always comfortable) arrangement; as noted especially in the *Sonate* and the Piano Concerto (see this chapter, pp. 133–40).

72 Brée, *The Groundwork of the Leschetizky Method*, pp. 36–48.

73 Prentner, *The Leschetizky Method*, p. 44.

74 *Ibid.*, p. 45.

75 See Chapter 2, pp. 109–10.

76 An indication of Stravinsky's achievement in this regard may be sensed in Prokofiev's own judgement on his rival's transformation. In November 1924 he wrote to Myaskovsky: 'Just look at Stravinsky who suddenly ups and becomes a pianist, that's courage! Tcherepnin has dreamed all his life about playing his [own] concerto, but up until now he's never [found] the nerve; but Stravinsky sticks with his exercises for a year and a half, then suddenly makes an appearance. Now he's got more engagements than I have'. S. S. Prokofieva and N. Ya. Miaskovsky, *Perepiska* [*Correspondence*], compiled and ed. M. G. Koslava and N. R. Yatsenko (Moscow, 1977), p. 206. Quoted in Malcolm Hamrick Brown, 'Stravinsky and Prokofiev: Sizing up the Competition', in *Confronting Stravinsky: Man, Musician, and Modernist*, ed. Jann Pasler (Berkeley: University of California Press, 1986), p. 48.

77 White, *Stravinsky: A Critical Survey*, p. 112.

78 See Chapter 2, pp. 79–84.

79 Edwin Evans, *Music and the Dance* (London: Jenkins, 1948), pp. 89–90. Evans goes on to comment that he considers the episode to have influenced *Les Noces* and particularly its 'strange final pages'. Walsh, on the other hand, bases his view on the sketchbook where these bell notations figure alongside 'a fragment of a melody which … provided the second tune for the opening song in his next work, *Pribaoutki*'. Walsh, *Stravinsky: A Creative Spring*, p. 237.

80 V. Stravinsky and Craft, *Stravinsky in Pictures and Documents*, p. 127.

81 Fabian Stedman (1640–1713) devised and first published calculations of all the variations possible by the call-change method (*Tintinnalogia*, 1668, and

Campanologia, 1677). Stedman was an early member of the Ancient Society of College Youths (founded 1637), an all-male association that provides the ringing at St Paul's Cathedral to this day. The 'College' of the title refers to the College of the Holy Ghost founded in the City of London by the Lord Mayor, Richard Whittington (1358–1423). John Camp writes that, according to Stedman's calculations, 'the order of ringing of three bells could be changed six times ($3 \times 2 \times 1$) and the variations possible on four bells amounted to twenty-four ($4 \times 3 \times 2 \times 1$). But the majority of churches [have] more than four bells … On six bells [as is the case at St Paul's, the possibilities] number 720, while eight bells could be varied 40,320 ways.' John Camp, *Discovering Bells and Bell-Ringing* (Princes Risborough: Shire, 2001), pp. 9, 11.

82 This process is addressed in the Prentner volume via Chapter 9, 'To Stretch a Small Hand', whose opening paragraph reads: 'A contracted stretch is one of the greatest hindrances to the acquirement of a brilliant technique. A small hand can, however, with absolute certainly be aided in gaining a normal stretch by the making use of the combined exercises intended for this purpose … these exercises [are] to be repeated and repeated until the desired result is attained.' Prentner, *The Leschetizky Method*, p. 65.

83 Taruskin, *Stravinsky and the Russian Traditions*, pp. 1501–2. The glossary (pp. 1677–9) gives: '*Drobnost'*: Lit., "splinteredness"; the quality of being formally disunified, a sum-of-parts; *Nepodvizhnost'*: Immobility, stasis; as applied to form, the quality of being nonteleological, nondevelopmental; *Uproshcheniye*: Simplification (positive nuance).'

84 In fact Taruskin views the impact of these Turanian virtues to extend well beyond the portfolio of this one composer: 'Stravinsky's Russianness bequeathes a *russkiy slog* ['Russian morphology'] to the whole world of twentieth-century concert music.' *Ibid.*, p. 1675.

85 In his summary of *drobnost'*, for example, Taruskin writes: 'Some of Stravinsky's instrumental works of the Swiss period can indeed support this description (*whether they invite it is another question*).' *Ibid.*, p. 1452 (emphasis added).

86 *Ibid.*, p. 1449.

87 Notes accompanying performances by the London Philharmonic Quartet (February–April 1919), in Craft, *Stravinsky: Selected Correspondence*, Vol. I, p. 407; quoted in Taruskin, *Stravinsky and the Russian Traditions*, p. 1465.

88 'The twenty-three beat violin tune and the seven beat percussive pattern in the cello.' Taruskin, *Stravinsky and the Russian Traditions*, pp. 1465–6.

89 *Ibid.*, pp. 1466–7.

90 *Ibid.*, p. 1449.

91 *Ibid.*

92 Craft, *Stravinsky: Selected Correspondence*, Vol. I, p. 411; quoted in Taruskin, *Stravinsky and the Russian Traditions*, p. 1449.

93 Taruskin, *Stravinsky and the Russian Traditions*, p. 1451; *Vesnyanki* (from *Vesna* – spring) and *Petrivki* (from *Piotr* – Peter, i.e. St Peter's day in the Orthodox calendar) are seasonal songs and dances connected with the rites of spring and

autumn (apple harvesting) respectively. The tradition can be traced to Kievan Rus' (ninth–eleventh century) when the three nations – Russian, Ukranian and Belorussian – were established.

94 *Ibid.*, jacket text.

95 Namely: the musical mobile, the genre of (toy) automata, hypostatized ostinati and *nepodvizhnost'*.

96 *Die Tat* (Zurich, 14 October 1961); quoted in V. Stravinsky and Craft, *Stravinsky in Pictures and Documents*, p. 629n29.

97 Isidor Philipp (b. Pest, 1863; d. Paris, 1958) was Professor of Piano at the Paris Conservatoire from 1893 to 1934. He had studied at the Conservatoire under Mathias (a pupil of Chopin) and Ritter (a pupil of Liszt) though equal, if not stronger influences throughout his long life were the musicianship and pianism of Camille Saint-Saëns. Early in his career Philipp won renown as a soloist, later gaining an international reputation as a teacher – especially in France and in America – through his extensive range of didactic publications written over sixty years, of which the following is a selection of the principal titles: *Exercices quotidiens tirées des oeuvres de Chopin* (1897) – Preface by Georges Mathias; *Exercices pratiques* op. 9 (Durand, 1897/1948); *150 exercices d'extension pour les doigts* (Paris: Alphonse Leduc, 1898); *Ecole de mécanisme pour le piano* (Lyon: F. Janin et Fils, 1900/1904/1908); *Exercice technique quotidien* (Paris: Heugel & Cie, 1906); *Exercices élémentaires rythmiques pour les cing doigts* (Lyon: F. Janin et Fils, 1900); *Quatre études pour la main gauche seule d'après J.-S. Bach* (Paris: E. Fromont, 1903); *Gammes en doubles notes* (1904); *Complete School of Technic for the Piano* (1908); *Le Trille dans les oeuvres de Beethoven para I. Philipp et Supplement au «Trille»* (Paris: E. LeDuc, p. Bertrand et Cie, 1912); *Trois études de concert en doubles notes* op. 56 (Paris: Durand, 1918); *Finger Gymnastics for the Piano* op. 60 (1920); *Ecole des arpèges* (1923) – including an *étude* by Busoni specially composed for inclusion in this volume (Busoni had dedicated his 1915 edition of Bach's *Goldberg Variations* to Philipp); *Une demi-heure de préparation technique* (Paris: Heugel, 1925); *Exercices analytiques de l'oeuvre de Chopin* (1930) – Preface by Paderewski; *26 Special Exercises for the 4th & 5th Fingers*, Schirmer's Scholastic Series (New York: Schirmer, 1930); *Six Octave-Studies in the Form of Little Fugues* (New York: Schirmer, 1930); *Scale Technique for the Pianoforte* (New York: Schirmer, 1950).

The list of distinguished Philipp pupils includes (in roughly chronological order): Maurice Dumesnil, Paul Layonnet, Edmond Trillar, Cella Delavrancea, Madeleine Grovlez-Fourgeaud, Emma Boynet, Youra Guller, Marcelle Herrenschmidt, Guiomar Novaes, Ania Dorfmann, Madeleine Valmalète, Germaine Thyssens-Valentin, Denyse Molié, Genia Nemenoff, Jeanne-Marie Darré, Beveridge Webster, Jacqueline Blancard, Soulima Stravinsky, Nikita Magaloff, Jean Françaix, Phyllis Sellick, Monique de la Bruchollerie, Rena Kyriakou and Fernando Laires. Charles Timbrell, *French Pianism: A Historical Perspective* (Portland, OR: Amadeus Press, 1999), p. 79.

98 See above, pp. 108, 140.

99 Henry Bellamann, 'Isidor Philipp', *The Musical Quarterly* 29.4 (October 1943), 417–25 (p. 421; original emphasis).

100 Craft acknowledges that 'the composer of *Capriccio* exploits to perfection his own characteristics as a performer', that he 'tailored his piano music to his specifications as a performer' and that 'his abilities and limitations as a pianist are ... imprinted on his piano music'. Yet Craft denies that 'this personal requirement [in any way] restrict[s] the music's technical range'. V. Stravinsky and Craft, *Stravinsky in Pictures and Documents*, pp. 215–16.

101 Neither should one underestimate the high level of expectation that the musical public and press held at that time (indeed, ever since) with regard to the performances of a Russian pianist, particularly in a context where the reputations of two composer-performers of the calibre of Rakhmaninov and Prokofiev were already well established.

102 Stravinsky, *An Autobiography (1903–1934)*, p. 121.

103 Leonie Rosenstiel, *Nadia Boulanger: A Life in Music* (New York: W.W. Norton, 1982), p. 57.

104 Ernest Boulanger (1815–1900) won the Prix de Rome at the age of twenty, in 1835.

105 *Ibid.*, p. 93.

106 *Ibid.*, p. 155.

107 *Die Tat* (14 October 1961), quoted in V. Stravinsky and Craft, *Stravinsky in Pictures and Documents*, p. 629n29.

108 Peter Heyworth (ed.), *Conversations with Klemperer* (London: Gollancz, 1973), p. 61.

109 Walsh, *Stravinsky: A Creative Spring*, p. 480.

110 V. Stravinsky and Craft, *Stravinsky in Pictures and Documents*, p. 629n29.

111 Joseph, *Stravinsky Remembered*, p. 79.

112 *Ibid.*

113 *Ibid.*, p. 80.

114 *Ibid.*, p. 91.

115 See below, pp. 190–204.

116 Christopher Small, *Musicking: The Meanings of Performing and Listening* (Middletown, CT: Wesleyan University Press, 1998).

117 Timbrell, *French Pianism*, p. 94.

118 *Ibid.*, p. 97.

119 *Ibid.*

120 *Ibid.*

121 *Ibid.*

122 Gabriel Tacchino recalls how Long 'gave me some money before the Long–Thibaud Competition, and said: "Go to a restaurant and have a good steak, because the Russians are coming and they play very well ... you'll need your strength!"'. *Ibid.*, p. 98.

123 Martinus Sieveking (1867–1950) was a pupil also of Julius Röntgen. According to Loyonnet the Sieveking method called for:

strong, very articulated fingers. Only in that respect was it related to Philipp's concerns … In general the Leschetizky school was more romantic, with a freer approach to tempo … and was more concerned with the complete education of the fingers and the different kinds of attacks – so in that sense you can talk about colour. On the other hand, the French notion of 'the atmosphere of a dream' – in which the music can nearly approach silence, *pianississimo* – was contrary to Leschetizky's ideal that everything always had to sing, to have a round sound even when it was quiet. (*Ibid.*, p. 190)

124 *Ibid.*

125 Cortot directed the first performances in Paris of *Götterdämmerung* (May 1902). He also conducted *Tristan und Isolde* (Paris, June 1902) and, following the establishment that year of the *Société de festivals lyriques*, the first performances in France of *Parsifal* (in concert form).

126 *Ibid.*, p. 102 (emphasis added).

127 *Ibid.*, p. 195.

128 *Ibid.*, p. 196.

129 I am indebted to Laurence Dreyfus for pointing out an intriguing, alternative reading of Stravinsky's aversion to interpretation: that his notion of pianism was a perverse severing of technique from expression, which would never have been countenanced by those from whom he borrowed. For them, technique was, surely, only a tool to aid expression with which they could more effectively embrace interpretation.

130 From the Foreword (*Avant-propos*) to Isidor Philipp, *Exercices journaliers* (Paris: A. Durand et Fils, 1897) (original emphasis).

131 See above, pp. 136–7 (Example 3.2).

132 Philipp, *Exercices journaliers*.

133 T. P. Currier, 'Introduction' to Philipp, *Complete School of Technic for the Piano*, p. 4. Similar accent displacement is a feature of the Leschetizky method; yet this latter's use of accentuation is proof of a quite different (and very un-Philippian) concern: namely the development of muscular strength in every finger, as in his 'Preliminary Studies for Velocity in Scale-Playing', where only the fourth finger (considered to be the least independent of all and where, traditionally, the pianist needs to direct the greatest attention) is accented. Prentner, *The Leschetizky Method*, p. 27.

134 Philipp, *Complete School of Technic for the Piano*, p. 8.

135 Philipp's *Exercices pratiques*, 2nd series develops the 'extended ritornello' (p. 18, Exercise 5) and wide chord-spacings (Exercises 6 and 7). This latter technique is further developed in Philipp, *Complete School of Technic* (p. 20, Exercises 6 and 7).

136 This 'condensed *Accordgruppe*' forms the basis for an extended section of 'Arpeggio Exercise(s) on the Preceding Chords, also in Broken Octaves, from High and Low Wrist'. *Ibid.*, pp. 98–103.

137 Stravinsky, *Poetics of Music*, p. 68; *Poétique musicale sous forme de six leçons*, p. 106.

138 Stravinsky's empathy with Webern appears to have extended to his engagement with the piano as a composing tool. Walsh comments on the 'seemingly arbitrary comparison of his own habit of composing at the piano with that of [Webern's]', referring to the composer's comment on this subject in *Conversations with Igor Stravinsky* (1959). Walsh, *Stravinsky: The Second Exile*, p. 358.

139 Stravinsky, *Poetics of Music*, p. 24; *Poétique musicale sous forme de six leçons*, p. 78.

140 Janet Mills, 'Working in Music: The Conservatoire Professor', p. 184. To support her case Mills refers to Yehudi Menuhin, *Unfinished Journey* (London: Future, 1976), and Hilary du Pré and Piers du Pré, *A Genius in the Family: An Intimate Portrait of Jacqueline du Pré* (London: Chatto and Windus, 1997), but could also, of course, have included *Chroniques de ma vie*.

141 Stravinsky was not alone in owing his international debut and subsequent career to the Ballets Russes. 'Without Diaghilev I would not be here', Balanchine would later comment. In *Balanchine*, a television documentary directed by Merrill Brockway, PBS Dance in America series (Kultur: D2448).

142 Walsh, *Stravinsky: A Creative Spring*, p. 467.

143 Unlike Stravinsky, Balanchine had graduated in piano from the Petrograd Conservatoire (entering in 1919). He remained an active and committed musician throughout his career. On arriving in New York in the early 1930s he resumed his studies of musical theory with Nicholas Nabokov. Balanchine was an occasional song-writer and was adept at piano arrangement. His transcriptions of contemporary scores include works by Webern and Stravinsky, notably the first movement of *Three Pieces for String Quartet*.

144 Joseph, *Stravinsky and Balanchine*, pp. 8, 4.

145 Igor Stravinsky and Robert Craft, *Themes and Episodes* (New York: Knopf, 1966), p. 24 (emphasis added).

146 Joseph, *Stravinsky and Balanchine*, pp. 15, 18.

147 *Ibid.*, p. 18.

148 Igor Youskevitch, interviewed in Francis Mason, *I Remember Balanchine* (New York: Doubleday, 1991), p. 300.

149 Joseph, *Stravinsky and Balanchine*, p. 29.

150 *Ibid.*, pp. 18–19.

151 A. S. Eddington, *The Nature of the Physical World* (1928), (Ann Arbor: University of Michigan Press, 1981); quoted in Joseph, *Stravinsky and Balanchine*, pp. 8–9.

152 Quoted in Joseph, *Stravinsky and Balanchine*, p. 9 (emphasis added).

153 See the impressive photograph (by 'Vera Sudeikina'), reprinted in V. Stravinsky and Craft, *Stravinsky in Pictures and Documents*, p. 298. The caption reads: 'Autumn 1924, Berlin. Hotel Fuerstenhof. Exercising during a concert tour of Germany.' On 23 July 1923, Stravinsky, in Biarritz, wrote to Ernest Ansermet: 'I do my gymnastics every morning and I sunbathe from twelve to one o'clock.'

154 William King, *Cue* (24 April 1948), quoted in V. Stravinsky and Craft, *Stravinsky in Pictures and Documents*, p. 298.

155 The complete letter is reprinted in Taruskin, *Stravinsky and the Russian Traditions*, pp. 972–4 (original emphasis).

156 Roger Shattuck, 'The Devil's Dance: Stravinsky's Corporal Imagination', in Pasler, *Confronting Stravinsky*, pp. 82–8 (p. 84).

157 See Chapter 2, pp. 87–91.

158 Balanchine may be seen also, according to his individual path, to have 'folded his own Maryinsky training into … the newly modern forms [of *Apollon musagète*]'; Homans, *Apollo's Angels*, p. 338. It is an observation that Homans credits to Diaghilev.

159 'The first movement [of the Concerto] sports a thrice-recurring near-quotation from the slow movement of the Chaikovsky Fifth Symphony.' Taruskin compares the 'Fifth Symphony, II, mm. 67–68 (*moderato con anima*), clarinet solo' with the 'Concerto, I, 3 before [Fig.] 22, oboe solo'. Taruskin, *Stravinsky and the Russian Traditions*, p. 1608.

160 Joseph, *Stravinsky and the Piano*, p. 271.

161 Gretchen Horlacher, 'Sketches and Superimposition in Stravinsky's *Symphony of Psalms*', *Mitteilungen der Paul Sacher Stiftung* 12 (April 1999), 22–6; Lynne Rogers, 'Varied Repetition and Stravinsky's Compositional Process', *Mitteilungen der Paul Sacher Stiftung* 7 (April 1994), 22–6.

162 Ernest Ansermet, *Les Fondements de la musique dans la conscience humaine* (1961), quoted in White, *Stravinsky: The Composer and His Works*, p. 366.

163 Pieter C. Van den Toorn, *The Music of Igor Stravinsky* (New Haven: Yale University Press, 1983), p. 341.

164 Cross, *The Stravinsky Legacy*, p. 61.

165 *Ibid.*, pp. 202–3: a reference to Taruskin, *Stravinsky and the Russian Traditions*, p. 1462.

166 Stravinsky, *An Autobiography (1903–1936)*, pp. 161–2 (emphasis added).

167 'So common are these fingerprints that their natural transference to non-piano works is assumable in a classic *abeunt studia in mores* tradition.' Joseph, *Stravinsky and the Piano*, p. 246.

168 Joseph, *Stravinsky Inside Out*, p. 91.

169 See the first movement, bb. 17–21 (before Fig. 3), where the part for piano 1 (right hand) transforms from a predominantly 1,2,4,5 fingering to 2,1,4,5.

170 White, *Stravinsky: The Composer and His Works*, p. 417.

171 Stravinsky is prompted to elaborate this passage (for two pianos) on the very first page of his sketches for the *Symphony of Psalms*: see Fig. 3.4.

172 NB first movement (bb. 17–21): the *legato* melody (horn 1, solo violoncello), non-*legato* accompaniment and bass-line (piano 1, *gli altri violoncelli* – i.e. 'the other cellos', with double-basses) and *staccato* accompaniment (piano 2).

173 NB first movement (bb. 50–2; Fig. 9, bb. 2–4).

174 Stravinsky, 'Some Ideas about My *Octuor*', p. 576.

175 *Strawinsky: Sein Nachlass, sein Bild*, for example, is not only an exhibition catalogue but also, surely, a testament to Stravinsky's passion for musical calligraphy.

176 Ockleford, 'Relating Musical Structure and Content to Aesthetic Response', p. 109.

177 See, for example, the detail from *Babel* reproduced in White, *Stravinsky: The Composer and His Works*, p. 418.

178 See Example 3.6b p. 164. The many errors in these figures may reflect the authors' (and proof-readers') lack of expertise, in 1903, in such eighteenth-century matters. Yet, the inclusion of figures at all in this unlikely context may also be an indication of a desire to lend some neoclassical/neo-baroque 'respectability' to this drill, being the theoretical/academic kernel of Leschetizky's method.

179 Each hand is treated separately so that while one is exercised the other may rest; Leschetizky insists on this. 'Play … at first … slowly with each hand alone' (Brée, *The Groundwork of the Leschetizky Method*, p. 75). Prentner echoes this sentiment: 'Practise at first each hand separately and later both together' (Prentner, *The Leschetizky Method*, p. 84). In Brée's volume (Chapter 26, 'Practice and Study') one recognizes the typically Leschetizkian drive to develop physical and mental stamina in the pianist: 'A point for etude-playing in particular … is to play them – after they go well and quickly – several times in succession, as long as you can keep it up; *this promotes endurance*' (emphasis added). This latter tendency is central to the demands that Stravinsky makes on the performer in, for example, the 'Gigue' of *Duo concertant*, the 'Rondoletto' of *Sérénade en la*, in *Capriccio* as a whole and in the outer movements of the *Concerto for Two Solo Pianos*.

180 See Fig. 9. To the text 'Ne sileas' ('Hold not thy peace') the sopranos and tenors execute a tonic pedal on E, supported by cellos, double-basses and piano 2 (the alto and bass sections do not sing at this point). See also Fig. 12: '… mei. Remitte mihi' ('O spare me').

181 See Czerny, *Forty Exercises,* op. 337, (Peters Edition), no. 1.

182 Philipp, *Complete School of Technic for the Piano*, pp. 8–10: 'Exercises in Velocity', nos. 1–9.

183 Stravinsky's fair copy of the *Sonate* is without the upper A in this passage (Paul Sacher Stiftung: R91. PSS 114–0211); the note E alone provides the pedal point for this oscillation. The first edition (Edition Russe de Musique) contains the double pedal point, A/E. It is a revision maintained in the current edition published by Boosey & Hawkes. (See also *Les Cinq Doigts:* final bars of movements 3 and 4.)

184 Coincidentally, perhaps, the lower notes of the oscillation in the *Sonate* example, A–B♭, consist of the same semitonal outline as the two-note chant on E–F heard in the opening chorus of the *Symphony*.

185 See *Symphony of Psalms*, first movement (bb. 68–70; Fig.12, bb. 4–6).

186 Fig. 4 – altos alone; Fig. 5 – altos within an SATB texture; Fig. 7 – altos alone; Fig. 12 – fourth bar (three versions of this theme within an SATB texture: tenors (an exact statement), altos (as a 'varied repetition') and sopranos (entering in the next bar – as a second 'varied repetition')). Other statements of choral material closely related to the two-note chant can be found at: Fig. 10 – bb. 1–2, 4–5 and 6; Fig. 11 – bb. 3 and 4.

187 Rather than follow symphonic precedent – the 'various models adopted by custom' as Stravinsky refers to them – he has produced an orchestral 'invention'. This description can be justified by the composer's evident modelling of the work on Bachian references, particularly those that relate to this particular (keyboard) genre whose didactic function is two-fold, serving a useful purpose to composers and performers. The invention, like this Stravinskian movement, was monothematic and founded upon the creative manipulation of contrapuntal devices. At the premiere of *Symphony of Psalms* in Brussels the movements were given titles, although these were never used again in programme note or score. The third movement was 'Allegro symphonique'; the titles of the first two movements reflected their apparent inter-relationship and their Bachian allusions: 'Preludio' and 'Double-Fugue'. The Italian form chosen (*preludio*) – instead of the expected French *prélude* (to balance *symphonique*) – provides a curious parallel with the working title that Stravinsky gave to his first sketches of the *Sonate*'s first movement (see above, Figure 3.1). Perhaps that, too, was intended originally to lead into a slow fugue.

188 Stravinsky and Craft, *Themes and Episodes*, p. 58.

189 Van den Toorn, *The Music of Igor Stravinsky*, p. 440.

190 Joseph N. Straus, *Stravinsky's Late Music* (Cambridge: Cambridge University Press, 2001), pp. 228–9.

191 Watkins, *Pyramids at the Louvre*, p. 357.

192 'I prefer Latin to Greek and Slavonic because Latin is definitely fixed – as well as universal, thanks to its diffusion by the Church.' From *La veu de Catalunya*, Barcelona (March 1925), quoted in V. Stravinsky and Craft, *Stravinsky in Pictures and Documents*, p. 205.

193 See Taruskin, *Stravinsky and the Russian Traditions*, p. 1619 for comparison with an eighteenth-century form of *Otche nash*, as Orthodox chant, published in Moscow in 1775.

194 Walsh, *Stravinsky: A Creative Spring*, p. 501.

195 While the use of Latin reflects Stravinsky's approximation to Catholicism, the choral writing in these works is in complete contrast to that tradition, as Louis Andriessen has commented: 'My father always talked of [the *Symphony of Psalms*] with much admiration. His only criticism was that he found the choral writing too stiff, too square. It was a recurrent theme of his: as a Catholic composer, he was deeply rooted in brilliant choral writing (all those Masses in the French or Italian style).' From Louis Andriessen with Jonathan Cross, 'Composing with Stravinsky', in Cross, *The Cambridge Companion to Stravinsky*, p. 248–59 (p. 254).

196 Maritain, *Art et scholastique*, p. 3 (original emphasis).

197 This observation is made in the light of personal experience in using the *Accordgruppe* for piano study. The mental and physical effort engaged in the successful rendition of this marathon of arpeggios is such that, with familiarity, the desire to move the other hand, and so leave behind the harmonic monotony of the pedal harmony, may be seen as an inevitable and welcome consequence of this endurance test. One can only admire the discipline of those who were schooled within such rigorous traditions that would require the pupil to use the *Accordgruppe* exactly as it was designed – and to run the marathon 'to the bitter end'.

198 Walsh, *Stravinsky: A Creative Spring*, p. 501.

199 *The Industrious 'Prentice: A Favourite, and Enthralled by His Master*, from William Hogarth, *Industry and Idleness* (1747), in Ronald Paulson, *Hogarth's Graphic Works*, 2 vols. (New Haven; London: Yale University Press, 1970).

200 For a complementary yet contrasting view of this work as a Stravinskian landmark, cf. Van den Toorn, *The Music of Igor Stravinsky*, p. 269: 'For it can just in this referentially octatonic respect be deemed a matter of consequence that Stravinsky should have singled out the *Symphony of Psalms* as a point of arrival, as an ultimate in neoclassical accommodation and synthesis.'

201 'As Stravinsky, in response to some form of inner compulsion, does not make of his music an act of self-expression, his religious music can reveal only a kind of "made-up" religiosity.' From Ansermet, *Les Fondements de la musique dans la conscience humaine* (1961), quoted in White, *Stravinsky: The Composer and His Works*, p. 366.

4   Departures and homecomings

1 Walzer, *Charles-Albert Cingria: Correspondance avec Igor Strawinsky*, p. 83.

2 A prominent writer of the *vaudois* circle, Charles-Albert Cingria (1883–1954) was well known to C. F. Ramuz and other literary figures in Switzerland and to Jean Cocteau in Paris. He was an occasional contributor to *La Nouvelle Revue française* and wrote on a wide range of subjects (including medieval art and cycling). He maintained a close friendship with Theodore Stravinsky. Walzer's *Charles-Albert Cingria* documents fifty-nine letters, several of which – either in their entirety or in an abridged form – appear in translation in Craft, *Stravinsky: Selected Correspondence*, Vol. III.

3 Stravinsky, *An Autobiography (1903–1936)*, p. 170.

4 Walzer, *Charles-Albert Cingria: Correspondance avec Igor Strawinsky*, p. 79.

5 Stravinsky, *Chroniques de ma vie*, p. 207; *An Autobiography (1903–1936)*, p. 170.

6 *Duo concertant* was composed at Voreppe between December 1931 and 15 July 1932. It was premiered in Berlin (28 October) with further performances that year in Danzig (2 November) and Paris (8 December), this latter attended by Cingria as a guest of Theodore Stravinsky.

7 Cingria, postcard to Stravinsky [December 1932], in Walzer, *Charles-Albert Cingria: Correspondance avec Igor Strawinsky*, p. 27.

8 *Ibid.* The postcard represents the Fontaine-de-Vaucluse. Cingria probably chose this image of France's largest spring deliberately to evoke, for the delectation of its addressee, mythological connotations of abundant creativity.

9 *Ibid.*

10 Stravinsky, 'Some Ideas about My *Octuor*', p. 577.

11 Michael Oliver, *Igor Stravinsky* (London: Phaidon, 1995), p. 191.

12 Cited in Stravinsky, *An Autobiography (1903–1936)*, p. 170.

13 Igor Stravinsky, letter of 28 December 1932 to Cingria, in Walzer, *Charles-Albert Cingria: Correspondance avec Igor Strawinsky*, pp. 28–9. English translation in Craft, *Stravinsky: Selected Correspondence*, Vol. III, pp. 113–14.

14 Stravinsky, *An Autobiography (1903–1936)*, p. 170.

15 *Ibid.*, pp. 170–1.

16 In the light of considerations discussed above (in Chapter 1, pp. 55, 64) regarding Stravinsky's weekly lessons with Rimsky-Korsakov, the phrase 'orchestral as well as instrumental' presents an interesting distinction.

17 Cited in White, *Stravinsky: The Composer and His Works*, p. 372.

18 Isidor Philipp, *Trois études de concert en doubles notes* op. 56 (Paris: Durand, 1918).

19 White, *Stravinsky: A Critical Survey*, pp. 141–2.

20 Igor Stravinsky, 'The Owl and the Pussy-Cat' (1966) for soprano and piano. Words by Edward Lear.

21 Adriano Banchieri (1568–1634). Cingria refers to this composer erroneously as Oliviero Banchieri.

22 White, *Stravinsky: The Composer and His Works*, p. 374.

23 Charles-Albert Cingria, *Pétrarque* (Lausanne: Editions L'Age d'Homme, 2003 [1932]), p. 49.

24 (1) At the end of *The Shrove-Tide Fair* (Fig. 56): side-drum without snares (arrowhead accents) and timpani (high F♯). (2) At the end of *Danse russe* (Fig. 91): side-drum and timpani (wooden sticks; high F♯) *marc. articulato*. (3) At the end of the Valse (Fig. 160): side-drum (without snares) and timpani (low F♯).

25 '"Sadko – the wealthy merchant" is an ancient Novgorod *bïlina*, one of the gems of our *folk*, unwritten literature … This legend is full to overflowing [with] the element of music. It all just asks to be set to music, since the hero himself, Sadko, is also a *guslyar*, a virtuoso player of the *gusli*.' A. N. Serov, 'The Seventh Russian Musical Society Concert', *Music and Theatre* 15 (1867). Serov 1895, 4, pp. 1841–5, cited in Campbell, *Russians on Russian Music, 1830–1880*, p. 187. A *bïlina* is a Russian folk epic song-narrative recounting the deeds of *bogatïri* (heroes).

26 Campbell, *Russians on Russian Music, 1830–1880*, p. 187.

27 I am grateful to Ulrich Mosch for the suggestion that Stravinsky's fast '*ritornello* music', aside from its *pal'tserazvitiye* spirit, may also be a reflection

of that general toccata idea adopted by several neoclassical composers as a reference, *en hommage*, to the eighteenth-century *clavecinistes*. A notable example of this would be the final movement of Ravel's suite for solo piano, *Le Tombeau de Couperin* (1914/17). However, any interest on the part of twentieth-century composers in toccata as a form of composition is surely underpinned by a fundamental respect for the rounded, indeed 'ideal', musicality of these pre-Romantic composer/performers, whose virtues are encapsulated in the 'pure' keyboard dexterity of their finger-based virtuosity.

28 Boris de Schloezer, writing in the *La Nouvelle Revue française* (1 July 1938), 152–3.

29 From Igor Stravinsky, '"Quelques confidences sur la musique": Conférence de M. Igor Strawinsky faite le 21 novembre 1935', reprinted in White, *Stravinsky: The Composer and His Works*, Appendix A/6, p. 581.

30 *Ibid.*, p. 584.

31 Jonathan D. Kramer, 'Discontinuity and Proportion in the Music of Stravinsky', in Pasler, *Confronting Stravinsky*, pp. 174–94 (p. 177).

32 Translated from Stravinsky, 'Quelques confidences sur la musique', p. 584 (original emphasis).

33 See the epigraph to this section, p. 213.

34 White, *Stravinsky: The Composer and His Works*, p. 409.

35 For example, the sketches of a *concertante* piano work (in the first movement) and the re-use of material originally intended as a film-score for *The Song of Bernadette* (in the Andante).

36 Stravinsky and Craft, *Dialogues and a Diary*, cited in White, *Stravinsky: The Composer and His Works*, p. 431.

37 Craft informs us, on his jacket note to *Dearest Bubushkin*, that this was 'Vera Stravinsky's pet name for the composer during their fifty years together – from 1921, when Diaghilev first introduced them in Paris, to Igor's death in 1971'. The term appears to be derived from three principal sources, including the verb *bubnit'*, used colloquially to mean: grumble, mutter, drone (or ramble) on. *Bubushkin* seems to combine *bubnit'* with *babushka* ('Granny') to form something teasing along the lines of 'Granny's little grumpy boy'. Whatever the word's more distant resonances, its close similarity with 'Pushkin' ensures that this term of endearment is never disrespectful. Robert Craft (ed.), *Dearest Bubushkin: The Selected Letters and Diaries of Vera and Igor Stravinsky*, trans. Lucia Davidova (London: Thames and Hudson, 1985).

38 Stravinsky, 'Quelques confidences sur la musique', p. 585.

39 In the 1933 publication of *Duo concertant* by Editions Russe de Musique (copyright assigned to Boosey & Hawkes in 1947) these movements are titled 'Eglogue I' and 'Eglogue II'.

40 Igor Stravinsky, *Elegy/Elégie* (1944), in *The Stravinsky Collection: 9 Pieces for Violin and Piano* (Boosey & Hawkes).

41 Between Figs. 88 and 90, Figs. 100 and 101 (varied), and Figs. 109 and 111.

42 Igor Strawinsky, *Concerto en ré pour violon et orchestre (Réduction pour violon et piano par l'auteur)* (Mainz: B. Schotts Söhne, 1931).

43 While Alexandre Tansman had noted Stravinsky's reference at the time to writing a piano concerto – Alexandre Tansman, *Igor Stravinsky: The Man and His Music*, trans. T. and C. Bleefield (New York: Putnam, 1949), p. 251 – the composer (who was dismissive of Tansman's book) took the opportunity later to comment: 'The first movement of the symphony was written in 1942; I thought of the work then as a concerto for orchestra', in Stravinsky and Craft, *Expositions and Developments*, p. 77.

44 To this listener the passage is reminiscent of similarly declamatory and syncopated chords in the first movement of Beethoven's Symphony no. 3, 'Eroica'.

45 See *Symphony in Three Movements*, Fig.71.

46 See *Ebony Concerto*, Fig. 9a.

47 Walsh, *Stravinsky: The Second Exile*, p. 182.

48 See Chapter 1, pp. 35–7.

49 Taruskin, *The Oxford History of Western Music*, Vol. IV, p. 447.

50 White, *Stravinsky: The Composer and His Works*, p. 263.

51 PSS 123–0336/7 contains 'LIED OHNE NAME für zwei Fagotten'; twenty-eight bars; no date; 'Igor Stravinsky' is written after the final bar in Church Slavonic script: i.e. 'printed', not autographed with his usual florid signature. The manuscript is located immediately prior to the sketches for *Three Pieces for Clarinet Solo*, whose first movement is dated (also in Church Slavonic script) '11–14 October 1918, Morges'. Both works are notated in identical handwriting and page layout, which would suggest that Stravinsky worked on these woodwind miniatures in close proximity to each other in the autumn of 1918.

52 See Stravinsky, 'Some Ideas about My *Octuor*', p. 574.

53 Rimsky-Korsakov, *Principles of Orchestration*, Vol. 2, p. 119.

54 Goubault, *Igor Stravinsky*, p. 263.

55 In some editions of Petrarch's sonnets this is listed as no. 217, not 218. Schoenberg sets the translation by K. Förster: 'O könnt' Ich jeder Rach' an ihr genesen' ('Ah! That my vengeance soon be flaunting / On her who has destroyed me with her glances.')

56 From 'Notice par Christophe Calame' in Cingria, *Pétrarque*, p. 141.

57 *Ibid.*, p. 115.

58 Igor Stravinsky, 'Misunderstood! Stravinsky Says Audience Did Not Hiss Enough', *Weekly Dispatch* (12 June 1921), cited in Walsh, *Stravinsky: A Creative Spring*, p. 331.

59 Milan Kundera, 'Improvisation in Homage to Stravinsky', in *Testaments Betrayed*, trans. Linda Asher (London: HarperCollins, 1995), p. 78.

60 White, *Stravinsky: The Composer and His Works*, p. 551.

61 Igor Stravinsky, 'The Composer's View' (Paris, 16 August 1964), in Paul Griffiths, *Igor Stravinsky: The Rake's Progress*, Cambridge Opera Handbooks (Cambridge: Cambridge University Press, 1982), pp. 2–3.

62　A fuller debate in these terms can be found in Robert Moevs, 'Mannerism and Stylistic Consistency in Stravinsky', in *Stravinsky (1882–1971): A Composers' Memorial.* Special double issue of *Perspectives of New Music* 9.2, 10.1 (1971), 92–103.

63　Charles Koechlin, 'Le "Retour à Bach"', *La Revue musicale* 8.1 (November 1926), 1–2.

64　Strawinsky, *Poétique musicale en forme de six leçons*, p. 92; Stravinsky, *Poetics of Music*, p. 46.

65　Griffiths, *Igor Stravinsky: The Rake's Progress*, p. 96.

66　*Ibid.*, p. 86.

67　D major–F♯ minor (e.g. bb. 1 and 3); F major–F♯ minor (e.g. bb. 2–4); G major–G♯ minor (e.g. b. 5).

68　Griffiths, *Igor Stravinsky: The Rake's Progress*, p. 73.

69　Igor Stravinsky, 'The Composer's View', in Griffiths, *Ibid.*, p. 4.

70　See Chapter 3 above, pp. 131–40.

71　See the instrumental list at the front of the full score.

72　See, respectively, Chapter 3, p. 139 (Example 3.3b), and Chapter 2, p. 81 (Example 2.1e).

73　Milton Babbitt, 'Order, Symmetry, and Centricity in Late Stravinsky', in Pasler, *Confronting Stravinsky*, pp. 247–61 (p. 248).

74　Stravinsky and Craft, *Dialogues and a Diary*, pp. 55–6.

75　Stravinsky and Craft, *Themes and Conclusions*, pp. 23–4.

76　Ivan Turgenev, *Sketches from a Hunter's Album* (1847/51), trans. Richard Freeborn (London: Penguin, 1990), p. 42. Turgenev is referring to the oft-visited 'raspberry waters' of the river Ista.

77　Stravinsky and Craft, *Themes and Episodes*, pp. 23–4.

78　Straus, *Stravinsky's Late Music*, p. 48.

79　Igor Stravinsky and Robert Craft, *Conversations with Igor Stravinsky* (London: Faber and Faber, 1979), pp. 15–16.

80　Straus, *Stravinsky's Late Music*, p. 49.

81　Volker Scherliess, '"Torniamo all'antico e sarà un progresso": Creative Longing in Music', in Boehm *et al.*, *Canto d'Amore*, pp. 39–62 (p. 39).

82　'Do not be astonished if I say nothing about Spanish folk music. I do not dispute its distinctive character, but for me there was no revelation in it.' Stravinsky, *An Autobiography (1903–1934)*, p. 64.

83　See *Movements*, first movement, for example, bb. 42–42b. It is a passage full of fast repeated notes and fleeting triplet phrases, both of these imprints recalling, in fragmentation, the introductory bars of the *Sonate*.

84　Taruskin argues in favour of Bartók's *Bagatelle* op. 6, no. 12 for piano (1908) as the seed-bed for such patterns of acceleration. See Taruskin, *The Oxford History of Western Music*, Vol. IV, p. 394.

85　Susannah Tucker, 'Stravinsky and His Sketches: The Composing of *Agon* and Other Serial Works of the 1950s', D.Phil. dissertation (University of Oxford, 1992), p. 263.

86 Straus, *Stravinsky's Late Music*, p. 40.

87 Cited in White, *Stravinsky: The Composer and His Works*, p. 538. Huxley's 'novel of ideas' *Point Counter Point* (1928) may have been at the back of Stravinsky's reference to married couples, for this work is, in the manner of *Vanity Fair*, a rich and droll commentary on faithful (and fickle) relationships.

88 One ponders the effectiveness of this song in another guise: voice and harp.

89 Cf. Philipp's instruction on how to practise his *Accordgruppe* cited above in Chapter 3, p. 183 (Example 3.10).

90 Cited in White, *Stravinsky: The Composer and His Works*, p. 543.

91 Milton Babbitt, [untitled article], in *Stravinsky (1882–1971): A Composers' Memorial*, p. 107.

92 Boris de Schloezer, 'Chronique musicale', *La Nouvelle Revue française* 178 (1 July 1928), 104–8.

93 Walsh, *Stravinsky: The Second Exile*, pp. 381–2.

94 The December 1920 issue of *La Revue musicale* contained a music supplement ('Tombeau de Claude Debussy') wherein Stravinsky published his arrangement for piano of the final section under the title 'Fragment des *Symphonies pour instruments à vent à la mémoire de Claude Achille Debussy*'.

95 Igor Stravinsky and Robert Craft, *Dialogues* (Berkeley: University of California Press, 1982), pp. 69–70.

96 Stravinsky and Craft, *Themes and Conclusions* (London: Faber and Faber, 1972), p. 92.

97 'J'aime mieux une boîte à musique qu'un rossignol'; cited in Daniel Albright, *Stravinsky: The Music Box and the Nightingale* (New York: Gordon and Breach, 1989), p. 4.

98 Stravinsky and Craft, *Conversations*, p. 20.

99 See Chapter 2, p. 118.

Conclusions

1 Lucians Berio, 'Adieu', in *Stravinsky (1882–1971): A Composers' Memorial*, special double issue of *Perspectives of New Music* 9.2, 10.1 (1971), 129–30.

2 In Walzer, *Charles-Albert Cingria: Correspondance avec Igor Strawinsky*, pp. 28–9.

3 The original materials, being Stravinsky's personal copy of Bach's score and his own transcriptions in manuscript (in pencil), are held at the Paul Sacher Stiftung.

4 Stravinsky, *An Autobiography (1903–1936)*, p. 113.

5 *Ibid.*, p. 81.

6 *Ibid.*

7 Roy Harris (1898–1979) has commented, regarding *Le Sacre du printemps*, that (even in this unlikely context) 'nearly all the materials [can] be found in the piano exercises of Czerny'. One might concur with Harris that this work is 'full of Alberti basses, trills and broken chords, with a little Russian folk tune and some

eighteenth-century ornamentation', though not, surely, that this indicates 'all has gone into the packaging'. On the contrary, a reading of such passages from the perspective of *pal'tserazvitiye* would consider such elements (1) as testimony to Stravinsky's long-standing utilization of pianistic idioms as central to his creative substance, and (2) as confirmation of his superlative skill in disguising this within the 'packaging' of early-twentieth-century ('Russian') orchestration. In Vivian Perlis and Libby Van Cleve, *Composers' Voices from Ives to Ellington: An Oral History of American Music* (New Haven; London: Yale University Press, 2005), p. 344.

8 Ivan Goncharov (1812–91), *Oblomov* (1859), trans. David Magarshack (London: Penguin, 2005 [1954]), p. 163.

9 Joseph, *Stravinsky and the Piano*, p. 271.

10 Joseph, *Stravinsky and Balanchine*, p. 208; Stravinsky's own comments about *Orpheus* – see liner notes to Igor Stravinsky, *Ballets: Vol. II*, audio CD (Sony Classical, 1991) – indicate that he recognized the pianistic morphology of the instrumental writing in this work. By denying that this derives from Czerny, the composer may be seen to admit the possibility of this in other works.

11 Joseph, *Stravinsky and Balanchine*, p. 208.

12 The transcriptions seem to have escaped this fate. Publishers have left them alone for reasons of economy, perhaps. There would have been less justification to fund an editor for these artistically reduced items.

13 This must be considered another topic touched upon, but ultimately inadequately handled, on this occasion. The path is open, however, for later exploration; it may be an important aspect, for instance, to understanding the nature of Stravinsky's engagement with fingerings as digital choreography.

14 Rosenblum, *Performance Practices in Classic Piano Music*, pp. 209–10. Rosenblum's sections on 'Beethoven's Exercises and Other Fragments' (pp. 204–9) and 'Fingerings by Clementi and Beethoven' (pp. 209–15) present an intriguing case for these composers' more extraordinary 'musical' fingerings.

15 Stravinsky, *Poetics of Music*, pp. 133–4.

16 Shattuck, 'The Devil's Dance', p. 83.

17 Martha M. Hyde, 'Stravinsky's Neoclassicism', in Cross, *The Cambridge Companion to Stravinsky*, pp. 98–136 (p. 99).

18 Theodore Strawinsky, *Catherine and Igor Stravinsky: A Family Album* (London: Boosey & Hawkes, 1973), quoted in Walsh, *Stravinsky: A Creative Life*, p. 187.

19 Stravinsky, *Poetics of Music*, p. 12.

20 Jonathan Pitches, *Meyerhold* (London: Routledge, 2003), p. 55.

21 Eugenio Barba, *Meyerhold's Etude: Throwing the Stone*, videotape, Archive no. 1 (Exeter: Arts Documentation Unit, 1997).

22 Hyde, 'Stravinsky's Neoclassicism'. Her discussion of heuristic imitation may be found on pp. 114–22.

23 Taruskin, *Defining Russia Musically*, p. 382.

24 André Gide, *The Counterfeiters* (London: Penguin, 1926), p. 181.

25 Kundera, *Testaments Betrayed*, p. 95.

26 Richard Taruskin, 'Back to Whom? Neoclassicism as Ideology', *19th-Century Music* 16.3 (1993), 286–302.

27 Stravinsky and Craft, *Dialogues and a Diary*, p. 124.

28 Igor Stravinsky, 'Sonate für Klavier' and 'Konzert für Klavier und Bläser': recorded in 1926 (French Columbia); *Stravinsky: Early Recordings by the Composer*, The Condon Collection (690.07.006); *Sérénade en la*, recorded 6/7 July 1934 in the Salle Gaveau, Paris (Columbia LF 139/140); *Igor Stravinsky Plays Igor Stravinsky*, Vol. III, Vogue (VG 665/665002). The performance manner described is better suited to the other (equally absorbing) early recording included in the above collection: a solo piano version of *Der Feuervogel: Ballett in 2 Akten*, recorded in '1929/30' (duration: 47 minutes).

29 Stravinsky's extensive recording catalogue evidently provides a wealth of relevant material in this regard. However, for his performing legacy to be adequately re-considered in the light of this study, considerably greater space would be required.

30 Isaiah Berlin, *Russian Thinkers*, ed. Henry Hardy and Aileen Kelly (London: Penguin, 2008), p. 330.

31 Stravinsky, *Poetics of Music*, p. 65; 'le sourire mélodique', in Stravinsky, *Poétique musicale sous forme de six leçons*, p. 104.

32 See Chapter 2, pp. 87–91.

33 Shattuck, 'The Devil's Dance', p. 88.

34 Ernest Ansermet, *Les Fondements de la musique dans la conscience humaine*, 2 vols., Vol. I (Neuchâtel: A la Baconnière, 1961), p. 498.

35 Alastair Williams, *Constructing Musicology* (Aldershot; Burlington: Ashgate, 2001), p. 14.

36 Boris de Schloezer, 'La musique', *La Revue contemporaine* (1 February 1923), quoted in Messing, *Neoclassicism in Music*, p. 130.

37 Richard Freeborn, *The Russian Revolutionary Novel: Turgenev to Pasternak* (Cambridge: Cambridge University Press, 1982), pp. 221–2.

38 Quoted in Gerig, *Famous Pianists and Their Technique*, p. 320.

39 Taruskin, *Stravinsky and the Russian Traditions*, p. 1675.

Bibliography

Abraham, Gerald. 'Nikolay Andreyevich Rimsky-Korsakov'. In *The New Grove Dictionary of Music and Musicians*, 20 vols., Vol. XVI, ed. Stanley Sadie. London: Macmillan, 1980, pp. 26–41

    Rimsky-Korsakov: A Short Biography. New York: AMS Press, 1975 [1945]

Adorno, Theodor W. 'From "The Culture Industry: Enlightenment as Mass Deception (1947)"'. In *The Norton Anthology of Theory and Criticism*, ed. Vincent B. Leitch. New York: W. W. Norton, 2001, pp. 1223–40

    Philosophy of Modern Music, trans. Anne G. Mitchell and Wesley V. Blomster. London; New York: Continuum, 2007

    Quasi una fantasia: Essays on Modern Music, trans. Rodney Livingstone. London: Verso, 1992

Agawu, Kofi. 'Schubert's Sexuality: A Prescription for Analysis?'. *Nineteenth-Century Music* 17.1 (Summer 1993), 79–82

Albright, Daniel. *Stravinsky: The Music Box and the Nightingale*. New York: Gordon and Breach, 1989

Andriessen, Louis with Jonathan Cross. 'Composing with Stravinsky'. In *The Cambridge Companion to Stravinsky*, ed. Jonathan Cross. Cambridge: Cambridge University Press, 2003, pp. 248–59

Andriessen, Louis and Elmer Schönberger. *The Apollonian Clockwork: On Stravinsky*, trans. Jeff Hamburg. Amsterdam: Amsterdam University Press; Amsterdam Academic Archive, 2006

Anon. [Eric Walter White?]. *Igor Stravinsky*. Miniature Essays. London; Geneva: J. & W. Chester, 1925

Ansermet, Ernest. *Les Fondements de la musique dans la conscience humaine*, 2 vols. Neuchâtel: A la Baconnière, 1961

Asaf'yev, Boris. *A Book about Stravinsky*, trans. Richard F. French. Ann Arbor: UMI Research Press, 1982

    Kniga o Stravinskom. Leningrad: Muzïka, 1977 [1929]

Ayrey, Craig. 'Stravinsky in Analysis'. In *The Cambridge Companion to Stravinsky*, ed. Jonathan Cross. Cambridge: Cambridge University Press, 2003, pp. 203–29

Babbitt, Milton. 'Order, Symmetry, and Centricity in Late Stravinsky'. In *Confronting Stravinsky*, ed. Jann Pasler. Berkeley: University of California Press, 1986, pp. 247–61

    [Untitled article]. In *Stravinsky (1882–1971): A Composers' Memorial*. Special double issue of *Perspectives of New Music* **9**.2, **10**.1 (1971), 103–7

Barba, Eugenio. *Meyerhold's Etude: Throwing the Stone*. Archive no. 1 (videotape). Exeter: Arts Documentation Unit, 1997

Bartlett, Rosamund. 'Stravinsky's Russian Origins'. In *The Cambridge Companion to Stravinsky*, ed. Jonathan Cross. Cambridge: Cambridge University Press, 2003, pp. 3–18

Bartók, Béla. *Béla Bartók Essays*, ed. Benjamin Suchoff. London: Faber and Faber, 1976

Bellamann, Henry. 'Isidor Philipp'. *The Musical Quarterly* **29**.4 (October 1943), 417–25

Bely, Andrei. *Petersburg* (1916), trans. Robert A. Maguire and John E. Malmstad. London: Penguin, 1983

Benois, Alexandre. *Reminiscences of the Russian Ballet*. London: Putnam, 1941

Berio, Luciano. 'Adieu'. In *Stravinsky (1882–1971): A Composers' Memorial*. Special double issue of *Perspectives of New Music* **9**.2, **10**.1 (1971), 129–30

Berlin, Isaiah. 'Fathers and Children: Turgenev and the Liberal Predicament'. In Ivan Turgenev, *Fathers and Sons*, trans. Rosemary Edmonds. London: Penguin, 1975, pp. 7–61

Russian Thinkers, ed. Henry Hardy and Aileen Kelly. London: Penguin, 2008

Bie, Oscar. *A History of the Pianoforte and Pianoforte Players*, trans. and rev. E. E. Kellett and E. W. Naylor. New York: Da Capo Press, 1966 [1899]

Bloom, Harold. 'From "The Anxiety of Influence" (1973)'. In *The Norton Anthology of Theory and Criticism*, ed. Vincent B. Leitch. New York: W. W. Norton, 2001, pp. 1794–805

Boehm, Gottfried, Ulrich Mosch and Katharina Schmidt (eds.). *Canto d'Amore: Classicism in Modern Art and Music, 1914–1935*. London: Merrell Holberton, 1996

Boekaerts, M. and M. Niemivirta. 'Self-Regulated Learning: Finding a Balance between Learning Goals and Ego-Protective Goals'. In *A Handbook of Self-Regulation*, ed. M. Boekaerts, P. R. Pintrich and Moshe Zeidner. San Diego: Academic Press, 2000, pp. 417–51

Bohlman, Philip V. 'Ontologies of Music'. In *Rethinking Music*, ed. Nicholas Cook and Mark Everist. Oxford: Oxford University Press, 2001, pp. 17–34

Boretz, Benjamin and Edward T. Cone (eds.). *Perspectives on Schoenberg and Stravinsky*. Princeton: Princeton University Press, 1968

Bowen, Catherine Drinker. *Free Artist: The Story of Anton and Nicholas Rubinstein*. New York: Random House, 1939

Braun, Edward. *The Theatre of Meyerhold: Revolution on the Modern Stage*. London: Methuen, 1986

Brée, Malwine. *The Groundwork of the Leschetizky Method: Issued with His Approval by His Assistant Malwine Brée with Forty-Seven Illustrative Cuts of Leschetizky's Hand*, trans. Th. Baker. New York: G. Schirmer, 1902

Brown, Malcolm Hamick. 'Stravinsky and Prokofiev: Sizing up the Competition'. In *Confronting Stravinsky: Man, Musician, and Modernist*, ed. Jann Pasler. Berkeley: University of California Press, 1986, pp. 39–50

Butler, Christopher. *Modernism: A Very Short Introduction*. Oxford: Oxford University Press, 2010

'Stravinsky as Modernist'. In *The Cambridge Companion to Stravinsky*, ed. Jonathan Cross. Cambridge: Cambridge University Press, 2003, pp. 19–36

Camp, John. *Discovering Bells and Bell-Ringing*. Princes Risborough: Shire, 2001

Campbell, Stuart (ed. and trans.). *Russians on Russian Music, 1830–1880: An Anthology*. Cambridge: Cambridge University Press, 1994

    Russians on Russian Music, 1880–1917: An Anthology. Cambridge: Cambridge University Press, 2003

Carr, E. H. *The Romantic Exiles*. London: Serif, 2007

Chaliapin, Fyodor Ivanovich. *Chaliapin: An Autobiography as Told to Maxim Gorky*, ed. and trans. Nina Froud and James Hanley. London: Macmillan, 1968

Cingria, Charles-Albert. *Pétrarque*. Lausanne: Editions L'Age d'Homme, 2003 [1932]

Clementi, Muzio. *Introduction to the Art of Playing on the Piano Forte*. London: Clementi, 1801

Coleridge, Samuel Taylor. *Coleridge: Selected Poems*, ed. Richard Holmes. London: HarperCollins, 1996

Cortot, Alfred. 'Igor Strawinsky, le piano et les pianistes'. *La Revue musicale* **20**.191, special issue on Igor Stravinsky (May–June 1939), 24–68

    La Musique française de piano, troisième série. Paris: Presses Universitaires de France, 1944

Craft, Robert (ed.). *Dearest Bubushkin: The Selected Letters and Diaries of Vera and Igor Stravinsky*, trans. Lucia Davidova. London: Thames and Hudson, 1985

Craft, Robert (ed.). *Stravinsky: Selected Correspondence*, 3 vols. London: Faber and Faber, 1982–5

Craft, Robert. '*The Rite of Spring*: Genesis of a Masterpiece'. In Igor Stravinsky, *The Rite of Spring: Sketches 1911–1913*. London: Boosey & Hawkes, 1969, pp. xv–xxv

    'Roland-Manuel and the "Poetics of Music"', *Perspectives of New Music* 21.1–2 (1982–3), 487–505 (p. 487)

    Stravinsky: Chronicle of a Friendship 1948–1971. New York: Alfred A. Knopf, 1972

    Stravinsky: Chronicle of a Friendship. Rev. and expanded edn. Nashville; London: Vanderbilt University Press, 1994

    Stravinsky: Glimpses of a Life. London: Lime Tree, 1992

Cross, Jonathan. *The Stravinsky Legacy*. Cambridge: Cambridge University Press, 1998

    'Stravinsky's Theatres'. In *The Cambridge Companion to Stravinsky*, ed. Jonathan Cross. Cambridge: Cambridge University Press, 2003, pp. 137–48

Cuddon, J. A. *The Penguin Dictionary of Literary Terms and Literary Theory*, rev. C. E. Preston. London: Penguin, 1999

Dahlhaus, Carl. *Foundations of Music History*. Cambridge: Cambridge University Press, 1983

    Nineteenth-Century Music, trans. J. Bradford Robinson. Berkeley: University of California Press, 1989 [1980]

Dannreuther, Edward. 'Henselt'. In *The New Grove Dictionary of Music and Musicians*, 20 vols., Vol. VIII, ed. Stanley Sadie. London: Macmillan, 1980, p. 489

'Study'. In *Grove's Dictionary of Music and Musicians*, 9 vols., Vol. VIII, ed. Eric Blom. London: Macmillan, 1954, p. 156.

Dawes, Frank. 'Pianoforte, Section II: Piano Playing'. In *The New Grove Dictionary of Music and Musicians*, 20 vols., Vol. XVI, ed. Stanley Sadie. London: Macmillan, 1980, pp. 711–14

Dostoyevsky, Fyodor Mikhailovich. *Crime and Punishment* (1865-6), trans. David McDuff. London: Penguin, 2003 [1991]

Drewal, Margaret Thompson. 'Constructionist Concepts in Balanchine's Choreography'. *Ballet Review* **13**.3 (Autumn 1985), 42–7

du Pré, Hilary and Piers du Pré. *A Genius in the Family: An Intimate Portrait of Jacqueline du Pré*. London: Chatto and Windus, 1997

Dyachkova, L. S. ed., with Boris M. Yarustovsky. *I. F. Stravinskiy: stat' i i material'i*. Moscow: Sovetskiy Kompozitor, 1973.

Evans, Edwin. *Music and the Dance*. London: Jenkins, 1948

Fay, Amy. *Music Study in Germany*. New York: Dover, 1965 [1880]

Ferguson, Howard. 'Study'. In *The New Grove Dictionary of Music and Musicians*, 20 vols., Vol. XVIII, ed. Stanley Sadie. London: Macmillan, 1980, p. 304

Figes, Orlando. *Natasha's Dance: A Cultural History of Russia*. London: Allen Lane, Penguin, 2002

Foss, Lukas. 'Thirteen Ways of Looking at Igor Stravinsky'. In *Stravinsky (1882–1971): A Composers' Memorial*. Special double issue of *Perspectives of New Music* **9**.2, **10**.1 (1971), 61–2

Freeborn, Richard. *The Russian Revolutionary Novel: Turgenev to Pasternak*. Cambridge: Cambridge University Press, 1982

Garden, Edward. 'Anton Rubinstein'. In *The New Grove Dictionary of Music and Musicians*, 20 vols., Vol. XVI, ed. Stanley Sadie. London: Macmillan, 1980, pp. 297–300

Gerig, Reginald R. *Famous Pianists and Their Technique*. New York: Robert B. Luce, 1974

Gide, André. *The Counterfeiters*. London: Penguin, 1926

Gladkov, Aleksandr. *Meyerhold Speaks, Meyerhold Rehearses*. London: Harwood, 1997

Gloag, Kenneth. 'Russian Rites: *Petrushka, The Rite of Spring* and *Les Noces*'. In *The Cambridge Companion to Stravinsky*, ed. Jonathan Cross. Cambridge: Cambridge University Press, 2003, pp. 79–97

Goddard, Scott. '"Chronicle of My Life", by Igor Stravinsky'. *Music & Letters* 17.3 (July 1936), 253–5

Goehr, Lydia. *The Imaginary Museum of Musical Works*. Oxford: Clarendon Press, 1992

Gogol, Nikolay Vasilievich. *Dead Souls* (1842), trans. Robert A. Maguire. London: Penguin, 2004

Goncharov, Ivan. *Oblomov* (1859), trans. David Magarshack. London: Penguin, 2005, [1954]

Goubault, Christian. *Igor Stravinsky*. Paris: Librairie Honoré Champion, 1991

Grace, Harvey. 'Igor Stravinsky: *Chronicle of My Life*'. *The Musical Times* 77.1120 (June 1936)

Griffiths, Paul. *Igor Stravinsky: The Rake's Progress*. Cambridge Opera Handbooks. Cambridge: Cambridge University Press, 1982

Griffiths, Graham. 'Fingering as Compositional Process: Stravinsky's Sonata Sketchbook Revisited'. *British Postgraduate Musicology Online* (May 2005), available online at www.bpmonline.org.uk/bpm7/griffiths.html (last accessed 14 August 2012)

Grover, Stuart R. 'The World of Art Movement in Russia'. *Russian Review* 32.1 (1973), 28–42

Gutman, David. *Prokofiev*. London: Omnibus Press, 1990

Hamilton, Kenneth. 'The Virtuoso Tradition'. In *The Cambridge Companion to the Piano*, ed. David Rowland. Cambridge: Cambridge University Press, 1998, pp. 57–74

Herzen, Alexander Ivanovich. *Childhood, Youth and Exile* (1853), trans. J. D. Duff. Oxford: Oxford University Press, 1994 [1923]

Sobraniye sochineniy v tridtsati tomakh, 30 vols. Moscow, 1954–66

Who Is to Blame?, trans. Margaret Wettlin. Moscow: Progress Publishers, 1978

Heyworth, Peter (ed.). *Conversations with Klemperer*. London: Gollancz, 1973

Hill, Peter. *Stravinsky*: The Rite of Spring. Cambridge: Cambridge University Press, 2000

Hipkins, Edith J. *How Chopin Played (Notes of A. J. Hipkins)*. London: J. M. Dent, 1937

Hofmann, Josef. *Piano Playing with Piano Questions Answered by Josef Hofmann*. Philadelphia: Theodore Presser, 1920

Homans, Jennifer. *Apollo's Angels: A History of Ballet*. London: Granta, 2010

Hoover, Marjorie L. *Meyerhold and His Set Designers*. New York: Peter Lang, 1988

Horlacher, Gretchen. 'Sketches and Superimposition in Stravinsky's *Symphony of Psalms*'. *Mitteilungen der Paul Sacher Stiftung* **12** (April 1999), 22–6

Hullah, Annette. *Theodore Leschetizky*. London: John Lane; The Bodley Head, 1906

Hyde, Martha M. 'Stravinsky's Neoclassicism'. In *The Cambridge Companion to Stravinsky*, ed. Jonathan Cross. Cambridge: Cambridge University Press, 2003, pp. 98–136

Ingarden, R. *The Work of Music and The Problem of Its Identity* (1928), trans. A. Czerniawski, ed. J. G. Harrell (Berkeley; Los Angeles: University of California Press, 1986

Iwaszkiewicz, Jarosław. *Wiadomosci literackie (Warsawa)* 46 (1924). In Viktor Varunts, *Igor Stravinskiy: Publitsist i sobesednik*. Moscow: Sovetskiy Kompozitor, 1988

Jameson, Frederic. *Postmodernism; or, The Cultural Logic of Late Capitalism*. London: Verso, 1991

Jorgensen, H. 'Student Learning in Higher Instrumental Education: Who Is Responsible?'. *British Journal of Music Education* **17**.1 (2000), 67–77

Joseph, Charles M. *Stravinsky and Balanchine: A Journey of Invention*. New Haven;
London: Yale University Press, 2002
Stravinsky and the Piano. Ann Arbor: UMI Research Press, 1983
Stravinsky Inside Out. New Haven; London: Yale University Press, 2001
Stravinsky Remembered. New Haven; London: Yale University Press, 2001
'Stravinsky's Piano Scherzo (1902) in Perspective: A New Starting Point'. *Musical
Quarterly* **67**.1 (January 1981), 82–93

Kashperova, Leokadiya Aleksandrovna. 'Vospominaniya'. In *Muzïkal'noye nasledstvo: Sborniki po Istorii Muzïkal'noi Kul'tury SSSR*, Vol. II, Part II, ed. M. P.
Alekseyev. Moscow: Muzïka, 1962, pp. 135–68

Kentner, Louis. *Piano*. London: Macdonald and Jane's, 1976

Kerman, Joseph. *Contemplating Music: Challenges to Musicology*. Cambridge, MA:
Harvard University Press, 1985
'How We Got into Analysis, and How to Get Out'. *Critical Inquiry* 7.2 (1980),
311–31

Kermode, Frank. *Pleasing Myself: From Beowulf to Philip Roth*. London: Penguin,
2001

Koechlin, Charles. 'Le "Retour à Bach"'. *La Revue musicale* **8**.1 (November 1926),
1–2

Köhler, Karl-Heinz. 'Felix Mendelssohn(-Bartholdy)'. In *The New Grove Dictionary of
Music and Musicians*, 20 vols., Vol. XII, ed. Stanley Sadie. London: Macmillan,
1980, pp. 134–59

Kramer, Jonathan D. 'Discontinuity and Proportion in the Music of Stravinsky'.
In *Confronting Stravinsky: Man, Musician and Modernist*, ed. Jann Pasler.
Berkeley: University of California Press, 1986, pp. 174–94

Kundera, Milan. *Testaments Betrayed*, trans. Linda Asher. New York: HarperCollins,
1995

Kunin, Josif Filippowitsch. *Nikolai Andrejewitsch Rimski-Korsakow*. Berlin: Verlag
Neue Musik Berlin, 1981

Kutateladze, L. and A. Gozenpude (eds.). *F. Stravinskiy: Stat'i, pis'ma, vospominaniya*.
Leningrad: Muzïka, 1972

Leitch, Vincent B. (ed.). *The Norton Anthology of Theory and Criticism*. New York:
W. W. Norton, 2001

Lenz, Wilhelm von. *The Great Piano Virtuosos of Our Time from Personal Acquaintance*,
trans. Madeleine R. Baker. New York: Da Capo Press, 1973 [1899]

Levinski, Alexei. *Meyerhold's Biomechanics: A Workshop*. Archive no. 10 (videotape). Exeter: Arts Documentation Unit, 1997

Lhevinne, Josef. 'Good Tone Is Born in the Player's Mind', transcribed by Harriette
Brower. *The Musician* 28.7 (July 1923), 7

Lourié, Arthur-Vincent. 'La Sonate pour piano de Strawinsky'. *La Revue musicale*
6 (1925), 100–4

McAllister, Rita. 'Sergey (Sergeyevich) Prokofiev'. In *The New Grove Dictionary of
Music and Musicians*, 20 vols., Vol. XV, ed. Stanley Sadie. London: Macmillan,
1980, pp. 288–301

MacDonald, Malcolm. 'Preface' to Igor Stravinsky, Pétrouchka: *Revised 1947 Version*. London: Boosey & Hawkes, 1997, p. v

McGraw, Cameron. *Piano Duet Repertoire*. Bloomington: Indiana University Press, 1981

Maguire, Robert A. and John E. Malmstad. 'Translators' Introduction' to Andrei Bely, *Petersburg* (1916), trans. Robert A. Maguire and John E. Malmstad. London: Penguin, 1978, pp. vii–xxi

Maritain, Jacques. *Art et scholastique*. Paris: Art Catholique, 1920

Mason, Francis. *I Remember Balanchine*. New York: Doubleday, 1991

Meierkhold, V. E. *Meyerhold on Theatre*, ed. and trans. Edward Braun. London: Methuen, 1969 [1913]

Perepiska 1896–1939. Moscow: Iskusstvo, 1976

Menuhin, Yehudi. *Unfinished Journey*. London: Future, 1976

Messing, Scott. *Neoclassicism in Music: From the Genesis of the Concept through the Schoenberg/Stravinsky Polemic*. Ann Arbor: UMI Research Press, 1988

Michelson, Kari. 'Thomas Tellefsen'. In *The New Grove Dictionary of Music and Musicians*, 29 vols., Vol. XXV, ed. Stanley Sadie. London: Macmillan, 2001, p. 244

Milhaud, Darius. 'Preface' to Igor Stravinsky, *Poetics of Music in the Form of Six Lessons*. London: Geoffrey Cumberlege; Oxford University Press, 1947, pp. v–vii

Mills, Janet. 'Working in Music: The Conservatoire Professor'. *British Journal of Music Education* **21**.2 (2004), 179–98

Moevs, Robert. 'Mannerism and Stylistic Consistency in Stravinsky'. In *Stravinsky (1882–1971): A Composers' Memorial*. Special double issue of *Perspectives of New Music* 9.2, 10.1 (1971), 92–103

Montagu-Nathan, M. *Rimsky-Korsakoff*. London: Constable, 1916

Moore, Jerrold Northrop. *Edward Elgar: A Creative Life*. Oxford: Oxford University Press, 1984

Museu Villa-Lobos. *Villa-Lobos, sua obra*. 2nd edn. Rio de Janeiro: MEC/DAC/ Museu Villa-Lobos, 1972

Myaskovsky, N. Ya. '*Petrushka*, Ballet by Igor Stravinsky', *Music* **59** (14 January 1912), 72–5

Sobraniye materialov, 2nd edn., 2 vols. Moscow: Muzïka, 1964

Nestyev, Israel V. *Prokofiev*, trans. Florence Jonas. Stanford: Stanford University Press, 1960

Neuhaus, Heinrich. *The Art of Piano Playing*, trans. K. A. Leibovitch. London: Barrie & Jenkins, 1973

Newcomb, Ethel. *Leschetizky as I Knew Him*. New York: Da Capo Press, 1967 [1921]

Ockleford, Adam. 'Relating Musical Structure and Content to Aesthetic Response: A Model and Analysis of Beethoven's Piano Sonata Op. 110'. *Journal of the Royal Musical Association* **130**.1 (2005), 74–118

Oliver, Michael. *Igor Stravinsky*. London: Phaidon, 1995

Ortega y Gasset, José. *The Dehumanization of Art*, trans. Helene Weyl. Princeton: Princeton University Press, 1968

Paddison, Max. *Adorno, Modernism and Mass Culture: Essays on Critical Theory and Music*. London: Kahn & Averill, 2004

   Adorno's Aesthetic of Music. Cambridge: Cambridge University Press, 1993

   'Stravinsky as Devil: Adorno's Three Critiques'. In *The Cambridge Companion to Stravinsky*, ed. Jonathan Cross. Cambridge: Cambridge University Press, 2003, pp. 192–202

Partch, Harry. *Bitter Music: Collected Journals, Essays, Introductions and Librettos*, ed. Thomas McGeary. Urbana; Chicago: University of Illinois Press, 2000

Pasler, Jann (ed.). *Confronting Stravinsky: Man, Musician, and Modernist*. Berkeley: University of California Press, 1986

Paulson, Ronald. *Hogarth's Graphic Works*, 2 vols. New Haven; London: Yale University Press, 1970

Perlis, Vivian and Libby Van Cleve. *Composers' Voices from Ives to Ellington: An Oral History of American Music*. New Haven; London: Yale University Press, 2005

Philip, Robert. 'Pianists on Record in the Early Twentieth Century'. In *The Cambridge Companion to the Piano*, ed. David Rowland. Cambridge: Cambridge University Press, 1998, pp. 75–95

Philipp, Isidor. *Complete School of Technic for the Piano*. Philadelphia: Theodore Presser, 1908

Piston, Walter. *Orchestration*. London: Victor Gollancz, 1973

Pitches, Jonathan. *Meyerhold*. London: Routledge, 2003

Pleyel, Ignaz and Jan Ladislav Dussek. *Méthode pour le pianoforte*. Paris: Pleyel, 1797

Potochka, comtesse Angèle. *Theodore Leschetizky: An Intimate Study of the Man and the Musician*, trans. Geneviève Seymour Lincoln. New York: Century, 1903

Prentner, Marie. *The Leschetizky Method*, trans. M. De Kendler and A. Maddock. London: J. Curwen & Sons, 1903

Prokofiev, S. S. *Autobiography, Articles, Reminiscences*, ed. S. Shlifstein, trans. Rose Prokofieva. Moscow: Foreign Languages Publishing House, n.d. [*c.* 1954]

Pushkin, Aleksandr. *Eugene Onegin: A Novel in Verse*, trans. Vladimir Nabokov (1956), 2 vols., Vol. II. *Commentary and Index*. Princeton: Princeton University Press, 1990

Rayfield, Donald with Jeremy Hicks, Olga Makarova and Anna Pilkington (eds.). *The Garnett Book of Russian Verse: A Treasury of Russian Poets from 1730 to 1996*. London: Garnett Press, 2000

Reed, John. *Ten Days that Shook the World*. London: Penguin, 1977 [1919]

Rimsky-Korsakov, Andrey. 'Chronicle of N. A. Rimsky-Korsakov's Life during the Period Not Included in *My Musical Life* (September 1906–June 1908)'. In N. A. Rimsky-Korsakov, *My Musical Life*, ed. Carl Van Vechten, trans. Judah A. Joffe. London; Boston, MA: Faber and Faber, 1989 [1923], pp. 425–61

Rimsky-Korsakov, N. A. *My Musical Life*, ed. Carl Van Vechten, trans. Judah A. Joffe. London; Boston, MA: Faber and Faber, 1989 [1923]

Practical Manual of Harmony, trans. from the 12th Russian edn. by Joseph Achron, ed. Nicholas Hopkins. New York: Carl Fischer, 2005

Principles of Orchestration, ed. Maximilian Steinberg, trans. Edward Agate. New York: Dover, 1964 [1922]

Ritterman, Janet. 'On Teaching Performance'. In *Musical Performance: A Guide to Understanding*, ed. John Rink. Cambridge: Cambridge University Press, 2002, pp. 75–88

Rogers, Lynne. 'Varied Repetition and Stravinsky's Compositional Process'. *Mitteilungen der Paul Sacher Stiftung* 7 (April 1994), 22–6

Rosenblum, Sandra P. *Performance Practices in Classic Piano Music: Their Principles and Applications*. Bloomington: Indiana University Press, 1988

Rosenstiel, Leonie. *Nadia Boulanger: A Life in Music*. New York: W. W. Norton, 1982

Rubinstein, Arthur. *My Many Years*. New York: Knopf, 1980

Rudnitsky, Konstantin. *Meyerhold the Director*, trans. George Petrov. Ann Arbor: Ardis, 1981

Sachs, Harvey. *Arthur Rubinstein: A Life*. London: Phoenix, 1997

Safonov, Vassily. *New Formula for the Piano Teacher and the Piano Student*, English edn. London: J. & W. Chester, 1915

Said, Edward W. *On Late Style: Music and Literature against the Grain*. London: Bloomsbury, 2007

Reflections on Exile and Other Essays. Cambridge, MA: Harvard University Press, 2003

Samson, Jim (ed.). *The Cambridge History of Nineteenth-Century Music*. Cambridge: Cambridge University Press, 2001

Chopin. Oxford: Oxford University Press, 1996

Sankt Peterburgskaya Konservatoriya. *Dokumentï i Materialï*, Vol. I. St. Petersburg: Forteks, 2002

Sargeant, Winthrop. 'The Leaves of a Tree', *The New Yorker* 38.47 (12 January 1963)

Schaeffner, André. *Strawinsky*. Paris: Les Editions Rieder, 1931

Scheijen, Sjeng. *Diaghilev: A Life*, trans. Jane Hedley-Prole and S. J. Leinbach. London: Profile, 2009

Schenker, Heinrich. *The Art of Performance*, ed. Heribert Esser, trans. Irene Schreier Scott. Oxford: Oxford University Press, 2000

Scherliess, Volker. '"Torniamo all'antico e sarà un progresso": Creative Longing in Music'. In *Canto d'Amore: Classicism in Modern Art and Music 1914–1935*, ed. Gottfried Boehm, Ulrich Mosch and Katharina Schmidt. Basel: Kunstmuseum Basel; Paul Sacher Foundation, Basel, 1996, pp. 39–62

Schloezer, Boris de. 'Chronique musicale'. *La Nouvelle Revue française* **178** (1 July 1928), 104–8

Schmidt, Paul (ed.). *Meyerhold at Work*. Austin: University of Texas Press, 1980

Schnabel, Arthur. *My Life and Music*. Gerrard's Cross: Colin Smythe, 1970

Scholes, Robert. *Structuralism in Literature: An Introduction*. New Haven: Yale University Press, 1974

Schonberg, H. C. *The Great Pianists*. London: Victor Gollancz, 1963

Shattuck, Roger. 'The Devil's Dance: Stravinsky's Corporal Imagination'. In *Confronting Stravinsky: Man, Musician, and Modernist*, ed. Jann Pasler. Berkeley: University of California Press, 1986, pp. 82–8

Silver, Kenneth. *Esprit de corps*. Princeton: Princeton University Press, 1989

Sloboda, John A. *The Musical Mind: The Cognitive Psychology of Music*. Oxford: Clarendon Press, 1985

Small, Christopher. *Musicking: The Meanings of Performing and Listening*. Middletown, CT: Wesleyan University Press, 1998

Smirnov, Valeriy. *Tvorcheskoye formirovaniye I. F. Stravinskovo*. Leningrad: Muzïka, 1970

Souritz, Elizabeth. 'The Young Balanchine in Russia'. *Ballet Review* **18**.2 (Summer 1990), 67–8

Souvtchinsky, Pierre. *Un siècle de musique russe (1830–1930)*. Arles: Actes Sud; Association Pierre Souvtchinsky, 2004

Steinberg, Maximilian. 'Editor's Preface' (1912) to Nikolay Rimsky-Korsakov, *Principles of Orchestration* (1922), ed. Maximilian Steinberg, trans. Edward Agate. New York: Dover, 1964, pp. vii–xii

Straus, Joseph N. *Remaking the Past: Musical Modernism and the Influence of the Tonal Tradition*. Cambridge, MA: Harvard University Press, 1990

'Stravinsky the Serialist'. In *The Cambridge Companion to Stravinsky*, ed. Jonathan Cross. Cambridge: Cambridge University Press, 2003, pp. 149–74

Stravinsky's Late Music. Cambridge: Cambridge University Press, 2001

Stravinsky, Igor. *An Autobiography*. New York: W. W. Norton, 1936

An Autobiography (1903–1934). London; New York: Marion Boyars, 1990

'Ce que j'ai voulu exprimer dans *Le Sacre du printemps*'. *Montjoie!* 8 (29 May 1913). Reproduced in *Igor Stravinsky: Le Sacre du printemps. Dossier de presse*, ed. François Lesure. Geneva: Editions Minkoff, 1980, pp. 13–15

Chronicle of My Life. London: Victor Gollancz, 1936

Chroniques de ma vie. Paris: Editions Denoël, 1962

'The Composer's View'. In Paul Griffiths, *Igor Stravinsky: The Rake's Progress*. Cambridge Opera Handbooks. Cambridge: Cambridge University Press, 1982, pp. 2–4

'Foreword' to Edward E. Lowinsky, *Tonality and Atonality in Sixteenth-Century Music*. New York: Da Capo Press, 1961, pp. vii–ix

'Interview avec Serge Moreux de L'Intransigent pour la Radiodiffusion, Paris, 24 December 1938'. In Eric Walter White, *Stravinsky: The Composer and His Works*. London: Faber and Faber, 1966, Appendix A/7, pp. 585–7

'Love Music!', trans. Sarah S. White. In Eric Walter White, *Stravinsky: The Composer and His Works*. London: Faber and Faber, 1966, Appendix A9, pp. 591–2

Poetics of Music in the Form of Six Lessons, trans. Arthur Knodel and Ingold Dahl. New York: Vintage, 1956 [1947]

Poétique musicale sous forme de six leçons, ed. Myriam Soumagnac. Paris: Harmonique Flammarion, 2000

'Pushkin: Poetry and Music', trans. Gregory Golubeff (1940). In Eric Walter White, *Stravinsky: The Composer and His Works*. London: Faber and Faber, 1966, Appendix A8, pp. 588–91

'Quelques confidences sur la musique'. Conférence de M. Igor Starwinsky faite le 21 Novembre 1935. In Eric Walter White, *Stravinsky: The Composer and His Works*. London: Faber and Faber, 1966, Appendix A6, pp. 581–5

'Quelques mots de mes dernières oeuvres'. *Muzyka* **1**.1 (1924), 15–17

The Rite of Spring: Sketches 1911–1913. London: Boosey & Hawkes, 1969

'The Sleeping Beauty', trans. Edwin Evans. In Eric Walter White, *Stravinsky: The Composer and His Works*. London: Faber and Faber, 1966, Appendix A1, pp. 573–4

'Some Ideas about My *Octuor*'. *The Arts* (January 1924). In Eric Walter White, *Stravinsky: The Composer and His Works*. London: Faber and Faber, 1966, Appendix A2, pp. 574–7

Strawinsky: Sein Nachlass, sein Bild. Basel: Kunstmuseum Basel; Paul Sacher Stiftung, 1984

Stravinsky, Igor and Robert Craft. *Conversations with Igor Stravinsky*. London: Faber and Faber, 1979

Dialogues. Berkeley and Los Angeles: University of California Press, 1982

Dialogues and a Diary. London: Faber and Faber, 1968

Expositions and Developments. London: Faber and Faber, 1962

Memories and Commentaries. London: Faber and Faber, 1960

Themes and Conclusions. London: Faber and Faber, 1972

Themes and Episodes. New York: Knopf, 1966

Stravinsky, Vera and Robert Craft. *Stravinsky in Pictures and Documents*. New York: Simon and Schuster, 1978

Strawinsky, Theodore. *Catherine and Igor Stravinsky: A Family Album*. London: Boosey & Hawkes, 1973

Le Message d'Igor Strawinsky. Lausanne: Librairie F. Rouge, 1948

Taneyev, Sergey Ivanovich. *Invertible Counterpoint in the Strict Style*. Wellesley, MA: Branden, 1962

Podvizhnoy kontrapunkt strogovo pis'ma. Leipzig and Moscow, 1909

Ucheniye o kanone, ed. V. M. Belyayev. Moscow, 1929

Tansman, Alexandre. *Igor Stravinsky: The Man and His Music*, trans. T. and C. Bleefield. New York: Putnam, 1949

Tappolet, Claude (ed.). *Correspondance Ansermet–Strawinsky (1914–1967)*, 3 vols., Vol. II. Geneva: Georg, 1991

Taruskin, Richard. 'Back to Whom? Neoclassicism as Ideology'. *19ᵗʰ-Century Music* **16**.3 (1993), 286–302

Defining Russia Musically. Princeton: Princeton University Press, 1997

On Russian Music. Berkeley; Los Angeles; London: University of California Press, 2009

The Oxford History of Western Music, 5 vols., Vol. IV. New York: Oxford University Press, 2005

'Revising Revision'. *Journal of the American Musicological Society* **46**.1 (Spring 1993), 114–38

'Russian Folk Melodies in "The Rite of Spring"'. *Journal of the American Musicological Society* **33**.3 (1980), 501–34 (p. 502)

Stravinsky and the Russian Traditions: A Biography of the Works through Mavra. Oxford: Oxford University Press, 1996

'Stravinsky and Us'. In *The Cambridge Companion to Stravinsky*, ed. Jonathan Cross. Cambridge: Cambridge University Press, 2003, pp. 260–84

Timbrell, Charles. *French Pianism: A Historical Perspective*. Portland, OR: Amadeus Press, 1999

Tucker, Susannah. 'Stravinsky and His Sketches: The Composing of *Agon* and Other Serial Works of the 1950s'. D.Phil. dissertation. University of Oxford, 1992

Turgenev, Ivan. *Fathers and Sons*, trans. Rosemary Edmonds. London: Penguin, 1975, *Rudin*, trans. Richard Freeborn. London: Penguin, 1975

Sketches from a Hunter's Album, trans. Richard Freeborn. London: Penguin, 1990

Van den Toorn, Pieter C. *The Music of Igor Stravinsky*. New Haven: Yale University Press, 1983

Varunts, Viktor (ed.). *I. F. Stravinskiy: Perepiska s russkimi korrespondentami. Materialï k biographi*. 3 vols., Vol. I. Moscow: Sovyetskiy Kompozitor, 1998 [1977]

Varunts, Viktor. *Igor Stravinskiy: Publitsist i Sobesednik*. Moscow: Sovyetskiy Kompozitor, 1988

'Strawinsky protestiert …'. *Mitteilungen der Paul Sacher Stiftung* **6** (March 1993), 35–7

Vlad, Roman. *Stravinsky*, trans. Frederic Fuller. Oxford: Oxford University Press, 1960

Volkov, Simon. *Balanchine's Tchaikovsky*. London; Boston, MA: Faber and Faber, 1985

von Riemann, Oskar. *Rachmaninoff's Recollections as Told to Oskar von Riemann*. London: George Allen & Unwin, 1934

Walsh, Stephen. *Stravinsky: A Creative Spring. Russia and France 1882–1934*. London: Pimlico, 2002

Stravinsky: Oedipus Rex. Cambridge: Cambridge University Press, 1993

Stravinsky: The Second Exile. France and America 1934–1971. London: Jonathan Cape, 2006

Walzer, Pierre-Olivier (ed.). *Charles-Albert Cingria: Correspondance avec Igor Strawinsky*. Lausanne: Editions L'Age d'Homme, 2001

Warrack, John. 'Ludwig Deppe'. In *The New Grove Dictionary of Music and Musicians*, 20 vols., Vol. V, ed. Stanley Sadie. London: Macmillan, 1980, p. 380

Watkins, Glenn. *Pyramids at the Louvre: Music, Culture, and Collage from Stravinsky to the Postmodernists*. Cambridge, MA: Belknap Press, 1994

White, Eric Walter. *Stravinsky: A Critical Survey*. London: John Lehmann, 1947

Stravinsky's Sacrifice to Apollo. London: Leonard and Virginia Woolf, 1930

Stravinsky: The Composer and His Works. London; Boston, MA: Faber and Faber, 1966

Whitehead, A. N. *The Organisation of Thought.* London: Williams and Northgate, 1917

Whittall, Arnold. *Romantic Music.* London: Thames and Hudson, 1987

Williams, Alastair. *Constructing Musicology.* Aldershot; Burlington: Ashgate, 2001

Yastrebtsev, V. V. *Reminiscences of Rimsky-Korsakov,* abridged and trans. F. Jonas. New York: Columbia University Press, 1985

   Rimsky-Korsakov: Vospominanya, 1886–1908, 2 vols., ed. A. V. Ossovsky. Leningrad: Musgiz, 1959–60

Zamyatin, Yevgeny Ivanovich. *We,* trans. Clarence Brown. London: Penguin, 1993

Index

Abraham, Gerald, 86
  on Rimsky-Korsakov, 288n174
Accordgruppe, 111, 161, 163–5
  and bell 'changes', 168–70
  and pedal-notes, 199–200
  as compositional material, 166–8
  in *Symphony of Psalms*, 192, 199–200
Adams, John
  and 'personalisation', 119
  Grand Pianola Music, 285n136
Adorno, Theodor
  on neoclassicism, 103, 254
  'Vers une musique informelle', 274n189
Agawu, Kofi, 108, 140, 173
Akimenko, Fyodor Stepanovych, 260n10
  as Stravinsky's teacher, 15, 29
  piano music, 32
Alberti bass, 50, 83
Albright, Daniel, 247
Andriessen, Louis, 106–7
  on Stravinsky and Bach, 121
  on Stravinsky's style, 101
  on *Symphony of Psalms*, 302n195
Ansermet, Ernest
  correspondence with Stravinsky, 120
  on *Symphony of Psalms*, 203–4, 303n199
  on *Three Pieces for String Quartet*, 171
arpeggios, as compositional material,
  168–70
Arts, The, 273n160
Asaf'yev, Boris
  on *Five Easy Pieces*, 278n21
  on Skryabin, 38
  on *Three Easy Pieces*, 278n21
Auden, Wystan Hugh, 235
automata, 171, 172

Babbitt, Milton, 246
  on Stravinsky as serialist, 239
  on Stravinsky's neoclassicism, 94
'Bach', 119, 121
  and counterpoint, 119
  and 'impersonal' style, 37
  and neoclassicism, 13
  and objectivity, 116

as exemplar of good compositional practice,
  119
as Stravinsky's creation, 121
Bach, Johann Sebastian
  and Vivaldi, 121
  B minor Fugue, 1
  B minor Mass, 288n165
  Clavierübung pt.4 '*Goldberg Variations*',
    119, 124
  piano transcriptions of, 50
  Stravinsky arrangements of, 1–3, 260n3,
    261n13
  'Three-Part Inventions': Sinfonia no. 1 in C,
    BWV787, 121, 302n185
  Wohltemperierte Klavier, Das, 1, 2, 3, 119, 249
Balakirev, Mily
  and Glinka, 126
  B♭ minor Sonata, 18
  on Bach, 287n160
  on Chopin, 287n160
  on Mendelssohn, 287n160
Balanchine, George, 185–9
  as pianist, 299n143
  'noodling', 291n35
  on Diagilev, 299n141
Banchieri, Adriano,
  'Canzone italiana per organo', 208, 231
Barba, Eugenio
  Meyerhold, *Throwing the Stone*, 309n21
Bartók, Béla
  Concerto for Orchestra, 242
  Fifth String Quartet, 242
  Music for Strings, Percussion and Celesta,
    242
  night music, 242
bass-treble separation, 22–3, 50
bassoons, 225, 226
Baudelaire, Charles Pierre, 113, 247
Beethoven, Ludwig van
  compositional methods, 74
  fugues, 123
  piano fingerings, 252, 309n14
  Piano Sonata op. 110, 123, 286n151
  Quartet in E♭-flat major op. 127, 126
  Symphony no. 9, 119

bell 'changes', 168–70, 294n81
bell-figuration, 47–9
Bellamann, Henry, 173–4
Bely, Andrei, 11
Belyayev, V. M., 128
Berio, Luciano, 'Adieu', 3, 249
Berlin, Isaiah, 310n30
Bie, Oscar, 22
bïlina, 212, 304n25
Bloom, Harold, 122
Blumenfeld, Felix, 42
Boehm, Gottfried, 99–100
Bohlman, Philip V., 10, 56
Borge, Victor, 28
Borodin, Aleksandr Porfiryevich,
    Tarantella, 49
Boulanger, Nadia, 174, 220
Boulanger, Raissa, 174
bowing (as Russian gesture of respect), 128,
    288n178
Brée, Malwine, The Groundwork of the
    Leschetizky Method, 156, 159, 161–3, 164
Britten, Benjamin, War Requiem, 124
Brodsky, Joseph, 263n9
Bülow, Hans von, 22
Busoni, Ferruccio, 120
    Sechs Stücke zur Pflege des
    polyphonischen Spiels 120
Butler, Christopher, on stylistic variation, 83

Calame, Christophe, on Cingria, Pétrarque,
    229
Camp, John, 295n81
Canille, Théodore, 126
Carter, Elliott, 124
Casadesus, Gaby, 179, 180
celesta, 64
Chaliapin, Fyodor Ivanovich, on
    Rimsky-Korsakov, 289n181
change ringing, see bell 'changes'
children, music for, 78, 84–7
Chopin, Frédéric, 49
    and Bach, 109
    and Clementi's Introduction, 160
    and the French piano school, 180
    Etudes opp. 10 and 25, 109
    Nocturne in E♭, op. 9 No.2, 23
    technique, 20
chord playing, 22–3, 158, 161–8
Cibiel, Dominique, 260n1
cimbalom, 67, 95
Cingria, Charles-Albert, see also Pétrarque 94,
    205–6, 303n2

on Symphony of Psalms, 203
Clementi, Muzio
    Introduction to the Art of Playing on the
    Piano Forte, 160
    scale exercises, 160–1
Coleridge, Samuel Taylor, 93
    'Lecture on Poetry', 279n35
    Lyrical Ballads, with Pastoral and Other
    Poems, 279n34
Copland, Aaron, 99
Cortot, Alfred, 180
    as teacher, 178, 180
    on Stravinsky's music, 25, 268n85
counterpoint, 1–4, 119–25
Craft, Robert 24–5, 111, 124, 175, 240, 305n37
    on Capriccio, 297n100
    on Isidor Philipp, 175
    on Stravinsky and Skryabin, 271n132
    on Stravinsky's Bach arrangements, 1
    on Stravinsky's fingerings, 131
    on Stravinsky's keyboard skills, 290n11,
    297n100
    on Stravinsky's memoirs, 111, 264n30
    on Stravinsky's Russianness, 10
    on The Rite of Spring, 77
    on Three Easy Pieces, 172
Cross, Jonathan
    'Composing with Stravinsky', 302n195
    on Perséphone, 101
    on Symphonies d'instruments à vent, 61
    'Stravinsky's theatres', 281n69
Cui, César, 25, 278n24
Currier, T. P., 298n133
Czerny, Carl
    and Capriccio, 176
    and pedal points, 200
    edition of Das Wohltemperiertes
    Klavier, 249
    40 Daily Exercises, 108, 138, 147–9, 301n181
    Kunst der Fingerfertigkeit, Die, 79, 80,
    153–5
    Stravinsky's regard for, 79

Dahlhaus, Carl, 99
    on reception history, 282n71
Dannreuther, Edward, 109, 283n89
Dargomïzhky, Aleksandr Sergeyevich
    Slavyanskaya tarantella, 25, 26, 47–9, 86
Darré, Jeanne-Marie, 179
Debussy, Claude, 174, 246
    Images pour piano, 246
    on Petrushka, 61
defamiliarization, 93–4

Dehn, Siegfried, 270n112
Diaghilev, Sergey Pavlovich
  and Pergolesi, 82
  and *The Sleeping Beauty*, 264n25
  at Landowska concert, 273n158
  on St Petersburg, 11
diminution, simultaneous, 198–9
Dostoyevsky, Fyodor Mikhailovich
  Crime and Punishment, 65, 128
  on St Petersburg, 55
double-bass, 96
Dreyfus, Laurence, 298n129
drobnost' (sum-of-parts), 170
du Pré, Hilary and Piers, 299n140
Dushkin, Samuel, 4, 205, 220, 256
Dussek, Jan Ladislav, 160
Dyachkova, L. S., 16, 18

Eddington, Sir Arthur Stanley, 187
Edition Russe de Musique, 70, 134
eighteenth-century music
  imitation of, 100–1, 257
  role of keyboard instruments, 99
  Romantics' view of, 100–1
  transcriptions, 100–1
Eikhenbaum, Boris, 280n37
Einheit, 120
Eisrich, Karl, 126
émigrés, Russian, 51
enculturation, 17, 104, 253–4, 265n44
Essipova, Annette, 158, 161
Etude (magazine), 174, 292n54
études, artistic merit, 108–9, 255
Evans, Edwin, 168, 294n79
Evenings of Contemporary Music, 32
expressionism, 99

Farrell, Suzanne, on Balanchine, 187
Ferguson, Howard, on studies, 109
Figes, Orlando
  on Russian émigrés, 51
  on *The Rite of Spring*, 95
Findreizen, N. F., 276n223
Formalist theory, *see* Russian Formalism
Foss, Lukas
  as Vengerova pupil, 292n48
  on *Histoire du Soldat*, 61, 274n187
Franco-American Conservatory
    (Fontainebleau), 174
fugue
  and Beethoven, 123
  as exemplar of musical form, 119–20, 121–2

objectivity of, 119
Stravinsky's appreciation of, 2

George, Stefan, 131
Gerig, Reginald R.
  on Leschetizky's method, 159
  on Rubinstein, 22
  on Russian pianists, 161
Gide, André, 255
  on classicism, 66
Glazunov, Aleksandr Konstantinovich
  as pupil of Rimsky-Korsakov, 127
  piano sonatas, 18, 32
  Raymonda, 27
Glebov, Igor, *see* Asaf'yev, Boris
Glinka, Mikhail Ivanovich
  Jota Aragonesa, La, 287n163
  keyboard fugues, 30, 270n112
  Life for the Tsar, A, 14, 25, 128
  Prince Kholmsky, 126, 287n162
  Recuerdos de Castilla, 287n163
  Ruslan and Lyudmila, 25, 30, 126
  Spanish Overtures, 128, 287n163,
  studies with Siegfried Dehn, 270n112
Gloag, Kenneth, on *The Rite of Spring*, 129
glockenspiel, 64
Gnesin, M. F., on Rimsky-Korsakov, 289n185
Goddard, Scott
  review of *An Autobiography*, 118, 248
Gogol, Nikolay Vasilievich, 1, 262n4
Goncharov, Ivan, 250
Goncharova, Natalia, 95
Gorodetsky, Sergey Mitrofanovich, 47
Goubault, Christian
  on *Symphony in Three Movements*, 228
  on *The Rite of Spring*, 70
Gozenpude, A., 25
Grainger, Percy Aldridge
  piano notation, 267n78
  Rosenkavalier Ramble, 268n78
Grandes sonates, 32
Grieg, Edvard, *Peer Gynt*, 47
Griffiths, Graham, 'Fingering as
    Compositional Process: Stravinsky's
    Sonata Sketchbook Revisited', 289n1
Griffiths, Paul, on *The Rake's Progress*, 234
grotesk, 253

habitualization, 93, 94
Hamilton, Kenneth
  on Romantic piano tone, 268n78
  on teacher-pupil relationships, 22–3, 155

hand position, 158–9
harmonium, in *Les Noces*, 95
harp, 57
  and piano, 66, 244
  in *Symphony in Three Movements*, 220, 230
harpsichord, in *The Rake's Progress*, 234–5, 236
Harris, Roy, on Stravinsky and Czerny, 308n6
Henriot-Schweitzer, Nicole, on Long, 179
Henselt, Adolph von
  and Chopin, 21
  teaching career, 156
  technique, 20, 21
Herman, Woody, 225
Herzen, Alexander Ivanovich
  on St Petersburg, 13
  on Turgenev, 121, 257
  on youth, 9
Hill, Peter, 268n83
Hipkins, Alfred, on Henselt, 21
Hipkins, Edith J., 267n64
Hogarth, William, and the 'industrious apprentice', 203–4
Horlacher, Gretchen, 190
Horowitz, Vladimir, 91
Horsley, Sophie, 160, 293n60
Horsley, William, 160
Hughes, Edwin, interview with Leschetizky, 159, 292n54
hurdy-gurdy, in *Petrushka*, 67
Huxley, Aldous, *Point Counter Point*, 308n87
Hyde, Martha, 252

Igor Stravinsky plays Igor Stravinsky, 310n28
imitation, 254
improvisation, 152, 166
index-finger-over-thumb overlap, 78–80
intervals, in serial composition, 141–2
Iwaszkiewicz, Jarosław, 140, 262n28

Jakobson, Roman, 93, 280n37
Jameson, Frederic, 119
Joseph, Charles M.
  and 'tactile models', 193
  on accuracy of Stravinsky editions, 251
  on *Apollo*, 138
  on *Capriccio*, 138
  on Czerny's influence on Stravinsky, 145
  on Philipp's influence on Stravinsky, 5, 175–6
  on *Scherzo*, 29
  on Stravinsky and Balanchine, 138
  on Stravinsky's hands, 138

Stravinsky as 'piano composer', 190, 250
Joyce, James, 83
junge Klassizität, 120
Juslin, Patrik, on aesthetic theory, 287n152

Kalafati, Vasily Pavlovich
  as Stravinsky's teacher, 15, 29
  piano music, 32
Kallman, Chester, 235, 260n7
Kanille, F. A., *see* Canille, Théodore
kantele, 67, 212
Karatïgin, V. G., on Lyadov's *The Musical Snuffbox*, 272n154
Kashperova, Leokadiya Aleksandrovna
  and Rimsky-Korsakov, 266n56
  and Rubinstein, 18, 20, 155
  and Solovyov, 266n56
  and Wagner, 266n57
  as Stravinsky's teacher, 15, 16, 18, 24–5, 47, 104, 109, 166
  career, 18–19, 161
  'Recollections of Anton Grigor'yevich Rubinstein', 155
  Stravinsky's view of, 19–20, 24–5
Kermode, Frank, 129, 274n193
King, William, on Stravinsky's exercising, 188
Klemperer, Otto, 173, 174–5
Koechlin, Charles, 233
Konzertstück form, 65–6, 275
Koussevitsky, Sergei, and Stravinsky's soloist career, 91, 282n80
Kramer, Jonathan D., on *Agon*, 213
Krenek, Ernst, 241
Kukolnik, Nestor Vasilievich, 287n162
Kundera, Milan, 231, 256
Kutateladze, L., 25

Lamond, Frederick, 157
Landowska, Wanda, 50, 67, 273n158
Lateiner, Jacob, 158–9
Layonnet, Paul, 179–80
Lazare-Lévy, 180
legato and *staccato*, simultaneous, 39, 49, 50, 195–6
Lenz, Wilhelm von, 21
Leschetizky, Theodor, 18, 152, 155–70
  finger-development exercises, 113
  founds St Petersburg Conservatoire, 156
  on chord preparation, 160
  on hand position, 159, 160
  on Marie Prentner, 294n70

Leschetizky, Theodor (*cont.*)
   on tempo, 23
   on *The Groundwork of the Leschetizky
      Method*, 156, 293n65
   piano method, 47, 49, 110–11, 156–7, 199,
      298n133
   teaching method, 163
   technique, 23
Lhevinne, Josef, 156, 158, 161
Lhevinne, Rosina, 156, 161
   and chord visualization, 158
Lind, Jenny, 293n60
Liszt, Franz, 157
   piano transcriptions, 91
Long, Marguerite, 178–80, 259
Lourié, Arthur-Vincent, on the *Sonate pour
      piano*, 123
'low' art, 92–4
Lowinsky, Edward E., 261n15
Loyonnet, Paul
   as pupil of Philipp, 179
   as pupil of Sieveking, 179, 298n123
   on Leschetizky method, 297n123
Lyadov, Anatoly Konstantinovich, 127
   Canons on a Cantus Firmus, 261n11
   Chopsticks, Valse and Gigue, 278n24
   Fuga, 2
   fugal writing, 121, 126
   as model for counterpoint, 122
   Musical Snuffbox, The, 49
   Six Pieces, 30
   Three Canons, 261n11
   Twenty-four Canons, 2
lyricism, 206, 220

MacDonald, Malcolm, 66
Maguire, Robert, 11
Malmstad, John E., on St Petersburg, 11
Maritain, Jacques, 113, 120
Mason, Francis, 299n148
Massenet, Jules, 100
Mathias, Georges, 180
Mendelssohn-Bartholdy, Felix
   G minor Piano Concerto, 16, 24, 66
   Octet in E♭, 92
Messing, Scott, 120
   on neoclassicism, 6–7
   on *Sonate pour piano*, 286n140
Mey, L. A., 288n175
Meyerhold, V. E., 253, 254
Michelsen, Kari, 'Thomas Tellefsen', 293n60
Mills, Janet, 266n49, 299n140
Milstein, Nathan, 291

Miniature Essays, 262
modernism, in music, and neoclassicism,
      99–100
Moevs, Robert, 307n62
Moiseiwitsch, Benno, 161
Montagu-Nathan, M. 126
Morhange-Motchance, Marthe, on Cortot, 180
Mosch, Ulrich, 99–100, 261n22
   on toccata form, 305n27
Moscow
   and avant-garde art, 11
   as Russian city, 11
   rivalry with St Petersburg, 11–12
Moscow Linguistic Circle, 93
Mozart, Wolfgang Amadeus
   Gran partita K. 361, 92
   Musikalischer Spass, Ein, 28
   Nozze di Figaro, Le, 42
   Rondos K. 382 and K.386, 275n207
   wind serenades, 92
Mukařovský, Jan, 280n37
musical mobiles, 168, 171, 172
Musorgsky, Modest Petrovich, *Boris Godunov*,
      47
Myaskovsky, Nikolay Yakovlevich
   on *Petrushka*, 68–9
   on *The Firebird*, 40

Nabokov, Nicholas, 299n143
   and Stravinsky's Bach arrangements, 1
Nabokov, Vladimir, on Moscow, 263n11
neoclassicism
   and modernism, 99–100, 101
   and objectivity, 101
   national differences, 99, 100
nepodvizhnost', (immobility) 170–2
Neue Klassizität, 99
Neumann, Vitaly, on Vengerova, 158
Newcomb, Ethel, 293n57
Newmarch, Rosa, 277n16
Nijinska, Bronislava, 95
Nijinsky, Vaslav, 290n11
   training methods, 271n134
note tenue, 200
Nouvel, Walter, 111, 191

objectivity, 5, 8, 93, 101–7
   and Stravinsky's music, 103–5
   of fugue, 119
Ockleford, Adam, 123, 145, 287n152
orchestral piano, 62, 64–77
orchestration
   as 'exercise', 198

Rimsky-Korsakov's view, 56–61
Russian view of, 56
organ point, 30
in *Pastorale*, 51
Ortega y Gasset, José
and neoclassism, 101
and Stravinsky, 101
Ossovsky, A. V., 31
on Rakhmaninov, 30
ostinato, 45, 49, 86, 172

Paderewski, Ignacy Jan, 23, 161
pal'tserazvitiye, 110–18, 165–6, 172, 214–17,
    256, 285n135
in *Symphony of Psalms*, 190
Paraphrases on the Theme of 'Chopsticks',
    278n24
parody, 100, 281n65
Partch, Harry
eighteenth-century music, role of keyboard
    instruments, 99
Pasternak, Boris, 258
Pasternak, Leonid, 273n158
pastiche, 100
Paul Sacher Stiftung, 190, 261n22, 275n209,
    289n4
pedal-point ostinato, 47–9
in *The Faun and the Shepherdess*,
    47–9
pedal points
in *Scherzo*, 30
in *Symphony of Psalms*, 199–200, 201
in *The Faun and the Shepherdess*, 47
pedals, use of, 20, 50, 179
by Stravinsky, 20
in Russian school, 20–1
in *Two Melodies of Gorodetsky*, 49
Pergolesi, Giovanni Battista, 82
transcription by Thalberg, 100–1
Pétrarque, 205–6, 208, 229
Petrivki, 172, 296n93
Petrova, O. A., 15
Philip, Robert, 157
Philipp, Isidor, 49, 139, 173–85
accent displacement, 181–2
career, 296n97
*Complete School of Technic for the
    Pianoforte*, 4, 175, 182, 217, 261n22
Exercices pratiques, 181, 221–3
main publications, 296n97
pupils, 296n97
Rameau transcription in *L'Art pianistique*,
    100

piano
and harp, 66, 69
fingering: 'for musical purposes',
    251–2; gap widening, 161, 295n82;
    index-finger-over-thumb overlap, 78–80,
    193–5, 239; velocity, 160–1
grand versus upright, 64, 66–7
playing, 108–9; French school, 178–83;
    Romantic performance practice,
    23, 36; 'virtuoso', 22; recordings,
    157; transcriptions, 86–94; of
    eighteenth-century music, 100–1; status
    of, 91; of violin playing, 88
Picasso, Pablo, 83, 100
Piston, Walter, *Principles of Orchestration*, 64,
    279n30
Pleyel, Ignaz, *Méthode pour le pianoforte*, 160
polarity, 114
Prague Linguistic Circle, 93
Prentner, Marie,
Leschetizky Method, The, 156, 161, 163–5
progressive extension, in *Symphony of Psalms*,
    195
Prokofiev, Sergey Sergeyevich, 30
on *Sérénade en la*, 7
on *Sonate pour piano*, 6, 7
on Stravinsky as concert pianist, 294n76
Pushkin, Aleksandr Sergeyevich
and Stravinsky, 14
and *Tucha*, 41
Bronze Horseman, The, 11
on St Petersburg, 289n188
Prologue to *Ruslan and Lyudmila*,
    263n12
Trud ('The Work'), 260n1

Rakhmaninov, Sergey Vasilyevich
and counterpoint, 12, 264n22
Piano Concerto no. *4*, 35, 271n120
style of playing, 30
Ravel, Maurice Joseph, *Le Tombeau de
    Couperin*, 305n27
Reed, John, 288n178
rehearsing, as compositional process, 195
Reich, Steve, 106
Richter, Nikolay Ivanovich, 30
Riemann, Oskar von, 12
Rimsky-Korsakov, Andrey, 55
'Chronicle of N. A. Rimsky-Korsakov's
    Life during the Period Not Included in
    My Musical Life (September 1906–June
    1908)', 273n168
Rimsky-Korsakov, Nadezhda, 51

Rimsky-Korsakov, Nikolay Andreyevich
and other composers: Bach, 126, 128,
288n165; Balakirev, 126, 287n160;
Beethoven, 126, 280n51; Glinka, 14,
126, 128; Handel, 126; Schumann, 126;
Tchaikovsky, 126, 127, 128
life: and Kashperova, 19; as Stravinsky's
teacher, 4, 55–6; early musical life, 57;
last days, 273n168; on composition: and
counterpoint, 128; and eighteenth-century
music, 126; fugues, 121, 126; on
'compound timbre', 274n184; on
orchestral piano, 64–5; on orchestration,
56–61, 63, 96; on percussion instruments,
274n179; on stringed instruments, 96; on
Two Melodies of Gorodetsky, 47; on wind
instruments, 57, 58–60
style: academism, 127; affinities with
Stravinsky, 125–30; and classical myths,
128; and the gusli, 212; as internationalist,
13; as model for counterpoint, 122;
Russianness, 129
works: Christmas Eve, 19; Four 3-Part
Choruses for Male Voices, 288n166; Four
Variations and a Fughetta on the Theme of
a Russian Song, 288n166; Iz Gomera, 127–
8; Legend of the Invisible City of Kitezh,
The, 226–8; Maid of Pskov, The, 30; May
Night, The, 57; Nausicaa, 127; Paraphrases
on the Theme of 'Chopsticks', 86, 278n24;
Piano Quintet, 288n166; Sadko, 47, 212,
304n25; Servilia, 127, 288n174; Sextet
for Strings, 126; Six Choruses without
Accompaniment, 288n166; Six Fugues for
Piano op. 17, 288n166, 288n166; Three
Pieces for the Piano, 288n166; Tsar's Bride,
The, 127, 288n175; Two 3-part Choruses
for Women's Voices, 288n166
writings, speeches and interviews:
My Musical Life, 273n168; Practical
Manual of Harmony, 30; Principles of
Orchestration, 56, 57, 58, 63, 64, 97–6
Roerich, Nikolay Konstantinovitch, 212, 276n221
Rogers, Lynne, 190
Roland-Manuel, Alexis, 8, 111, 284n98
Rosenblum, Sandra P. 251–2
on Beethoven's piano fingerings, 309n14
on Clementi's piano fingerings, 309n14
on rubato, 34
Rosenstiel, Leonie, 174
rotational arrays, 241, 246
rubato, 39

agogic, 34
contrametric, 34
Rubinstein, Anton, 20–2, 152
and eighteenth-century music, 100
and rubato, 23
and Wagner, 266n57
at St Petersburg Conservatoire, 156
influence, 13
Suite for Piano, 100
Rubinstein, Arthur, 25, 268n86
Russian Formalism, 93–4
and Stravinsky's 'low' art, 93–4
and the author as cipher, 93
and unimportance of the art-object, 94

Sacher Foundation, see Paul Sacher Stiftung
Safonov, Vassily Ilyich, 156, 158, 161
St Petersburg, 55, 130
as cultural centre, 54–5
as non-Russian, 10–11
pianistic tradition, 155–6
rivalry with Moscow, 11–12, 273n165
Saint-Saëns, Camille, 174, 269n97
Sammlung Igor Strawinsky, 74, 275n209
see also Paul Sacher Stiftung
Samson, Jim
on Chopin études, 109
on musical education, 108
on parody, 281n65
on reception history, 282n72
Schaeffner, André, 40, 271n127, 271n133
on Four Studies, 38, 271n136,
Scheijen, Sjeng, 263n6
Schenker, Heinrich
on études, 140
Scherliess, Volker, 241
Schloezer, Boris de
on Concerto for Two Solo Pianos, 213, 214
on Concerto in E♭ ('Dumbarton Oaks'),
98, 213
on Symphonies of Wind Instruments 258
Schnabel, Artur 292n53
on Kashperova's teaching, 161
Schoenberg, Arnold, 94, 120
and Petrarch, 229
Five Piano Pieces op. 23, 141
Pierrot lunaire, 286n137
Serenade op. 24, 141, 229
String Quartet no. 2, 289n2
Suite for Piano op. 25, 141, 229
Scholes, Robert, 279n33
on Formalism, 93

Schönberger, Elmer, 101, 106–7, 271
  on Stravinsky and Bach, 121
Schubert, Franz
  Octet in F D.803, 92
  Quintet in C D.956, 92
Schulhoff, Julius, 160
Shattuck, Roger, 252
Shklovsky, Viktor, 93, 94, 280n37
Shvetsova-van-Eker, Olena, 163
Sieveking, Martinus, 179, 298n123
simplification, *see uproshcheniye*
Skryabin, Aleksandr, 38–9, 156
  and counterpoint, 264n22
  Etudes, 39
  Piano Sonata no. 3, 32
Sloboda, John
  theory of cognitive development, 17
Small, Christopher, 178
Smirnov, Valeriy 129
  on *Tarantella*, 25, 26–7, 268n87
Snyetkova, Aleksandra Petrovna, 15, 16–17,
  25–6
Society for the Study of Poetic Language
  (OPOJAZ), 93
Solovyov, Nikolay, and Kashperova, 19
Song of Bernadette, The 305n35
Souvtchinsky, Pierre, 111, 284n99
Spalding, Albert, 134
staccato and *legato*, simultaneous
  in *F# minor Sonata*, 35
  in *Four Studies*, 39
  in *Pastorale*, 50
  in *Sonate*, 195
  in *Symphony of Psalms*, 195–6
  in *Two Melodies of Gorodetsky*, 49
Stedman, Fabian 295n81
Steinberg, Maximilian, 58
Stockhausen, Karlheinz, *Klavierstücke*, 246
Straus, Joseph N
  on Stravinsky's memoirs, 111
  on Stravinsky's 'musical stutter', 202
  on Stravinsky's pianism, 240–1
  on Stravinsky's serialism, 285n135
Stravinsky, Fyodor Ignatyevich, 263n7
  bass roles, 41, 42–4
  death, 272n143
  role in Stravinsky's training, 25–6
Stravinsky, Igor Fyodorovich
  LIFE:
  and other composers: Bach, 2, 109, 121, 128;
    Britten, 124; Carter, Elliott, 124; Chopin,
    17; Czerny, 5, 79, 143–5; Debussy,

246; Glinka, 14, 128, 287n163; Lyadov,
  261n11, 288n167; Pergolesi, 82; Prokofiev,
  6–7, 30, 294n74; Rakhmaninov, 35;
  Rimsky-Korsakov, 13, 55–6, 97–8;
  Schoenberg, 120, 285n113; Taneyev, 12;
  Tchaikovsky, 12–13, 24, 98, 128, 207;
  Weber, 66; Webern, 299n138
and other musicians and colleagues:
  Balanchine, 186; Klemperer, 174–5;
  Rubinstein, Anton, 266n55
and the piano: and pianism, 254–6;
  arpeggiating modal chords, 107; as concert
  pianist, 4, 7, 153–4, 282n80, 297n101;
  finger drills, 28–9; on fingering, 80; piano
  colour, 98–9; piano practice, 4, 115–16,
  165–6
attitudes and beliefs: and Catholicism,
  302n195; and Orthodoxy, 62, 120, 202,
  252–3; and physical exercise, 188; attitude
  to the past, 118–19; Russianness, 9, 10,
  80–2, 95, 129, 189, 253; self-referentiality,
  256–7; compositional methods: and
  objectivity, 103–4, 153; bell 'changes',
  168–70; composing as craft, 5, 112–13,
  117–18, 203, 206–7; composition as
  a process, 27, 112, 116, 124–5, 239;
  compositional freedom, 113–14, 184;
  compositional processes, 27, 140;
  'compound timbres', 61; contrapuntalism,
  49, 99; counterpoint, 2–3, 119–24, 127,
  128, 250–1; diatonicism, 114–15; early
  improvisations, 26, 28, 29, 269n97; early
  neoclassical tendencies, 37, 39, 50–1;
  early working methods, 103–4; fingering
  as a compositional process, 131–40,
  152–3; fingering, as choreography,
  309n13; Hyde theory of imitation,
  254; improvisation, 152, 253, 255–6;
  Konzertstück form, 65–6; orchestral
  colour, 97, 98; *pal'tserazvitiye*, 114–19;
  rubato, 34; serial composition,
  141–2, 237–48, 285n135; Stravinsky as
  'piano composer', 4, 27–8, 190; tonal
  centring, 114, 115–17; transition to
  neoclassicism, 80–4; 'virtuoso' works,
  213–14; 'wrong' notes, 28; affinities with
  Rimsky-Korsakov, 128–9; birth, 10, 15;
  early life, 26; Iberia visit 1917, 287n163;
  schooling, 15; undergraduate life, 15;
on art and music: childrens' music,
  84–7, 92; classical myth, 214; dance, 188;
  'emotive force', 140; 'low-art' music, 77;

Stravinsky, Igor Fyodorovich (*cont.*)
and Meyerhold, V. E., 253–4; music for
'amateurs', 39; on art, 94, 112, 124; on
dramatic plots, 117; on music, 219, 233;
Spanish folk music, 307n82; on his own
music, 102; *Movements for Piano and
Orchestra*, 240; *Octuor*, 94; *Pastorale*,
277n10; piano music, as 'vessel' 5;
Pulcinella, 249–50, 277n10; *Rite of Spring,
The*, 280n47; *Sonate pour piano*, 97
on instruments: guitar, 241; harp-piano
combination, 244; orchestral piano, 64–
70; stringed instruments, 91–2, 95, 96–7,
207, 210, 219–20; wind instruments, 95–
6, 97; zither, 212; photographs, 261n20,
269n93, 289n181, 291n23, 299n153;
recordings, 125, 257, 310n29
scores and texts: Church Slavonic texts, 202;
hand-writing, 198, 301n175; in-score
fingerings, tempi and text, 23–4, 105–6,
251; Latin texts, 202, 302n192
teachers: Akimenko, 260n10; and St
Petersburg Conservatoire tradition,
21, 24; Kalafati 15, 29; Kashperova,
15, 16; Philipp, 4, 139, 173–5, 221–3,
261n22; Rimsky-Korsakov, 37, 55–6, 64,
128–30, 254; Snyetkova, 15, 16–17, 25–6;
Timofeyev, 15
writings, speeches, interviews: accuracy
of published editions, 251; and wind
instruments, 96; *Autobiography, An*, 13,
64, 174, 248, 261n12, 263n7; Berlin 1924
interview, 102–3, 282n77; *Chroniques
de ma vie*, 102, 108, 261n12; Harvard
lectures, 184; *Komsomolskaya Pravda*
article, 277n7; memoirs, authorship
of, 111, 264n30; *Memories and
Commentaries*, 19; Moscow 1962 speech,
10; *Muzyka*, interview with, 2; on his
early years, 14–15; on his own music,
102–3, 121; Paris 1938 radio interview,
289n180; *Poetics of Music in the Form
of Six Lessons*, 66, 102, 111–14, 116,
284n98; pre-concert talk, November
1935, 213–14; 'Quelques confidences sur
la musique', 305n29, 305n38; '*Sleeping
Beauty, The*', 264n24, 268n82; Some
Ideas about My *Octuor*, 4, 7, 54–5, 96,
102, 105, 106, 137, 140, 191; *Themes
and Conclusions*, 244; Warsaw 1927
interview, 102; *Wiadomosci literackie
(Warsawa)*, 1924 interview in, 281n57

WORKS:
Agon, 214
Apollo (Apollon musagète), 127, 185, 224,
285n137; instrumentation, 96; pianistic
figurations, 138
Babel, 198–9
Bach arrangements, 1–3, 9, 249
Berceuses du chat, 84
Cantata (lost), 31
Capriccio, 79, 80; as neoclassical 'manifesto',
184; Czerny motifs in, 138, 176;
index-finger-over-thumb figure, 79;
instrumentation, 97; technical demands,
301n179; as neoclassical Scherzo, 50
Cinq Doigts, Les, 39, 49, 85, 125, 135,
282n79
Concerto for Two Solo Pianos, 206, 213–18,
219
index-finger-over-thumb figure, 79
performer demands, 301n179
première, 4
Concerto in E♭ ('Dumbarton Oaks'), 98
Concerto pour piano et instruments à vent,
see Piano Concerto
Creed (Simvol' Veri), 202
Duo concertant, 4, 205–13, 256;
composition, 303n6; movement titles,
305n39; performances, 303n6; as
ritornello, 110, 301n179; as neoclassical
Scherzo, 50
Ebony Concerto, 225
Elégie, 220
Elegy for J. F. K., 202
Etudes op. 7, *see Four Studies*
Fairy's Kiss, The: instrumentation, 97
Fanfare for a New Theatre, 281n52
Faun and the Shepherdess, The, 38,
45–7; ending, 272n147, 277n2; orchestral
version, 42, 70; pedal point octave in,
49; piano reduction, 45; première, 45;
three-stave writing, 31
Firebird, The, 38; ending, 272n147;
orchestral colour, 61; piano part, 64, 65;
piano reduction, recording, 310n28
Fireworks, 32, 38, 65, 271n128, 275n201,
275n202
Five Easy Pieces, 39, 85, 105; and
nepodvizhnost', 171; fingering, 86
Four Studies, 37–40; as virtuoso work, 214;
fingering, 78–9, 80; index-finger-over-
thumb overlap, 78–9; tempos, 34
Funeral Dirge, 62–3

Histoire du soldat: and *nepodvizhnost'*, 172;
orchestration, 61

'How the Mushrooms Mobilized for War',
38, 42–5

Legend of the Invisible City of Kitezh, The,
orchestration, 226–8, 306n51

Lied ohne Name für zwei Fagotten, 226–7,
306n51

Mavra, 91; and *nepodvizhnost'*, 172;
influence of Glinka, 14

Movements for Piano and Orchestra, 80, 184,
240–7

Nightingale, The, 247; jazz elements, 253;
orchestral colour, 61; piano part, 64; plot
development, 117

Noces, Les: choreography, 94–9;
instrumentation, 94–9, 117

Octuor, 91, 106; as start of twentieth-century
music, 99; instrumentation, 96

Oedipus rex, 127, 128; instrumentation, 96

Orpheus, 106–7, 220; accuracy of editions,
251; as hieratic music, 285n137; rhythms
in, 106; role of harp, 244

Otche nash, 202

Owl and the Pussy-Cat, The, 208, 244–5

Pastorale, 38, 50–5, 83

Pater noster, 202

Perséphone, 101, 117

Petrushka, 38; and *nepodvizhnost'*, 172;
index-finger-over-thumb figure, 79;
orchestral colour, 61; pianism in, 77;
piano part, 65–70, 80

Piano Concerto, 141, 143–9, 151, 173;
as neoclassical work, 4, 154, 184;
composition, 7; double basses, 96;
Klemperer conducts, 175; passage-work
in, 141; Philipp's model for, 176; première,
7, 131, 173, 282n80; recording, 310n28;
Stravinsky's fingerings, 135–7, 181;
Stravinsky's playing in, 4, 257; three-part
counterpoint, 121; *Vorstudien*, 141, 151

piano duets, 85–6, 93

Piano-Rag-Music, 49, 125, 253

Pribaoutki, 84, 253

Pulcinella, 83–4, 249–50; and
nepodvizhnost', 172; instrumentation, 96

Quatres chantes russes, fingering, 86

Ragtime, 212

Rake's Progress, The, 233–7

Requiem Canticles, 172, 185, 231

Reynard, 212, 274n186

Rite of Spring, The, 70–7, 309n7; and
nepodvizhnost', 171, 172; anticlassicism

in, 77; bassoon solo, 61; orchestral and
piano versions, 70, 276n218; orchestral
colour, 61; *pal'tserazvitiye*, 309n7; pianism
in, 70–1, 75–7

Roi des étoiles, Le, 62, 274n191

Sacre du printemps, Le, see Rite of Spring, The

Scherzo fantastique, 32, 38, 40, 51

Septet, 184, 237–9

Sérénade en la, 50; as neoclassical work, 4,
184; composition, 7; Philipp's influence,
176; *ritornelli*, 110; simultaneous
diminution in, 198; Stravinsky's recording
of, 257, 310n28

Sermon, a Narrative and a Prayer, A, 244

Simvol' Veri, 202

Sonata for Two Pianos, 206, 214–17

Sonata in F# minor, 24, 32–7, 40, 225
rediscovery of, 272n139

Sonate pour piano, 4, 51, 97, 208, 241;
and Bach E minor Prelude, 286n140;
as neoclassical work, 4; composition,
7; first performance, 119; index-finger
overlap, 277; neoclassical characteristics,
51, 184, 191; passage-work in, 141; pedal
points, 200, 301n183; recording, 310n28;
ritornelli, 110; simultaneous diminution,
198–9; sketches, 250–1; Stravinsky's
fingerings, 131–4, 137–8, 140, 161;
Stravinsky's recording of, 257, 310n27;
Vorstudie, 145, 151

Svadebka: see also Noces, Les
as Russian title, 94; cimbalom parts, 212

Symphonie concertante, 220

Symphonies of Wind Instruments, 61, 105,
196, 258

Symphony in C, 218–19, 233

Symphony in E♭, 37

Symphony in Three Movements, 207,
218–33
role of harp, 244

Symphony of Psalms
and *pal'tserazvitiye*, 190; arpeggios in,
142; Bachian references in, 302n187;
compositional processes, 190, 191;
fugue subject, 182; harmonies, 115;
index-finger-over-thumb overlap,
193–5; instrumentation, 97; movement
titles, 302n187; opening chorus, 228;
orchestration, 63, 198; passage-work
in, 141; pedal points, 201; scoring,
92; two-note oscillations, 201–2, 203;
Vorstudie, 149–51, 152

Tarantella, 25–9, 40, 268n87

Stravinsky, Igor Fyodorovich (*cont.*)
　Three Easy Pieces, 39, 85, 86, 105, 171
　Three Little Songs, 84
　Three Movements from Petrushka, 67, 214, 268n86
　Three Pieces for Solo Clarinet, 306n51
　Three Pieces for String Quartet, 171, 172
　Three Symphonic Movements, 220
　Trois histoires pour enfants, 80, 84, 168
　　fingering, 79, 80
　　index-finger-over-thumb figure, 79
　　ostinati in, 86
　Tsvetochniy Val's: and *nepodvizhnost'*, 171
　Tucha, 41
　Two Melodies of Gorodetsky, 38; Novice, La, 49; *Scherzo*, 47–50
　Two Poems of Verlaine, 31, 272n144
　Two Sacred Songs, 231
　'Valse' from *Histoire du soldat*, piano fingerings, 226
　Valse pour les enfants, 226
　Variations (Aldous Huxley in Memoriam), harp and piano in, 244
　Violin Concerto, 207, 220; tempo markings, 23–4; violin and piano reduction, 223–4; *Zvezdoliki, see Roi des Etoiles, Les*
Stravinsky, Soulima, 4, 138, 139
Stravinsky, Theodore
　on Stravinsky's composing at the piano, 241, 286n145
Stravinsky, Vera, 218–19
　on Isidor Philipp, 175
　on Stravinsky's Bach arrangements, 1, 175, 260

Tacchino, Gabriel, 179
　on Marguerite Long, 297n122
Taneyev, Sergey Ivanovich, 263n18
　as academic, 12
　Invertible Counterpoint in the Strict Style, 264n21
　on St Petersburg, 11–12
　Study of Canon, The, 264n21
　Symphony no 4, 12
Tansman, Alexandre, 224, 306n43
Taruskin, Richard
　musical mobiles, 168
　on Bartók's *Bagatelle*, op. 6, no. 12, 307n84
　on *drobnost'*, 36
　on F♯ minor Sonata, 24, *34*
　on *Grande sonates*, 32

on 'How the Mushrooms Mobilized for War', 42–4
　on *nepodvizhnost'*, 170–2
　on organ point, 30
　on *Otche nash*, 302n193
　on *Pastorale*, 50
　on Rimsky-Korsakov, 55, 127
　on Romantic attitudes to eighteenth-century music, 100
　on *Scherzo*, 29–30
　on *Sérénade en la*, 7
　on Snyetkova, 265n42
　on *Sonate pour piano*, 6, 7
　on Souvtchinsky, 111, 264n30
　on start date of twentieth-century music, 99
　on Stravinsky and Tchaikovsky, 189
　on Stravinsky's early life, 15
　on Stravinsky's memoirs, 264n30
　on *Symphonies d'instruments à vent*, 62
　on Taneyev's Symphony no.4, 12
　on *Tarantella*, 26, 269n90
　on the Piano Concerto, 189
　on *The Rite of Spring*, 289n184
　on *Two Melodies*, 47
　on *uproshcheniye*, 92
Tchaikovsky, Pyotr Ilich, 14
　as model for counterpoint, 122
　C♯ minor piano sonata, 29
　Capriccio italien, 25
　Grande Sonate, 32
　on Glinka, 287n162
　Sleeping Beauty, The, 12
　Symphony no.5, 32
teacher-pupil relationship, 155, 157, 266n49
Tellefsen, Thomas, 293n60
Thalberg, Sigismond
　Pergolesi transcription, 100–1
　'three-handed writing', 33
Thomas, Ambroise, 100
Timofeyev, G. H., 15, 16
tonal centring, 114
Toorn, Pieter van den, 202, 303n200
training phase (of development), 17
transcription, 87–94
tremolo, 41, 45
Trubetskoy, Nikolay Sergeyevich, 280n37
Tucker, Susannah, 242
Turgenev, Ivan Sergeyevich, 257
　Fathers and Sons, 283n85
　Rudin, 121
　Sketches from a Hunter's Album, 307n76

twentieth-century music, starting date, 99

uproshcheniye (simplification), 86, 170

Valéry, Paul
    on Perséphone, 101
    on poetry, 231
varied articulation, 195–9
Varunts, Viktor
    caption to Stravinsky photograph, 166
    on Stravinsky's teachers, 15
Vengerova, Isabelle, 158–9, 161
Vesnyanki, 172, 296n93
Villa-Lobos, Heitor, 85
Vivaldi, Antonio, and Bach, 121
Vorstudien, 141–51

Wagner, Richard
    Meistersinger, Die, 30
Walsh, Stephen, 102
    on Stravinsky's Bach arrangements, 1
    on Stravinsky's early life, 15
    on Stravinsky's view of Kashperova, 267n61
Watkins, Glenn
    on Stravinsky and Orthodoxy, 202
    on Stravinsky's compositional methods, 104
Weber, Carl Maria von, 66
    Freischütz, Der, 41
    Grand duo concertant, 213

Konzertstück in F minor, 66
Webern, Anton, String Quartet op. 28, 141–2
White, Eric Walter
    on Duo concertant, 208
    on The Faun and the Shepherdess, 47,
        272n147
    on The Rite of Spring, 70, 276n218
    on Stravinsky's neoclassical works, 5–6
Whitehead, A. N., theory of cognitive
    development, 17
Whittall, Arnold
    on The Rite of Spring, 289n184
    parody and pastiche in neoclassicism, 100
Wiadomosci literackie (Warsawa), 262n28
Wiener, Jean, 119, 124, 286n137
'will to style', 101, 102
Williams, Alastair, 258
wind instruments, sonority, 92
wind transcription, of Pastorale, 51–4
Wolf, Hugo, Spanisches Liederbuch, 231
Wordsworth, William, 92, 279n34

Yanovich, Y. M., 16
Yastrebtsev, V. NA.
    on Pastorale, 50, 272n156
    on Stravinsky's improvisation, 28
Yelachich, Aleksandr Frantsevich, 35

Zamyatin, Yevgeny Ivanovich, We, 84

Manufactured by Amazon.ca
Bolton, ON